WOMAN TO WOMAN
THE CONVERSATION

PART II

MOTHER, DAUGHTER, SISTER, FRIEND

by Kristin A. Crage

Photos Credits: unless otherwise credited, all photos, letters and postcards are from the author's collection. Every effort has been made to identify copyright holders, in case of oversight, and on notification to the publisher, corrections will be made in next edition.

In honor of my mother, Mary J. Crage

****

This is a true story, although certain names have been changed.

FOREWORD

"It is a woman's inherent right to be free, independent of any and all restraint. To harm a woman in any way is to harm the strongest, most progressive part of society. Let all human beings strive for the day when Women's Rights is no longer a movement but a way of life!"

Kristin A. Crage

****

On Anger…

At its foundation, anger is energy. It can be used it to create, sustain, and imagine as well as suffocate and destroy. If not careful, it can lead to the downfall of the human spirit. If we can work through anger and feel the pain, there's a good chance we'll get to its opposite: love and forgiveness.

On Love…

At its foundation, love is life sustaining but it does not have to be all-encompassing. Love needs room to breathe, grow and flourish. Humans and animals alike simply cannot live without it.

As the years went by, I began to know more anger and less love. I wasn't sure where, internally, if I was growing. I only know my experiences were profound and jolting. My mother always said, "We ask for the circumstances that come into our lives, even if they're painful." My feeling is some, yes and some, no way. Some circumstances are thrust upon us. How we deal with them is the journey.

As I grew into a young woman, my dreams of becoming a professional dancer faded; yet hopes of living a beautiful, simple life and being free remained. Things turned out, differently.

I don't know where to begin.

Start from a quiet place and write your truth. Never mind what others think.

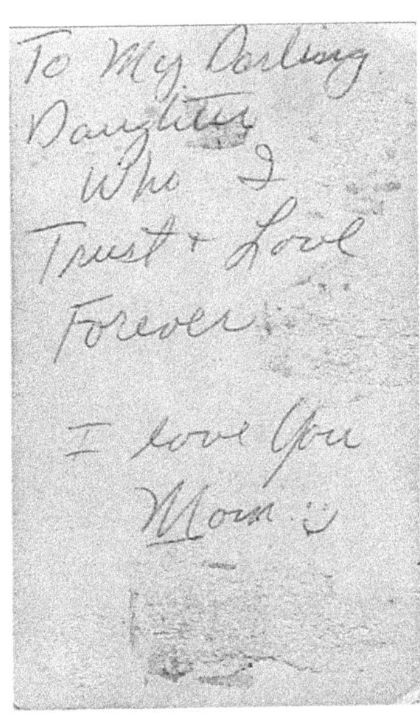

THE UNBREAKABLE BOND

1990

"As a child of God, I do not need to fear separation
Because separation is impossible.
It's only possible to feel separate.
Not to be separate.
As a child of God, I do not need to fear separation
Because separation is impossible.
There is no such thing as separation.
It is possible for the mind to create what does not exist.
As a child of God, I do not need to fear separation
Because separation is impossible.
I cannot die unless I want death.
My life urge is stronger than my death urge.
As a child of God, I do not need to fear anything.
For there is no absence of good.
I am one with God."

Mary J. Crage, 1990

"Cancer is a belief system.
It has no reality other than the reality I give it.
Cancer is nothing but a concept; a thought form.
It [Cancer] is a thought form.
Cancer is a belief system.
I cancel my belief in Cancer.
The etheric body is a blueprint for the physical body.
Heal the etheric body.
I would like to see this in truth, and I ask for a miracle."

Mary J. Crage

How are you feeling my sweet?

Okay.

Good. Do you feel like this is helping you?

I do.

I'm glad. I would do anything and everything for you.

I know and you have.

I think this was a great idea.

I think so too. Talking about the past can be emotionally draining at times though right, or is it just me?

No, it can be. We're going through and writing some painful experiences. I'm glad you've retained your sense of humor though. That helps.

Being there for each other helps too.

Absolutely. So, I know you said you knew what you wanted to talk about next.

Right.

I do too.

****

The Buffalo General Hospital
100 High Street
Buffalo, New York 13210

"Admittance Date: September 25, 1990

Principal Diagnosis: None

Secondary Diagnosis: Confusion"

Department of Radiology

"September 25, 1990

CT Scan of the Brain

There is no evidence of infarct or intracranial hemorrhage. Please note that a non-contrast CT scan will be markedly insensitive to metastatic breast CA within the brain. No obvious large masses are detected on non-contrast scan. Bone windows appear unremarkable.

Impression: Negative non-contrast CT scan of the Brain."[1]

"September 26, 1990

Chest

Re-examination of the chest as seen in AP and lateral upright projections.

A right central venous catheter is in place, the tip lies in the region of the right atrium. The right lung field reveals no evidence of vascular congestion or recent infiltration. A small nodular density overlying the fifth rib anterior on the right may be vascular. On the left there is loss of volume throughout. There is some residual pleural change, not as marked as previously. The question of a parahilar mass on the left cannot be ruled out. Again, unfortunately, the patient is rotated, and it is very difficult to evaluate accurately. There is some residual interstitial change in the lower lung field on the left. Specific nodules other than the parahilar lesion on the left are not demonstrated. The visible skeleton revealed no evidence of a destructive process.

Impression: There appears to be a decrease in the pleural change on the left. The question of a parahilar mass on the left must be considered. This could represent a right nodule or adenopathy."[2]

"September 27, 1990

Whole body bone images were performed in the anterior and posterior projections after the intravenous administration of Techneticum 99m methylene diphosphonate.

The images revealed focal areas of abnormal increased radionuclide accumulation involving the sternum, the anterior aspects of the left 3rd and 4th ribs and the lateral aspects of the left 5th and 6th ribs, the posterior aspects of the left 11th and 12th ribs.

Impression: The areas of patchy increased radionuclide accumulation involving the spine and knees are felt to most likely represent degenerative arthritic changes with the areas of more increased radionuclide accumulation involving L5 and the upper aspect of the sacrum either representing areas of more active degenerative change or possible metastatic involvement. The focal areas of abnormal increased radionuclide accumulation involving the sternum. Left ribs and right sacroiliac joint region are felt to most likely represent metastatic involvement at these sites."[3]

"September 29, 1990

Lumbosacral Spine, Pelvis and Hips.

Examination of the lumbosacral spine, seen in AP projections, including pelvis and hips, lateral and oblique views were obtained.

Impression: Examination of the lumbosacral spine, including pelvis and hips reveal degenerative disc disease at levels L4-5 and L5-S1. Degenerative arthritis at these levels is also noted bilaterally. There appears to be a hemangioma of L2. No evidence of a destructive process could be identified."[4]

"October 5, 1990

CT Scan of the Abdomen

Axial scans of the upper mid abdomen were obtained after administration of oral contrast material, before and after administration of intravenous contrast material. Non-ionic contrast was utilized due to contrast allergy.

Impression: Left pleural thickening. No evidence of intra-abdominal metastasis.

Ribs

Examination of the thorax, rib detail, bilaterally.

Impression: Examination of the thorax, rib detail revealed no evidence of metastatic disease."[5]

"October 25, 1990

Mrs. Crage received five 12 MeV electron beam treatments to the left posterior 11th and 12th ribs. The treatments were administered from 10/4/90 thru 10/12-90 and the tumor does was 2250 at a depth of 2.7 cm. At the completion of therapy, the patient's pain improved, however, she was on morphine sulfate."[6]

****

"Dear Dad,

This letter has been a long time in coming. It's so hard for me to write it and I keep finding ways to avoid it. Even after all these years. I still miss you, but I realize I must let you go. So, from this moment on I release you and let you go. Also, Dad, I do not have to die to be close to you or love you anymore than I do. So please Dad, let me go. I want to live. Release me with your blessing for life eternal. My love for you is eternal and always was. Thank you, sweet father.

As I look back on the years of our lives together. I remember how much I wanted to please you. I know you wanted a son and I tried my best to be one but, in the process, I lost that part of my womanhood that cares for herself. Dad I have associated myself with you so much that I even got cancer just like you. Only I lost my female organs in my effort to be a "good son." I am so hurt and angry over that. I guess I keep saying that it's okay because you didn't mean to hurt me in the way you did, but deep down it's not okay. I am still mad because my body is still hurting. I've had many operations and still my body has not healed. In addition, my mind is not healed. I think of all the times I wanted to yell at you the way you yelled at me and call you stupid the way you called me stupid, but it wouldn't matter now. I just can't understand why you couldn't appreciate me as a woman. I had so many good qualities and it seemed like you didn't recognize them at all. And sometimes I wanted to scream at you for your hypocritical thinking. I was so hurt when I would ask you to pray the rosary with me and you would angrily refuse, and you were the one sending me to Catholic School. If you didn't want me to come home with ideas like that why did you send me there? And why did you get so angry when I would ask you to do such simple things? When I was real little, I played the violin and the piano, and you never seemed pleased with that either. Mom had to force you to come to my dance recitals and you were usually too busy for those too. There doesn't seem to be much I do to get your approval. Even as a grown girl you didn't want me to go to college because you said I would waste my education by ending up getting married. You always assumed I wouldn't do well. Once in a while you would have some confidence in me and then something would come up in you and you'd be back to criticizing me or just being distant. I'm not saying it was all bad because you were loving and affectionate and took good care of me. As a matter of fact, no man has taken care of me like that since you. I hope you can help me understand why that is. Sometimes I think I'm trying to let men know that I don't need them because if I need them – they will reject me. No matter where you are please embrace me for who and what I am; just me, Mary. I want this pain to end. I don't want to die to be with you or to be like you. I just want your love. I am asking your forgiveness for all hurt and harm I have done to you knowingly and unknowingly and I forgive you, you bastard. I forgive you and I forgive myself. It is done."

That is so powerful. It hurts me that Grandpa hurt you so much. You're loveable and worth being loved Mom for all that you truly are. Your kind, intelligent, generous, beautiful, strong, nurturing, open, caring, warm. I could go on and on and I know I do but that's because I want you to hear the truth of who you are, as often as possible.

My beautiful daughter, this is one of the many reasons I love having you so close to me. You make me feel the way I wish my dad made me feel – worth all things good.

That's because you are. Grandpa starved you of that knowledge and if he were alive, I'd let him know it.

I know you would and you're right, and because I was never taught any self-worth, I let him. Unlike you with your father.

Please don't blame yourself Mom. Grandpa conditioned you to believe you weren't worth anything. Yet you broke through that. You did. You got away from Dad. You went to school. You marched for Women's Rights. Most of all, I'm so grateful to you for so many things, but particularly for teaching me self-worth and self-respect. You accomplished what you set out to do and that is break the cycle of negative self-image with your girls.

I wish you sister paid more attention to the lessons I gave.

Well, that's her journey that she didn't, and I don't want to speak to that. For me, I can say that Dad hurt me with his absence, his anger and his refusal to be a father but I never let him put me down. Not that either is better but because of what you taught me I, at least, felt worthy enough to stand up to him when he did come around.

I know you did. I was always so proud of you when you did.

Once, after you first separated, he tried to condescend me with something. It wasn't too long after you wrote that saying to me.

What saying?

"A woman of equality is not threatened by a man of Quality." I wasn't completely sure what it meant at that time. I just know it had to do with being a girl and feeling good about yourself - woman/girl empowerment. I don't remember what Dad's comment was. I only remember making a sharp comment back and him giving me a dirty look. After that, he knew I'd never let him put me or you down the way he did to you in the past. No matter what my feelings were about him I always either stood up to him or showed him indifference. It was my way of protecting and standing up for you. My way of saying, "You can't mess with my mother or me without consequence you shit." With you, I never felt I needed Dad. That's how loved I feel by you.

I'm so glad baby. I think for the reasons you just stated you intimidated Dad. He didn't know how else to get to you, so he went in the opposite direction.

Yeah, he knew I wouldn't let him put me down so for or him to feel good about himself he had to wine about how hard his life was. That's why I stayed away from him. He was the opposite of Grandpa. Both were nothing short of disappointing children in the bodies of men.

That's true.

Mom?

Yeah.

Why were you so afraid to express your feelings to Grandpa?

I was always afraid of losing my father's love, and even after he died, I still looked for his approval in everything I did and all the things I felt.

I hear your need to be accepted and loved by him so prevalent in your letter.

Yes. This letter wasn't easy. The way Grandpa was with me dictated the men I chose and how I was with other people; men, women and my children. That's why this was my last letter to him and at the end I write "It is done." I was done allowing him to control the decisions I made in my life. I wanted the hurt and pain I felt from my father over. I know my Dad loved me but like I wrote, he never seemed happy with me.

He was always putting me down and making me feel bad about myself and Grandpa made it very clear to me that he wanted me to be a boy. Imagine being born a girl and always having your father tell you he wished you were a boy. He wanted his son but instead he got a girl. Talk about chauvinists. Grandpa was the epitome of chauvinists. As I've said, he felt girls were good for two things - marriage and having babies. The more I did things to please my father the more I lost sight of me, as a person and a woman, and that continued on in through my marriage. I wanted to please your father and completely neglected myself. My relationship with my Dad was similar to what you feel with your Dad. There was a lot of anger and resentment there. I know for you there still is.

Yes, there is.

Grandpa was emotionally distant, and I married a man just like him and now my daughter is suffering because of it.

It's not your fault.

It is. Don't sugarcoat this. Dad and I knew what each other were like before we got married and we got married anyway. I mean don't get me wrong we loved each other but we were doomed from the start. We just never saw eye to eye on anything.

I know you wanted him to be there for us while I was going through all this but, honey, your father was a lot of things - strong was not one of them. I'm sorry Dad was the way he was with you – distant and completely and totally lacking in responsibility, but that's who he is and that's who my Dad was. We have to accept these things in our fathers even though they're painful and we don't like them. Once we accept what and who we cannot change, we can then let them go. Otherwise the only person we hurt us is ourselves with our constant reminder of what we needed from our fathers - never got and never will get. The good news is that you're not like Dad and you won't marry a man like Dad.

That's for sure.

All these things we're talking about are the other reason I was so intent on your attending and graduating college. I didn't want to let Grandpa's put downs and feeling that "it wasn't worth it to educate women" to become a legacy with the females in our family. I wanted my girls to have opportunities and as I've said, college opens your mind which opens doors for you in life. With an education you're smart enough to know you have options. You're never stuck. Sometimes it just feels that way.

If Dad was around and helped more, we wouldn't have had to be so dependent on charity organizations, food pantry's and people we should have never had to depend on like your friends, who were never really able to help us and rarely could. Yet they tried, more than my own father did. Most of all, if Dad stepped up, we wouldn't have had to move to Buffalo and deal with the negative energy from your family. How can anyone have hope, get well or beat the impossible with negative energy around them? To your family cancer means death and that's exactly how they treated you from the time of your diagnosis, like you were about to die, always.

I agree with you, 100%. I do. My sisters were negative. They were always like that. That's why I didn't want to go back to Buffalo to live. I felt like I was going backward and not forward like I should have been, but I had three children to think of and a diagnosis of breast cancer. Believe it or not I was thinking of you kids when I made that move.

So, you've said.

Honey, we didn't just move to Buffalo to be near family. Buffalo has the cancer institute, Roswell Hospital. Syracuse had yet to even have a cancer wing let alone a whole center.

I know. Still. More help from him, or anyone for that matter, would have meant less dealing with the crazies.

Remember what I've always told you, just because you're born into a family doesn't mean that's your family. Family is what and who you make it. I understand why you feel as you do though. I do. I think with you kids' things were harder. Your childhoods were marked with a lot of heartache and loss. My older sisters often thought if I settled down and found one person that things would be easier for me and my children. My response was always the same, "you try finding someone who wants to take on a woman with breast cancer and three emotional children." It's not like I wanted to be alone honey. I was alone. I mean aside from you kids. I know that the instability in our lives affected each of you differently. My sisters' kids, all of them, like you said, had both their parents even though those relationships weren't perfect there was always, at the very least, financial support which certainly helped my sisters more than they care to admit. At least your uncles were around for their kids. We struggled - big time. If my sisters felt I was secretive it's because there were many things, I knew they would criticize me about or put me down for and I just couldn't deal with that. I had enough people putting me down just for being lesbian. Then I had my father's voice in my head, and I wasn't about to let anyone else hurt me, up to and including my sisters. I had more than they'll ever know on my plate and I did a damn good job managing all our lives.

You did Mom. I was there and you did. I'm so glad you're my mother and not any one of your sisters. I'm really grateful to the Universe for that.

Me too. Your father left a pain in each of his children that, I feel, is just as great, if not greater, than the pain I experienced with my Dad. This is what I mean by allowing Grandpa to affect me in terms of the choices I made in men. The man I chose replicated my childhood pain in my children.

Do you know how much it bothers me that you chose Dad for a husband?

Yes.

He never could understand the reason I didn't want anything to do with him is because of how little he gave to us and how much shit he left us with. I couldn't love a man that consistently took advantage of and treated my sick, struggling mother like she was of no value. That was unacceptable to me.

That's the drinking. He probably can't remember who, what, where or why of anything from his past.

Probably, but I was never one to tailor my feelings or how I express them to suit anyone. So, Dad got from me what he gave to me, nothing. Every time he opened his mouth to complain I wanted to shove my fist in it and make him choke on it.

Well I'm glad I chose Dad because if I didn't, I wouldn't have had my three beautiful children. Just think we would have never met if it weren't for me and Dad.

Na, I would have found you somehow☺.

Oh, you would have, would you?

Yup.

So, in talking about Dad and needing help from others I know that this is leading up to that place you weren't happy with. You know what I'm talking about?

Yeah, when you went to stay with Trudi. You never liked going there in the first place. You shouldn't have had to do that. Why did you go there?

Honey, first of all, it was only for a couple of weeks. Caring for me and caretaking in general is your thing. You liked it and you're good at it but there was a time or two when I needed help while you were away. When it comes to illness the things that get most people down don't affect you like that. In fact, that's when you're at the top of your game but not everyone is like that. I was in the midst of, yet another round of chemo and you know how intense those treatments are. Besides, it was only for a few days.

I know. I know. When you say, "not everyone is like that" you're referring to Andrea, whom you asked to come home while I was at school so she could help you so you could be comfortable and cared for in your own home. Not shuffled back and forth to Trudi's house. Trudi was a dictator, "Do this! Do that! Go here! Go there!" Ugh and that ugly stiff upper lip. It never moved even when she tried to smile. That stiff lip stayed in place. What the fuck was up with that thing?

Oh honey. You are funny, but yes, you are right. Your sister couldn't handle helping me the way you did.

It got to a point where the only thing good about coming home was you. I felt like I was a stranger in my own house. Andrea would tell me how easy I had it because I was at school and how hard things were for her at home. I couldn't believe I was hearing this from my sister who, only a year earlier, left for Florida to stay with Sandy telling you that she wanted to become more independent and what did she do down there? The same thing she did at home. She drank, drugged and was so irresponsible that Sandy told her she had to go if she couldn't get her shit together. So, what does she do? She goes to live with people she'd only just met to drink and do more drugs. I'll never forget that phone call you got from her. You know the one I'm talking about, right?

Yes, and it was gun wrenching. No parent wants to get a call like that from their child.

Of course not. Your daughter called you from a thousand miles away to tell you that she's in a phone booth, on some drug she's not sure of because she was out partying and can't remember if she had sex with someone or if she was raped. You didn't raise us to behave that way but that's how Andrea allowed herself to become. I was so mad at her for putting you through that.

That was my breaking point with her. It really was.

I know. I was there when you got that call. I could hear her screaming on the phone. Your face turned white then red with anger.

Oh boy did she get it from me. I told her, "You come home now, or you never come home at all." I never thought I would say that to my child, but she put me through years of her antics; like stealing and destroying my car costing me thousands of dollars, coming home at all hours of the night, drinking and drugging. She put me through one too many catastrophes.

When she tried starting in on me, I told her, "I've been caring for and doing everything our mother needed since Mom was diagnosed, including taking care of the house and our dog! Stop whining and help our mother because she wants me at school because all you did from the time I could remember was fuck up!" She blamed me and my going to school for the reason she had to come home and that wasn't the case. She had to come home because she conned you into footing the bill for her to go to Florida and conned your ex-girlfriend into letting her stay with her promising, she'd be respectful, responsible, etc. and she did just the opposite. She disregarded everyone's generosity toward her and ruined their trust in the process. She was always doing that Mom. She was always fucking up then blaming me because "Mom loves you more," or "You're a little goody two-shoes," or using some feel sorry for herself excuse to try and rationalize her shit behavior. Like you didn't have enough stress in your life. Her selfishness pissed me off because she just kept adding to the massive amount of stress you already had. Man, I used to straight up tell her, "Get your shit together and stop blaming me and everyone else for your screw-ups!"

I know. I heard the arguments.

Your son and your daughter could not handle life's challenges, be they episodic or on-going. That was evident by the amount, of drugs and alcohol they ingested by the time they were in their twenties. I was so sick of them. I really was.

You had every right to be sick. You were like the second Mother in the house.

Someone had to maintain some order in the house, and you were too tired to have to keep on them and they needed it. The fact that they were both out so much helped things. The house was peaceful when they were out.

I know you and your sister argued all the time. Not only did you have to deal with your brother, but you also had your sister and her harping on you to contend with too.

Thank you for acknowledging that because that wasn't easy. I particularly didn't like the way Andrea tried to prepare me, before I came home, as to how sick you were getting as if I didn't know. I was in constant contact with you and we'd been dealing with the ups, downs, ins and outs of your illness all the years before this. She should have given the speech to herself. She was the one who needed preparing. I knew what you were going through and how lonely you were. My brother and sister dread hospitals and can't take being in them because they weren't in them like I was. I, on the other hand, feel comfortable in hospitals. They're like a second home to me.

Being at school was hard for me because our home became an open door for your sisters and their unwelcomed comments. Even your nieces and nephews started making comments about our family based on what their mothers told them. I just wanted your family to be nice and help where you needed it and to keep their nasty comments to their selves. Your nieces and nephews assumed that since their mothers were in our home that it was now their home too, and our business was now their business. They were wrong. More importantly, they were hurtful by being invasive and insensitive to the pain of having a mother that was so sick. They behaved with such disregard because you couldn't defend me, us or our home.

Everyone wandered in and out of our home like it were theirs. They had no respect for you or the life you built. They rummaged through your things and did what they wanted. Can you imagine if I or you did that to them? They would have freaked out! Your sisters formed your care around what was easiest for them. Every time I reminded them of what you wanted; be it the way you were being cared for or how you wanted the house kept. Or if I voiced my opinion about how badly I felt one of the home healthcare nurses was treating you. I was reminded time and again to let them handle it because I wasn't around on a day-to-day basis and they were. Trudi was the worst. No one stood up to her except me and you know how we butt heads.

Yes, I do. The two of you are very, very strong minded.

We fought about what you wanted versus what she thought was "best" for you. Since I had to return to school, she got her way. I never understood why she just didn't do what YOU wanted.

Your aunt was head strong, stubborn and self-righteous.

Yeah, everything was her way or the highway. Everyone made me feel like I abandon you.

I know. Tell me how. I need to know the details.

While I was at school, your family called me an "absent" daughter.

They said that.

Yes. The truth is they resented me because I was no longer with you on a day-to-day basis, preparing your meds, keeping the house clean, running errands and tending to whatever you needed whenever you needed it. I liked doing all that because of my love for you. Now, after years of focusing solely on their miserable lives, drinking, drugging, screwing who they wanted and raising fucked up kids, they finally had to step up and help out. All I heard was how hard it was for them to be with you because they had their own lives to live. All they did was whine and complain about the fact that they had to come over and help. Trudi once said to me, "Well if your mother's so-called friends were here, I wouldn't have to be." She was right but she had no right to say something so awful about you.

She said that.

Yes.

First of all, I moved to Buffalo because my family spent years telling me they would help me those little shits. Now they're pissed off, resentful and giving my daughter shit because they have to do what they promised?

Exactly. They made you out to be an inconvenience and that really pissed me off. Prior to my being in school, they never had to worry about doing anything with or for you before because I was there. Now, the tables were turned, and they were blatantly ugly, mean and resentful and all that was directed toward me. One time, in one of your hospital stays one of the nurses asked your sisters how many children you had. Do you know what their response was?

What?

They said you had only two children. They listed Andrea and Codardo, who was much like his father, absent in your life, and Andrea who was noted as "suicidal" and "strongly urged" to see a psychiatrist.

Oh my gosh. The more you tell me the more I regret having moved us back to Buffalo. I really do.

Me too. I couldn't believe it. The only thing I can think of is that I must have been at school at the time of this hospital visit.

That's no excuse! Every time I think they can't get any lower they do, and the bar gets lower and lower.

I wanted to strangle them. Your sisters and their intrusive children are selfish, unfeeling, mean fucks. Every decision they made was all about what was easiest for them, not best for you. They turned our home into one big dramatic circus. We had no privacy. They had no respect for our lives. All I wanted to do was come home and be with you minus the judgment. I couldn't talk to you about any of this because you were busy fighting for your life. I want you to know that every day I was at school I was with you. I was with you Mom. You were on my mind all the time.

I know.

On one of my weekends home Darlene and I were in the bathroom talking. I needed someone to confide in so much. I made the big mistake and confided in Darlene that I didn't think the decision your sisters were making were in your best interest. I told her that everything centered around what everyone else wanted, not what my mother wanted for herself and that I was fighting for you. Darlene responded in a matter-of-fact tone, "You don't even know what's going on with your mother. You're not here." Then she proceeded to tell me that I should be home taking care of you because my sister wasn't used to caring for you. I shoved her against the wall, and we started arguing. Louisa and Carolyn came in. I told them what Darlene said to me, but the argument was still my fault. According to them I was overemotional and angry. That was the first time I felt your absence in a powerful way. You couldn't protect me because you needed your own protection and I was left without a net. I was a constant free for all for anyone to say whatever they wanted to me and anytime I defended their hurtful words I was branded with one word, "ANGRY." I must have heard it a thousand times. Frankly, all of it was none of Darlene's damn business and I kick myself for confiding in her. We were none of her business.

That's right. She wouldn't have gotten away with that comment if I was there. That's for sure. Honey don't beat yourself up. You needed someone and Darlene let you down plain and simple. Her mother is the same. I had to be another mother to Louisa. She wasn't someone I could rely on, at all.

I know. Your family didn't talk to me they talked "at" me.

Like they did me.

Yes. Trudi was too much the way she just swooped in and took control as if our house was her house, your brain was her brain, and her feelings were the only feelings that mattered. She decided who would and wouldn't come and visit you and at what time. I spoke but no one heard me. When I defended you or me, I was told to "leave things to them [your sisters]."

I can't believe they were saying these things and taking advantage of my not being able to defend my daughter. Darlene, obviously, has her own issues as does her mother. You're more than anger baby. You know that don't you? Kristin?

Yeah but back then I felt like my every word was being used against me. You, in all your life, were never and could never be as hurtful to your sisters' children as they were to me. You asked me to make sure your sister's kept things a certain way while I was away, i.e. whether it be making sure you were given your vitamins and herbs; had your friends that made you smile. Trudi was the hardest to deal with and made things so difficult because she's such a miserable, bitter woman. She kept telling me, "Where are your mother's friends now, now that she needs help getting up, getting dressed, preparing her meds." The bottom line, Trudi was pissed because she had to help you while I was away. She would say things to me like, "You should be home caring for your mother. I have my own family to care for Kristin! Do you hear me!" Then she'd graduate to yelling. "I can't be doing this!" I couldn't believe she would say such things.

While I was at school, she took it upon herself to do away with all that you'd built and surrounded yourself with. Gone were your friends, Buddhist chants, holistic and macrobiotic diets. In place were the drugs, rosary beads, and one picture after another of Jesus with blood dripping from his face hanging from a cross. Any body movement for you was a "no-no" according to Trudi. Your visualization tapes were tucked into drawers. I had to search through the house to find them. All the things that meant "health" and "healing" were out of your reach and Trudi was incorrigible to your friends. The reason your friends stopped coming around as often, according to them, was that they couldn't take her. They said when they came over, she would tell them what to do, what not to do and they couldn't have any privacy with you. She didn't agree with alternative healing which is what they were all into. I should have been able to protect you from all this drama and I didn't.

I didn't want you involved in that. I was trying to protect you from their bullshit. That's how my sisters were, drama, drama, drama. And your cousins should never have said anything to you or been so hurtful.

Rather than be supportive or caring your emotionally unstable, rageful sister took control of everything you built in your life that was good and loving and turned it into darkness.

Kristin, I may have been on a lot of drugs, but I knew what was going on. I don't care what my sisters say. I knew what was going on. I just didn't have the energy to fight them. With that, I felt I lost control of my life. I had to completely let go. That was my lesson. I had to let go and trust in the Universe. What hurts me the most is my little girl was out there fighting for me and all the things you knew I wanted, and you were alone getting all this pushback from my sisters and their kids. That's not right and not what I wanted, at all. I'm sorry. Wasn't there anyone that supported or helped you?

No and the other challenge was that I had no support from my brother or sister. I lost count how many times they told me to "keep your mouth shut," and not make waves. Remember when Spencer came to visit you. I wanted her to stay longer but Trudi made her go.

I remember. She looked just the way I remembered her and, of course, her hair was still the same☺. Spencer didn't change much in all the years we knew each other. She sat at my bedside and told me how much she loved me; how sorry she was she couldn't be there for me the way I needed her all those years ago. That it didn't mean she didn't love me, she did. She just couldn't leave the responsibilities she had at home. Me, cancer, you kids, what she had going on was more than she could handle. You don't know how much this conversation meant to me.

I'm glad. Her apology was long overdue.

Spencer and I had one last good time before she left though.

Oh no, I don't want to know.

We had a beer together silly. Of course, Trudi had a hissy, but I didn't care. I loved that Spencer still knew me so well. When I was with her, we reminisced about the first time we met and all the fun we had. We just wanted to laugh and have a good time. It took a lot for Spencer to come and see me. Your father sure as hell didn't and I had three children with him!

You wanted Dad to visit you, didn't you?

I hoped. I needed him too. You think you have some things you need to get off your chest. I had a truck load for your father.

You were let down in so many ways by a number of people. So was I.

I choose to see things differently.

How do you mean?

How lucky was Mom to have had so many people in her life to love? Some drove me crazy, betrayed me, hurt me deeply but I learned about love with each and every person that came into my life. I learned I had so much love to give, and I chose to give it without ever expecting anything in return. Breathe baby, breathe. How do you feel?

Tired, sad and angry.

Kristin, I know the family made you feel terrible about being at school. They can be very judgmental, downright hurtful and they have a tendency to add salt by the pound to any wound. However, don't let them bring you down to their level of anger, hatred and meanness. You're better than that. You deserve better. I know you harbor extreme guilt for staying at school and you have no reason too. It's okay honey. It's okay. Kristin? Honey talk to me.

What's there to say? They had a point. I should have come home.

They didn't have a point! They never will. Don't you ever say that. You gave up your entire childhood and teenage years for me. You gave up your life as a kid, dance, time with friends, boyfriends you could have had to be with me; to go with me to the hospital every time I had to go; to help me when I was sick and vomiting and didn't want to call my sisters so they could drag me to the hospital when I didn't want to go. You got my prescriptions, cookies, groceries and anything else I needed. You cleaned, did the laundry, ironed my clothes and took care of our baby,

Sophie. Most of all you never said no to me. Anything and everything I wanted you gave me and supported me. I wish you could see my gift to you was to send you away. Not having you in the house was excruciating for me but it would have been worse if you weren't where I wanted you to be, and that's school. I wanted my kid to have a break. I'll remind you a hundred times if I have to. I told them that and they should have never made you feel as bad as they did or treat you so badly. Please stop beating yourself up. There's nothing to forgive. Only you and I know the inside of Kristin and the agony you were going through.

I love you Mom. Your unselfishness will forever bring to me tears and make my heart both happy and break into tiny pieces. I missed you so much. I cried every day. Sometimes I would have to leave class just to go to the bathroom to cry. Then I would pull myself together only to have to do the same thing all over again. It was hard to stand my ground to your family because I was always outnumbered, and the fight became exhausting. I try not to let them get to me but when they outnumber you as they do, it's challenging. They're challenging.

I know. I know exactly how you feel. Sometimes after a conversation with my sisters I felt like I was out of breath and my heart would be racing. I felt like I was defending the very essence of my being to them. You know why they do that?

Why?

They saw your strength and wanted to bring you down with them, to the place of lost hope and you didn't let them. With all the hardships you faced you never gave up because you're my daughter, and guess what? Neither did I☺.

The only reason I never gave up is because I learned that from you. You taught me to keep going and never give up until the day you cross over.

We are each other's teacher and student. Let's give ourselves a breather and switch gears for a second. How were things with you and Ethan during this time? You stopped talking to me about him.

I didn't want to bother you with what any of that stuff.

Why not? I would have liked you to "bother" me.

I didn't want to tell you that we went from not being able to take our hands off each other to arguing all the time. The first two years were great but then he started to get critical and condescending about the things I was passionate about like animal welfare. I always stood my ground, but the arguing just got worse afterward. One of the reasons for this was the ferret.

The ferret? What ferret?

Ethan's roommate had a friend that asked him to watch his ferret. Well, the asshole friend never came back for the little one and rather than care for the ferret, Ethan's roommate stuck it in a cage and then put it in a closet with no light and only fed and gave it water once a day. The callous shit didn't even clean his cage. That poor little one had no positive interaction with anything or anyone. It was forced to sit in a filthy cage in a dark room all by itself while listening to people on the other side of the door because the closet was in the living room. It must have been terrified.

Oh, my goodness! Are you kidding me?

No. I was sickened when I found out.

How did you find out about?

Well, I spent a lot of time at Ethan's apartment and one night he told me. It had been in the closet for a couple of days before he told me.

Oh, I can't believe this. This is just so horrible.

I know. That night he told me I ran to the closet and just about lost my shit on Ethan. I bellowed, "How can you allow this to happen to a defenseless animal. He's stuck in a filthy cage in pitch black with no positive interaction and scared out of his mind! What the fuck is wrong with you? Where is your conscience?"

What did Ethan say?

He said he tried to tell his roommate to treat it better, but the guy wouldn't listen, and he didn't know what else to do. So, I told him, "You call the local humane society you self-righteous know-it-all!" This was one of the defining moments for Ethan and me. Here I am, actively involved in animal welfare and he could condescend my knowledge in that area but not be smart enough to ask his well-informed, intelligent girlfriend what to do about an animal that is being abused and neglected right under his nose.

I gather you took action.

Oh yeah, that's an understatement. I almost stole the ferret and brought it to the local shelter but realized I could go to jail for that. That night I made Ethan clean the cage with me and let the little guy run around to release some energy. I also took his cage out of the closet and put it in the living room. The next day I called the local animal shelter and told them the condition I found the ferret and asked them to come and do a home check. They said they couldn't get anyone out there for a few days. So, I went over to Ethan's once a day and made sure the little one was fed, had water, cleaned his cage and let it run around until a shelter employee could come over.

Good girl. Did they?

They did.

And, what happened?

I don't know because after that Ethan's roommate banned me from their apartment.

Are you serious?

Yeah, talk about behaving like a child. Rather than take responsibility for his shit actions this guy reverted to the age of 10.

Wow, that is sad.

I agree. Ethan said that the ferret was gone that same week. I hoped the roommate took it to the shelter but probably not. We're not talking about men with a conscience.

This is just heartbreaking.

Yeah, it's hard for me to talk about.

I'm sure.

Do you believe that Ethan didn't even stick up for me?

Oh my gosh! This story just gets worse!

Oh yeah, he sided with his roommate stating that he had to live there, and I made his living arrangements stressful because I pissed his roommate off.

What was your response?

I said, "Fuck you! You allowed animal abuse to happen under your nose you asshole, and rather than support me or help that animal you cowered like a weakling to your roommate whom you should have had the balls to stand up to. Any decent human being would have protected that animal and supported his girlfriend you jerk!" I was so pissed. I really was. I think I ended things with him for a little while. This was around the time we started to break up and get back together and break up and get back together. It wasn't fun.

That is a very upsetting story. I thought Ethan was smarter and more compassionate than that.

Yeah, so did I. I was learning a lot about him that I didn't like. He reminded me of Cody when he would get like that and the feeling made me sick to my stomach. My relief was coming home to you on the weekends. Ethan stayed at school on my visits home to you. You remember he was a year ahead of me, so he wanted to be with his friends on the weekends. I was hurt because while I understood how he felt, I really needed his support.

Hearing the ferret story, it's not surprising he wasn't supportive.

He was focused on graduating and I understood that. However, he didn't take the time to understand that you and I were dealt a horrible experience and who wants to deal with that when you're a 21-year-old, on the outside of it all and about to graduate.

Still, if you love someone you help that person through anything. It's called "Love."

Yeah, that's what I thought too. It was becoming clear to me that what Ethan and I shared wasn't love.

What do you think it was?

I feel like it was more about me being a young woman, experiencing deep feelings for the first time and being on that journey with someone I truly did care about – even though he had some serious flaws. When I was alone all I did was cry and not so much about Ethan.

What about?

I was overwhelmed with sadness and anger at Cancer ever having entered our lives and now destroying it.

I'd say that's pretty normal. You didn't have anyone to help you with the things you were doing for me. At the same time, I can understand why Ethan felt the way he did. He wanted to do what most college kids do - study and have fun. I always hoped Ethan loved you. You deserved and needed some tenderness in your life.

Love is unconditional. Ethan "loved" me when things in my life seemed okay. Now that things were getting harder for you and me, I felt him pulling away. At the same time, my feelings for him were shifting too. As time went on, I had less and less respect for him. I'll never get over the ferret incident, but I'll move on for the sake of our conversation.

Yes, and for the sake of yourself too. That little ferret has long since crossed over and is at peace now.

I hope so Mom because that really hurt me to see that little one so mistreated, you know?

I know baby. I know how hard the mistreatment of animals hits you. You don't recover from reading or learning about such things let alone witnessing them.

Yeah. Meanwhile, me and Ethan's relationship was changing for the worse and that was hard too.

You two were really hitting some very challenging times.

Yes, we were, and it was hard for me to just let go. Ethan and I were together for a long time, since the first year of college for me. In the beginning, we had so much fun. We traveled a lot to see Dead Shows. We studied, ate and slept together. We did everything together. I mean we liked each other as friends even before we started going together. We hung out with our friends and made each other laugh. Then, I don't know, you were getting sicker and things started to go bad and I'm not saying it's your fault, not at all.

I know. I didn't feel that.

Between trying to manage my studies, coming home and dance the situation felt impossible. We weren't on the same level anymore. I was dealing with some very serious, grown-up issues and he was a college kid that wanted to party. We weren't communicating as well as we used too, and he was showing a side of himself I didn't want to know.

Give me an example?

Another one besides the ferret story? That one is enough for me.

Yes, another one. I need to hear these things.

Okay, one time, we went to visit some of his friends, people that he hung out with prior to our getting together so I didn't really know them all that well. They were all gathered in this one bedroom. Ethan and I were greeted by one of the guys in the living room and he asked us to come into the bedroom where everyone was. So, Ethan said to me, "Stay here for a second," motioning for me to wait for him on the sofa. I thought that was weird since we were both asked to hang out in the room. Then I thought, maybe he just needs to get something and he's coming right back, but I sat there for about ten minutes or so. I remember getting super pissed off hearing them all laugh and toke it up in this bedroom while I'm feeling pathetic on this sofa all by myself. In my head I'm thinking, "No he did not just go into a room to hang with his friends and leave me out here alone," but that's, indeed, what he did. One of the guys opened the door and said, "Ethan, why did you leave your girlfriend out here by herself?" The guy apologized on behalf of my boyfriend who was behaving like a jerk and said to me, "Kristin, I'm sorry, come on in." So, I did. I sat next to one of the other guys and literally ignored Ethan the whole time. That's how I pissed I was. In fact, when he said, "C'mon honey, let's get going," I told him, "Go ahead. I'm staying a little while longer."

Oh my gosh. What did he say to that?

He got this look of complete and utter emasculation on his face. He tried to get me to come with him, but I stood my ground. He knew I wasn't someone he could control.

Good for you.

Yeah, I mean, everyone could see how pissed I was, including Ethan.

Boy, hearing these things about Ethan are very disappointing and I'm not liking them.

Ethan was charming and sweet, but he could also be ignorant at times, that's for sure. Also, I got the feeling he was threatened when it came to women's rights. He wasn't always supportive when I talked about it.

Really? Now that's surprising.

Yeah, right because he wasn't always like that but now all of a sudden, he could be downright critical if we were in a group together and I'd speak on either of those subjects. He'd act embarrassed when I was vocal on those issues because they weren't important to him. Or, he'd be condescending and say something like, "I don't think you meant to say that." Or, "I don't think that's what that person was saying." You know, comments that were belittling to me when I was trying to make an informed intelligent point on something, he knew nothing about. I always stood up for myself, but it was embarrassing - for him because I'd shut him down.

Oh my gosh! I never knew he could be like this. He always seemed so polite and friendly.

Yeah, to you.

I hope you told him to shove it.

Of course, I did. A few times I had to tell him to mind his business and keep his mouth shut when I was speaking and to not interrupt me - ever! I never interrupted him, but he thought he could interrupt me, no, not happening. I told him that I felt belittled when he'd behave that way and I didn't deserve it nor was I going to take it! Then our friends would say, "Ethan, she has a right to say what she feels."

How did he take that?

Well, then we'd have a small argument, but he'd do this in front of our friends, and I don't like that. Disagreements should be hashed out in private. It was uncomfortable.

Did he do this often?

No, the things I'm talking about weren't the norm for him or I wouldn't have stayed with him for so long, but they do stick out in my mind that's for sure.

I know that feeling.

Another incident that sticks out is the time he picked me up in his car and I noticed another woman's shoes in the backseat. This one I told you about.

Oh yes. You were very upset about this and rightfully so. Cheating is unforgiveable for you.

That's right. I asked him why another woman's shoes were in his car just to see what kind of bullshit response I'd get.

What did he say?

He said that he was working on a group project and he gave one of the girl's in the group a ride home and she left her shoes in the backseat which is a possibility but...

But...

I remember we talked about this, how I wasn't really sure what happened and maybe he was telling the truth. You didn't influence me one way or the other. That's what I love about you. You always just talk things out with me and let me make my own decision as to what to do about a situation I'm in conflict with.

That's right. It's important to me that you weigh both sides of any given situation and then make whatever decision you need to from there. As opposed to making rash decisions. Do you remember what you did?

I ended it right there, for a while anyway.

You guys got back together.

Yeah.

One of your break-up/get back together moments?

Yeah, he pleaded with me to give us another try and swore up and down that he didn't cheat on me. I don't know. Until this day I'm not sure about that but I gave him a second chance anyway.

Oh, my goodness. You two sure went back and forth a bit.

I think we had to – as part of the acceptance of letting go process.

I understand that very well.

Then there were one of the two weekends he came home with me. You were just finishing your chemo. You'd lost all your hair, were frail and curled up in a blanket in your favorite chair. When he saw you, his energy got heavy. I think it scared him to see you that way because he'd never seen anyone so sick and he wasn't used to seeing you so frail. Plus, my attention was totally on you, not him. He left the next morning. I was dealing with these major issues and I just couldn't handle the arguments we were having. He had all these freedoms and support of his family. In a way, I envied him. I envied the closeness he had with his family and how loved he was. I envied how carefree he was able to be.

You were loved Kristin.

No, I know. I don't mean to imply that I wasn't. I never felt more loved by anyone but you and there was the problem. The only person I felt loved by was sick, very sick and I felt vulnerable to the dragons that surround me. Ethan didn't like your sisters. He thought they were, how did he put it, "fucked up."

Oh, he did, did he?

Yeah. I thought that was funny. His feelings validated that it wasn't just me when it came to your sisters.

I told you that too.

Yes, you did. So, anyway, cancer, amongst other things, was taking its toll on me and my relationship with Ethan. The second time he drove me home is a memory that serves as a distinct reminder of how much I hated that belittling factor that cancer brought upon us.

What do you mean?

From the way the doctors and/or nurses treated you to how much it drained your already drained finances. We were broke. With cancer in our lives we were brought one notch above poverty. This left us with few choices across the board. This brings me to the second and last weekend Ethan came home with me. This was one a real doozey for Ethan, me and you.

I know. Cancer made our lives miserable. I won't deny that. I don't remember this weekend you're recalling. Refresh me.

While we were home, we had an argument and it was in front of you.

Oh, yes, now I remember. This one was a doozey.

It sure was. We were talking about women's rights. We weren't yelling or anything, just discussing and I don't know, I guess he felt threatened. Whatever it was he got so mad at the topic that he got up, walked away and without looking back, threw the papers he had in his hand behind him. Unfortunately, it was a large stack and they hit me in the throat. It was an accident but still, I lost it, went after him and just started punching him. Accidental or not, no man is going to get physical with me. No way. It was horrible. I was hitting him so hard and fast all he could do was try to cover himself. Things got so heated you had to step in, pull me off him as best as you could with your one arm and calm us both down. I didn't want to drive back with him. I wanted him as far from me as possible and take the bus back. Unfortunately, you had no money. Ugh, this next part just breaks me up. You pulled me aside, tears in your eyes and said, "Honey, you have to go back with Ethan. You have to. I have no money for the bus. Please, please, do this for Mom." I had the solution, stay home period. Again, you insisted that staying home was not an option. So, I had to drive back with Ethan. It wasn't a fun ride for either of us.

Yes, this was not a situation I ever wanted my daughter in. I remember speaking to Ethan and he apologized and agreed to take you back with him. He understood how grave our situation was. He wasn't nasty or anything like that to me. He was very respectful and polite.

Of course, he was polite. What was he going to say to you, no? Ethan would never be rude to you. It's just that times like these made me feel like cancer had backed us into corners we, otherwise, would never allow ourselves to get into and would fight like hell to get out of. Now, in the face of cancer, we were forced to accept circumstances that were more than uncomfortable.

Did he apologize to you?

He did, on the way home and boy was it was a long drive back.

I bet.

The air was so thick you could cut it with a knife. You could hear each of us breathing that heavy, painful, anger breath. He tried to talk to me, but I couldn't stand the sound of his voice or the sight of him. I put my headset on and blasted my music. I despised him for behaving like a child and causing you and I more heartache when he should have been caring, supportive and compassionate. After a while I took my headset off. We fought more and then, boom. Just like that, the anger turned to silence and hurt. From that point on everything around me felt shaky. I wanted something in my life to be steady and it wasn't. This was the beginning of the end of our relationship. I guess I...

You didn't want any more instability in your life.

Exactly. I think what also disturbed me was that I could feel myself getting a little too used to the arguing. I didn't want that. The relationship Ethan and I had wasn't sweet or passionate anymore and it wasn't doing either of us any good.

That's very self-aware of you Kristin.

Yeah, well, I mean what I saw was a young man who couldn't handle illness. He actually became visible uncomfortable around sick people and would flee the scene like a fugitive on the run. This was never more apparent than when he was around you.

It was heartbreaking for me to find these things out about Ethan. I thought, "If this guy can't handle my mother being sick what is he going to do if something happens to me, or him?" I didn't want a man that was going to run in the face of adversity, like my father. I wanted a man that was going to stay in love and crisis. I know illness is hard for some people, but I'd been dealing with it for so long that I knew I wanted someone emotionally stronger than I felt Ethan to be. I also wanted someone that loved animals, wanted to help them as I do and supported Animal Rights and Women's Rights. Ethan wasn't that person. When I'm objective about this relationship, I should have ended things after the ferret incident but there was more to it for me.

I was just going to ask why you didn't walk away from him after that.

While our relationship wasn't stable, it was tangible. Something I could feel, and touch as opposed to cancer which was this untouchable cloud with the unknown hanging over our heads. Aside from that, I also always fantasized that I would spend my life with the man I gave my virginity too. I know it sounds naïve, but I did.

That's not naïve babe. I know you did and there's nothing wrong with that.

Realizing that wasn't the case with Ethan and me was really upsetting. It felt like we wasted four years. I mean we didn't but that's how it felt. I needed to let go of that fantasy so I could let go of us.

I understand. Oh honey - I wish I knew about these things so I could have helped you through them. I wish you would have talked to me about all these things.

I couldn't Mom. I mean some you did know about but others I just didn't want to, as I said, bother you.

You were never a bother, ever. While Ethan behaved in some pretty despicable ways at least you were finding these things out about him before you two went any further into your relationship, like living together or marriage. The way I did with your father.

Well, it's safe to say I was definitely going in the opposite direction of Ethan. So yeah, I guess that was the plus side. Ethan wasn't a bad person Mom. I'm just highlighting some of his worst moments that were memorable.

I know. He just was a lot younger in his heart and mind than you and didn't know what to do with the heaviness you were dealing with and, at times, acted badly. Still, that doesn't excuse his actions.

Not it doesn't and that's a very good way of putting it.

You were really going through a lot and taking on so much, too much. I'm surprised you didn't have a nervous breakdown.

I couldn't. Like you said, there was too much to do and take care of. You were my priority. There was only one other being next to you, who was, without a doubt, my only support, friend and comfort and one that no one really thought about.

Who?

Sophie.

Of course. I don't even know why I asked "who."

She clung to you and knew you so well. She could sense something was wrong with you. You weren't your playful, funny self with her, and you couldn't pick her up the way you used to. Sophie knew what was happening, but everyone dismissed her and her fear of the unknown that I saw in her. Animals sense when the energy around them shifts for the better and worse. It made her sad for you to be so sick. With you, I had my adult responsibilities but with Sophie, I not only felt that need in me to care for her, but I could also be my kid self with her. We grew up together. I was the kid I couldn't be with you. You, on the other hand, were the "adult" person she'd go to. Remember how she used to climb into your lap? You couldn't pry her out of your arms.

I do. She was the same with you. I also remember who she slept with every night, walked her, fed her, hugged her, played with her, took her to the vet and never left her side. You two used to jog every day together; rain or shine, cold or hot. Our neighborhoods knew "Kristin and Sophie" as one being, and if one was without the other people questioned why.

I loved her so much I wanted her to come to school with me. I missed her when I was away.

I know. She missed you. She was sad without her other half.

Sophie was my best friend in the world.

I thought I was your best friend in the world.

You are - you both are but like I said. I was different with Sophie. I told her all my thoughts, dreams and feelings. I took Sophie everywhere, not just jogging, but everywhere; the store, Grandma's, you name it. My favorite was our picnics in the park. I learned the art of stillness through Sophie. I loved it when we'd be outside, and she'd sit with her face toward the sun. Sophie was always drawn to the sun. She'd stare with a look of peace and thoughtfulness while the sun illuminated her black/brown/white fur. It was like she was sifting through the wisdom she acquired for the day.

Like a Buddhist monk.

Exactly. Everything was okay for me with Sophie in my life and she never lost that look. We were each other's rock.

Sophie loved you honey. I don't know where you got it from but from the time you were young, you were as nurturing and maternal as any mother could be - particularly to Sophie and to me.

What sickens me is that your family knew how much Sophie meant to me and still spoke of her as if she were dispensable. I don't know how many times I heard your sisters tell me that we should make "our situation" easier and give Sophie away. Oh my gosh I wanted to smack them so hard.

Well my sisters never understood the depth of the human/animal bond the way you do. I learned how deep a relationship humans can have with animals through you. I don't know why my sisters would say that though. They had their family dogs, and NO ONE was allowed to say anything about their animals or god-for-bid even suggest they be being given away. I'm glad you had Sophie and I know she was always glad she had you. Talk about inseparable. You two adored each other and she knew who her "mommy" was, and it wasn't me☺. All those times Sophie got hit by a car you were the none that nursed her back to health. How many times did she get hit by a car?

Three; twice in Syracuse and once in Buffalo. She was fast, much faster than me. When she was little, I had to be careful because she liked to dart out the front door and into the street and, of course, into any oncoming traffic there was. Those few times she got by me and I wasn't fast enough to catch her before she got hit. I saw each accident and I swear, each time, my heart felt like it was jumping out of my chest. Remember the first time, you were there. She was only a year old and she was running around the front yard. Granted this was in Syracuse and there were hardly any cars around but this particular incident there was, and her hind leg got nicked by one. She was thrown about the road and then actually limped to the side of the road and collapsed. I was calling for you and ran as fast as I could to her. I put her in the car, and we drove to the Vet.

I remember that. I didn't know what happened. You screamed for me to get my purse and keys and we had to go! Poor honey. Sophie was bleeding from her mouth and trying to gasp for air, and you were shaking like a leaf. That was traumatizing, even for me but she made it through, bandages, stitches and all. She made it through. When we got home from the vet you brought all her meals to her so she wouldn't have to get up, and you slept on the floor with her in the living room because she couldn't go up the steps. You were completely devoted to her, just as you are to me.

Yes. Oh gosh Mom, remember when she got pregnant! We were in Syracuse and it was by accident but poor little Sophie. She had just gone into "heat" and was still just a baby herself. You agreed to babysit your friend's dog and he smelled Sophie's heat and that was it.

Oh, that was all I needed, puppies!

Mother how could you agree to babysit your friend's dog when you knew Sophie was in heat? She was raped. You traumatized her Mom.

I was trying to do a favor for a friend who also helped us out from time to time. Why are acting like this is my fault. I told you to keep them separate.

I did keep them separate but the dog got through all the barriers I put up and found his way to Sophie anyway. You should have said told your friend you couldn't help her just this once due to Sophie being in heat.

I couldn't. She needed my help, or her dog needed our help.

Well her dog raped our dog. I can't erase the look of fear on Sophie's face from my memory. It's as clear as the day it happened. She cried and I cried with her. Those big eyes had actual tears in them. She didn't know or understand what was happening. She just kept looking at me as if to say, "Get him out of me, please, please help me." All I could do was pet her and tell her it would be over soon. Of course, you had the brilliant idea, while they were "stuck" together of throwing cold water on them in an effort to shock them into "un-sticking." Okay, FYI, that doesn't shock them into "un-sticking." It just shocks them period. Nice Mom, very nice. I'm so mad at you for that.

I'm sorry! What did I know? It works with people☺.

Oh - My - Gosh. Well, it doesn't work with dogs.

Obviously.

We should have kept the puppies, all of them!

Oh, her little babies were so cute. Honey, how could I keep her babies when I could barely feed all of us?

I don't know.

I know how upset you were/are, still. I remember how you slept on the kitchen floor with Sophie and her babies. You could tell she was happy to have you there. If only to help her sleep and help her babies eat.

Poor honey I had to. Sophie was just a baby herself and she had absolutely no interest in nursing her babies. Every time they would start to nurse, she would get up while the babies were nursing, and she'd drag them from one spot to the next. She didn't want any part of them. I had to calm her and help her lay still.

Sophie was their Mom and you were Sophie's Mom.

I was so sad when we had to give them up. Even though she didn't want to be a mom I know it hurt Sophie too. She looked for them after they were gone. So, did I.

Kristin, what do you want me to say except that I'm sorry a thousand times over.

Tell Sophie you're sorry.

I do, every day and you know what? She's more forgiving than you are.

Is that so?

Yes, that's so. Is there anything else you want to say about this, or can we close this subject?

You did some really dumb things sometimes.

Like mother like daughter.

You're right. Let's close this.

Good idea.

Well, getting back to where you were at with cancer. Thanksgiving came around. The family arranged to have dinner brought to you. Everyone brought a dish.

It would have been nice had I not been in that place. I hated being there. I told Trudi to get me out. I didn't care how overwhelmed and spent she was. She knew I didn't want to be there, and I would have never done that to her.

You were on this terrible roller coaster. You went from being in the hospital to going home for a few weeks to that horrible place. She wouldn't put her husband there or her children, but she put my mother, her sister there. That's how well she DIDN'T take care of you. She stuck you in that place and I couldn't do anything about it. I despised Trudi. I truly did. When I talk about all this, I feel that anger come up and want to…

I know.

My ass Trudi had your best interests at heart. I had your back from the time I was born. Your family was just more weight on your back you didn't need.

I told Trudi I was prepared to come home. She said "For what? It's better if she goes where people can care for her around the clock. I can't do it anymore." Even if I dropped out of school, I couldn't do anything anyway. You already made her POA (Power of Attorney). I couldn't believe you did that. I was the one who had your true best interests at heart, and you let Trudi take control. Look what she did to you, to us? Look where she put my mother? How could you do that Mom? How could you give her POA? What were you thinking? I'm so hurt and mad at you for doing this.

I'm sorry but I had to. I thought, I don't know what I thought. She told me, she assured me if I made her POA I could trust her with everything.

She lied.

Who else was going to take that responsibility on? Who Kristin? Your drugged-out brother and sister? My other two sisters who couldn't handle boo and barely managed their own lives? I had no one else. I had to trust Trudi!

You had me! You had me! How can you say you had no one else when you had me? Do you have any idea how much it hurts to hear you say that? You could have had arranged for me to be your POA before things got bad for you. I mean if you had to keep me at school you could have, at least, given me that. You know I could have handled it.

Kristin, listen to me. I know I had you, but I didn't want you dealing with all the pressures of me anymore. I wanted you focusing on school. I knew you were the only one, out of my three kids, that had it in you to finish school. I wasn't going to let my illness get in the way of my daughter getting a college education.

Even Spencer would have been fine, anyone besides that god-for-saken vile bitch!

I'm sorry. I screwed up. I'm sorry.

She got off on the power. Every time I tried to say anything, suggest anything or advocate for you she squashed everything I said with her newfound status. After this my cousins felt even more privy to our home. They began going through your things while you weren't there. I actually caught them divvying up some of your clothes, pictures, jewelry, you name it. I threw them out of our house, and this is where the fighting got worse. I fought for the privacy of our home. I fought for my mother's respect. I fought for the right to hurt without being called names and miss my mother in a way they would never have to know. I fought to keep my only best friend, next to you, Sophie. I had to fight Mom because any other way didn't work. Trudi treated me like I was a visitor in your life, not your child. You went from that horrible place to having to go back into the hospital. Both places you hated and feared the most.

My sister didn't know what she was doing. I know that and she does too. She was like a crazed lunatic making all the wrong decisions, telling everyone what to do and yet she didn't know her head from her foot. I know you wish I could take it all back, but I can't, we can't. We have to go forward.

The Buffalo General Hospital
100 High Street
Buffalo, New York 13210

"Admittance Date: November 30, 1990
Principal Diagnosis: Disorientation/Confusion"[7]
****

I wish Mom had more options than Trudi honey. I really do.

I know. I understand. I guess. After Thanksgiving we were on a downward slope. You were so sad. You had a hard time responding to me. Your movements and speech were markedly slow. It took a long time for you to lift your arm, ask for something to eat or drink, anything. At one point I helped you to the bathroom. While you were on the toilet you asked me to hug you. At first, I was a little hesitant and then you said, "It's okay." I didn't want you to think I didn't want to. You know how much I loved and needed our hugs. I just couldn't bear to see you in such pain. You went from being a full-figured woman to being almost emaciated. I was scared for you. When I hugged you, I could feel every bone in you as you gave me the weight of your fragile little body. We cried and I assured you that you were going to be okay, that this was just a setback for us, like so many times before and we were going to beat this, again. Like so many times before.

I remember. I never thought you didn't want to hug me. I also knew that you were scared for me, but we had hope, didn't we?

We sure did. The hospital had you on pretty much the same drugs except this time they gave you a combination of Morphine and Haldol. Haldol was another drug used to treat psychotic disorders. I also wrote these side effects down too. The side effects in bold are the ones you had. Side effects include: **drowsiness, dry mouth**, increased saliva, blurred vision, **loss of appetite, constipation, diarrhea, heartburn, nausea**, vomiting, **difficulty falling asleep or staying asleep, blank facial expression**, uncontrollable eye movements, **unusual, slowed, or uncontrollable movements of any part of the body, restlessness,**

agitation, nervousness, mood changes, dizziness, **headache**, breast enlargement or pain, breast milk production, missed menstrual periods, difficulty urinating, fever, muscle stiffness, **confusion**, fast or irregular heartbeat, sweating, decreased thirst, **neck cramps**, tongue that sticks out of the mouth, tightness in the throat, difficulty breathing or swallowing, fine, worm-like tongue movements, uncontrollable, rhythmic face, mouth, or jaw movements, seizures, eye pain or discoloration, decreased vision, especially at night, seeing everything with a brown tint, rash and yellowing of the skin or eyes.[8]

Haldol was the drug Trudi was screaming they give you, not your pain meds but your Haldol, the psychotropic drug. The one that in conjunction with the Morphine, put you in a slow-motion state of la la land. I missed you. I missed us. Everything was so crazy. Your family couldn't understand how much I was hurting. They just kept adding more to the pain I was already feeling.

Do you think it was my fault that things got so bad, because I made my sister POA?

No Mom, nothing was your fault. We were left totally vulnerable. With all the comings and goings of everyone you and I had few moments alone but there was one that sticks in my mind. It was while you were in the hospital. I crawled into bed with you just like I used to when I was a little girl and the most beautiful memory of us popped into my head.

Tell me.

It was about a year and a half prior to your diagnosis. I was nine and you were thirty-nine. We were living in Kings Park Apartments. I was getting ready to go to school. I was in Elmcrest Elementary. School was close enough for me to walk to back then. You told me to come and sit next to you on the couch. Fourth grade was my favorite year because I had that teacher who gave us gobstoppers every time, we answered a question correctly, remember?

I remember.

I was worried about being late. You told me to come and sit by you anyway and that if I was late you would write me a note. I sat next to you and you took my little hands in yours and said, "I want us to look at each other for a few minutes." I asked you why and you said, "I don't know. I just do. I want you to always remember me like this, just as I am now. I want you to always remember my face. When you get sad or down. Remember how much I love you. Will you do that?" I told you I would. For the next few minutes we stared at each other.

A warm breeze came in through the sliding screen doors that led from our living room to the patio, and the fresh smell of early morning spring air filled the room. Flowers were beginning to bloom about our complex. You sat in your favorite white robe; the sun glistened off your dark brown, shoulder length hair. You wore it straight back then. Your olive toned skin and big smile captivated me. They still do. You were smiling as you stared at me with those big brown soulful eyes. You gently brushed my hair from my face. The minutes went by and I got lost in you and forgot about having to get to school. I felt so good sitting next to you. The world was a good, kind, safe place with my hands in yours. When I was laying next to you in the hospital this is the memory I held in my mind and replayed over and over as my hand clasped yours. You were now 50 and I'd only been 20 for a couple of months.

I remember that morning. My little minute. It wasn't easy to get you to sit still.

Did you know something bad was going to happen to you?

I always knew I'd be stricken with cancer. For me, it was just a matter of when. That was my unshakeable fear. You know that.

Right.

I cherish those moments between us. I hope you do too and keep them, remember them when things get tough. That's why Mom gave them to you. They're better than material gifts, aren't they?

Yes. I never said thank you for that memory Mom. Thank you.

Thank you, Little Minute.

While you were in the hospital one of the nurses told me that Trudi was yelling at the nurses and demanding they give you your medication before you needed it. Then she would accuse them of leaving you in dirty bed sheets, but the nurse assured me that they kept your bed sheets clean. She said that Trudi was hard to deal with, that they couldn't communicate with her because she was yelling at everyone all the time or she would refuse to discuss things. I think the most upsetting remark for me was when they told me that she made you nervous and when she was out of the room you were less agitated. Do you agree with that?

Trudi did make me feel agitated. She was filled with rage, even before I got sick, and it was all consuming for her. I could feel it before she entered the room. It wasn't just Trudi that made me nervous it was the family in general. They would come to my bedside and cry like I was dead.

I know. I actually told them to stop crying in front of you.

What did they say?

They got mad at me. I was lonely for you to talk to me. I talked to you all the time, even when I was at school. Did you hear me?

I did. I was lonely for my daughter, my best friend and my companion. We did everything together, always. There were so many things I wanted to be Kristin, so many things I felt I was robbed of because of cancer.

Like What?

For starters I wanted to be unafraid of cancer, unafraid of death, happy, healthy, a healer, a Rebirther, a good mother, a good listener, a good friend, kind, patient, peaceful, thin, organized, calm and serene. I had all these dreams for me and my children to live beautiful, happy lives and while my sisters thought I was crazy for thinking this I had fantasies about going back to Syracuse, living in our family home on Davis Road and getting my independent life back.

I don't think that sounds crazy. I would have loved to go back to Syracuse. I bet if we stayed there, I'd still be living there. I loved the idea of living in the same town I grew up in, where everyone knows you. Anything would have been better than where we were. By the way, you were always a good mother, listener, kind, patient and a good friend to everyone. You weren't in the hospital too long and then you came back home. You were happy to be home and so was I.

I was having more episodes of confusion, wasn't I?

Yes, but it was also from the myriad of meds you were on too. There was no need for you to be on psychotropic drugs. You had anxiety and were depressed but you weren't crazy. There were other ways of coping with anxiety and depression but it's like you said, no one had the patience for the alternatives and your family didn't believe in them. They believed in pills and lots of them. Then Trudi made the decision to put you back in that place. I don't know why she did that. You had home health care help. I begged her not to put you there. I told her you hated it there, but she insisted. All she kept saying was how tired she was. What did she think you were? What did she think I was? We were all tired. I couldn't think of anything more selfish on her part. She claimed to be taking care of you but in reality, she wasn't. She just passed you onto strangers.

I got that feeling too. I felt locked inside a box where I could hear what was happening around me, but I just couldn't get my mouth and body to react the way it used too. The nurses were nice, but I knew where I was. The worst part was that I couldn't express how much I didn't want to be there. You're right about those drugs. I was in la-la land. It's hard to say or do anything on those things.

I know. Mom?

Yeah babe.

I want to talk a little bit more about how Trudi putting you in that place affected me.

I know. Go ahead. I'm listening.

I was really angry and devastated she did that and while I was at school no less and didn't tell me until I came home so I couldn't stop her. I reminded her she was supposed to care for you. Not pass you onto strangers and that you didn't belong there. It was the last place you wanted to be. I insisted on taking a leave from school and staying with you, but she said she already signed all the necessary papers and the decision was made. I felt everything in me collapse as though someone cemented my jaws together and I couldn't speak. I felt stuck; caught between two places neither of which was to your benefit. I felt guilty and powerless at what was happening to you, and sadness and fear at what was happening to us. I was ashamed for not being stronger. I promised I'd protect you and make sure that all your wishes were adhered to. Trudi made all these decisions and none of them had anything to do with what you wanted. To me your sisters were behaving like spoiled brats waiting for their Daddy to come and save them. They were women who depended on being taken care of. Strength wasn't their strong suit. I knew how you felt and why you found it so hard to stand your ground with them. It was difficult for me because your sisters were argumentative, controlling and downright mean.

All these decisions were made before anyone told me anything. I had a phone at school. Someone could have called me and said, "This is what I'm thinking we should do. What are your thoughts and what do you want to do?" I should have been a part of the decision-making process. Just because Trudi had POA didn't mean she had to execute it without taking me, your fucking child, into consideration. I was home on the weekends and still no one talked to me about what they were planning until after the fact. Trudi completely abused the privileges of being your POA. She made all the decisions and while silently saying "screw you and your children Mary." Leaving you in that place at night made me want to die. All I could think was how lonely and scared you must have been all by yourself. I despise those weak, bitter, messed up, low life, pieces of garbage sisters of yours. I truly do. I'm an advocate for women but not these women. I get why their husbands walked and for Trudi's husband. My heart went out to him. I'm surprised he didn't cross over sooner. I'm sorry Mom. I'm so sorry I let this happen to you. I'm sorry you went to that place. Please forgive me.

I understand your anger. I do. I think I'd feel the same way and sweetheart, I'm not the one who needs to forgive you. When will you forgive yourself? For all the adult things you were handling you were still young in your mind and heart. You were a little girl watching her mother suffer and that's enough to frighten anyone. Yes, I was lonely and scared. Who wouldn't be in a place like that? More than anything else I missed my children. I knew no one would heal my babies' broken hearts like their mother. You know what I felt guilty about?

Tell me.

No one would or could love you kids more than me, not ever. What I felt guilty about was letting my children down by being sick whether it was my fault or not. I was sick and unable to be the mother I wanted to be for my children who were all hurting so much, and your brother and sister were rapidly going down self-destructive paths. I wished I was a magician who could reach into your hearts, pull out all the pain and leave only peace, love and joy.

What was happening to us was surreal. A winter like no other set upon us. Buffalo or Syracuse winters are no joke. The cold is a bitter one. It's the kind that freezes your face the minute you step outside. I went back and forth to that place. What are you thinking about?

It's dreary out today. The clouds have rolled in. It looks like rain.

I see them. I want to talk about that day.

Me too.

Today looks like that day, the one where you and I were sitting together, hand in hand, except these were a different kind of clouds. It was Buffalo, New York and there were several feet of snow. You couldn't bundle enough clothes on.

I wanted so much to talk to you, but I couldn't get the words out, no matter how hard I tried. I wanted to get up and get out of that place. I wanted to be healthy and happy with my kids. That's all I cared about was my kids and seeing you grow and do all the things you wanted to do with your lives and being a part of that. My heart ached every day I couldn't share in all the ways you kids were growing up because I was so sick. There were so many times I felt bad. I felt like cancer prevented me from being a better mother.

You were and always will be the best mother I could have asked for and the only mother I ever wanted.

You always made me feel better whenever I felt bad about myself. I wish you would do the same for yourself.

If I were as important to me as you were, I would.

Be important to you Kristin – be as important to you as you are to me and more!

Everyone was busying themselves, preparing for Christmas. I had all your gifts. They were all set for when you got home. The tree and all the decorations were up. I couldn't wait for you to come home.

My little Christmas Angel.

I couldn't wait to see you; watch you get better and get you out of that place. I got to you early in the morning. Andrea said she would be there later after she took a shower.

I couldn't wait for you to get there. I had so many things to talk about with my little minute.

I missed you so much. For days before you were completely non-responsive. The only noise you made were the ones that came from your gurgling stomach. You hadn't eaten in days. You didn't look peaceful Mom. You looked like you were fighting something or someone.

I was.

I could see the cancer protruding from your skull from the inside out. Lesions were starting to show through your ribs. You were pale, emaciated yet I knew you were there. I knew this was just another setback for us. I knew you were going to come out of it. I knew you were going to come out of it because you always came of out of these setbacks. That's what made you Mary, my amazing, beautiful, strong mother. The woman I revere.

I was still there. I could hear and see everything that was going on around us. Everybody was talking amongst each other in the hallway. With me was your brother, your cousin Sal and you. You sat at my bedside. Your little face was so tired. I could see the years weighed heavy on you. You had dark circles like I'd never seen before. My baby girl. No one can know what we went through and don't you let people second guess yourself. Don't do that. For Mommy, don't let anyone do that to you, okay?

Okay.

Do you know the comfort I felt when you turned on my meditation music? I needed something to soothe me and you know how much I love my meditation music. You know me like no one else. You knew I was so scared. My fear of the unknown was all encompassing. That's what I was fighting, the "what ifs" of everything in my life that was still pending and undone. I was thinking about my children - my beautiful babies. There was no way in my life I could ever leave you. No one would love my babies the way I do and you kids still needed so much love and tenderness in your lives. All three of your pain and anger was constantly being misjudged and mislabeled but you mostly. Still, Mom knew. Mom knew how hard you kids had it from the time you were all so little. We struggled and inched our way from one hard time to the next without so much as a break in-between. We really could have used a few breaks, here and there couldn't we.

Yes. You could have. You were one woman handling the load of several.

We all could have honey. I tried so hard to make things as easy as I could for us, but cancer just kept pulling us back and back and back until before I knew it, we had so long to go before any healing could take place. This was the biggest part of my life that was undone; the healing I knew my children needed. You were only 20. That is so young. Nothing is figured out when you're this young and I needed and wanted to be there for you kids as you figured yourselves out. I was talking to you and telling you how much I loved you. What a beautiful, strong woman you were growing into; how beautiful you danced and how proud I was of you. Despite everything, you were still doing so well in school. You amazed me then as you do now. I was thanking you for all the days you never left my side; for all the help you gave me. I reminded you that nothing could separate us, not even God. Did you hear me?

Yes. I sat beside you and watched the sun trying to beam its way through the clouds. The freshly fallen snow silenced everything around us and lent itself to a calm I welcomed. I told you I would never leave you and take care of you forever no matter what. I told you I was here for you always and that my hand would stay in yours, forever. I told you I loved you and that love began even before we met. I told you the same thing; that nothing would separate us, not even God. Did you hear me?

Yes baby. I heard every word. I felt your soft little hand in mine and all of a sudden, I felt like I was going to be okay. I felt safe and I was no longer afraid of the unknown.

My hand was there to remind you of the connection between you and me - we are forever. You had three seconds between each breath. You were struggling for each one, but I knew in my heart this was all just a setback Mom. I know I keep saying it but it's true. It was just a setback. Right?

That's right.

I knew you would come back to me. Everyone told me to "let go." Yet they, with all their self-righteous indignations, could never "let go" of their significant other(s), parent(s) or children. None of them could prepare themselves for such a moment yet they became experts on our journey. You were just tired that's all. You were just tired and needed a rest and I understood that. I understood Mom. No one understood that more than me. Only you knew I could never live this life without you.

My baby girl, my sweet baby girl. Don't you know? Don't you know that Mom could never leave her children, no matter what?

Yes Mom. I know and I couldn't wait for you to, once again, prove everyone wrong. I knew you wanted out of that place and would pull out of this state of mind. All but the sounds of your breath and the beautiful mediation music filled the air. I waited and waited and waited. The minutes agonized by like snails crossing a street. My cousin Sal stared out the window waiting for a sign of something, anything from you. He loved you so much.

And I, him – my first-born nephew.

I watched you intently. I caressed the side of your face. I dabbed the corners of your crusted mouth with the lemon cotton swabs you liked so much. I breathed with you, one breath every three seconds. I knew you would feel me rubbing your hand. I knew you would feel me and wake up. I couldn't wait to get you out of that place. So, what if we had to go to more doctor appointments or hospital stays. Anything was better than this; the silence was too much. I hated it. I longed for the sound of I.V. drips, nurses chatter, the sound of the bed automatically going up and down at the push of a button; the vision of white coats entering and leaving the room after they've just told you about your diagnosis in words that sound like letters were thrown together; the horrible taste of hospital food and the cards and flowers that would flood our home when you came home. I just wanted you out of that cold, empty place. There was no way you could get better - not where you were. It took a long time didn't it? For you to respond but you finally felt me and heard me. I knew you would.

I love you. You are my beautiful child and nothing you do or say could make me love you any less.

I felt that love all my life and couldn't imagine a day without it, and just like that, just like that you did it! You squeezed my hand, my heart raced. I jumped from my chair. I screamed with joy for you, "Mom!" "Mom!" I was so excited I thought I was going to burst with happiness! Your eyes opened wide; you took one big gasp of air. I kept telling you, "I'm here Mom! I'm here!" And just like that you released your hand from mine, those big, beautiful brown eyes rolled to the back of your head and that gasp of air was your last.

I'm here sweetheart. I'm here.

I froze, everything in me froze. I held my breath, my mouth draped open from the blood curdling screams that morphed into your name and my body began to shake. It wasn't real. The moment wasn't real until I draped my body over yours and felt the life in you sucked out. I placed my ear to your chest desperately trying to find your heartbeat but there was only silence. Your body transformed from soft and warm to cold and hard in a matter of seconds. Sal uttered two words I'll never forget, "She's gone" he said.

It was December 18, 1990, 10:30 a.m. and "the place" we've been talking about is Hospice of Alden, New York - the place where people go, not to get well, but to cross over.

Baby girl, I love you. Feel my loving arms around you every day of your life. When I felt your little hand in mine, I knew everything would be okay. I waited as long as I could. I stayed as long as I could, but I was so tired. My body was so tired. I didn't have any more fight in me.

Mom! Mom! I need you! I wish you back every day, still! There's this huge pit of pain, longing, wonder of what would have been for you and me, and loneliness for you at the center of my being. We have so much to do, say and see! I need you! I love you! You're the love of my life Mom. You're the love of my life, always and I'd give anything to have you back.

I'm here my beautiful baby girl. I'm here. Feel my love surround and enfold you.

How could this have happened to you, to us! How could this have happened? What didn't we do right? It's not fair. All those years of struggle and this is what we got! Silence! After praying and clinging to hope for almost a decade we got silence! I was prepared to fight for you, forever. Cancer made me strong enough for the both of us. I could have kept us both going. You didn't have to go Mom. You didn't have to go. Why did you go?

I saw you Kristin. I saw you draped over me, still hanging onto me. I heard you crying out, "Mommy! Mommy! Mommy come back to me! Please come back to me!" These were the last words I heard before a peace overcame me like I'd never felt before. I felt so good. My body felt like I'd been healed. I saw this beautiful, bright, white light and was drawn to it. I was drawn to its peace and most of all. I was drawn to who was walking toward me from the other end. You know how much I missed him. His arms were outstretched to me and I ran to him. Just like a little girl I ran straight into my Daddy's arms. There was no anger between us - no hurt feelings. He loved me unconditionally. I loved him just the same. There was only forgiveness and love. Oh, the love honey. I can't describe in words the love that's here. It's beautiful and intoxicating. Everyone here loves each other. There is no evil or wrongdoing here. There is only love and forgiveness. Forgive me. Forgive Mom. I didn't want to go. I didn't want to leave my children. I was just so tired baby.

There is nothing to forgive Mom, but I will never get over your crossing over, never. How can I not understand this after the journey we had? You got the break you needed but it was the most painful break of my life. Mom?

Yes baby.

Did you feel pain when you crossed over?

No honey. There was no more pain for Mom. That was the intoxicating part for me. I had years of agonizing pain and suffering; my body being tortured like some test tube and now, now there was nothing but peace and love. I felt and still feel light, unlike anything I'd ever felt before.

I was hoping you'd say that. I feel guilty when I tell you that after all the years of hard work we put into fighting cancer. I needed you to come back to me.

Don't feel guilty. I wanted to come back but honey, my body was so deteriorated there was no turning back. There was no strength or life in me to fight anymore. My body had been tested and treated beyond its max.

I know. The things you went through were horrible. All the times you cried like a little girl before your tests and procedures. All the moments you begged for the doctors to leave you alone were in the past. I wanted nothing but peace for you. I just…

Kristin, if there is one thing, I could pick the most to do over again it would be to figure out how I was going to say goodbye to my children. I couldn't fathom ever leaving you kids. I asked God so many times, to give me strength to say goodbye to my children, but how does a mother that loves her children as much as I love you kids say goodbye? It's not possible. That's why I always tell you, "Nothing can separate us. Not even death. No even God."

You kids were hurting so much already. To know that my departure was about to cause you an immeasurable lifetime of pain was more than I could bear. I knew the only thing that would heal my children's pain was me and now, I wasn't able to do that. We never said all the things we needed to say because I couldn't. I just couldn't and I should have, to better prepare you for what was to come.

No one in this world knew how lost I would be without you except you. I thought for sure you would understand this and stay. Is that selfish?

No.

For years we beat cancer. We were supposed to win. Instead, we lost, we lost, and I got lost. In that one last breath, my mind, body and everything about me got lost somewhere between April 1, 1982, the day of your diagnosis and December 18, 1990. My life as I knew it ended. I had no idea of the things that would happen to me - things where I would need my mother. When I realized you crossed over, I went into another room and I unleashed years of pain and anguish. I screamed obscenities, cried from the bottom of my gut, threw chairs, tipped tables and then...

You walked out of the Hospice building and stood in the open snow-covered grounds.

You saw me?

Yes. I called to you, over and over. When you didn't respond I knew I'd crossed over and there was no coming back. I called to you honey. I reached for you. I put my arms around you and held you as tight as I could as you buried your face in your hands and this is where it happened.

What? What happened?

The disconnect between you and me.

I know. I'm sorry. I just got so scared. I didn't understand what happened. I didn't understand what went wrong. I didn't understand anything period Mom. I was so scared without you. I felt like my home and my life were taken away.

They were baby.

I had nowhere to go inside or outside myself. Everything that was safe, good and real was you and you weren't there anymore. I felt like someone thrust me into the abyss. I went from feeling strong and confident to feeling scared and vulnerable. You were my strength.

You are your strength.

I screamed for God to send you back, that I would be a better daughter and do everything perfect and the way God wanted if it would just send you back.

You couldn't have been a better daughter baby. God is everything that is good, light and beautiful. God is the reason we met, and God is the reason we will stay together for as long as we want. Isn't that beautiful? Isn't that exciting? Sweet baby girl don't cry.

No matter what I do, where I go, who I meet or how hard I try to fill my life with things that are supposed to make me happy, they don't. There is an emptiness in me that will never be filled. Many times, I tried to hear or talk to you but there was this block in me. Your words and your hugs and kisses were intangible. I couldn't hear and see you the way I did when you were in your physical body and it scared the life out of me. I'm sorry I closed us off. I'm sorry I did that. I didn't mean to. I…

Shhh. You didn't close us off. I never left. Don't you know I've been following you around since the day I crossed over. I could never leave you. Even God knows that. Come here baby. Rest yourself in my arms where it's safe, where you're loved just the way you are, forever.

I miss you. I miss you still, after all these years.

I know but sweetheart, you don't have to miss me. I'm right here, in your heart, always. You don't know how good it feels for me to have us talking again, just like we used too. You've come to a place of acceptance and understanding of how Mom has transitioned and transcended. We're still the same "us". We're just communicating differently that's all. Right?

Yeah, I guess.

We sure have had some unbelievable journeys, haven't we?

Yes, we have. The aftermath of your crossing over was hard, really hard. I thought you put your wishes of what you wanted after your crossed, on paper.

I didn't. I had no energy. I didn't think I had to. I thought my sisters would have respect for my kids' grief and know that the wishes you expressed on my behalf came straight from me.

I told them that, but they did what they wanted. Do you remember the time Carolyn and I were sitting next to you in your bed? This was before you went into Hospice for the second time.

Yes. Carolyn thinks I don't, but I do. I remember what I asked of you. I wanted Carolyn to be a witness to help you in case Trudi tried to bull doze you. I thought if you had another adult helping you Trudi would back off.

She didn't. I kept it and I want it here in front of their faces. Carolyn wrote part of it and you wrote the other part because you could barely write at the time. Yet you were still coherent enough to know what you wanted and didn't want, and all you wanted was to have your wishes heard and executed. You were entitled as a woman and as a person with a terminal illness to be heard. That was your right. They took that away from you and justified it with self-centered reasons having nothing to do with you. I kept the note. It reads:

Dec 13, 1990
Dec. 113 1990
This is part of my last will
and testament.
I donot want to be
embalmed under any circumstance
I want to be creamated.
Marry I donot want my face
Signing: covered.
marry C Crage

"December 13, 1990, this is part of my last will and testament. I do not want to be embalmed under any circumstances. I want to be cremated. I do not want my face covered. Signed Mary J. Crage."

I remember this Kristin. I had a terrible fear of embalmment and suffocation. That's why I didn't want my face covered. I signed my name twice. I could barely see the paper, but I felt the pen in my hand and the paper underneath my skin. I knew what I was doing. Just because I couldn't speak or write well didn't mean I couldn't feel or think. I trusted my sister would help my daughter and me. Why didn't they do what I asked? Why weren't my wishes carried out? What happened?

Your sisters are what happened. They took over. You were embalmed at your sisters' insistence and then there was the funeral service you never wanted. Then they cremated you.

I never believed in embalmment or funerals. I didn't want any of that. I saw what they put you through. I saw honey.

My sister and brother didn't want any part of any of the before or aftermath decision making so that left me to try and make sure your wishes were followed through. I showed the note to Carolyn and Trudi before we went to the funeral parlor. Trudi told me it didn't mean anything and took control of the funeral services you never wanted. Then I showed Carolyn the note hoping to remind her of what your wishes. She said you didn't know what you were writing, and we shouldn't pay any mind to the note.

You told her she was wrong right?

Yes, oh yes. I told her you did know what you were writing and that was the whole purpose of writing it. I told her that you expressed these same wishes to me long before you became so sick, years before as a matter of fact. I told her that even so, you were still a person and your wishes needed to be respected. I told her that just because you were having a hard time communicating didn't mean your words and feelings should be ignored. That's exactly when they should have listened more closely to you instead of hearing and doing what they wanted. You expressed yourself. So, what if it wasn't the way they wanted. You still expressed yourself and they completely ignored your fears, concerns and wishes. The reason you wrote those words was to ensure you would be heard, even after you crossed over.

That's right. That's exactly right. What else?

I told her I promised you I would make sure your wishes were carried out, that I needed to do that for you, and they took that away from me. My heart sank into a bottomless pit. I lost you and slowly, I was losing my voice. They had you embalmed. A stranger cut you open and injected you with formaldehyde and put all that horrifying makeup on you. They wanted me to pick your outfit. I couldn't. I felt sick to my stomach. I felt like someone chopped my heart into tiny pieces. That's when I knew their love for you wasn't real. It's not love when you disrespect someone and everything they want in their last days and afterward. Then continue to disrespect your child when she's trying to make sure your wishes were followed through.

Did they let you have a say in anything?

They let me choose your prayer cards and we weren't even fucking Catholic anymore. I was filled with grief, rage at your family and utter despair.

Oh, my goodness. Oh Kristin. Oh, my sweet girl.

I tried to find something as non-religious as possible, but it wasn't possible. The funeral home was a traditional Italian Catholic funeral nightmare. I couldn't believe what they were doing and every time I tried to do something of what you wanted, they wouldn't let me. I had no say because you also made Trudi Executor of your Will.

I was there. You were there but to them, we didn't exist. The only people that existed was themselves. Your sisters believe that because someone is gravely ill and unable to respond as they normally would and crosses-over, that your rights as a person with dignity and respect are no longer. They dishonored you and caused a hurt in me they'll never understand or care about. I needed to execute your wishes as you wished. That was my closure. They took that away too.

Kristin, I am so sorry. None of what happened is your fault. It's okay. I know you tried. I know you did. I'm sorry my sisters did this. I knew how intimidating they could be and it's my fault for giving Trudi Power of Attorney. I made an even bigger mistake by making her Executor of my Will. I just didn't know what else to do and even if I did, it was too late. The damage was done, and I couldn't undo it. I'm sorry honey. I'm so sorry this happened, and you hurt so much.

I did more than hurt Mom. A huge part of me was traumatized forever. For two days your lifeless body lay in a casket you specifically asked not to be in. Your sisters were upset with me because I only came to the ridiculous funeral service and wake Trudi set up once. That was all I could bare. I couldn't see you like that. Every time your friends walked in Trudi gave them nasty looks. Spencer came, despite Trudi telling her not too and that she had no business being there.

Are you serious?

Oh yeah. What happened between you two was your business. Apparently, Trudi thought that being Executor of someone's Will meant playing God. Anyway, your sisters wanted me and Andrea to say a few words at the funeral service. I wanted to tell them, "Are you kidding me? You want me to speak at the funeral service my mother never wanted while she's laying, embalmed I might add, in a casket she also never wanted and feared with everything inside her would happen. Fuck you bitches."

I bet. I'm getting sick just listening to all this. So, what did you do?

Andrea said she didn't want to stand up there alone and practically pleaded with me not to make a scene. I didn't have the energy to make a scene. I knew if I confronted them anymore than I tried I would have been carted away for physically hurting them.

I understand and just as an aside, you would have been justified if you did.

So, we're standing there reading a passage from the bible with your casket directly in front of me. All I could think was, "I'm at my dead mother's funeral she never wanted, standing inside a Catholic Church she never went too reading from the bible she stopped reading because she never agreed with its philosophies." You hadn't been inside a Catholic Church in almost two decades. It had been longer since you ever read anything from a male-centered chauvinist book of stories and myths like the Bible. Your book was the Course In Miracles - a more progressive, philosophical approach to God, Spirituality and the Universe. I wanted to read from that, but your sisters threw a fit when I suggested it.

I should have been stronger. I am stronger than this, but every time I stood up to them, I was bombarded by your family and my siblings telling me to "stop being difficult and causing problems."

Oh, really? Seeing to my wishes was "being difficult and causing problems."

Yes. I felt like I was in a fog - a daze that wouldn't go away. My reactions went from being spot on to slow motion. I couldn't shake the nausea I felt. I was sickened by what I allowed to happen to you. I tried to override Trudi being the Executor but couldn't. Her status was legal. Everything between you and me was verbal. Her words overrode mine. I'm your daughter and that heartless, cheap excuse for a woman silenced both our voices. I was there all those years before she was. I know you. Most importantly, I respect you and what you wanted. To add salt to the already excruciating wound in me some of your nieces called the house demanding that the flowers that were sent to us be given to their mothers because it was their sister they lost. I finally had enough and told them that we are your children and we will decide who gets what, if anything. They called me "angry." I didn't care. I refused to let anyone in our home unless I was there. I guarded everything that was yours like a hawk. They told me I had no business guarding your things like that. I, again, reminded your family that I am your daughter and your children were the only ones who had the right to your things, not them. When the funeral services were over Trudi caught me off guard with yet another stunt. You promised me the only picture we had of your grandparents, my great grandparents. It hung in the dining room. A couple of weeks after you crossed over Trudi stormed into our home without knocking, pushed me out of the way, took it off the wall and said, "I'm taking this, and don't you dare try and stop me." I was in such shock I actually froze and didn't move until a minute or two after she was gone. I never got the picture back.

For your sake I want you to know that the picture was intended for you kids to take turns keeping. I would have never done that to her children. I know how much you loved it, but I don't want you to bother yourself with the picture. You've been through enough. It seems more like a symptom of the pain she caused you. Besides, I know Trudi. You won't get it back.

I missed you so much. I was left with nothing but hurt and disgust for your sisters. Oh! I get so angry when I think about all of this! I should have done more. God damn me! I should have done more. I should have told them all to go fuck themselves and leave us alone! They disrespected you in life and dishonored your spirit and I had no one to stand by me on this. If it's one thing Ethan and I did agree on it's the fact that your sisters are fucked up!

Kristin?

Yes.

Please don't do this to yourself. Please, honey. Don't hurt yourself anymore with anger for them. They're not worth it. You were acting on my behalf and I couldn't have asked for a better confident or daughter. Please hold onto that baby. You did nothing wrong. You were doing what you did for me in life, fighting for me against family who didn't have Mom's best interest at heart. I want my sisters to know that had the shoe been on the other foot I would have never hurt them or their children as deeply as they hurt my children. Their heads were filled with pills, alcohol and rage. I would have executed everything they wanted to a T and their children's grief would have been foremost on my mind and in my heart. I would have helped mend their kids' broken hearts, not add to their pain the way they did you.

I know you would have. Guess who finally showed up the last day of the funeral?

Dad.

Yup. I don't know if you remember but you asked for him when you were at Hospice. He didn't even have the human decency to show up.

I remember.

When Uncle Martin, Carolyn's ex-husband, went to your bedside, you looked him at him and said, Joe? You thought it was Dad. My heart ached for you. I know you needed closure with Dad. Still, after all those years he couldn't find it in himself to show up until after all was said and done. Of course, he had incentive.

What did he want?

Take a wild guess?

Money.

I couldn't stand to touch him let alone look at his ugly fucking face. Cody and Andrea hugged him and cried. I looked at them with disgust at how they could even feel any kind of love for a man who treated us and our mother so badly. Then, after giving a terrific performance of fake tears and hugs, your classy ex asked the question I knew he was waiting to ask.

Which was?

"Did your mother leave any insurance money for me?"

That's typical of your father.

All I could think as I watched my brother and sister embrace their father was "It should have been him, not my mother, my best friend, my sister."

Kristin don't say that.

Why not? It's true. You were the one that was there for me and the person I needed every day, not him. You always helped that man no matter how badly he treated us and how little he was in our lives. You were the person he counted on when he was down on his luck. Yet we couldn't count on him for anything, ever.

Kristin…

Listen to this. Listen to what I found:

"Dear Mary,

You called my office on November 2nd asking for copies of the 'Separation Papers.' In response to your inquiry, there are no Separation Papers that I am aware of. I checked the papers on file in the Onondaga County Clerk's office and I am enclosing for your information copies of the Court Orders dated August 2, 1982 and June 26, 1983. These have to do with your Support. You will recall that after we obtained these Orders, your husband pretty much disappeared from the face of the earth and we were never able to make service upon him or to file the Orders with any of his employers in order to enforce your judgment.

There are no additional papers on file in the Onondaga County Clerk's office. I am afraid that the enclosed documents are the only information that I can give you at this time.

Very truly yours..."

Oh my gosh. Where in the world did you get that letter?

It was a letter from your attorney dated November 29, 1989. We were in Syracuse at the time. It was with all the rest of your papers. You were still trying to get support from that scumbag. After 1976 that man never gave you, us, a fucking dime and you were still trying to get something, anything from him almost ten years later. That's almost two decades of hurt, anger and hardship he put all of us through.

I know Kris. Don't you think I know that? He took so much of my energy. I tried to get him to understand I couldn't support all four of us but all he kept saying was how hard he had it, how he had no money and blah, blah, blah. If only he knew the garbage, I had to feed my children just so you kids could eat.

What in the world made you help that man? Really, I want to know.

I think it was more projection of my father issues than anything else. I felt if I could get your father to be friends with me and accept me for whom I was, then I would feel the love and acceptance I always needed from my Dad. That's not the truth but that's how I felt.

Oh my gosh Mom. I wish you weren't put through so much. I really am sickened by both our fathers.

I wish you weren't being put through so much.

Things were awful, right to the core. Between your ex's disgusting illusory hope that you left him anything and the constant grief and anger from your family, I wanted to break out of Buffalo faster than a rocket.

Kristin, for years your plate was fuller than any kid could handle, and you carried that weight for years. I think the only way you could deal with all that was happening was to go so deep inside yourself that it made it difficult for me to communicate with you. I couldn't communicate with you at all. The wall was up and behind that wall were fear, anger, loss, grief and as you say, utter despair. It was like I was watching you through a glass window waving my arms to try and get your attention. Yet with all my attempts you never heard or acknowledged me.

Everything that was real now felt surreal. Where you were once a person, you were now handed to me in an Urn filled with ashes. All the things you taught me about spirituality, having faith in our spirit guides and the afterlife, etc. went out of my mind because it wasn't supposed to apply to us. That was for the books we read, not Mary and Kristin. You were all I had - my whole world. There was so much to do and so many things I had to take care of that I had to shut down inside. I could only let so much into my head. Others well-meaning comments such as, "Time will pass and you'll feel better," "God needed an angel," "Life goes on," "You'll move on," "Move on," "Everything happens for a reason," "She's in a better place," and best of all, "Let go" were uttered so many times I wanted to start punching the people who expressed such ignorance just because they didn't know what else to say. It seemed unfathomable that all those comments were about us and well-meaning or not, they were stupid. Who made them up in the first place? All I wanted to do was breathe because from the time you crossed over, I couldn't catch my breath. I felt as though I'd been running for years chasing hopes for a cure for breast cancer and dreams of what we would do when you were cured. Now I felt like we ran into a brick wall head on.

I know baby. I know. I'm so glad you went back to school. Your new semester was starting and going back to school was better for you than staying home.

For me, I had to go back. For us, I went back. My only other option was staying around your family. No way. I couldn't do that. Still, there was the issue of Sophie. Neither Cody nor Andrea wanted the responsibility of her. They both knew I would take Sophie and so did I. Sophie was sad without you. We brought her to Hospice so she could see and smell you. I hoped she would understand you weren't coming back, but Sophie waited for you anyway. Her grief went deep. I could tell. She waited everyday of every minute for you to come home. Her face went from being open, bright and happy to being long, drawn and sad. She moped from one spot to another.

I missed my Sophie too, but she saw me from time to time.

I knew it. I could tell. Sometimes she would look at something, like the sofa or the chair you used to sit in and respond as if someone was talking to her.

I was talking to her, letting her know I was okay and telling her to take care of you.

Animals are amazing like that. Their minds and hearts are free of guilt, anger and resentment. They have these direct pathways of communication, here and in the afterlife.

That's true, they do.

The hardest part about me going back was that although I would be Sophie's sole parent from now on, I still had to ask Andrea to watch her while I was in School.

Your brother wasn't there?

He was but you know he never took an interest in caring for her. I'm just feeling regret for not having taken her back with me.

Why?

Like I said, they didn't want the responsibility of her. They could barely handle themselves. From the time Sophie was little I was her parent and when you crossed, I was the only one that acknowledged her grief because she felt it. Forget about whether my siblings could or would take care of her or not. At the end of the day it was me that wanted Sophie the most. She was my love, my family and always my responsibility. We were inseparable all our lives. Now we were dealing with these intermittent periods throughout my college life where I had to leave her and that was gut wrenching for me. I wanted to be there for Sophie, and I let her down. I had that small apartment my last year of school. I could have taken her back then. I should have taken her with me. I'm so mad at myself for leaving her with my siblings.

Honey stop looking back because you did what you could. I know Sophie missed you, but she was okay with your sister. It was only for a short time. I know you guys needed each other but you keep beating yourself up on these things honey. I think the fact that you went back to school at all is commendable.

No, we would have been fine together I just wasn't thinking clearly about anything. What I was thinking was it would be better for her to stay in familiar surroundings but with each weekend I came home, I saw our surroundings become less familiar. Cody and Andrea weren't taking care of the house, at all. The place was always a mess. I regret not taking her back.

Sophie understands you couldn't take her. She does. You have a lot of regrets about this time period babe. I mean while I was sick and afterward. Too many.

I do.

You seemed to do okay with school.

The Director of Hospice was kind enough to write a letter to all my professors explaining what was happening with you. This enabled me to get extensions on all my exams for the winter semester. My grades were good, so I only needed the time to make up the tests. All my work was done. While you in Hospice I would bring all my books and homework and study at your bedside. I would read you my essays. You always liked reading my essays. You had your little criticisms here and there, but you liked my writing. You said I put things that were incomprehensible into more comprehensible language.

That's right. You did and still do.

All those days we were in Hospice I read, wrote and watched you. School felt like the only safe place for me. I longed for your loving arms to enfold me. I brought some of your clothes back with me. I held them, used them as blankets at night and sniffed them in the morning when I awoke. I used to go to the Library where they had these little rooms for a single person to study, and cry. I'd keep my back to the door so no one would see my face and stay for hours letting the tears flow being as silent as I could. I prayed your death was a nightmare that I would awake from - that it was all a mistake and you'd be coming back to me healthy, and we'd go on living our lives just as we planned. I'd have my career, fall in love, have my animals and most of all, you.

We'd be together every step of the wayside by side - just as we began and as we always said we'd remain. You know what Mom?

What baby?

Something in me knew we didn't have much time together. I didn't care if we were co-dependent or not. I just wanted to spend as much time with you as I could. It was one of those things we didn't talk about but should have.

I felt the same way. You're right Kristin. We should have. I'm sorry.

Me too. I listened to your favorite song every day, "Holding Back the Years" by Simply Red. There's a line in the song that reads, "I'll keep holding on..." Every time we heard that song you used to say to me "I'll keep holding on Kristin. I'll keep holding on," and you did for a long time. I know you held on for as long as you could, but I wanted more time with you. I needed more time for us. The irony is, looking back, as hard as those days were, I wish I could go back to them because you were there. I wanted to go back to all the places you were. Sometimes I still do.

I wished you weren't in so much pain. It almost debilitated you and you had so much life ahead of you.

I didn't feel that way. School was a distraction, but Sophie and dance are where I felt like I could express some of my grief. It's also where I felt the closest to you. At school, I busied myself by auditioning and getting into the school dance company. The professor/choreographer changed each semester. One semester it was a modern dance company and the next semester it was West African/Caribbean Dance Company. We used to travel and perform in and around Brockport and Central New York. When I was in the modern dance company we traveled to a very special city, well special to me anyway. Guess which one?

Well I know right off the bat you're not referring to Buffalo.

No, thank goodness. Syracuse! We went to Syracuse and performed at the Syracuse Civic Center. Spencer came to see me.

Well, talk about coming around full circle.

I know. Can you believe it?

The Civic Center - isn't that where I once took you for an audition.

That's the one. I loved going back home. That's my home, Syracuse, not Buffalo. I missed it so much. I asked Spencer to take me by the old house. We parked the car in front and I just stared. All kinds of memories flooded my head but the one that never left is the one when I was little and was awakened by that favorite sound of mine.

The sound of planes flying overhead from a distance.

Yeah. I thought about you and us. I thought about the friends I'd grown up with, most had moved away. I loved being there because everything reminded me of you, pre-cancer. I missed your hugs when I got sad.

Honey, I saw how sad, alone and lonely you felt. You cried every day you were at school. You stared at the walls and cried into your pillow. You woke up and cried. You cried yourself to sleep but I want you to know that Mom would never leave you alone to cry like that. My arms were and still are around you, loving you, enfolding you in my love.

Every now and again I would feel something brush my hair from my face. Was it you?

I loved those moments. The ones where you felt me but weren't sure if it was me. At least I had some connection with you, even if it wasn't what we have now. It was something. Sweetheart, spirits can miss those they depart from even when they cross over. You missed me and guess what baby? I missed you desperately. I hated seeing you go through so much pain without me by your side loving you and healing your pain. That was one of my fears before I crossed over, remember? That I wouldn't be able to be there for you in your pain. I was so glad you went back to school. School was the best place for you, not home with your siblings. Things weren't good between you guys there. You argued too much. You were trying to keep the house as it was before I crossed, and they were beyond disrespectful to the home I created for us. I wasn't happy about.

I wanted you to be in a place that would give you some sense of grounding and I knew school would do that for you. I knew school gave you hope for a better life and dance kept you on solid ground and gave you a place to express your feelings. You could let go in your movement and be free to be who you are and feel whatever you need to.

There are no more of your beautiful writings, birthday cards, Christmas cards or any other cards or writings from you after 1990. Everything I wrote and gave you was cremated with you.

I have everything you gave me that matters - the immense, unconditional love from you in my spirit and soul.

I don't want people to remember you sick Mom. I want people to remember you the way you were: a free, warm, loving, passionate, full of life, caring, funny, generous, open, compassionate, spontaneous, strong, intelligent, open, always wanting to learn about others, accepting, non-judgmental woman with an infectious smile. What photograph do you think captures all that?

You know which one. I love it! It's me!

Mary J. Crage
June 9, 1940 – December 18, 1990

Now it's your turn.

My turn for what?

It's your turn to read me the beautiful poetry you wrote. Mom always loved the poems you wrote, especially the ones you wrote for me. Read me what you wrote to heal yourself.

1991 - 1992

Light emerges from the glimmer of your reflection
Tis' then I'm reminded of my greatest vision of you:
Shadowy, bright, surreal
Yet always magnificent

I worship you
I look for you everywhere, still

I, once or twice, thought I felt
Your hand gently push my hair from face

They say I'm obsessed
They say I must go on
They say I will never be clean if I don't forget

I say nothing
I feel everything
I sit

I watch for your laughter
I listen to you dance under rays of sunlight
I feel your touch
I let go
I am freedom besieged through memory.

Kristin A. Crage ©1991

So, were you and Ethan doing any better through all this nonsense?

No, but my relationship wasn't as prevalent on my mind you know.

Yes, I'm sure.

That first year without you didn't seem real. I felt like I was walking around in a daze. When I wasn't in a daze I vacillated between grief, anger, rage and utter hopelessness and despair. I sank, emotionally, and felt like I couldn't get out of where I was. Your mail still came and people that we didn't know to contact still called. Every day I woke up wanting to die just so I could be with you. The best part of me died the day you crossed over. Ethan and I continued to do the things we normally did. We studied together, spent time with friends and he prepared to graduate. School was a big distraction for me, and I was glad I had it. I needed some sort of schedule to stick too. Surprisingly, Ethan did something sweet for me.

Oh, what was that?

I was so down Mom. I couldn't lift myself out of the black hole I felt like I fell into. Ethan took me on vacation to his parents' cottage in downstate, NY to try and lift my spirits. It was a nice break and I really appreciated it.

That was nice of him.

It was. The cottage was on a lake. We went in the dead of winter and it was so beautiful. Everything around us was silent except the birds that hadn't flown south for the winter and the sound of the water swishing back and forth. The sky was a perfect blue with a few white fluffy clouds here and there. I wanted to stay longer but we could only stay a few days. Still, it was good to get away. I missed Sophie. She was my only consolation. I was trying so hard to keep my head above water. Then I got a call from Darlene.

Your cousin?

Yup. She said she wanted to come and visit me. Given out contentious relationship and my absolute disdain for her my knee jerk reaction was to say, "no thank you." Yet I really needed someone to talk to. I couldn't talk to the friends I had at school. Any time I started to talk about you they would get uncomfortable or try to change the subject. They tried but, you know, we were all gearing up to graduate so the crossing over of someone's mother was a downer for them. Do you know what I mean?

I do know what you mean.

I mean they weren't being mean; they were just being themselves, soon to be college graduates that wanted to party and have fun.

So how was the visit with Darlene?

I was hoping to see a compassionate side of my cousin. I longed for someone to tell me that everything I was feeling was okay and normal.

Oh no. Honey…

Yeah, I know. Darlene's idea of being supportive was to tell me how angry, sad and depressed she thought I was - how I needed to let go of you and move on and not express myself so much to your sisters. I defended myself and reminded her she didn't know the whole story of me and your sisters. That I'd spent years caring for my mother and best friend and now just watched her cross over. Then I asked her how she thought I should feel?

What did she say to that?

She said, "I don't know but that's why the rest of the family doesn't want to be around you." I responded by telling her I wasn't aware the rest of the family didn't want to be around me but thanks for the info. It hadn't even been a year since your passing. It was one jab after another with her. Finally, I just told her thanks for coming but that I thought she should leave the next morning. That was the last full conversation I had with her. I knew not to trust or talk with her. In my vulnerability I just made a mistake and confided in the wrong person.

It's heartbreaking when the people we thought or wanted to trust aren't trustworthy at all. Or, in Darlene's case, aren't compassionate, understanding or even kind for that matter. Wow, you're right. It was one dig after another with her.

Yeah, after you crossed, I found myself trusting and/or accepting help from people I would have otherwise not dealt with. I felt vulnerable to other peoples' influences that were already toxic relationships in my life.

Like the family.

Specifically, your family. Their meanness and toxicity were suffocating me. There are people that will take the opportunity to kick while you're down for the sole purpose of making themselves look better. I felt like your family was doing that with me.

I understand and know those feelings all too well. Sometimes when you're not paying attention to how lonely you truly feel you let people into your life that you'd be better off without. It's hard to keep perspective when you're in the thick of it.

It is hard, really hard.

What about Dance? Dance and movement in general were always your touchstone - your saving grace that kept you on an even keel.

Dance was going great, except for the little hiccup I encountered with my back.

I know and I wanted you to know I was there for every moment of it.

I was really thrown off guard. One minute I was dancing, going to class, working out and the next minute I was thrown for a loop. You know, it's funny, just when you think all the hard stuff is over there's more and more to come, at least for some of us.

Yes, for some. You were so brave.

I had no choice. When I first went to the doctor, he told me I would have to have an MRI in order for him to see what was going on and find the root of the pain. When he told me this I freaked! I knew from going with you how small the MRI machines were and you know how claustrophobic I am.

Do I ever.

I couldn't believe I was going to have to have an MRI. This was before they even came out with open MRI's. All they had were the closed ones and the only opening was the one you entered from. It was like being in a, big, round metal casket. Twenty minutes in a closed metal tunnel, UGH! While I waited for them to call my name, I was talking to you, telling you how afraid I was and how I didn't want to die in an MRI machine. I had this fear it would collapse on me or something. I was asking you to be with me and hold me.

They put me on this conveyor then strapped me down. My heart raced a mile a minute. Then, they left the room, pushed a button, and I slowly glided into the tunnel, they told me "Don't Move." All this loud clinging and clanging was happening, and my face was about one inch from the top and sides. I actually couldn't move. Even to think about it makes me want to break out which is what I wanted to do at the time.

I remember those, boy do I remember those. Mom always hated them too. I used to just shut my eyes and try to go to sleep.

What! Sleep! Are you nuts! How could you possibly sleep?

It's called Valium.

Oh right☺. Why didn't I think of that? I do remember feeling something soothing while I was in there though. After about one minute of being inside the machine my heart began to slow down and I just felt, calm. Then I felt something brush the side of my face. That was you?

Yes. I hated seeing you go through that and I knew how scared you were. I lay next to you in the machine. You were crying, a very careful cry because you knew you couldn't move. I was rubbing the side of your head and telling you to think of rainbows and walking through an open field on a sunny day - that you were okay, and it would be over soon, very soon.

I didn't hear you, but I know I felt you when that calm feeling came over me. Whenever I would get scared or nervous about things you always gave me that exact visualization - to think of rainbows and open fields. You made me think of good things or memories to chase away the negative thoughts. So, I did just that. I thought of rainbows and open fields and it helped.

You see☺.

If I got distracted from my rainbows and open fields I switched to a funny memory.

Which one?

I thought of the time you took us kids to confession. We were little. It was my first time in a confessional. I remember the dimly lit tiny booth with one chair and not wanting to go in there because of my claustrophobia. Back then I was also afraid of the dark.

What do you mean "back then", you still are.

I am not.

Yes, you are. You sleep with nightlights in each room of your apartment.

Hey, I'm in the middle of a positive memory here. What are you, stalking me in my sleep?

Maybe.

Can I finish the story please?

Go ahead, (Kristin's afraid of the dark. Kristin's afraid of the dark, na, na, na, na, na).

You know what? You're fired!

Okay, okay, keep going.

You closed the curtain and all I saw was the tiny screen that separated me and the priest. I wasn't sure how loud I needed to speak for the priest to hear me. How did I know you had to speak softly? Did my mother tell me? No.

I thought you knew. Your brother and sister went before you.

Yeah but I was so little I barely reached the screen. Plus, I didn't know where the priest was in relation to the screen.

What do you mean you didn't know where the priest was? Where did you think he was dear, speaking from heaven ☺?

I just thought since I couldn't reach the screen that I'd better speak up that's all.

Oh, little minute. Your brother and sister and I were laughing so hard we almost wet our pants when we heard this tiny voice screaming at the top of her lungs, "BLESS ME FATHER FOR I HAVE SINNED…" and you confessing all your sins in number format. "Number 1…" You actually organized your sins, numerically.

I hope things are organized where you are because if not it's going to be a very unsettling transition for me. Do you have organic decaf there? I only drink decaf now-a-days☺.

You don't need anything here but you. You'll be fine sweetheart. Well, the priest heard you alright and so did everyone else in the church.

The priest was nice. He said, "Shhh, my child. I can hear you. You don't have to yell." I think I heard him laughing a little too.

I wouldn't doubt it. It was funny.

When I was done, I saw you, Cody and Andrea laughing so hard you all had tears in your eyes. I couldn't figure out what you guys were laughing at. In a way I didn't care. The fact that we were all laughing made me happy.

That was a good moment. I have to hand it to you Kris.

What, the nerd crown?

No silly. You could be a funny kid when you wanted too. Even if it meant making a fool of yourself.

I like making people laugh. It's good when it happens.

Why don't you try stand-up? You'd be great at it.

Na, I'd rather just make a fool of myself in everyday life. It's much more fun. Besides, Stand-Up is the only vocation where I actually fear people won't laugh at me. Anyway, while I was in the MRI my tears turned to laughter which I had to hold in. Then I thought of another funny memory. Want to hear it?

Of course.

Oh, you'll love this one. It was the time you helped me with my math homework, and I got an "D" on it.

I don't think we need to recall this one. Don't you have any others?

There are many funny memories with you, but certain ones stick out the most, like this one. I was in fifth grade at Lakeshore Elementary in Cicero, NY and while math was never my strong suite, I was still able to hold anywhere from a c+ to a b- in it. That all changed with one assignment.

You're exaggerating and that never happened.

I hate to break it to you Mary, but it did. My homework was on some equations I can't remember. When I saw my first "D" I was so mad at you. Of course, typical Mary, decided to call my math teacher and challenge her by telling her she was wrong and that all the problems were done in such a way so no one could understand them. Smooth, very smooth. You may have been right, but she really liked me after that phone call.

Okay, now I remember. Is that why you never asked for my help with your homework again?

Let me think, YEAH!

Every time I offered to help you with your homework you immediately said no. That hurt Mom's feelings.

Too bad.

Brat. Well I was right, and your teacher was horrible! So was your reading teacher. Come to think of it I didn't like that school in general. I'm glad you were there only there one year.

Yup, one year and off to another school. Between grammar school and high school, I changed schools seven times.

You did not.

Yes, I did.

Seven times? No. Really?

Yes, really.

No.

Yes.

Name them.

Bear Road Elementary (North Syracuse, NY), Elmcrest Elementary (Liverpool, NY), Lakeshore Road Elementary (Cicero, NY), Gillette Road Middle School (North Syracuse, NY), North Syracuse Junior High School (North Syracuse, NY), Bennett High School (Buffalo, NY) and finally to end my high school career at the Buffalo Academy of Visual and Performing Arts High School (Buffalo, NY).

You have a good memory. I'm sorry about that babe. I wish you didn't have to change school so many times.

It's alright. Like you said before, I adapted pretty well, I think.

You adapted well for a person who hates change.

It kept things from getting boring, except for Lakeshore Elementary. I didn't like that school.

Why?

You have to ask?

Oh right. That's when you went to school with Lucy Spinnetz and the whole spelling bee thing and...

I'm over it Mom. I am. I mean, I wish you wouldn't say her name but whatever. It is what it is. N-E-C-E-S-S-A-R-Y.

Okay sweetheart. It's okay. Mommy's here.

Thank you and I appreciate the Mommy love.

Of course, dear. Wasn't you're teacher also a little, different? Didn't he have a fear of children or something like that?

Yeah, it was weird. If one of us kids got to close to him, he would hug whatever wall or object was nearest to him to put as much distance between him and us kids.

I wonder why they kept him.

Who knows? He was nice just a little standoffish.

Well he seemed harmless.

He was. With all my funny "Mary" memories, before I knew it the MRI was over and a few days later I had my diagnosis; a slipped/herniated disc at L4-L5.

Just like Mom.

Just like you.

I'm so sorry you went through that. You had the same problems with your discs and joints.

More commonly known as degenerative disc disease, or Osteoarthritis.

That's right but you had an early onset of it.

Yeah. I didn't even know I had it or what it was until the doctor told me, but it's not just limited to my spine. I have it everywhere in my body. It's okay, I mean it's workable except in the rain and really cold weather. Then it can be a pain, literally. When I walk it feels like someone is pushing against my legs and the rest of me trying to prevent me from going from point A to point B.

I didn't know you had it either honey. If I knew you had it, I would have told you and we would have done something about it. It never occurred to me get you any bone or body scans. You were always working out, dancing and so healthy and fit. I didn't think I needed too. We had so much going at the time. Plus, with all that Mom went through, getting you to go to the doctor was like pulling teeth.

I know. After seeing what you went through, I hated going to the doctor. I was so afraid she/he might find something. I don't blame you at all. It was just painful. I mean, seriously painful. I felt like it happened overnight, but Osteoarthritis is a gradual process and while I was diagnosed at age 20, the doctor said it started before that.

I think I may have been young too when it started for me and didn't realize it. You know, we just didn't check for things like that when you're that young. Anything with the word "arthritis" was for "old" people, at least that's how it was viewed back then but believe me, I know the pain very well.

Yeah, everything was agonizing; sitting down, going to bathroom, standing up and forget about dancing. I had to take a couple weeks off from dance class. Back then they used an anti-inflammatory called Dolobid. I was on that for a few weeks. The disc slipped to where it needed to (thankfully not near my spinal cord) and it's been there ever since. I made it through. Every now and again it flares up but it's okay.

That's good. I'm so glad you didn't have to have surgery.

Me too. I was trying to keep it together Mom. I really was. During this last semester I was thankful for my own apartment. It was hard for me to process anything in my head, it was so cluttered with thoughts, memories, disbelief, anxiety, depression, etc. Having my own space helped. It was good to be able to cry when I needed too. After my disc healed, I threw myself into Dance even further. I did my best to make it through that year. Each day I would tell myself you just have to make it through today.

Kristin, you did more than make it through. My goodness, after your back ordeal you were in two dance pieces - a solo and a duet with one of your girlfriends. I couldn't believe how talented you became. I saw every bit of each one. They were beautiful honey.

I knew you were there. I could feel this amazing light and love around me. I knew it was you.

Of course, I was there. I wouldn't have missed any of the wonderful things you did. Your energy and passion for movement came through clear as day on stage. When you danced you could tell you were someone who loved movement just for the sake of moving, not so much to perform, although your performances were dramatic and captivating. I loved the title of your solo, "7921 Davis Road."

The address of our old house in Syracuse.

That's what the piece was about, our old house?

Yes, and how much I missed it and the woman who wanted so much to return to it one day.

My favorite piece was the one you choreographed all by yourself. It was a beautiful masterpiece and a great sending off to yourself for your senior year.

That was the Graduate/Undergraduate Dance Concert. All of us had the opportunity to choreograph and/or perform our own piece. All the while I was dancing and choreographing all I would think about is, "I wish my Mom were here and I wonder what she would say if she were?"

She was and she would say she was filled with pride that her little girl was growing into a woman - accomplishing all the things I hoped she would and more! You kept going honey, that's the important thing. You kept going and look what you did with your grief. You expressed it through your art. That's healing and life affirming. Seeing all these things you were doing made me even more glad you stayed at school. You needed this creative outlet, if for nothing else than to help you heal.

Your right. Dance was my savior.

I know it was. The girls in the piece danced so beautiful. I couldn't believe that was my little minute up there giving direction to the sound and stage people and you were very soft spoken, not that loud, obnoxious tone that so many artists use. Sometimes people yell and demand just to hear themselves talk and their hard to deal with.

I wanted to be respectful and very nice. After all, who was it that used to say, "You get more bees with honey." Hmm, I wonder?

That's right, and did you?

I did.

All of the dancers had long hair. Was that on purpose?

It was. I like long hair. I like the way it flows with the body and I think it adds a dramatic effect to any piece. They were beautiful dancers.

Why didn't you dance in it?

I felt too close to the subject matter and thought it would be better if I stepped back and worked the process from behind the scenes. I don't think it was a masterpiece, but I thank you for saying that. It was a good first piece of choreography for me. I like working behind the scenes just as much as I like performing.

You can tell and it was a masterpiece! What did you call it again?

"Silent Screams." The main theme was animal rights, specifically stopping animal testing. It was about the unheard suffering animals endure while being held in laboratories and tested on.

That is a very serious subject and very close to you. You were smart to work it from the behind the scenes. My favorite part was the end, the most important part!

The beautiful picture of you, the one you love so much with you waving appeared at the end as my dedication to you.

I loved that dedication. I felt your love so strong and beautiful. Did you feel mine?

Sometimes, not like I do now. I needed you in all the ways a daughter needs her mother; for guidance, life education, love, support, to talk and do things with, argue and grow with.

I know you did. It was hard watching you and not being able to help you. You fumbled a lot.

My entire life after you crossed has been one big fumble. Everyone loved the dedication to you and the picture. I learned how difficult it is to be objective with your art when you're in such a subjective place. I did the best I could and enlisted the help of faculty whenever I needed it.

That's true but the end result was amazing!

Thanks. One of the students on the school paper did a critique of all the performances and highlighted mine.

What did they say?

The headline read:

"Student dancers dazzle audience." The critique of my piece is as follows:

> "The most impressive piece was 'Silent Screams,' choreographed by Kristin A. Crage. The piece was performed to Sinead O'Connor's 'Stretched on My Grave' and used props such as slides and chairs. It was dedicated to Mary Crage, the choreographer's mother, who died of cancer."

Wow!

There's more:

> "The dancers, with long hair hanging down, used many clawing motions as they flew around the stage. The piece downgraded the use of animals in experiments. Crage said, 'It's all try me stuff. That's the same thing they did with my mother. Experimenting with radiation and chemotherapy. It was torture.'"

I mean, looking back my quote was not altogether what I wanted to say. I was so emotional I…

Why do you feel you have to justify yourself?

I don't know. I wish I said something more intelligent.

That was pretty good for a first timer. It's how you feel right?

About the animals, yeah. You know how strongly I feel about animal welfare.

No, I mean about me and the radiation and chemo, that it was torture to me?

I didn't mean to hurt or disrespect you in anyway, I just…

Kristin, is that how you feel?

Yes. I feel the doctors stopped looking at you like you were a person; a woman and it was like, "Let's try this," or "Let's try that" and here we were left with the roller coaster of hope and lost hope. In the end, you're right. Your body had enough. I saw that, emotionally and physically.

Honey don't ever apologize for the way you feel. I taught you to express yourself and you do it in the most appropriate of ways, through your creative process. I felt the same way too you know - like I was being tortured. I would ask myself, "How much more do I have to go through? When is this all going to be enough and will it ever end? What are they going to do to me next that ISN'T going to work? How much more will my children have to see me suffer?" I felt like a test tube.

The piece was beautiful honey. I'm amazed at what you did with all those feelings you had. You poured them into your art. I was so proud of you Kristin. I can't tell you how proud I was of you. My heart was overjoyed. Were you proud of yourself?

I wanted to be, but I wasn't. On the outside I gave the appearance that I was rising above grief and loss, but I was actually slowly sinking into it in an intense way. After you crossed, something happened.

What?

I came home from school one weekend. I called Trudi and we had a huge argument. I think the essence of the argument was that she had her hands in everything just before and after you crossed and now, she was nowhere to be found. In the midst of our arguing she called me a "Fucking little bastard," and then told me to grow up.

She's a fucking little bastard to say that to my kid. What did you say?

While we were arguing all these things ran through my head.

Such as?

I thought about the picture of my great grandparents and the way she basically stole it out of our home. I thought about the friends she turned away while you were in the hospital and at the funeral you didn't want. I thought about how she embalmed you and all the other things she did to you that you didn't want done. Then I thought about how now that you crossed, she told me I should give Sophie away and I finally just told her.

Told her what?

I told her to go to hell. I wanted to say a whole lot more, believe you me but I didn't. Looking back, I should have. I should have told her all the things I felt. You know, all the things I've been talking about with you.

You should have. She deserved it.

She did but I didn't have the energy. I knew she'd tell the rest of your family and the fact that she called me a "fucking little bastard" wouldn't mean shit. The only thing anyone would come down on is me and whatever I said which is what happened. I hung up on her, but the rest of the family got wind of Trudi's crazed out version of the argument. Like clockwork, what she said didn't matter. It was my fault according to them. After that, I was blacklisted even more than I already was from the family.

I believe that. Give me an example of what they did.

Once I needed a ride back to school. This wasn't too long after the argument. I called Trudi's son-in law, who never liked our family in the first place. He said he would be happy to give me a ride. When Trudi's daughter found out he was going to help me she called back to say he wouldn't be able to "for personal reasons."

Wow.

Wow is right. I never asked for anyone's help after that. I already knew the answer. All I kept hearing from your family was, "I know how much you're hurting but it's time for you to grow up." They felt that now that you crossed, I was of an adult age and should be able to handle everything on my own. Even though they promised you they'd be there for me. Yet your sisters' kids that were my age or older, were still kids and still needed their help. Of course, they got it, way into their forties as a matter of fact.

You were of an adult age, but you still needed guidance. I can't believe they said that to you.

I can. That's them, cold hearts or no hearts and all.

You know why they felt that way?

I don't care.

I know. I wouldn't either.

Bottom line is they didn't want to be bothered, with your illness, your crossing over or your kids. They were always like that. What your sisters and their children don't get is that they had their parents through graduations, first jobs, job losses, money problems, birthdays, holidays, engagements, weddings, births and everyday life in general, etc. I had my anchor ripped from beneath my feet and nothing to ground me but grief and despair.

An uncomfortable silence entered my life when you crossed. I missed the sound of I.V. drips, back and forth trips to the hospital and the adrenalin rush of worry and/or fear. I wanted to worry for you. I was used to it. I wanted to go to the hospital, my second home. The smell never bothered me. In fact, I was starting to miss it. I missed the scheduling of your meds and all the characters I used to come up with to make you laugh so you wouldn't feel so depressed taking them. I missed watching you finally doze off for the night after struggling to stay awake. Toward the end, you feared going to sleep. You were sure you were going to die, and you always said you weren't ready.

I looked for you everywhere. I hoped the funeral home would call me to tell me they made a mistake - that they realized they had the wrong body and my mother was still alive, and I could go and get you. All I needed was the address. I jumped when the phone rang. I hoped it was you, happy, healthy and asking me to come and pick you up from somewhere, anywhere. All I wanted to do was go home and see my Mom. Yet I had no idea where home was anymore.

My little Kristin. I love you. I love you.

I couldn't accept that I would no longer hear you calling me from another room only to forget what you wanted.

Tell me you love me.

I love you so much it hurts, still. I knew from as far back as I can remember that no one would love me the way you love me. My future looked bleak without you. In fact, I couldn't see my future at all. Where things were clear now seemed like such a blur. What was I going to do, about anything and everything? There were so many things we never talked about and then there were things I knew I would need you to talk to and couldn't. While I was 20, I was in no way a woman. I missed my entire childhood and was still a daughter/child who needed her mother. I couldn't believe that in order to see my mother grow old I would have to imagine her and never have the beauty of experiencing this process for ourselves. In one moment, you were physically here. The next, you were an image and collection of memories. How could that be? I had no idea how I would reconcile not having you for any milestones in my life such as my 21st birthday or college graduation. The one thing you wanted so much for me and I wasn't' even sure I would get that far. The one and only person in my life who would feel the most proud and excited for me for such an accomplishment wasn't going to be there. I wanted to call you so many times and actually picked up the phone and pretended we were talking.

What did we talk about?

The usual. You asked me how school was, how dancing was going, was I having fun? You know all the things we always talked about. Then you told me not to worry so much, that everything was going to be okay and WE would be okay.

That conversation was real honey. It was real. I missed you too. It made my energy feel heavy to see you so sad. It still does.

I cried to you, for you and I haven't stopped. Am I not normal?

No one can say or judge what's normal. You are your normal. You and I both have things that are undone. That's why the tears still flow.

I was hurting and all anyone could see was anger. I couldn't breathe without your family calling me angry and who wouldn't get angry at that. I would get angry at them calling me angry and other derogatory names and this only reinforced their words.

They didn't know you then Kristin and they don't know you now. My family likes to focus on everyone but their selves. Your cousins had it easy compared to you. My sisters try to argue this because they need some justification for their misery but there really isn't any. They're just miserable, angry, mean women who had pretty good lives compared to most. They have no reason to be so awful, none whatsoever.

The worse I did the better they felt about themselves. I wasn't going to have it. I wanted to prove them wrong and show them that you raised a strong, independent woman who could overcome anything.

You are a strong, independent woman who can overcome anything.

Back then, I didn't feel that way. I remember you wanted your ashes scattered in a serene, beautiful place, somewhere in nature. I told my Cody and Andrea that and we argued. They insisted on keeping them on a shelf. With their usual two against one I was outnumbered. The most difficult part of this transition was how they turned our home into their own personal drug bin and a "crash zone" for all their drugged-out friends.

I know. This is what I was referring to when I said they were beyond disrespectful to the home I created for us. They did what they wanted and not what I asked of them. Sometimes your siblings reminded me very much of their aunts and that's not a good thing.

Oh my gosh Mom. I couldn't believe what they were doing.

Do I want to hear this?

No, but you need too.

Oh no.

They rented out your bedroom to losers with no jobs who barely showered and did drugs all day. The "boarder" slept in your bed and used your closet. Then they sold your hospital bed; the one that automatically moved up and down.

They sold my bed!

Oh yeah. That's not the worst of it.

Ugh, I feel sick already.

It was a constant change of someone renting your room. Some asshole would come for a few months and leave and then another asshole would come and so on. Not too long after you crossed Cody decided he would turn part of your room into a "grow" room.

A "grow" room?

Yeah, you know, for marijuana.

Oh, you've got to be kidding me.

No. I'm all for smoking pot and even the legalization of marijuana but not the way he did it. He was so lax-a-daisy about growing. He and Andrea let anyone and everyone into our home. They always forgot to lock the door and the place was in constant disarray. Every time I came home it was a mess. They never cleaned the place. Cody was an irresponsible grower and he could have gotten himself and everyone in that house arrested if someone said something. Thinking about it, that probably would have been good for them.

I was just going to say that.

I tried to keep our home the same. I wanted something, anything to stay the same. Everything was changing and it was all too much. I tried for weeks to convince them to let our house be as it was minus the strangers that came and went but they ignored me. I had no say because I was at school most of the time. I wished they didn't treat our home with such disrespect. We didn't even own it. I felt like they were also disrespecting our landlord who was always so kind to you.

They were those little shits. They were always a handful those two.

You're telling me. I had no home or family anymore. I had nothing but school and Sophie. I worried for Sophie when I wasn't there.

She was okay, wasn't she? They were taking care of her right? Or, at least, your sister was.

She was okay. They were feeding her, letting her out and giving her some attention but I was anxious to get her with me. Then, my siblings made a decision that I, again, objected to but to no avail.

I can't imagine how awful you felt. You were trying to maintain my wishes and I know you think no one listened but I heard you baby, and that's enough for Mom. I know the decision they made was hard for you to take.

It was like swallowing a golf ball. For me, it was unforgiveable. Until this day, when I think about it and my heart sinks because I know how much our house in Syracuse meant to you. I remember all the times you and I went back and forth to fix it up between tenants. Those drives were so special and important to me. We talked about so many things on those drives; politics, boys, memories, food, dance, animals, LGBT issues, etc. That house was the place where I began Mom. It was the place where I wanted to end.

I know honey.

You wanted us kids to keep the house "just in case" you always said. You left us each some insurance money, not a lot, but enough to get through us through for a year or two. Financially, we were doing just fine with what you left us and whatever jobs we held although, Andrea didn't work that first year you crossed. She basically spent all her money on drugs, alcohol, and whatever money Louisa and Darlene would hit her up for as well as other useless things she didn't need.

Louisa and Darlene would ask her for money?

Oh yeah, "loans" here and there that were never paid back. They completely took advantage of her and she let them. I used some money to pay for housing and went back to school and put the rest away until I needed it. Cody went back to his job and Andrea continued to be totally and completely irresponsible and destructive and Louisa was her drinking and drug partner.

I couldn't control what my little sister or your sister did when I was in my physical body and I had a feeling that would be the case when I crossed over. However, honey, that was their journey.

It was and I couldn't watch the pain Andrea was causing herself. I told her, "The pain you're putting yourself through with drugs, alcohol, bad relationships, not caring about yourself, bad diet, is all you. No one is hurting you but you. You need to get yourself together or you're going to die."

What did she say to that?

She didn't care. She told me to mind my own business and called me "goody two-shoes." So, whatever, I never said a word to her again about what she was putting her body and mind through, but I knew one day it would catch up with her.

Anyway, I wanted to keep the house for the same reason you did, "just in case." It was also good income. Andrea and Cody argued that there was no one to keep it up but I told them I would have. I did it with you and I liked it. I knew what went into renting the house out, the trips back and forth. I knew how you had to keep tabs on it, but my Andrea and Cody didn't want the responsibility. All those two lazy, self-serving, greedy jerks saw were dollar signs. Not a home that had a past, present and future that we built.

I worked so hard, sacrificed so much for you kids to have it and keep it as you said, just in case. I never wanted my kids to be without a home and this was the home any one of you could have returned to if you needed it.

That's how I felt but "two against one" prevailed. I was pissed, really pissed and disgusted by them. All they kept saying was, "Who's going to going to maintain it?" When I reassured them, I would they told me that they wanted to sell it so they could get the money. Every day since then I've regretted signing the papers to sell. I should have held out and been stronger. I just felt so vulnerable and penetrable without you. I held out as long as I could but all I got was pressure from my siblings and Trudi. The same pressure you got yet you defied them.

I had you in my corner, always. Now, you had no one. There was another reason I never sold the house honey.

Tell me.

There was that practical part of me that knew I was going to cross over and, that this time around I wouldn't beat breast cancer. There was also that part of me that remained hopeful that a miracle would happen, and all my prayers would be answered. I'd be miraculously well and be able to go back home, to Syracuse and have my life back. I missed my independence like you wouldn't believe.

I know Mom and you know what?

What?

I held that same hope right up until the moment you crossed. Why shouldn't we, right?

That's right. Hope can only help and heal.

I poured the pain and loss of you and our lives into dance but the hollowness in my gut still grew.

I know. You danced a beautiful solo. That must have helped you express your feelings.

It did, sort of, for the moment anyway.

How much did the house sell for?

I don't remember the total amount. Trudi took all the papers. I just remember that after all the liens on the house, the mountain of debt your ex left you with and the attorney's fees, us three split $30,000 or $40,000.

Oh, my goodness. I'm not going to sugar coat this. I'm going to be straight forward in how I feel.

Please do.

Your brother and sister should have never sold our home and my sisters went against everything I wanted and believed in. They didn't respect my wishes because they knew I never wanted to sell the house. They should have helped you kids keep it. I know you would have done whatever was necessary to do so.

That's exactly what I told them. They were just lazy and wanted everything in your life to be closed up so they wouldn't have to deal with anything. Everything about your life was a bother to them and they had no bones about letting me know it. I mean they would flat out tell me they didn't want to deal with this and that. I never forgave them.

I don't blame you.

That was our home and they treated it like they treated your things in the house in Buffalo, like it all meant nothing; like you meant nothing. I did my best to try and change their minds to see the house the way you and I did, as income and a future place for one of us but just like that, it was gone. Every home inside and outside of my heart was gone. I needed you so much.

Once, when I was walking home from class, I thought I saw you. I stopped and my heart began to race with this uncontrollable excitement. Then, I blinked, and you were gone. After that day I prayed to the higher power to give me one more day with you. I just wanted to be with you, see you and feel your arms around me.

I needed to feel your love. I didn't care where we went or what we did or said. I just wanted to be in your arms.

I heard you honey. I heard you.

You did and you came back to me. I knew you would. I was home on one of my breaks from school. I fell asleep in your reclining chair, the one you loved so much and sat in right up until you went to Hospice. I dreamt I was at your funeral service. I was standing over your casket watching everyone pay their respects to you. I was crying that you were in the casket at all. Vinnie, Dad's brother, bent over to kiss your cheek and that's when it happened. You opened those big brown eyes wide as can be. I was startled but not scared. You smiled and slowly got out of the casket. You came over to me, put your arms around me and held me tight. I threw my arms around you. I didn't want us to separate ever again. Tears of happiness and sadness flowed. Happy because you were awake and sad because I missed you so much. Yet with you in my arms I felt whole again. In an instant I was safe and home again. My heart was bursting with love and joy! You released us from our hug, outstretched your hands to mine and said, "C'mon on Baby" and motioned for me to follow you. I asked you where we were going. You smiled and responded, "C'mon, let's go." You took my hand and off we went. I don't know what we did or said. I just know my hand was in yours and I didn't let go, neither did you. Then I woke up.

I have news for you sweetheart.

What's that?

That wasn't a dream. That's the day you asked for and it's going to last forever. What do you think of that?

I think that's the best news I've had in a long time.

I'm always here for you Kristin. Remember that.

I do it's just sometimes things are so hard and not having you here to journey with me through all this stuff is harder.

I know. I'm sorry. I wish I could make things easier for you. I wish I had that power but honey, you have a knack for forging onward in a big way.

Well look who I get it from.

No, no no. Don't sell yourself short. You're moving forward in ways I only dreamt of. Look at what you did with school. Most kids, your cousins even, probably wouldn't have been able to even go back to school, yet you did. To top things off then you went out with a bang by dancing with a slipped disc, choreographing your own dance piece while simultaneously honoring your Mother and dancing a solo. I couldn't have been prouder of you. If I were physically there, I would have been telling everyone, "That's my daughter! That 's my daughter!"

I know and I would have loved every minute of it☺. We would have had a great time afterward too huh.

We sure would have.

What would we have done?

Well a celebration dinner for starters, and then we would have gone for drinks because you would finally be of age for me to drink with. This time I wouldn't have to be your guardian like the time we went to the bar when we first moved to Buffalo, and you got stinking drunk and danced all about the dance floor. That was cute, funny and cute.

Oh my gosh, don't remind me. I made a fool out of myself.

A little but who cares. The point is we would be together sharing in your accomplishments and joy the way I always wanted. I'm your mother and not even death can change that.

Mom? Mom? Mom, what is it? You're sad. Please don't be sad.

I'm feeling all the things I missed with you kids as you grew and all the beautiful memories I hold in my heart of my beautiful children. No one knows how hard it was for me to leave you kids, no one but God. I want you to know, my love grows for each of you every day in every way. Please believe me when I say I fought hard to get well I just, I just never got well. The few months prior to my crossing over I went through every memory I had with my babies. With all the hard times we had you kids drove me beautifully crazy☺!

Remember when Andrea was, maybe 10 and I was 8. We were still on Davis Road and Andrea was always doing handstands on your bed. One afternoon she decided to teach me how to do them.

Oh boy, you two!

You had two nightstands with lamps on either side of your bed. Andrea told me to keep doing the handstand until I got it right. Well I did. Unfortunately, I wasn't very adept because I did a handstand that lasted about two seconds before I tumbled over onto your nightstand, over the lamp and then to the floor, gouging my head. You had to rush me to the hospital.

I knew anytime I heard a thug, tumble or any kind of ruckus that it would probably end up with a trip to the hospital.

I had to have stitches and the doctor had to shave a portion of my head.

The wound was deep but not deep enough where you had to be put to sleep. The doctor gave you a topical but me and two other nurses had to hold you down while they sewed your cut.

All I remember about this time is you telling me the story of the three bears and asking me to finish the end. I don't remember if I did. Did I?

No. I could barely get you to hear me tell the story. You were hysterical. Your sister and brother were in the waiting room and they said they could hear you from the other end of the hallway.

Well yeah, they should have knocked me out. I still have that scar.

I know. I can see it. How about the time you were riding your new yellow bike down the street? Remember that bike? It was your first?

Oh my gosh I loved that bike! I had it for years.

Yeah and you loved riding it.

So, I was riding it down the street, and then what?

You ran into a mailbox, more stitches.

Oh yeah, that's right. They should have given you your own room in the hospital. It would have been cheaper for you☺.

Or better yet, rather than extra flying miles I could have tallied up extra ER visits and gotten an extra visit for free. You know, pay for three get one free! Then there were times all three of you would be at me at the same time, each of you wanting something, "Mom I need this. Mom I need that. Mom, Mom, Mom." Sometimes I felt like "Mom" was all I heard. Often, I had to scrape, borrow and beg to get you kids what you needed but I did it.

You were amazing the way you provided for us living on such little means.

When you're a single mother you learn how to be creative and resourceful. I don't know if you remember this but one time, this is when we were living in Kings Park Apartments. I was having a very, very bad morning. I woke up crying and thinking, "Oh my gosh. I have three kids I have to get ready for school, feed and clothe and I don't even have the time for the nervous breakdown I really need to have." So, I got you kids up, started making the cream of wheat you kids loved and, as usual, I was doing three things at once and the cream of wheat overcooked and got lumps in it. I hated when I overcooked my cream of wheat. I liked it smooth and perfectly cooked, the way my mother used to make it. Not this time. This time it was cream of lumps, but you kids were my little angels. I poured the cream of wheat into each of your bowls while crying at the same time and blaming you kids for making me overcook the cereal and making it lumpy.

What did we do that we made you overcook the cereal?

Nothing. That was just it. You didn't do anything. It was me. I was stressed, tired, angry and depressed and rather than just say "Sorry kids. I overcooked the cereal and it has lumps." Out of frustration I blamed you kids, telling you that you distracted me and made me overcook the cereal and you know what?

What?

You three didn't say a word. You let me rant and rave and you ate that cereal and told me how delicious it was. Then you, my little Kristin said, "Mommy, I like it with the lumps. From now on I want my cream of wheat with lumps". Your brother and sister rolled their eyes and said, "Oh brother," but you made me laugh. My bad morning turned into a good day because in my pain, I was reminded that I had three faces of joy to look forward to every day. These were the memories that ran through my mind prior to my crossing over. I kept asking myself, "How does a mother day goodbye to her children and all that they shared?" It's not possible. Not for me anyway. I love you baby girl.

I love you too Mom.

I know things were hard, but you were doing great in your senior year of college. You really were. Weren't you taking some sort of mind/body movement class that last year?

I was taking Dance/Movement Therapy classes. I wanted the option of graduate school and the DMT (Dance/Movement Therapy) classes were credits toward my master's. DMT was about mind/body connection. I liked it. Classes were still held in dance studios, so people had room to move. The movement was different and took on a whole new meaning.

What do you mean?

DMT is similar to rebirthing except that it uses movement and breath as its modality to heal places where a person feels emotionally stuck and there's very little discussion during the sessions. Discussions occur after the movement. In class, my professor gave us themes to move on. It was pretty powerful for me.

What kind of themes?

Well, for instance, we would be doing what's called "Authentic Movement." My professor would have all of us sit on the floor and then she would say, "Above you is your father, below you is your mother. You have fifteen minutes to move however you need to."

Wow!

Yeah "wow" is right. Everyone had strong, emotional responses to this exercise, including me.

What was your movement like?

You have to ask? I couldn't get off the floor. All of my movement was floor movement.

Oh honey.

Then we'd write about our experience as part of the exercise. I liked the writing part just as much.

How healing that must have felt.

It was. I couldn't wait to get to my DMT classes. I really thought that I wanted to pursue it as a career, but I think it was more stability that I was looking for.

I agree.

Ethan graduated and we were up in the air. Yet I liked being free from that relationship. Between the arguing, how different we were and some of the not so positive things I experienced with him, a long-term relationship didn't seem very probable. At least on my end it wasn't. We were going in different directions and I didn't want to be tied down, with anyone. I didn't know what my plans were or where I was going. I started applying to Graduate Schools on the East Coast in the MS (Master of Science) programs for Dance Movement Therapy. Filling out the forms was easy. I was so used to them by now. You know, I wanted to have a Plan B even though I wasn't sure about Plan A.

You were right on the ball Kristin. Every move you were making was right in line with where you needed to be.

Yeah?

Absolutely.

I was never really sure. I only knew that I wanted to have something solid and secure in my life. I needed to feel some sense of security and I knew no one could give that to me but me.

Well you did and look at what you did. I take it back when I said I was never more proud of you when I saw your dances. There was another time I was and still am filled with pride for you.

Which time was that?

College Graduation - June 1992, SUNY Brockport

The day you graduated college! You did it baby girl, for me, for you, for us, you did it! My heart overflowed with pride and joy and excitement at the new life you were about to embark on.

I love that picture. I look so happy. It was a great day. The sun was shining and all us students were happy to be graduating. I was really proud of myself too. It took a lot for me to focus and pull myself together to study as hard as I needed to so I could graduate. I worked hard to fulfill our dream. It was important to me that I graduate for one reason only, because it was important to you. You sacrificed so much for me, so very much. I wanted you to have your dream. Graduating college was a dream come true for both of us.

It was honey. I don't know how to put into words the happiness I felt that day. To see a dream for your child come true and by their own doing, there are just no words to describe that kind of happiness. You did it. You got yourself a college education.

WE did it Mom! We got me a college education. Graduating college is what I'm most proud of because of how much we struggled to get there. There was only one thing missing about this day and that's you. I wanted you there so much. I looked for you in the bleachers. I just, I don't know. I just thought maybe…

I know baby. I'm sorry I couldn't be there the way you wanted but I was there.

I know. I smiled and celebrated but the day wasn't complete without you. I was glad but empty. My feelings were mixed and then I just wanted to blow my top because...

I know, I know. Your father showed up with his southern girlfriend.

Can you believe him! The man was starting to make a habit of showing up after all was said and done. He had nothing positive to do with my life! There was nothing in me that could forgive him for not being my father or being around for us. I didn't know what to make of his appearance, or why he would think I would want him there and with his girlfriend who used to send you pictures of them no less. I don't know what he was thinking.

Who invited him?

Who do you think?

Your sister and brother.

Of course, I mean, c'mon. It was fine they wanted to be in his life every six or seven years because that's about how often he contacted them. However, they should have minded their own business when it came to my life. They knew how I felt about him all the years prior to this and they just disrespected me and in such a painful way. I couldn't believe them. I really couldn't. I didn't want to see his face. I barely looked at him and then went about my day with my friends. I didn't even greet him. He was a stranger to me and didn't deserve to share in that moment, you did. You raised me, not him. I resented him for being there. Given how indifferent and angry I was toward him as a child and young woman I'm surprised he had the audacity to show up. That's how clueless the man was to his own child. He never cared about me or loved me. He only cared about himself and what he wanted. You have to earn the right to celebrate your children's successes and he had no right to be there. You don't just show up when it's convenient and you want to claim the glory of your child's hard work. Every time he decided to show his cowardly face, I was reminded of all these painful memories of you struggling to provide for us. Or the way he used you when he was down on his luck for a place to crash, or a compassionate ear when no one else would listen to him. He knew you barely had anything to give yet he took from you anyway knowing you'd never say "no" when it should have been the other way around. He should have been the one giving to us. Your ex had no interest in seeing or helping his children grow yet he somehow felt justified to blame us for not loving and respecting him the way he wanted, according to his fucked-up letters. It took years for me to understand that his leaving wasn't because of me rather, because of him.

After we separated and Dad stopped seeing you kids, I used to beg him to come and visit with you. All he would tell me is, "Mary, I have my own problems right now. I wouldn't be any good to the kids."

He was right.

Kristin, your father was a shit. It was never your fault that Dad wasn't a good father. I wish he would have stayed in our lives for you kids.

I know. In the beginning, I wondered, "What did I do to make my father not want to be in my life?" When I saw how sad he made you I wished he would disappear off the face of the earth.

I wish there was something I could do or say to erase the negative imprint he left in you.

You know, I asked him a few times why he didn't help us, even if he didn't want to be around, just help us because you were going through so much with your cancer. Do you know what he would say?

What?

"What do you want me to say Kris?" Or, he would give me a blank stare. He never understood that I didn't want anything to do with him because he was so indifferent to what he put us through. Dad never understood the concept, "you made your bed now lay in it."

I understand baby, very well. The relationship we have with our parents, without a doubt, affects us as adults and the relationships we have. I hurt because of my father - you hurt because I hurt and because of Dad. Back then, we just couldn't get away from the pain.

It felt like sadness and hard times followed us everywhere. Sometimes I still feel that way but...

But what?

At least you and I had each other. Inbetween the sadness and dark days we still managed to make each other laugh and have fun, didn't we?

Yes, we did.

See, so what I was thinking back then was "Fuck him. He's not going to ruin this special day for me, no way." It was June 1992. I was 21 years old and Graduation Day was the last day I would ever see my father again, by choice, my choice.

I support your decision Kristin. Whatever is going to make you happy, I support you.

Some of your family showed up. I didn't bother with them either. I paid more attention to my friends. For a while I swallowed the hurt and anger, they caused me. It was so much I couldn't even think about dealing with it. No, truth be told. I didn't want to deal with it. There was still a lot for me to think about and do. I couldn't afford to lose control of my emotions.

I saw and felt you swallow a lot honey and I knew that was going to come back to you later on, big time.

I know. A part of me knew that too. I didn't know how or when, but I could only deal with so much you know?

I do. You gave me another gift in addition to your graduation, both of us.

I did. Can you believe it!

You were long overdue for you own adventure.

Me, traveling, anywhere. The furthest I'd ever traveled up to that point was Florida.

I was thrilled!

I was so nervous.

I know. What made you decide to do it?

You. You always told me to get out, see the world, experience new people, places, enjoy life and live only for the moment. I remembered how you wanted to see the glass makers in Italy. That was on your list of "Things to do."

It made me sad to think of all the things I wanted to do and knew I'd never get the chance to.

I know. It made me sad too but that's why I needed to travel. I wanted to change that for both of us.

That was my hope for you as well. I wanted you to expand your horizons beyond what was immediately around you. My spirit felt stifled seeing you holed up in your little apartment crying day after day, night after night. I wanted you to travel and boy did you ever. You never do things small honey. I gotta hand it to ya. When you do something it's usually in a big way. That's the Leo in you.

This is true. Everyone was very surprised when I announced I would be traveling around Europe, by myself. I asked my sister many times if it was okay, she stayed with Sophie while I traveled. She assured me time and again it would be. I didn't like leaving Sophie again, but I had to do this. I guess you could say this was my test. I thought, "If I make it back alive there's a good chance, I'll make it period."

You were so ballsy!

I was also scared but excited too. I took some of the money you left me and began making my plans. It was June 1992 and back then my airfare was $1,274.00 round trip leaving from NYC's Kennedy Airport to Amsterdam, Netherlands with a stop in Germany. I got my passport all squared away and bought a two-month Eurail pass for $652.00 and picked up a "Let's Go Europe" book. I packed only the necessities: my toiletries, one pair of shorts, one pair of jeans, one summer dress, two tank tops, one pair of sandals, I wore my hiking/walking shoes and as many underwear as I could fit into my backpack. My chest was so small I never even owned a bra so that saved some space. I rolled a blanket up and tied it underneath my backpack and that was it. I was all packed and ready to go! I purposely packed light because I knew I would buy a few items while I was traveling. I planned to stay in hostels the whole time and eat only bread and cheese allowing myself one meal per city, just to get a sense of the food culture and I stuck to it. It made my money stretch further too. Since Ethan was originally from Yonkers, NY I stayed with him for a few days before I left while taking care of last-minute travel plans. He was also planning to backpack around Europe. He was a little upset that we weren't traveling together but I really needed and wanted to do this trip alone. With this, I was feeling disconnected from Ethan and wanted to be sent off with a positive vibe. I was more than prepared to take a cab until an unexpected, happy surprise showed up. In fact, it was just the positive vibe I needed.

Oh yeah, what's that?

At one of the graduation parties, a group of us were all talking about our "post-graduation" plans. I let everyone know that I was traveling Europe. One of my friend's, who just happened to live in Queens, NY at the time, told me to call her while I was in the city so we could get together. So, when I got down to New York I did. While we were talking, she asked me how I was getting to the airport. I told her I was taking a cab and she exclaimed, "A cab! Oh no, you can't take a cab. I'll take you." It was fate! I loved what she had to say next.

That was fate or maybe a little angel☺. What did she say?

I agree. She said, "Kristin I wouldn't let you go to the airport all by yourself when you're leaving for Europe. You can't leave for a trip like that alone. You need someone to send you off with a smile and a hug and wish you a safe journey." That's exactly what she did. She said the same thing, that it was fate we met up before I left. Her name is Gabriela, a true New York Italian through and through with a huge heart. I couldn't have asked for a better send off. I appreciated her kindness on this very important part of my journey into the abyss.

That was so sweet of her and off we went – into the European abyss! I was so excited for you. I was excited period. I was finally going to get to fulfill my dream of seeing Europe and I couldn't have asked for a better companion.

Me too Mom. You know, when I think back on this time it's almost surreal to me that I even went given how reserved I was/am. I'm so glad I did because I so longed to learn of the world you talked to me about when you went on your travels. I refused to make an itinerary. I decided to wing the whole trip and hoped for the best. I was fortunate. While everyone thought I was nuts for traveling alone it turned out to be to my advantage. I met a lot of people my age who were super friendly and invited me to travel with them, which I did a few times, particularly in the beginning. Meeting up with people in the same boat as me, backpacking around Europe, was a good way for me to get my feet wet before I ventured on my own. I had a few places in mind I wanted to see.

Like what?

Like the "Free City" in Copenhagen, Denmark I once read of where everyone lives behind these gates closed to the public, and the people pretty much govern themselves. For you, I wanted to see the glassmakers in Italy, although I was excited to see them up close too. The rest I was looking forward to playing it by ear. Each city/country had so many historical landmarks. I had quite a few places I wanted to see. I knew I could pick only a couple of landmarks for each one if I wanted to get to all the countries I was hoping to get to. I did exactly what you wanted me too Mom. For two months we traveled throughout Europe meeting so many wonderful people, visiting and experiencing amazing places I'd only read of.

So, let's talk about where we first began again.

First stop, Stuggart, Germany!

THE TRAVELS
SUMMER 1992

Let the travels begin!
I simply must go, alone.
I must walk this journey solo.
Spirit and soul remain on either side of my entangled mind.
I know where to go. I know what to do
I can take care of myself. I am descending,
Spiraling downward deep into the unknown
I am. I am. Who am I?
What's happening?
Let go – let go!
I am lost. Will I ever be found?
I'm okay, not really.
Insidious thoughts have slipped from eyes.
If the tremble isn't a dead giveaway, what is?
My reality? My reality is dance, music, photographs, poetry
and it's all mine, mine I say!
Are you leaving? I wish you wouldn't.
The mouth of chaos has all, but my feet
wedged tightly between its lips.
I need to flow INTO THE AMAZON
if only to sort things out, or perhaps I'll just die.
It's Sunday, and there is very little to do.
I'll close my eyes and rest for a while.
The journey is not over.
When I awake, please Lord, let me feel the safety and warmth
of the sun on my face and body.
Let it shine with a power so strong it seeps into my veins.
Let its passion enter my blood
so that I may give something back to someone, somewhere.

Kristin A. Crage ©1992

STUTTGART, GERMANY

Church in Stuttgart

Stuttgart was the beginning of the summer of 1992 travels! I was only in Stuttgart for a day. I didn't see much but I did meet two guys that were traveling together and two women, Mara and Elana, from New Jersey, also traveling together. The five of us decided to hang in Stuttgart for the very short time we were there. Unfortunately, we were there on a day when the weather wasn't all that great. First, you tell me your thoughts and/or feelings on Stuttgart and then I'll tell you mine.

Okay, does it have to be in that order?

Yes. Let's do this in an orderly fashion. We'll review the countries as they were traveled. If you veer off this, I'm afraid I'll have to remove you from the Premises☺.

Uh oh – okay Felix. I thought Stuttgart was, interesting, different, historic.

"Interesting," "Different" which translates into you didn't like it much.

Ah, I could take it or leave it. I liked the architecture of the buildings in the area we were in. They looked like they'd been standing for centuries. Stuttgart had a gothic feel to it. The people seemed nice and pleasant to talk to. I wished we had a longer stay to get a better feel.

Gothic is a good word to describe it. Since we weren't there for very long, I don't think I got a good feel for it, so it really wasn't my cup of tea.

Sometimes you can get a feel for a person or place right away. I know you get those feelings even before you meet someone or visit a place. You're sensitive in that way. When you were little, you'd dream of things that had yet to happen but eventually would. That was freaky for Mom. You tuned into other energies around you without realizing it.

Yeah, my dreams are like stories. They often foretell who will be coming into or leaving my life. I listen to my dreams and never brush them off as "just a dream" even if it's a nightmare. Those too tell a story of what I'm feeling and/or what's affecting me on a darker level.

That's true. So, what was your feeling on Stuttgart?

The architecture that I saw was amazing, but I have to say, I never liked hearing people speak German.

Really?

Yeah. The language sounds harsh to me.

Huh, that's interesting.

You know, some places, events and people affect me like that. I might meet someone, go somewhere or experience something and realize it's just not for me. That's how I felt about Germany.

This is true and hey, if you didn't like you didn't like it. There's nothing wrong with that. Some places you connected with positively, some not and some you didn't connect with at all. This just happened to be the one you didn't connect positively with that's all.

Yeah, thanks Mom. You always have this way of appreciating everything even if you don't like it. I love that about you. Your opinion about people and places tends to remain neutral. You take them in as an experience, something to grow and learn from which is how they should be taken. I'm trying to learn to do that more.

You are and you do. I think you're just fierier about things. If something or someone affects you it really affects you in a big way and you react in a big way. You know who you are, and you know how you are. You don't have to be more like me. Just be you and like yourself the way you are. I do.

Thank you. Right back at you sister☺. With that, I was anxious to get to the place I really wanted to see, first and foremost. Whoop Whoop!

Oh dear, now this was definitely interesting. My daughter who was just branching out of her comfort zone now stepping into marijuana land – and lots of it.

AMSTERDAM, HOLLAND [THE NETHERLANDS]

Streets of Amsterdam

When I told Mara and Elana that I was going to Amsterdam they said they were too and invited me to go with them. Mara, Elana and I stayed together for a few countries and then went our separate ways. Do you hear that? "Stayed together for a few countries," that statement in and of itself is weird to say. I'm not talking about a city or a town - it's just a few countries, nothing big.

Na, nothing big, just country hopping.

Amsterdam was the place I felt like someone opened the cage door to my spirit and set me.

For me, it was the place I worried most for you and with good reason.

From the moment I stepped foot on Amsterdam concrete I was never the same and I mean that in a good way. When I got off the train, I took into the city from the airport it finally hit me and I was like, "Oh my gosh! I'm in Europe traveling on my own!" It was make it or break it time for me. I think I handled the initial shock of the situation pretty well.

Oh yeah, real well. You should have gotten yourself situated in your hostel and relaxed a little. No, not you. This once caged bird now free heads straight to a coffee shop, orders a large cappuccino with extra soymilk, four sugars and three purple sensei joints!

What can I say? I was 21 and just beginning to feel and find my way in the world. Most of the coffee houses had beverages, something to eat and various kinds of marijuana and hashish. Not only that but it wasn't just young people in them. It was also professionals having a coffee or tea with a cigarette that was half marijuana and half tobacco. I needed a little help calming down. I was freaked.

I understand but at one point during your stint in Amsterdam you got so high you almost got hit by a trolley car. Do you remember that?

Yes.

Do you know what could have happened to you?

Yes, and it was a mistake Mother.

A "mistake!" A "mistake!" The only reason you're alive is because a kind man pulled you by the arm and got you off the track. You didn't even hear the trolley honking its absurdly loud horn at you. Kristin, you almost died.

I know that Mom and as you say, "Let's focus on the positive." Besides, you're killing my memory high. I know what could have happened to me and I'm sorry okay.

Well, as fate would have it only a year later you were about to get a glimpse of what really would have happened to you.

Mom, can we move on please?

You should be very sorry.

I already said I'm sorry Mom. I'm very, very sorry.

Now you're just saying that.

Mother!

You scared me!

I made a few bad judgment calls here and there. I didn't mean to scare you.

Okay. Alright, let's talk about some of the highlights of Amsterdam.

Thank you. After getting a bed at the infamous Bob's Youth Hostel and spending most of my time in a coffee shop well known to backpackers called the Grasshopper. Mara, Elana and I decided to walk around and check out all the shops. That was fun.

I love the candy shop you visited. That couldn't be more fitting.

Oh yeah, that was a great shop. I love being surrounded by candy and chocolate. It makes me think of the stories you used to tell me of Grandpa when he owned his chocolate shop. Do you know, until this day and even when I'm broke, I'll only eat the best chocolates. Now-a-days I have to go sugar free because the sugar makes me edgy, but I know the good stuff, thanks to you.

You see. I taught you well. Knowing the best chocolates to purchase is one of life's necessities and Europe is filled with tons of the best of life's necessities☺.

That's for sure. Then there was The Red-Light District. Mara, Elana, myself and a few other people met up and had a few drinks at another coffee house called The Bulldog. The Red-Light District had a reputation for being a dangerous area to walk through and it was. You knew the area right away because the streets are all lined with red lights. Albeit the area was patrolled by cops until midnight, it still wasn't a good place to find yourself alone. Women were advertising their "services" in windows rather than street corners. It really hurt me to see human trafficking so up-close, and that's exactly what that was. I don't care what anyone says.

No, I agree with you 100%. That is one of the many dark sides of humans.

Yeah. It was really hard to see.

Hey, you okay?

Yeah, it's just seeing or knowing about abuse to women affects me hard. It makes me sink inward to a painful place that I don't like to go.

I know babe. Well I don't want you sinking now. How about the Anne Frank House? I know you went there right?

Yeah.

What did you think of that?

That was a piece of history I truly appreciated. I went there, again with Mara and Elana, and the experience was deep for all of us. The house isn't very big at all. I mean you could pass it easily from the street because the front looks like it could be a store. It doesn't stand on its own. It's connected to a row of what used to be other houses which are now shops in a high tourist area of Amsterdam. It's also a few stories high and not very wide. The stairs that led to the attic Anne Frank wrote from were these narrow steps that led to a very small room. It looked like it could only hold one bed. To think an entire family lived there for years gave me a reality check as to what people had to do to escape the atrocities of the Holocaust. At the time I was there it was the headquarters for the city's anti-fascist and anti-racist movements.

I'm glad you decided to go. It's an important part of history. To learn about Anne Frank and what she went through from books is one thing. To see her house firsthand is quite another.

Absolutely. There wasn't too much more that we saw of Amsterdam. We mainly "hung out" and went from coffee shop to coffee shop being as free as can be.

Well, I haven't forgotten about the parks and beautiful country roads you, Mara, and Elana rented bikes and rode through. That was my favorite part. It reminded me of when I was a teenager. I used to love to ride my bike through open roads. I felt so free. Amsterdam is a beautiful place and the people were friendly. It felt like there were few restrictions and everyone seemed happy.

Yeah. Mom?

What honey.

You grew up in Buffalo, NY.

That's right.

There are no open roads in Buffalo, NY, at least not where you lived.

Yes, there were.

Where?

I don't know Kristin, but they were there.

Oh, but...

Would you please let me have my fantasy?

Sorry☺. Anyway, Amsterdam was awesome.

Indeed, it was. You loved it!

I did.

Me too☺. I wanted to stay longer.

So, did I but we had to keep going. There was so much to do and see and so little time. Next stop...

PRAGUE, CZECH REPUBLIC
[Formerly Czechoslovakia]

Views from the streets of Prague

So, Prague was quite an experience huh?

Oh man, it was, definitely, a learning experience. Remember, this was a country going through major upheaval at the time. It was in the process of going from one country, Czechoslovakia, into two countries, the Czech Republic and The Slovak Republic.

The people were struggling very hard.

I know. It wasn't a good time to travel to Prague and for the record. I was so grateful to even have the opportunity to travel there.

Me to.

I particularly remember the train ride from Amsterdam to Prague. We arrived at the border during the night. I knew it was the border because the train was stopped right at the borderline and there were police checking everyone's passport and all their information, and dogs were sniffing through everyone's bags. You could see people along the railroad getting pulled off the train and frisked and/or arrested. I was still traveling with Mara and Elana. It was very scary for a couple of young people who were just backpacking through Europe for the first time that's for sure.

Oh my gosh. You must have been sweating up a storm.

I was. Everyone was, whether you had something to hide or not. The police in Prague were no joke. People were dealing with a lot of unrest. Scarcity of food and employment made people scared for their homes, families and everything that was once stable in their lives.

We know how that feels.

Yes, we do. When we got off the train, we were greeted by locals scattered throughout the train station offering travelers a place to stay, but we didn't accept any invitations because we weren't sure about the safety of that type of situation. Little did we know that was the only way, at the time, to stay in Prague unless you had money and could afford a hotel which I couldn't and didn't want to do anyway. Mara, Elana and I were looking through our "Let's Go Europe!" books. We were so hopeful we'd find a place, but all the hostels listed in the book had long since closed.

The three of us, with our backpacks in tow, walked the streets of Prague for hours in the hot sun. The streets were so bare it was like walking through a deserted town.

That's scary, especially when you don't speak the language and you don't know where you're going. Then again, as long as you weren't hurt, fumbling your way around is also the fun of traveling without an itinerary.

If we weren't so hot, we probably would have enjoyed the journey of finding our exhausted selves a place to rest more. Needless to say, we dragged our grouchy, dry mouthed, hungry, sweltering hot selves back to the train station and rented a room from a lovely mother and daughter. It was actually the mother's room but because of the language barrier we didn't realize this until the end of our stay. We felt horrible that they had to rent their own bedrooms as a means to bring income into their household. What an invasion of privacy. Yet for some, offering travelers' a place to say was their only income. We cleaned the room really well and bought them groceries and flowers before we left. They were so appreciative they cried. They said most people just come, do what they want and even destroy things. They don't care or have respect that they're staying in someone's house and leave without even cleaning up their mess. Can you even imagine? I could never do that to anyone. You were always such a stickler about teaching us to respect other people, their space and clean up after ourselves. Thank goodness Mara and Elana were taught the same values.

That was so sweet of you girls. We know how people can be with other people's property. I'm reminded of how some of the tenants were at our house. Remember?

Yes, assholes.

They changed our whole house without asking me and were completely oblivious to the fact that they were renting not owning - so rude.

I know.

Some people take others for granted, especially if they know that person(s) needs income.

That's so true and it burned me up that people would behave so disrespectfully. Us and the house are what I thought of when I was staying with this mother and daughter. I mean you could see in their eyes how desperate they were for income. How much they hated renting their bedrooms out, and how they could only hope that whomever they were renting too would have some compassion for them and be respectful. I couldn't imagine being anything but respectful. I had such empathy and respect for them.

That's right but you three girls gave them a positive experience of traveler's that cared. Sometimes when you get treated badly for so long and then someone finally comes along that cares it's an emotional experience that can bring people to tears.

I think you described it to a T. People had it hard there. In order to make a phone call, this was, of course, before the mass use of cell phones, we had to go to another building. Also, the mother and daughter had no shower, just a little basin they would wash up in and they were also living without any hot water.

You see. You never know how good you have it until you travel to places that have it much worse than you. That's how I felt when I went to India. I saw so much suffering and hopelessness, yet I also experienced a profound connection to God and spirituality. I realized how useless material things are, albeit I did buy some things when I first got there. The more I was there the more I asked myself, why do I need this rug or that picture? The answer always rests in the struggles I carried with myself and how I tried to fulfill the emotional holes with things. It never worked but I still kept trying. I'm glad you made it there okay and were experiencing many of things Mom did when I traveled. This is exactly what I wanted for you. I was very touched by some of the places you visited in Prague.

Which ones?

The Jewish Cemetery and what was that synagogue called?

The Staronová Synagogue.

Right, the Staronová Synagogue. They were very telling. I was most struck by the Synagogue that housed all the artwork.

Oh yeah. That was artwork made by children held in the Terezia Concentration Camp during the Holocaust. That was really profound work.

No book or painting will ever accurately capture the suffering those children and adults went through, ever. The artwork was one gruesome depiction after another of Hitler's reign. I don't know about you, but I couldn't take my eyes off it. While it was hard to look at it was also mind blowing. I'm glad you were able to see these things. They're an indelible part of history, again, the part of history you can't get from books. Yet when you see the things you saw up close, I think it brings a better understanding of what your teachers tried to teach you.

You're right. Throughout my education I felt like we got some watered-down version of the Holocaust and we did. I think the only way for me to have a true understanding of the atrocities of the Holocaust on a level that went beyond the obvious or superficial was to visit places like the Anne Frank Huis, The Jewish Cemetery and The Synagogue. These were all eye openers for me. It made me more aware to the suffering there is in the world. Not that I didn't know before but standing in a place like the Jewish cemetery in Amsterdam just has a way of putting things into perspective, you know?

I do.

What I was starting to question about in myself was what do I do with the intense grief and despair from the loss of my mother? How do I handle the effects it left me with? The answer to these questions was a work in progress, and often times, still is.

That's okay. There's no hurry. Who knows? Perhaps the answer is in the journey itself.

Yeah. Back then I felt like I was walking around in a daze trying to take in and deal with as much as I could, and whatever I couldn't - file it away to deal with later. Let me tell you, I was doing a lot of filing. I was so afraid to let myself feel my emotions fully and freely. I felt fragile, like I would completely break down and not recover if I let things get too close to me. So, I took things in only to a certain point. If something felt too threatening, I put the palm of my hand up and said, "Okay, that's enough. Whatever or whoever you are, you've come far enough. The wall is up and nothing's getting by."

You were like this for years. In some ways you still are.

Let's keep going Mom.

Oops, there's the hand and I just hit a wall.

Sometimes I really don't like you, but I've never loved anyone more since the day I met you.

Me too baby. What else about Prague, any other memorable moments or places for you?

I loved the Malá Strana which means, "Lesser Town". It was a great place filled with palaces, these old baroque churches and royal Gardens. It was like going back in time a few centuries. I felt a strong connection when I walked around the palaces; as though I'd been there before☺.

You never know. The fact that those places were preserved for so many years made them amazing in and of themselves.

Especially the gardens. Flowers evoke a sense of peace and stillness in me. I could sit in a garden four hours even a whole day and these gardens were like...

Heaven?

Exactly, at least that's how I picture heaven to be.

You're not too far off☺.

Seriously?

Seriously. Don't you get sad on me. I didn't mean to make you sad honey.

No, you didn't. My emotions are like being on a roller coaster. One minute I'm doing whatever, feeling okay and the next I'm crying. I'd love to get off the roller coaster you know.

I know. You will. I promise, and you're not sad all the time. You're funny too - recognize that in yourself. You make me laugh and I know you make others laugh. Right?

I guess.

No, not "I guess." Say "you're right Mom."

You're right Mom☺.

Good. Now why don't you make us both smile and describe the garden. You're so good with your descriptives.

Okay, close your eyes, and no peeking.

Okay, their closed.

Beautiful flowers of all colors and kinds were neatly placed one row after another. As soon as I entered the garden, I was greeted with a soft breeze followed by the aroma of roses and wildflowers that forced me to stop, and "smell the flowers." Colors were in full bloom from every direction. My sense of smell and sight were on overload yet taking in every intoxicating scent and magnificent, bright color. If ever I have a house, I hope to have a beautiful garden of flowers and vegetables.

That's a beautiful description. I always wanted a garden like that. I tried, when you kids were little, but it's a lot of work. You could do it if you have the time. It's relaxing to work in a garden - a good way to de-stress.

It seems like it would be.

What about the Town Square with the big fountain right in the center? That was fun too. Everyone hung out, musicians played and there were all those restaurants. It was a good place for people to relax and let go in a city filled with so much tension.

It was a good hang out, but I was unable to relax in Prague and I really needed too. Mara and Elana, again, invited me to continue on with them. I was looking forward to the mountains and fresh air. You know how peaceful I feel when I'm in nature, walking, hiking, or just sitting and taking in God's creation.

Me too.

Well, we were about to get a nice healthy dose of some nature, Swiss style.

INTERLAKEN, SWITZERLAND

The Swiss Alps

Oh Mom. Looking at my traveling photos brings back so many amazing, wonderful memories. Aside from my time with you, my travels were, by far, the best time of my life.

I knew they would be.

As I traveled from country to country, I would stick my head out of the train window and felt the air getting thinner, crisper and fresher.

It's exciting to see how different the environment and people are when you go to a different country.

It is. So, our next stop was Interlaken, Switzerland. The first thing I did when I arrived was check into the Balmer Herberge. It was a hostel but a little nicer. My room had a double window that opened to the outside with a breathtaking view of the Swiss Alps. Most of the locals spoke at least three languages, one of which was English, so that was refreshing.

That was helpful.

Most people in Europe speak English. Balmer's was good because it was all students, most of which just graduated college, like me. It was comforting to be around people that had no idea what they were going to do next on their journey in life. We were all just focused on getting from one country to the next, safely. Everyone was happy. There was all this smoke being passed around, people laughing and hanging out under the summer night sky until the wee hours.

Me and the girls rested the day we arrived and the next day we went hiking in the Swiss Alps.

Hiking is so up your alley too. Nature and the outdoors have always been the place where you find stillness and peace.

Yup. The guide, who didn't actually accompany us, let us know which trail would get us up to a high but safe altitude. He advised us to take sweaters because although it was in the low 90's when we started. He reminded us that the higher up we climbed the colder it would get. As we hiked, we passed by cows and their safe houses that were built for them along the hills when the weather got bad, several beautiful Chalets, some towns folk and then up, up and away we hiked - way away. The grass was greener than I'd ever seen. The guides put these marked sticks along the trail to help us stay on the right path. When we finally reached the top there was snow on the ground, it was cold, like an early winter day and people were paragliding off the mountain tops.

Why didn't you paraglide?

It was expensive and I don't know. You know the terrible fear of heights I have. It didn't interest me at the time nor does it now.

That's what I would have done.

I know you would have. I liked sitting on top of the mountain. It gave me time to take a few moments for a reality check and say to myself, "Wow. I'm in Switzerland hiking the Swiss Alps." Going down from the Alps proved to be a bit of a challenge because some idiot decided to pick up some of the sticks that were left to help the hikers stay on the trail and get down safely. I hiked down using my instincts and gut feeling. I didn't care if anyone followed me or not. I was going "this way" and if they wanted to come, they could and if they didn't, they didn't have too.

There's that sixth sense kicking in. You got a lot of experience from every place you visited. Your travels were more significant than you realize. What you gave yourself was a place to grow, on your own.

Yeah, I realize that now but back then all I knew was the moment. The only time I ever lived in the moment was when I traveled. I would like to try and do that more.

You can. Just think back to these days. So, we did the Swiss Alps which I, of course, loved. I could have lived in the Swiss Alps with "the ladies" [cows] as my neighbors, ate yummy Swiss cheese and lived simple and free.

Interlaken is beautiful. I loved the chocolate and ate lots of it!

I know! That's all you ate for breakfast, lunch and dinner was chocolate or things with chocolate in them. What was the other memorable fun thing you did while in Switzerland?

White Water rafting!

That's right. This was my favorite part of our Switzerland travels.

Mine too. White water rafting through the Swiss Alps was, to say the least, exhilarating. We went through waters that weren't dangerous but definitely exciting.

I was so glad you did this.

It was unbelievable. I loved being part of a group where everyone had to work together to stay safe and get down the river.

There were a few dips here and there that scared me. I thought the boat was going to tip over a few times.

It did feel that way. There were times we plunged down far and then were thrust way up. Then there were these absolutely beautiful, amazing, peaceful moments where the boat wade in the silence of the river as we gently glided though the mountains. I could hear drops of water coming down and felt the stillness of the mountain landscape that surround us with the blue sky above. Those were the moments I knew you were there. I knew because you would never miss a moment of such beauty. Nothing can keep you away from God's natural beauty.

You know me too well. Nothing could keep me from making sure my daughter was safe too☺. Well, I love remembering Switzerland but you're not yourself today. I can feel it. I think we should talk about it.

I don't feel like it.

C'mon. Don't let it fester.

I don't know. It feels like I try to create good things in my life, and I keep running into one brick wall after another. Sometimes I wonder if I was meant to have a good, happy life. Or, if maybe I was just meant to struggle.

No one was meant to only struggle baby. You can't appreciate success without struggle and vice versa. Why do you say this?

Every time I try to make my life better, I get knocked down again or something blocks the good thing I'm trying to create or make better. As I get older it's getting harder to get up and get going again yet there is this thing in me that won't stop trying. I maintain this stubborn hope that things will get better because giving up isn't in me.

I'd say that's a pretty darn good quality.

Having hope is causing me a lot of anguish. I've experienced so much loss because of having hope. There comes a point where I have to take the blindfold off and realize that perhaps good things just aren't going to come into my life.

Sweet girl, I'd say leave the blindfold on until you're ready to see the truth of you and your life. You have good things that I don't think you're taking into consideration.

Mom I...

Such as an independent life that you single handedly built and solely control; legs to take you where you need to go; arms and hands to help you grasp what you need and let go of what you don't; a roof over your head; a pantry with plenty of food in it; wonderful animals that you love and love you more than anything in this world; good health insurance; money to buy the things you need and want. You need to look around you and appreciate all the blessings you've got in your life little girl before they're gone. Then you'll really be crying. The blindfold, my darling daughter, is nothing more than your own distorted vision of all that is good and beautiful in your life. I wish I had what you have when I was alive but knowing that my daughter has these blessings brings me more joy than I can describe in words. Have fun, for Christ sakes honey, have fun and stop being such a worry wart!

Let's talk more about my travels please. By the way I am grateful for what I have. You make it sound like I'm not and I am.

I'm sorry. Do you remember when I told you that your travels were more significant than you realize?

Yes.

Do you know what I meant by that?

No.

Who got everyone down from the mountain when you went hiking in the Swiss Alps when the guide sticks were picked up?

Mom, it was purely a hunch on my part, and I told you, I just let people know which way I was going, that's all. I left it up to them to decide which way they'd go. Some followed, some didn't.

And those that didn't follow, what happened to them?

They came back super, super late. I thought it was funny because they were the same people that picked up the sticks in the first place☺.

Ah ha, you see but you had no fear at all about which way you were going did you?

No. Something in me was guiding me. I felt it clear as day.

Exactly and when we went white water rafting you were so scared to get into that boat you were shaking, and your heart was about to beat out of your chest. Not only do you have a fear of heights, but you have a fear of water too. Ever since Kings Park Apartments when your sister pushed you into the deep end of the community pool, albeit she was fooling around, you had no idea how to swim. You almost drown.

Yes, I remember that. Thank you for reminding me. That really affected me, still, until this day.

I know! You can't go in water unless you're able to touch the bottom. Yet even after the guide told you that the boat was going to be purposely tipped over, just as a fun thing at the end, you went anyway. Why did you go if you have such a fear of water knowing the boat would be tipped over and you still don't know how to swim?

Well, firstly, I can do the doggie paddle. I'm not at a complete loss in the water. I don't know. I was in Switzerland and wanted to do things I'd never done. I thought the whole purpose for me as I traveled was to expand my horizons, be open to new experiences and test my survival skills by tackling what seemed impossible. I wanted to push myself beyond my comfort zone whenever the opportunities presented themselves.

Precisely! You've taken on challenges that were completely opposite of your personality. You have a way of putting your fear in check and not letting it run your life. You thrive on overcoming what seems impossible. That's admirable. Your life is not only to struggle I assure you of that.

How do you know?

I'm your mother. I know everything, remember☺.

Right. Mom, you know how hard it is to piece your life together after it falls apart, but when it falls apart time and time again it makes me wonder why I'm even trying.

I know how low you feel. Believe me honey, I do. How many times has Mom had to piece her life together again only to have things fall apart right away? We barely had any breathing room before another tragedy hit us.

That's right and my adulthood is the same. Nothing has changed yet I keep trying and it's killing me. Why do I keep trying?

You keep trying because that's what you saw with me. There were many times I wanted to quit or give up. I was so emotionally drained that sometimes I prayed God to take me and then I'd feel guilty for praying God to take me. I felt like I was in a no-win situation all the time. My goodness I lost count as to how many nervous breakdowns I had. Yet I kept trying at everything I did no matter how excruciating it was or how terrible I felt because I had three mouths to feed. Giving up wasn't an option for me. I don't know what I could say that would make you feel any better. You've been through more than I could have ever imagined but giving up on anything is not an option for you either, ever. It's too easy.

Easy doesn't sound too bad right now.

Then you're not Kristin A. Crage. Honey?

What?

I've never seen anyone try as hard as you do with anything. Everything you do is with your whole heart and soul.

I want a better life for myself.

Me too, I want that for you and more. All these challenges make you strong.

I'm already strong. Enough is enough.

I think what you need is to do what you did on your travels.

What's that?

Take a break and then keep going.

FLORENCE (FIRENZE), ITALY

Il Duomo

The Countryside

Ah, Firenza (Florence), Italy.

Yay Italy!

I was so excited to get to Italy. I couldn't wait.

Me too.

We were drawn to Italy, weren't we?

Yes, we were.

Like magnets.

Exactly.

All the travelers I met, including Mara and Elana, were heading from Switzerland to Austria before they ventured to Italy. I decided to bypass Austria and follow the stars home. Italy was really special to me, all of it. I had a comfortable and safe feeling even before I entered the country. I felt like I was going home.

You were and you did, well another home. Now Italy is definitely a place I could have lived or had a second home in, and they DO have gay/lesbian communities throughout, somewhere.

Yes, they do. I wouldn't mind having a home there too. I'd spend summers or vacations in Roma (Rome). Even though I wanted to go to every city and town, I couldn't. Italy is so big that I had to choose which cities to venture too. So, I let my heart and gut do the talking. I began with Florence. While I was there, I met Melanie and Melissa, twins from Canada. They were funny blond haired, blue-eyed petite ladies who also just graduated. They cracked me up because all they did was banter and finish each other's sentences. It was like being in the company of a comedy team. They had such different personalities but were a lot of fun to be around.

It was so nice to see you opening yourself up to meeting new people. Everywhere you went you had a smile on your face and you really met some wonderful, interesting yet safe people Kristin.

I did. I felt fortunate in that respect.

I'm glad you gave the hostels a break and stayed in the Pensions. The hostels were fun, but they didn't seem too safe. The fact that you had to sleep with your money belt on and keep it with you at all times made me nervous.

You! I guarded that thing with my life. I missed hearing your voice and longed to feel your arms around me. The more I experienced all these faraway places and met so many different people the more I thought of how much you would have enjoyed these travels.

Oh, but I did through you!

I know but I was so bound with grief I talked to you as if you weren't really there. I couldn't and wouldn't let myself connect with you like I am now. I know it sounds ironic, but I missed you so much that I had to shut you out, you know.

Yes, I do and please don't keep beating yourself up. You did what you had to do in order to get through the day. I knew you knew I was there. I also knew one day we would talk as we are. I had enough faith for both of us.

That faith is what carried me from one day to the next. Once I entered the train station in Florence, I saw all these street kids ambush the tourists. They had this little scam going. They would hold their hands in the hopes of getting some cash. The second someone got distracted by reaching for her/his wallet they would take the whole thing. I saw it happen to an unsuspecting couple.

They were pretty fearless kids too.

Yeah, they were. I have to say, they weren't too bad to me, perhaps because I looked like someone that didn't have a lot of money. Wait a minute. I was someone that didn't have a lot of money.

Ah, ha, ha.

I was determined to find the glass makers you always wanted to see. I, too, was interested to see how glass was blown by hand. The fact that you wanted to see them so much set my determination in high gear. I asked everyone everywhere I went but still couldn't find the glassmakers. I didn't even know what part of Italy they were in. In fact, every time I asked a local, no one even knew the glass makers existed. That's when it occurred to me that maybe they weren't around anymore.

Hmmm, just goes to show you.

What?

Mothers always know best.

Yeah, yeah.

Well while searching we saw a lot in Florence, didn't we?

Yes, we did. What did you think of the Palazzo Vecchio, the town square that sat directly in the center of Florence?

That was my favorite. I liked sitting in the cafés drinking cappuccino and people watching. I could do that all day and be happy.

Yeah, we did that for a long time. I love to people watch, especially travelers. They're funny, dramatic, clueless, controlling, moody, always hungry and thirsty even if they just ate or drank. They're either in awe of their new surroundings or so exhausted from walking mile after mile that they can't quite appreciate the beauty and history they're in the midst of, at least not just yet - maybe after a snack. That's how I felt at times. The locals were all so friendly.

Of course, they were they're Italians! The Palazzo was neat because it was lined with all these shops and statues in the middle. One of the statues was a replica of the very famous what?

David! The real statue of David was moved to a place called the Academia due to some disfiguring that occurred from excavations that were being done under the Palazzo. I loved Il Duomo (The Dome). I loved it because it was this ginormous church with a dome shaped top along one of the busy streets. It was so big you could easily pass it by because it towered over the streets like a monument as opposed to a church.

Il Duomo was beautiful, but I really liked that other place we went. It had all the artwork in it.

Ah yes, the Uffizi Museum. It houses all the Italian Renaissance art. I only read of such beautiful art. I never thought I'd see it up close. Every piece was meticulous and vibrant and carried with it its own historical story. My two favorite pieces were La Primavera (Allegory of Spring) by Botticelli and the Madonna and Child with Two Angels by Filippo Lippi.

I loved the Madonna and Child too, but I also loved the Venus of Urbino by Titian. You know how much I love Venus, the Goddess of Love. Although this wasn't a painting of the actual Venus, to me, it depicts a woman who embodies both marriage and motherhood, yet she is also erotic and sensual. That's how I always wanted to be.

Are you serious? You were that way. People did a double take when they saw you.

No, they didn't.

Yes, they did.

No, you're exaggerating.

No, I'm not.

Hmm.

As I traveled throughout Florence, I was thinking about my next Italian city to visit. I asked a few of the locals about Venice but some people said it smelled, others said don't go there. So, the twins invited me to go to Roma (Rome) with them and I said, "Why not?"

That's my girl. Riding with the tide and going with the flow.

ROMA (ROME), ITALY

The Colosseum

The Vatican

I absolutely loved Rome. It was rustic, and the people were so friendly. They treated me like family and I so longed for that feeling.

I know you did. Rome was amazing. For years I dreamt about traveling throughout Italy and every country held its own beauty and special characteristics. No two cities were alike.

That's for sure. do you remember what happened to me in Roma?

Yes, and if I could have, I would have spanked you. How could leave your Pensione without a sweater or something to cover your shoulders knowing you were going to the Vatican? How?

I was…

How?

Firstly, it was June and…

We almost didn't get to see inside the Vatican because of that.

Would you let me finish please? I didn't know the Vatican didn't allow "bare shoulders" or anything showing above the knee. Man, they made you feel like a criminal for wearing shorts and a tank top, particularly when it came to women. It seemed we were more "suggestive" than men simply by virtue of our sex.

No shit. I lived with that my whole life.

Remember how hot it was that day? I think it was above 90° and the humidity was off the charts. I couldn't fathom carrying anything around my waist or on my arm or any place. Truthfully, being as non-denominational as I am, The Vatican didn't interest me. I just went because the twins said they were going, and I felt it was something I "should" see but didn't necessarily have to see. There was always something constricting about Catholicism and Christianity as a whole for me. Its rhetoric and ideologies were male oriented, guilt based and limiting in thought and human potential. However, even if you're not religious, the architecture is something else. When I walked in, I was taken by the Roman décor and history of the building. Not to mention it was massive. Every room was painted with such detail.

Oh, wasn't it? The ceiling and the intricate artwork throughout were amazing! All the colors and design, it was hard to believe they were hand painted. I loved it. So how did you get in again if you didn't have anything for your shoulders or your legs because you were in shorts right?

Right and I was just about to say that I was on a time constraint but, thankfully, two kind strangers let me borrow their tops because I needed one to cover my shoulders and one to wrap around my waist to cover my legs up to my knees. So, I couldn't stay in there too long because Melanie and Melissa had to continue with their day. It was so nice of these strangers to do that for me.

That was nice of them to let someone they didn't even know borrow their clothes.

Yeah, I was really grateful. I told them I was traveling around after college and really wanted to see the Vatican. They were happy to help. Believe it or not I actually did say a few prayers while in the Vatican.

Did you? What did you pray for?

I prayed for all abuse of animals to end and for the continuation of my safe travels. I also prayed for only good things to come into my life, whatever they may be.

Those sound-like good things to pray for.

I was more impressed with the Vatican City, those places around the Vatican like the Sistine Chapel, St. Peter's Square and St. Peter's Basilica. The Sistine Chapel was breathtaking. All that detail was just unbelievable.

It was.

The Arch of Constantine and The Colosseum were pretty impressive too huh?

Do you know why they called it the Arch of Constantine?

So, the Arch of Constantine is actually another huge arch structure that's situated between the Colosseum and the Palatine Hill. It looks like three of the Washington Square Arches in NYC put together.

It was pretty big right?

Yeah, The Arch of Constantine was erected to celebrate winning the Battle of Milvian Bridge in 312AD. After years of civil war, Constantine's army won over Maxentius. That win brought peace to the Roman Empire, so the Senate of Rome awarded

Constantine the Arch and dedicated it to him a few years later in 315AD. Hence, the Arch of Constantine.[9]

Isn't that interesting. I loved the detail that it was constructed with and all the statues that were so carefully crafted on the face of the Arch. Standing under it made you feel like an itty bitty tiny little thing next to it.

It is massive that's for sure.

Talk about massive - The Colosseum was certainly a sight to behold.

Now to say The Colosseum was Amazing is an understatement. That is the one place I'll never forget, ever! I've never seen anything so gargantuan in my life. I mean, it's this crazy maze surrounded by row upon row where spectators watched slaves, prisoners of war and condemned criminals fight to the death. It's unbelievable. I could feel the history as I sat in one of the columns. What's more interesting is that many people don't know that it was a full Colosseum, not the portion that remains today.

You're kidding. What happened to it?

An earthquake happened in 847 that forced the southern side to collapse. What's interesting is that the fallen pieces, some of which included the marble façade, were used to construct other monuments like St. Peter's Basilica.

Wow. I never knew that. Where did you read all these facts?

They have a plethora of information about the monuments, from beginning to end, when you visit them. We don't get this kind of detailed information in American schools.

That's true.

When I was walking around the Colosseum, I saw all these homeless kitties. Some were babies all cuddled together. I wanted to take them all back with me. They were all so friendly too.

I know. They actually made their home in the Colosseum.

Yeah, there certainly was enough space. It's really interesting to know how such wonders came to be. I love history and architecture from centuries ago. Together they tell a story of people and times from a different era that helped shape our world today. I wish I could have stayed in Rome longer. I wanted more time to do other things.

Such as…

I wanted to see as many of the architectural structures that I read of as possible. At the same time, I wanted to experience the city on a deeper level instead of being the typical tourist. Every morning I awoke to the smell of fresh baked bread just out of the oven cooling on the windowsills of houses across from my Pension. It was like staying in a little piece of Roman heaven. Romans express themselves with this strength and passion that I identify with.

Of course, you do! You're the same way.

I felt comfortable in Rome, like it was "home" or as if I'd been there before.

Who knows, maybe you were. What do you mean more time? You had plenty of time to do what you wanted.

Thinking back, I wish I would have stayed a few days extra just to walk around some more. I mean I did walk around with nothing planned for the day and relaxed in a few cafés, but my Euro-rail Pass was only for a couple of months and I was in need of a rest at some point soon. I wanted to find a place I could stay for a week or so before going back out on the road. I wanted to save some time for that. I was discovering that traveling, while fun, is also a lot of work. I lost count how many miles I walked and then there was the stress of having to find places to stay especially if my train got in during the early morning hours or late at night. Many hostels or Pensiones were closed and I'd have to walk to find an open café to rest before finding a place to crash. Sometimes if the train got in very early or very late, I waited on a street corner or in the train station until the sun came up and then would head out on my search. As I traveled, I thought about Ethan too. Every now and again a guy would show interest in me and then boom! Ethan would pop into my head. The mere attraction to someone else made me feel like I was cheating on him and we weren't even together.

Well, he was your first. It's hard to move on from your first but once you do, you do.

I was missing Sophie too. I wondered how she was fairing with Andrea and Codardo and all the people coming and going in our house. Everything felt so strange Mom. Everything was a fight with those two. I was trying to find a way to forgive them for disrespecting your home in Buffalo and selling our home in Syracuse. Their so-called friends were leaches with no direction, goals or means of supporting themselves. I particularly didn't like the way they were crashing in our home and making a mess of it. I wanted Sophie out of there. I missed you so and Sophie so much. I wished I could have taken Sophie with me. I really do.

I know honey but that would have been too stressful for her.

I know. Is it pathetic to tell you that I looked for you everywhere while I was traveling and for years afterward? I was so lonely without you.

I know baby. You didn't have to look for me because I was beside you the whole time. I was just waiting for you to acknowledge that.

Even though Ethan came to mind here and there, I mostly enjoyed being alone. It was good for me. I knew what I needed then, and I do now.

Yes, you do and I'm glad you were traveling on your own. It was a necessary journey.

I agree. I loved the southern tip of Italy so much that after Rome I spent a day in Bari and then went to Brindisi to catch the boat to Patras, Greece. I don't have any pictures of Bari or Brindisi but I have memories of wandering the streets, talking to the people, shopping at the local food stands and thinking how much I would have loved to live in Rome and make day trips to the nearby cities. I could have taken the boat to one of the Greek Islands, but I wanted to see Athens first, so from Patras I took the train to Athens.

I was so happy to see you exploring and doing things on a whim instead of planning every little detail out.

I have to admit it was unsettling for me but I kind of liked just throwing caution to the wind.

You see, you have an easy-going side to you. You just have to trust and have faith.

Yeah, I just like being organized. I feel more secure in my life that way.

That's probably because of all the instability we had. So, the boat ride was fun huh?

That boat ride to Greece was a great time. I didn't have enough money for an actual seat on the boat, but they allowed you to pay a small fee for a different kind of sleeping arrangement.

Which was?

I had to sleep on deck with my own sleeping bag. All the college travelers were doing it. It was safe and a whole lot of fun. The only downfall was that when I awoke the next morning, I had soot in my ears from the boat.

Yuck!

Yuck is right but, hey, it was worth it. I met some Italians that were also heading to Athens. They were living it up with dance and music and had everyone on deck laughing and dancing Greek style! I was dancing with one of the guys and accidentally clocked him in the face with my elbow. He was okay and laughed it off. I also met two American guys who just graduated Harvard and were traveling before going off to law school. They got so hammered they missed their stop. It was funny! Thankfully, the evening turned out to be warm with no rain or clouds. The full moon lit up the night sky. As I lay on the deck I gazed at the stars, listened to the swishing of the water and thought of you and Sophie. That night, there was a lightness and stillness in me I'd never felt before.

I lay with you that night, on the ferry boat. I held you like I used to when you were a little girl. I had no idea of the road that lay ahead of you baby. Honestly, I didn't. I only knew I had to be with you. Your grief was so raw, and I knew it would be for quite some time. I could see you were holding on for dear life. I saw how abandon you felt by me. You felt like I wasn't there for you anymore. That's why I knew I would need to start to remind you, from time to time, that in this life and beyond, I would never leave you, not ever – not for one second.

ATHENS, GREECE

The Parthenon

View of the Ancient Theater at the Acropolis

So here we were, in Athens! I have to say, Athens was the most trying part of my travels.

Athens was, different.

Yes, "different."

It wasn't quite like the more developed European countries you traveled to.

No, not at all. I was about to experience a whole different kind of living, Greek living that is. As soon as I got off the boat I was followed by this old man. He trailed me everywhere I went even if I stopped to use the restroom. It was spooky.

I'll say. What did you do?

I didn't do anything. I just kept on with my day and ignored him. He eventually went away. I was walking around trying to find a place to stay because the places listed in the Let's Go Europe book were closed and it was soooo hot. I'd say it never went below 100° while I was there, and the humidity was just as bad.

You also have to take into that it was summer too.

Yes, absolutely and "summer" let you know it too. For each place I traveled I tried my very best to speak the respective language, out of respect for the country and its people but Greek is a whole other world and it's not a language I picked up easily. I could barely speak a sentence and few people spoke English unless you happen to come upon another traveler. I felt very vulnerable there because of the language barrier. Thankfully the people at the "Hotel Lazanni," where I found a room, spoke English. I settled in and showered and guess who I happened to come upon?

Who?

Do you remember the twins, Melanie and Melissa from Canada, the ladies I met in Rome?

Oh yes, yes. You're kidding. You all met up there by chance?

Yup. That was a nice surprise. That was the good thing about traveling.

What's that?

Meeting up with the same people every now and again. Europe in the summertime is filled with college grads traveling from one country to another. It wasn't uncommon for me to meet the same people I'd met in prior countries I traveled to. It was good to see and hear about their travel experiences. With Melanie and Melissa, I didn't have to say a word. They did all the talking which was nice because between the heat and walking around I was exhausted. The first night I was there, rather than go out and about Melanie and Melissa invited me to go to this bar/tavern next door to the hotel. The bartender was from Ireland. He was also traveling and bartended between travels. He seemed friendly enough. He asked me where I was from and I told him. We talked for a bit as I sipped some local Greek soda then he asked me in his Irish accent,

"Have you ever tried Ouzo?"

I naïvely replied with a big, smile, "No. Is that another Greek soda?" I asked.

He laughed. "No. It's a traditional Greek Liquor. You should try it. It's reeeeaaaalllly good." He emphasized.

"Hmm," I thought, "Why not? I'm here to experience life as the locals do." So, with excitement at my first Greek experience I replied, "I'll take one, how do you call it again?"

"O-u-z-o." He slowly reiterated.

"Well I will take one O-u-z-o please." I said. He added one more pertinent detail about O-u-z-o.

"You have to drink it as a shot but don't worry. It tastes like licorice." My first thought was Sambuca, the Italian Liquor. Wait a minute. Why are you laughing?

I'm laughing because I know what Ouzo is.

Ah ha, well I wish you could have filled me in then on whatever it is you know now. It probably would have saved me from this night.

I doubt it. You would have wanted to find out for yourself anyway. Let's just say it's much stronger than Sambuca.

Ya think!

Remember how I used to pour the Sambuca into shot glasses, put a coffee bean in it, light it up and let the flame burn until it was nice and warm. You liked it. I was surprised given the fact that you don't even like to drink.

I still don't like the taste of alcohol, but I did like to sip the warm Sambuca. Only at Christmas time though. The other reason I don't like to drink is because I can't hold my liquor as noted in our bar excursion when I was sixteen.

You're right. You can't hold you're liquor. The rest of this story should be interesting.

Interesting is an understatement. Are you ready for the story?

I'm ready.

So, I was thinking since I've had Sambuca and that's a pretty strong drink, and this bartender made Ouzo sound sweet which to me, meant "not strong." I thought it would be okay if I took a shot. One wasn't going to hurt, right?

Right.

The key word here is ONE. Meanwhile, a couple of locals were sitting next to me telling me how delicious and sweet O-u-z-o is and how you can drink it like soda and blah, blah, blah. I had ONE shot and it was good, very good. It didn't even taste like there was alcohol in it.

What did it taste like?

It tasted like a refreshing licorice drink. I mean if you like licorice, which as you know I do, then you'll like this. Then I had another refreshing licorice drink, and another and another. Then I thought, "Hey, look who's holding her liquor?" Somewhere between the shots the bartender offered me a "refreshing Greek beer."

Oh, my goodness Kristin! You weren't doing all this drinking by yourself were you?

No. Melanie and Melissa were also with me along with some other people from the hostel, so it was all good and safe. That wasn't the problem.

What was the problem?

The problem was that after the beer the rest is a blur. All I can say is that I have a most poignant memory of this experience.

I'm afraid to ask but I will. What was the poignant memory?

The poignant memory of this night was finally being able to lay my head to rest after a long day of walking and then a long night of drinking, only to have to wake up and spend the remainder of the evening with my head in the toilet puking my guts out to the point of dry heaves. Do you have any idea how much I loved that toilet that night?

I bet! And for the record honey, the toilet loved you. It told me so.

Very funny. Oh my gosh, have you ever had dry heaves before from drinking or anything else?

Yes. It's awful.

It is. It's like your body is convulsing and trying to get something out but you've thrown up so much that there is nothing left to throw up so it's all dry, mucous...

Alright, alright that's enough. I know what you mean.

My stomach was killing me. I wished you were there to help me or rub my stomach. I was crying and sweating. I thought I was going to faint or pass out with my head stuck in the toilet.

Poor baby, good.

Good! What do you mean "good?" That's a terrible thing to say.

I hope you learned your lesson or lessons I should say.

Which one? Never to trust anyone that says a drink is "sweet" and "delicious?" Or, not to trust bartenders? How about never to drink with people that have iron for livers or maybe to find out exactly what it is I'm drinking before I drink it? There were so many lessons here. I just can't choose one.

I think you get the picture.

Mommy I was sooooo sick. Ouzo is really STRONG! I mean, what the hell is in that stuff, some sort of industrial waste fermented into liquor with licorice flavoring added to it? I bet if someone really knows what they're doing they could use it to build nuclear weapons. Is that what you would have told me BEFORE I tried it?

I would have tried to tell you but, as I said, you wouldn't have listened.

Uh huh. What'd I know? I was 22 and wanting to experience life like the locals do.

Well you did alright, but the locals have more practice honey, a lot more. They drink that stuff on a daily basis. How did you feel the next day?

I don't know. I was too busy looking for my liver. Pretty bad as I'm sure you can imagine. The following evening, I paid a visit to the bartender. As soon as he saw me walk in, he laughed and said,

"How do you feel American girl?"

"Ha, ha, ha." I told him. "You're a funny guy. What was that some sort of sick Irish humor? Maybe it's time for you to go to a different country for the sake of the new set of travelers coming in." He continued to laugh as he set up his bar. Then I told him I wanted my non-alcoholic drinks on the house for the rest of my stay for the little stunt he pulled. He agreed. Too bad I could only get water down. It seems I was his entertainment for the night.

It looks that way. You were mine the night we went out.

Thanks a lot.

Okay, okay. Well, you got through it in one piece, thankfully. Goodness gracious! The things you kids did were so different from my generation. When I was in my twenties I was married and already having babies!

I know. I could barely think about being in a relationship let alone being married at this time. There was still so much I wanted to do.

As painful as some of your experiences were, I'm glad you were having them. So, you got through the drinking and then what did you do?

I drank A LOT of water and forced myself to get out. I wanted to see some monuments and then get out of Athens.

You bought some beautiful dresses. I loved that black cotton, gauze dress you got and so cheap. I would have bought all kinds of things and sent them home, like I did when I went to India.

It's funny you mention that dress because today I was going through my closet and looking for things to give away to make more room and I was thinking to myself, "I wish I had that black dress I bought in Greece." It was one of my favorites and I gave it away.

What for? You should have kept it as part of your memories of Athens.

I know, I know. I don't remember why I gave it away. I think it was falling apart or something but you're right. I should have kept it.

Kristin, you have this thing with going through closets and giving things away. You give things away too quickly.

It's important to clean out the old and not be a packrat like someone I know.

I'm not a packrat. I didn't have a chance to be a packrat with you going through my things all the time. Do you remember how you used to do that?

Vaguely.

Vaguely my but. You used to go through my closets and drawers. You'd put all the things you thought should be given away in a big pile on the bed, which was always made, and you'd say, "Mom, when you get a chance can you go through this pile of 'stuff.' I think you can give these things away." I felt like a kid again with my mother. The best part is whatever I didn't give away found its way into the pile the next time around. What was that about? Were you hoping I wouldn't remember it the first time you put it there?

Now hold on there Mary J. That "pile" you're referring to were things you never used, and our apartment living didn't give us a lot of space. I was trying to make room.

For what, you're stuffed animals. You had a ton of those, and I never said anything.

Hey, hey now. Watch the stuffed animals. That's sacred ground you're stepping on.

Ah, you see. Well my "stuff" was sacred too. Besides, it was my "stuff" and we went through this little giving away process at least twice a month. How much can I give away twice in one month? It's good to keep some things from years gone by, for our memories.

I can't tell you what a feeling of accomplishment it was when you did give some things away. I felt like a fresh spring breeze blew into our bedroom in the form of empty hangers and new-found drawer space.

Kristin.

What.

Did I ever tell you what a weird kid you were/are?

Yes. It doesn't faze me as long as my closets are neat and arranged by season.

Oh yes, I forgot you arrange your closets by season. Lord help us all.

Hey, don't knock the cleanliness of this angel.

Oh yeah sure, angel shmangel.

At least I don't have to do the whole put the winter clothes away and make room for the summer clothes. Everything stays in the closet and drawers because there's space. It saves me the trouble of having to pack and unpack between seasons.

Yes, but you go through your closets at least once a month. Are you afraid you missed something the month before?

Exactly Mary. I'm glad you're finally getting with the program. It took a while, but I think you're finally getting on board with how blissful organization can be.

Organization - try OCD [over compulsive disorder].

Whatever you want to call it, just please, when expressing your feelings, have them all arranged beginning with the most recent.

Like I said, weird kid. So, what were some of the monuments you we saw before departing from your favorite city. Actually, before we get on that what was it specifically about Athens you didn't like?

Now, no offense to the Athenians but it was super crowded and as I said, hot. It was also a very dirty, smelly city that consists of a maze of streets all of which felt like they were on an incline, and you can't get sick or have a disease in Athens. From what the locals told me the hospitals and doctors aren't very well equipped.

Plus, all the stores, restaurants and homes were on top of each other. There was no space for people to breathe. Between that and the tourists it was hard to walk around without bumping into someone. I felt claustrophobic the whole time I was there. It's also very confusing if you don't read or speak Greek and the people weren't all that friendly or helpful.

Hmm, tell me what you really think about Athens.

Are you sure because I kind of feel like I was holding back a little?

No please, let your feelings go, by either time or date and starting with the most recent.

Finally! I knew you'd come around. Let's hug!

Keep going you Kook. Let's talk about more of the landmarks you saw.

I have two words for you, Acropolis and Parthenon.

I thought they were both incredible. Tell me something about each of them. What did you learn?

Here is an interesting fact about the Acropolis. It's actually the hill the Parthenon is built.

That is interesting. I never knew that. I thought it was another landmark.

Lots of people do. There's also an Ancient Theater at the Acropolis where elaborate performances were held. That's right up your alley. You love the theater.

I do. I wish you did. I was so hoping you were going to be my money child. That's what the gods told me before you were born anyway.

Right. Whatever stuff you were smoking before or during your pregnancy with me would explain a lot about me. In fact, it probably would have saved me in therapy costs. Is there anything you want to get off your chest?

No, and even if I did, I wouldn't tell you. Na ne na ne na na.

Okay, anyway, getting back to the Acropolis and the Ancient Theater which I have to say, was beautifully constructed. Now this is the Theater on the hill remember. The Acropolis is the hill.

Right got it.

The Theater is made of stone and it sits on the southern slope of the Acropolis. It's all open with lots of entrances and exits. The front part is this gigantic stone wall with holes or openings scattered throughout to resemble windows. The back part, which is shaped like a half moon, consists of rows of marble seats with a texture so smooth you could slide across them. That's what I did.

What an amazing sight. I thought the Acropolis and The Parthenon were awe inspiring. It's like a huge Greek Castle set on top of a hill built specifically for the goddess Athena.

IT IS a huge Greek Castle set on top of a hill built specifically for Athena.

I can see her now, standing between the columns overlooking all of Athens in her flowing white Greek gown, as the wind gust through her long, dark, silky smooth hair.

Oh brother.

Tell Mom what it felt like to be standing at the Parthenon? Were you in awe?

I was in awe. It was pretty spectacular. The columns evoked this sense of history combined with a feeling of pride in me. I don't know why pride. Greece isn't where we're from, but I still felt proud, of something.

Maybe yourself?

Yeah, I was just thinking that. Climbing to the Parthenon was an excursion in and of itself. I mean, you can't tell from the picture but sits at the top of the city. The walk up there pretty much took three quarters of the day. I didn't even realize how far I walked until I began looking down and the city got smaller and smaller and smaller. It was a surreal experience.

Isn't it exciting to be visiting a place so historic and one you've only read about?

Yeah, it was. I felt like that the whole trip. Many times, I had to stop and pinch myself that I was actually experiencing all that I was. Right before I left for Europe, I wrote down all the places I wanted to see but not really processing that I would, indeed, see and experience them. The Acropolis and Parthenon were just a few of those places. Now that I think about it. I pretty much saw everything I wrote down.

That's some accomplishment.

Yup.

Did you ever find out how the Parthenon lost much of its structure?

I did. That happened in 1687 during a battle with the Venetians. There was an explosion that caused the damage that is still seen today but they're working to repair it, slowly. The statue of Athena, which was originally made of silver, ivory and gold, used to be in its center.[10]

Interesting, so what happened to Athena?

Unfortunately, the statue was destroyed in a fire that, I believe, happened before the explosion in 1687.

Wow, you sure did learn a lot on your travels.

I did. Learning through firsthand experience as opposed to having my head buried in a book, was my sole impetus for going. I learn faster, easier and tend to retain more as well when I see things, particularly numbers. I guess that means I have a photographic memory.

You were always like that. If I explained something to you, you would often get a blank look on your face which, to me, meant you were "phasing out." However, if I showed it to you, you got it right away.

I'm still that way, although I also like to give blank stares just for the fun of it too. It tends to throw people off.

I noticed that. I was the same way in terms of learning. If I saw something or did it myself, I got it faster than if someone were verbally teaching it to me. So, the Acropolis and the Parthenon were the only two monuments you saw, weren't they?

They were. Like I said, I really needed to out of Athens. I felt so isolated from civilization. In order to get back to the ferry boat I had to take the train and I couldn't get there fast enough. Another person at the hotel gave me directions but I got lost. Since everything is written in Greek, I couldn't figure out which way to go and everyone I asked spoke little to no English. I was walking around in the sweltering summer heat for what seemed like hours and didn't see one car. I was starting to feel like I'd be stuck in Athens for a good portion of my twenties. In utter frustration I plopped my backpack on the street corner and sat there thinking what my next move would be out in no man's land with only one bottle of water left. It was do or die.

I don't know that it was quite that bad dear.

Are you kidding me? Yes, it was. I could feel myself getting weaker when, out of the blue, a cab came toward me. I ran to the middle of the road, dropped my backpack next to me so he couldn't get by and made him pick me up.

How did you know it was a cab?

The yellow color and the big sign on top that read, TAXI, was a subtle hint.

Oh.

I exhaustingly asked him to please take me to the train station in a combination of English and whatever other language I thought he might understand; "Traino, Trainnee, choo choo…" you name it. He laughed and just when I thought he understood me. Guess where he took me?

Oh no. Where?

To the train station but this train was heading southeast which would have taken me further into Athens, AHHHHH? I needed to go northwest, toward the coast. I was at my wits end and started to sob. The driver felt bad. "No cry miss, please, no cry," he said.

Poor honey. So, what happened? You obviously did get out of there.

I did. I told the driver, "train to America." Then he understood and took me to the train heading back up north. By this time, I really needed to rest. Between the man following me, drinking to the point of dry heaves and the four Swiss guys that ended up in the same room as I. I was pretty much done with Athens.

Well, that's the beauty of traveling. You take what you need and leave what you don't and learn from there. What did you learn?

That I cherish working telephones and the English language.

That's a start. Athens was a hard place to visit especially when you're alone, but I have to say, you navigated yourself pretty well. When in doubt, stand in the middle of the road with your backpack as a roadblock for an oncoming cab. Smooth Crage, very smooth.

You mean the only oncoming cab and thank you. From the train I finally caught the ferry boat. After my Athens journey, it was time for some much-needed R&R and I knew exactly where that would be.

This next spot was exactly what you needed!

Yes indeed.

THE ISLAND OF CORFU, GREECE

Mother and Daughter

View from the mountaintop

Oh gosh. I love, love, love these photos of Corfu. Anytime I get down I look at my photos of traveling, particularly of Corfu, and feel at ease.

Honey, you took some great shots. You feel at ease because that's what these photos invoke, ease and peace.

Looking at these photos reminds me of a much simpler time. Everything that seemed so hard back then was really just that easy compared to the present.

The past, for some of us, always seems like that and who knows baby. Maybe in a few years all that seems hard now will be easy.

Well, who knows?

I love that picture you have there, the one that says, "Mother and Daughter."

Of all the pictures I took in Corfu that's my favorite. Those two reminded me of us – it was symbolic of the way we used to play and have so much fun in each other's company. I guess that's why I clung to you so much.

And I you.

I was staying at The Pink Palace, a well-known hostel amongst travelers. I loved it because I had my own room with a view of the ocean which was only a few steps away. I went to sleep and awoke to the sound of gentle waves and the smell of fresh, crisp air blowing through my window. I was so happy.

Me too. I'm happy that you were allowing yourself to be so free.

Sometimes during the day or at night, I would put my headset on and dance around the room. I felt so uninhibited.

How cute. How did you afford your own room?

It was the same price as if I were sharing. They just weren't that full. I lucked out. I was also able to meet up with friends from the beginning of my travels like Mara and Elena, the two I met in Amsterdam and a few others. Along my travels I had a few constants with me; one was my cassette player and one tape, Earl Kluge's, Finger Paintings. We love that tape.

Love, love, love Earl Kluge. Earl Kluge takes me back to my carefree hippie days. His music always reminded me of being on a beach or island somewhere.

Yeah, it fit throughout my whole trip and I never got tired of it. I could dance anywhere to it. No matter how small my room was I found a spot and some alone time to dance and just let go.

What was another constant?

The high school graduation letter you wrote me. I brought it with me. I spent most of my time on the beach re-reading that letter and thinking of you and Sophie. Sophie was my tangible comfort. I knew I would be coming home to her soon. You, on the other hand, became this surreal, intangible unsettling state that I've never gotten used to.

What do you mean?

I've never gotten used to the fact that I can't hold or comfort you or vice versa. I never dreamed this physical separation would happen to us so soon.

Remember babe, nothing can separate or weaken our love. Do you feel that our love has decreased since I crossed, because I don't? I know it's gotten stronger every day, even in the bad times.

No. I feel our love everyday but, obviously, the physical separation is always present in my life. I don't think I'll ever get over not being able to hold you or have you hold me. We can't do things together. You know, that kind of stuff. You're with me but it's different.

I know we don't have that instant physical gratification of touch, but the feelings are just as real as when I was in my physical body.

What is it like if you don't mind me asking?

What?

Where you are.

It's nothing but complete love here Kristin. It's amazing. The moment you cross over it's like someone empties out all the anger, resentments, harsh feelings and whatever else that was negative in you and you become this entity made up of only love, forgiveness, warmth and good feelings. It's light here. I feel very light here. I felt heavy in my physical body, too heavy for me to keep going.

I'm glad Mom. You deserve light, peace, love and more.

Kristin?

Yeah.

It was time for me to go honey. My body had run its course. I wasn't able to hold on anymore. I couldn't baby, not even with the agonizing knowledge that my children would grow up alone.

I'm hurting without you, still. My life has been miserable since you left. No one understands this about me but you. For years if I wasn't being told I hung on to your memory too much then I was being told to let go of you. When you crossed, I was inundated with people offering the illusion that time would heal my loss and grief. What a crock of shit. There's just more time that passes between the present than when you crossed but the pain remains the same. There's this huge empty space inside me – the space where our lives together occupied. Nothing can ever fill it and not that I would want it to. Now, I find I'm just building my life around that space. That's all I can do. The pain of your absence in my life never goes away. I know you say we're still close, but our separation is more real for me than you. We can't go to lunch or a jazz concert or just be in each other's company.

Yes, we can. You make it real honey. You give separation too much power. Will you please try not to do that? The less power you give separation the more connected you'll be with me and more importantly, with yourself. Little minute?

What?

Look at me. I'm here. Can you see me?

No.

Take a moment, breathe and let go. Now do you see me.

Sort of.

What do I look like?

I see your smile, your big brown eyes, but the rest of you is foggy. It's kind of weird because it's not so much what I see but what I'm feeling. Now, you're more a feeling -a knowing. These conversations just come; you know. They're here and they happen and the "how" is difficult to put into words.

Exactly baby. That's because the "how" is God's way. We communicate effortlessly with love. The days you tell me you're struggling it's because you're fighting yourself.

I love you so much Mom. I miss you more than I can say. The holidays, Mother's Day, birthdays (yours and mine) have all come and gone for years now. Each year I go to the store to buy you a card. It doesn't matter what the occasion. I go through the same process. I stare at the card remembering how much you cherished cards from me more than my gifts because of what I wrote. Then I start to cry. I want to buy you flowers or take you out to dinner for your birthday. Christmas is the worst - only seven days from the anniversary of your crossing and I somehow muster up the energy to decorate my apartment and even bake. It's just me and my animals on the holidays but they love the Christmas lights and the smell of cookies baking. I continue the Christmas traditions because all the while I'm thinking of you and me and how silly we were with Christmas joy. Is that pathetic?

No! I love that you continue our holiday traditions. It brings you joy. I see your apartment. I watch you bake. I see all the cards you look at for me. I see you stand at the rows of flowers and feel you thinking of me. I see you my little girl. I see you. I love you. We're bound by the love of God and remain for each other. I want you to know you are not alone, ever. You are surrounded and protected by God angels and me, always. Remember that. I have an idea.

What's that?

The flowers you want to buy me.

Yeah.

Buy them for you. They'll look so beautiful on your kitchen table with the sunlight shining in on them. Will you do that for yourself?

I can do that.

And the beautiful dinners you want to take me too for my birthday...

Yes.

Go anyway. You deserve a night out Kristin. You deserve more than a night out, but a dinner is a good place to start.

I guess. Maybe I could order in.

Go out and take a friend. You have friends, don't you?

I have one or two people I trust but they're busy a lot, you know. They have families and what not. It's okay. You know I've always preferred animals over people. You were the "people" person between the two of us. I'm not good at meeting people Mom. I never was.

You are too, you just tend to go inward too much and stay there.

Precisely.

Well look at all the people you met on your travels. You must have something in you that draw people toward you because you never asked anyone to travel with them. They asked you.

It was short term. Everything is easier on a short-term basis - no commitments no promises, just pure fun, good times and lots of laughs. I wish life could be like that.

Life can be, sometimes.

Corfu was a good time wasn't it?

It was the best! You did something that I was so happy you did. You know what it was.

I went topless. Talk about freeing. I really enjoyed that.

Sunbathing nude is a wonderful way to free your body up.

I don't need to ask if you've sunbathed nude, I already know the answer.

Before my cancer I loved being nude. I mean there were things about my body I didn't like but I loved sunbathing nude and having my clothes off without feeling self-conscious. I particularly enjoyed that in the company I felt totally accepted by.

Even after your cancer you had a beautiful body Mom. Everyone thought so.

I wish I thought more of myself back then. I hurt myself a lot by having such low self-esteem. I don't what that to happen to you. As you say, "any who," let's talk more about Corfu!

Just hearing the word makes me smile. All I did was relax on the beach, bask in the sun, moon and stars. That's where the Mother and Daughter photo was taken. That beach looked like it jumped out of a travel magazine. The water was crystal blue, and I could see all the different kinds of fish swimming around me. You could see your feet even when you swam in the deep end although I didn't venture too much in the deep end.

That's where I would have spent most of my time too. Did you do any shopping or anything like that?

I did in Athens, but I wasn't really into shopping in Corfu. The most I did there was rent a mop-ed, rode around the island a bit and took some great shots.

Well that sounds like fun.

It was. I just wanted to relax.

I can understand that.

My most peaceful moments were when I'd stand at that place where the ocean meets the sand, look out into the vast open clear blue water - close my eyes and feel the lightness of the air softly brush against my face and body. I felt free yet lost; strong in the knowledge that before me held a life with unlimited possibilities yet I longed to have you with me every day, enjoying this freedom and these new places and faces I was encountering.

Me too but you were on a much-needed journey babe; physically, emotionally and spiritually.

I wished I knew what I wanted to do with my life. I felt free and uninhibited, but I also needed guidance, your guidance you know? I had no idea what I wanted to do or where to go or anything. I mean I loved to dance but I wasn't sure I wanted to make that my vocation. When you're a dancer you're not only trained to be disciplined but you're also trained to be self-conscience. I didn't like that part of dance.

No, I know. You were always so worried about not gaining weight, making sure you were strong and fit to the point of exhaustion.

I know. I actually liked being away from the rigidity I felt from the dance world. Yet I still really needed the help of someone that knew and loved me and had my best interests at heart. I needed you to bounce ideas off of, ask questions about anything and everything and so on.

I know how hard all of this was for you, but traveling was probably one of the best decisions you ever made. You always had me and still do. Now, the universe was demanding you to figure things out for yourself. It was time for you to be enough for yourself. That's been your lesson and challenge all along.

Yeah, Corfu was a good place to stop and take breather to think about all these things. It was also good to take a break from the hustle and bustle of country to country traveling. What did you like about Corfu?

It was peaceful there. I loved the sunrises and sunsets - the beginning and end of each day when everything was calm, and people were either just waking up or preparing to settle for the night. The sound of the water has always been soothing to me. Remember how I used to have all those cassettes of the ocean?

I do. I still have them you know.

Do you listen to any of them?

No, not lately.

Ah, well Corfu was like having my tapes of the ocean come to life right at my doorstep.

Me too. At night I opened my windows and felt a soft breeze pass through my room carrying with it the clean fresh scent of the clear blue ocean. I could see the moon and stars set against the warm night sky. While there I was at such peace, to the point of tears, good tears. The most peace I'd felt since you crossed. I didn't want to leave Corfu. This was the place where I finally grasped that there was an entire world out there waiting for me to see. All the different, beautiful people, cultures and places you told me about and those I read of were not only possible, but real as I was seeing them. My inner world was opening up and for the first time in a long time - I was feeling hopeful about whatever future lay in front of me. While traveling, I had only myself to relay on for safety and proper direction and surprisingly enough, I did pretty well. This trip helped me to understand that, while difficult, I had the ability to move forward.

I don't know why you would be surprised at that. Navigating through doctors and hospitals and all that garbage prepared you to learn how to ask questions and "get to the bottom of things" so to speak. Kristin, when I was sick you were a kid who was all about solutions, not lingering in problems. You could be a little dogmatic at times but sometimes that was necessary in order to get the answers and resolutions we needed. I don't know if you notice but your trip was as smooth as it was because of your ability to look at obstacles as challenges. I wish you would open your eyes and see what I see.

What?

For starters, the horrible things the family was saying about you weren't true. You were feeling the pain of my crossing over as well as the loss of any hope of having a supportive family to help you through such a hard time in your life and shame on them. They betrayed both of us and aren't worthy of your love, loyalty or trust.

You're right about that.

I wish you could have stayed longer in Corfu too but there was still so much to see and do. Remember how I was saying at some point I would need to start reminding you that I would never leave you?

Yes.

That point had arrived, and the reminder had to be big in order for me to break through some of those walls.

VENICE (VENEZIA), ITALY

The Canals of Venice

View from a water taxi

Happy Mother's Day Mom!

Thank you, baby! You too☺. So…

So…

Did you buy yourself the flowers?

Yeah, I did actually.

Yahoo! I'm so glad. I'll bet they look beautiful. They're on your kitchen table, right?

Right.

How did it feel to do something nice for yourself?

It felt good. Flowers are especially nice. They mean more to me than any material thing because they represent a renewal of life.

Yes, they do, and they represent growth which is exactly where you're at. You've loved flowers all your life. Even as a little girl. Remember when Mom used to have the rose bushes on the side of our house in Syracuse.

I do.

You picked roses for me, your teacher and anyone else you wanted to make smile. When they were gone you used to sneak into the neighbors' yards and pick their flowers for me you little peanut! Don't think I didn't know about that.

Oops, busted. Who told you?

Who told me? No one told me. Where else would you get all those beautiful flowers at 8 years old with no money? I know if you could grow your own flower garden you would. Sweetheart?

What?

You're worth all things good and a renewal of life.

Let's talk about Venice.

In a minute.

If I'm worth good things, then my life's experiences would reflect that, and they don't. I can't help but feel like I did something wrong somewhere.

Kristin, it's not your fault. We all screw up and make mistakes. Everyone messes up including Mom but that doesn't mean you deserve bad things to happen to you. Do you think I did something to deserve my cancer or for Dad to leave us or any other bad thing?

No, absolutely not. You deserved only good things Mom.

Then don't give in to the hurt that's been caused to you.

I went from having a handle on everything, being an independent woman to becoming dependent on others and not having any control over what was happening.

We'll get to how that happened, but you had control. It just felt like you didn't.

You're the only one that understands this weight I feel, like I'm 1,000 pounds. Sometimes I can just barely get myself out of bed.

Yet you do. You've been challenged with what feels like is beyond your means. I know.

I knew you would.

C'mon, let's talk about Venice.

Oh Venice, Venice, Venice. All I can say is VIVA Venezia!

There's my little traveler.

Oh man, Venice changed my life, for the better.

You changed my life, for the better. You almost didn't go to Venice you silly.

I know, well, everyone I met was talking about how romantic it was but romance was the last thing on my mind. Plus, I didn't want to get caught in the tourist zone. Corfu was just the rest I needed but as I lay on the beach of Corfu, I felt pulled to go to Venice. So, I went.

I was not going to allow you to bypass one of the most beautiful cities in Italy. I knew you would kick yourself if you didn't go and you knew how much I always wanted to see Venice. Besides there was something special we needed to do.

Once again, I hopped the boat from Corfu back to Brindisi. The ride was a lot of fun, but I was glad it would be the last time. I couldn't get used to waking up with soot in my ears. From Brindisi I caught the train to Venice, found a Pensione and relaxed on the balcony with a cappuccino. The coffee was so good in Europe.

Ever since I gave you your first sip of coffee as a little girl you were hooked.

Yes, and thank you! I remember when you tried to get me to drink that coffee substitute stuff.

Postum. It was all natural and better for you, but you made such a fuss it wasn't worth it.

Yeah, that coupled with the dry milk mix. Yuck. So, I found a Pensione right in the center of the market square. As soon as I walked out my door, I was smack dab in the midst of vegetable/fruit stands and a bustling shopping square filled with one pasty/café shop after another. I loved it. I loved waking up to the smell of fresh coffee. As it turned out I liked Venice more than I thought I would. There is something quite magical about it. I wandered the dimly lit cobblestone streets filled with late night restaurants packed with both locals and tourists. As I walked, I could hear the sounds of gentle splish splashing of the waves coming from the canals.

You see! I knew you'd like it.

You're right. Europeans, in particular Italians, know how to balance work and enjoy life. They never seem to overwork themselves, yet they get a lot done and still find time for siesta during the day. I wish Americans were like that. We probably wouldn't have so much disease and strife in our lives if we did.

You're right about that. I felt like that when I traveled too. The stress melted away from my body and mind.

I had a midnight meal at one of the restaurants tucked away on one of the side streets. It was fun and there were so many people out and about at the time, so it was safe.

I loved the Gondola ride.

Me too. I liked it when we went underneath the street bridges. That was quintessential Venice.

It was perfect. I thought it was neat the way the Gondola's all lined up together and rode side by side.

Yeah, I think there were six or seven that lined up one next to the other drifting alongside each other. Then the drivers sang beautiful Italian songs. With all these wonderful things we were doing I still looked everywhere but couldn't find them.

Who?

The Italian glassmakers you always wanted to see. I figured since I was back in Italy I might as well try finding them one last time. I asked everyone that could understand me, and all were clueless as to who, what or where they were. Again, I wondered if they even existed. Maybe I wasn't explaining myself properly. I don't know. I did meet someone very special though. I remember this day like it was yesterday. When I need to smile, I play this experience in my mind like a short film.

I'm ready for the movie to begin.

It was my last day. I'd been in Venice for two days roaming about eating, visiting museums, window shopping, sightseeing and what not. I was getting tired and decided it was time to move on. I went to one of the cafés, sat at an outdoor table and had a cappuccino. The day was beautiful. The sun was shining, everyone was smiling and there wasn't a cloud in the sky. I basked in the rays and people watched. The tourists meandered about from one fruit stand to the other while the locals bartered with that rustic Italian fire that comes out in their everyday conversations and makes non-locals think they're arguing but they're not.

They're just talking.

Right, it's conversation, Italian style. Italians converse a few octaves higher and much stronger than most. I loved being in Italy Mom. It was the closest feeling to "home" since…

Me.

Yes. Sitting alone at my table as I was, I couldn't help but feel like I let you down. I wanted so much to find and do the things we both wanted to do while traveling. I was upset I didn't find the glassmakers.

You could never fail me Kristin. Not in life or beyond.

I don't think I'm half the woman you were.

You fill me with pride every day. Tell me about the rest of your last day in Venice.

An elderly man, maybe in his 70's, came over to my table and asked to sit in one of the empty chairs. In Europe it's not uncommon for strangers to share a table with each other which is nice. Unfortunately, I wasn't in the most chipper of moods and wanted to be alone, but I didn't want to be rude. I responded, "Ci (yes)," with an accompanied hand gesture welcoming him to sit down. I was hoping he wouldn't say anything so I could be alone in my thoughts. I kept my head held down, indicating my desire to be left alone and started to write in my travel journal but that didn't seem to work. The gentleman started a conversation anyway.

"Buongiorno," he said.

"Buongiorno," I replied. There, I thought, good conversation. I returned my head to my journal, but the gentleman continued. It was interesting because when he said "Buongiorno" it almost sounded like, "I know you don't want to talk but let's talk anyway." He was of average height, gray hair and big brown eyes. He looked like your typical grandfather. He was nice and his manner of speaking was gentle. He had an unassuming demeanor and his presence was comforting. His English wasn't very good, but he started to ask me questions vacillating from Italian to English wherever he could. Every time he asked me a question, I brought my head back to my chest, but the tactic never worked. He would wait a minute or so then ask another question. Finally, I gave in.

I used my translation book to translate the words from both Italian to English and vice versa. With this, we were able to make out what the other was saying. With a charm only an elderly gentleman of some royal background could possess, he finally introduced himself. "Il mio nome è Pontini" (My name is Pontini). I introduced myself. Every time I fumbled through my translation book we'd laugh. It was funny. He asked where I was from and if I was a student. I told him I'd just graduated from college and was a dancer. His eyes lit up and he told me he and his wife used to ballroom dance.

I was so excited to hear that. He asked about my family, if I had any and so on. I told him I had very little contact with my father. I didn't respond to him right away about you. Every time someone asked me about you, I would choke up. I still wasn't used to saying you crossed.

Pontini noticed I didn't answer him, so he asked again. "E tua madre? (and your mother)." He asked.

I looked away and tears began to form in my eyes. He reached across the table, placed his hand over mine and repeated as if he knew and wanted me to say it, "E tua madre?"

A lump gathered in my throat. I took a sip of cappuccino to try and get it down, but it got bigger. There was no way for me to reply without the tears falling. I looked toward the clear blue sky filled with puffy white clouds. The same ones I used to look up at during the summer while laying on our backyard lawn in Clay, New York. I wanted my words to come out smooth. Instead, I swallowed a few gulps in-between words.

I replied, "Morta. Mia madre è morta (my mother passed away)."

I remember how you used to lay in the grass. Sometimes you'd be there for hours.

It gave me peace. The grass supported me. I liked being able to give something all my weight. It felt impossible to be little and have to constantly fight off someone twice your size.

Your brother?

Yes.

Do you want to talk more about that?

No, not now. Maybe later.

Okay, well I'm open and ready to listen whenever you need me to.

Thanks. Let's just stick with our travels for now.

You got it.

Whenever someone asked me about you it brought me closer to the fact that I no longer had a home - that place of comfort you created for me, inside and out even in your illness, where I could return for love, warmth, acceptance and safety. My stomach started to feel sick and for a moment I lost my breath. I tried but I couldn't hold my tears back. They just kept rolling down. Pontini gave a gentle squeeze to my hand and a charming wink.

"Mi dispiace (I'm sorry)." He said. We talked for a few more minutes until I realized I became so engrossed with our conversation that I'd lost all interest in my journal. I felt an immediate connection with Pontini. There was just something about him that drew me in. Our conversation paused for a moment and then Pontini asked me to go somewhere with him. My train was going to be leaving that evening, so I was a little hesitant. Pontini assured me he'd get me back in time.

You weren't nervous to go off with an elderly man you didn't even know.

No. I felt safe with Pontini. There is one thing I learned from my experiences with my brother and father.

What's that?

I learned on a gut level the difference between a man that can be trusted (one that won't hurt you) and one that can't. Pontini was a man to be trusted, not feared. After all, traveling was about new experiences. So, the first stop on my adventures with Pontini was his house to meet his wife!

How cute.

It was and she was sweet. He introduced me as his, "nuovo piccolo amico (new little friend)." He showed me around his Venetian home. A one level modest home filled with the smell of fresh baked bread and sauce. It was a short visit before we were off again. This time to his nephew that owned a bar/restaurant tucked along one of the streets. We were there for a few minutes while he greeted friends he'd known for years and then we were off again.

This time it was to a place I'd read about it in books but never thought I would have the opportunity to experience. It was hot that day. I had my black spaghetti strap camisole on and jean shorts with flesh colored sandals. My hair was long. I loved the way it felt on my back even when it was hot out. Pontini led us through several streets, turning left here, a right there, walking, walking, walking. I never asked where we were going or when we would get there. He seemed so sure of himself, there was no need to. Finally, after about thirty minutes of walking from one street to another we arrived.

It was two or three big open spaces connected by doors made of iron bars. The top of the walls finished with wire fences, like the ones you might see in a jail. In fact, each space looked like the outdoor recreational area of a prison. Cement comprised all four walls of each space which could probably hold about 100 people or so. There were these black stone carvings hanging on the walls and a couple of benches also made of cement. Pontini went and sat on one of the benches. He told me he would hold my things for me and motioned for me to walk around and look at the carvings.

When I glanced over at him, he looked like he was reminiscing about something. He looked sad. He caught me looking at him. He smiled, took out my camera and told me to stand next to the black carvings so he could take a picture. At first, I declined. I felt silly but he insisted, so I obliged. When I returned to Pontini I asked him what this place was. Pontini replied that he rarely came there but thought it would important for me to see. I assured him it was. He said he and his wife had been there many, many years ago when he thought their lives were over. I apologized and told Pontini I didn't understand. We went back and forth because I really couldn't understand what he was trying to tell me and then he used one word that explained everything and made me gasp for a breath of air.

"Hitler," he said. The large spaces, one connected to the other with the wire fences and iron bars for doors was where Hitler brought all the Italian Jews and held them there until they were to be transported to the concentration camps. This place came to be known as "Synagogue Square."

In Synagogue Square, Venice Italy, 1992

Oh my gosh.

Yeah, I was stunned. Never, in my wildest dreams did I think I would be sitting in such a place. My heart sank, tears welled in my eyes and Pontini held my hand. He pulled his hankie from his coat pocket and softly wept. He described watching all his friends and neighbors entering the areas - most of them separated from their families. He described the sounds of everyone around him crying their selves to sleep at night and screaming for their husbands, wives, sisters, brothers etc. during the day. He told me of peoples' faces filled with anguish, tears, bloodshot eyes, dark circles, parched dried mouths and lips. He recalled, like it was yesterday, his skin so dried and burnt from sitting under the hot sun with little food or water that it began to blister and bleed. Most disturbing were the inhibitions everyone was forced to let go of due to the lack of bathrooms. Everyone relieved themselves in corners of the holding area. Pontini recalled the loss of his life as he'd once known it - his home, his business and most importantly, the love he felt for his current wife, whom, back then he planned to marry.

This is gut wrenching.

I know.

What was Pontini's work?

He owned a restaurant. He said everything he experienced in his life up to that point seemed like nothing compared to what he was experiencing then. He didn't say anything more for several minutes but the tears flowing from his eyes elicited more tears from me. My heart ached for what he and everyone subjected to Hitler's regime went through. With gratitude and exhaustion, he began to tell me when he and his wife were sent to the camps, they got separated. It was near the end of the war. When he was able to return to Venice he immediately began searching for his wife. He wasn't even sure if she was still alive, but he continued his search. After months of looking he found her, and they were married. I asked him why he didn't leave Venice and the horrible memories it held to start a new life somewhere else and do you know what he said?

What?

He adamantly replied, "My home is inside me. Venice is my home and the place my family was born. No one will take my home from inside me." Pontini and his wife had children and built a simple life together. He said he was glad he stayed in Venice because rather than having a sad memory of the place he loved so much he filled it with beautiful memories with the woman he loved and the family they created. I wasn't feeling romantic when I got to Venice but talking with Pontini made me want to fall in love and live happily ever after. Here was a man who took a terrible situation and actually built something so precious and beautiful from it.

Imagine that.

I had enormous admiration and respect for him. I felt kind of uncomfortable that he took the picture of me standing in the place where thousands of people were waiting to be sent to die. Why do you think he wanted to take that picture?

Maybe he wanted you to remember that it's possible to take a terrible situation and build something so precious and beautiful from it. What an amazing man - one of God's angels don't you think?

Yes. You always said, "We're God's little angels. All of us."

Kristin?

Yeah.

I wish we could have talked then like we are now.

Me too. I'm sorry. I just didn't know how to handle the transition you went through - from body to spirit. I wondered, "Can she hear me? Can she see me? Can she prevent bad things from happening to me?" I wanted to know all these questions and just didn't know how to go on as we are now. I was a body in motion searching for you, always.

The answers to those questions are "yes," "yes," and as much as I wish I could, "no." If it were up to me only good things would happen to you and come into your life. I hope you know that.

I know and I do.

Tell me more about your day with Pontini.

The more time I spent with Pontini the more I thought about you. After we gathered ourselves from our emotional experience, I thanked him for sharing such an important part of his life with me. I promised I would cherish every word and memory. He said, "I know." I reminded Pontini that I only had a few hours left. He said he wanted to take me to one more place. I happily obliged. It felt so good to be able to trust someone again. I felt free with Pontini. The more experiences I had the more fulfilled I was feeling. I was being educated and opened to new places and people. I couldn't get enough. I thought, "This must have been how Mom felt when she traveled." That's another reason why you wanted me to travel isn't it? You get these new perspectives on yourself and your life from listening to other people's life experiences and vice versa.

That's it. I couldn't put it into words then but that's what I was hoping you would get out of your travels - a wider, different perspective of you and your life and the feeling that anything is possible because honey, anything is possible.

My whole trip I vacillated from deep despair to beginning to feel like I had my whole life in front of me and anything was possible. Pontini took me to one of the boat taxis. If you didn't walk to a place in Venice, you took a boat taxi. There were few if any cars around. I couldn't wait to see where we were going.

That's not like you either. You like everything to be planned and be in control.

I know. Well, living with cancer taught me to be in control of things otherwise my mother would have been disrespected and her concerns ignored by doctors who viewed her as a chart #.

Cancer taught you a lot.

Yes. While on the boat taxi Pontini saw one of his friends and introduced me. This time he called me his "other daughter" as translated by his friend. My heart felt like it was going to explode with joy when I heard that. I missed being someone's daughter.

I know you did but my crossing over hasn't and never will change that. You'll always be my beautiful daughter. Keep going.

The boat docked on a small piece of land with only one large building on it. Venice is surrounded by these little pieces of land with businesses, houses and what not on them. It's really beautiful at night when the city lights show the beautiful skyline with the water and historic buildings against it. Pontini was excited to show me this next part of our journey. His excitement was infectious. The building was old and made of the same kind of cement that most of the other buildings were constructed of. We got off the boat, Pontini stood still for a few moments. A big smile came over his face. He motioned me toward the double doors that slowly opened from the inside. A bright yellow light from inside illuminated the Venetian canal. Pontini stood hands clasped in front of him with a smile that went from ear to ear waiting for me to go inside. Atop of the doors was a sign that read, "Mauriano Glass Fabrique." I walked through the doors and just like that, after all my searching to my astonishment there they stood, as if they'd been there for thousands of years - THE GLASS MAKERS! I couldn't believe my eyes. Thank you, Mom! Thank you!

Thank you! Thank you for taking us on all these journeys. Tell me again what you saw.

I was instantly mesmerized. I watched in joyous amazement as men heated slabs of glass by blowing air through long pipes held over caves of fire. They twisted, turned, stretched and slapped glass onto concrete while molding it with heavy iron hammers to create all kinds shapes. There were rows filled with shelves of various vases, animals, dishes - you name it they blew it. Tears welled in my eyes as I slowly wandered from one row of glass items to the next being gently warned by the men to stand back from the fire. I stopped in front of one man making a unicorn, your favorite mythical animal. I felt Pontini looking at me. He nodded his head up and down in affirmation. I wasn't sure of what. I didn't care. I smiled the biggest smile back that said all I could say in that moment, "Thank you! Thank you! Thank you!" He gave me hope that you and I weren't lost somewhere in the midst of the abyss but found, every day in all kinds of ways, and sometimes through various people, good people. I loved Pontini so much. He watched me with reassurance. For the first time in a long time I felt accepted, understood, safe and loved. I never questioned how Pontini knew of the glass makers. I knew right away how he knew.

I had to find non-threatening ways to connect with you. I was so proud that my little girl was traveling Europe all by herself. How brave you are. I loved every minute of every place we were going. As a little girl I always wanted to see the glass makers, specifically the ones in Italy. To see them with my daughter went beyond my wildest dreams.

There was a moment I thought…

You thought what?

No.

Say it.

There was a moment I thought I saw you watching me watch the glass makers. You were standing in front of me smiling. That's when my tears started flowing like an endless down poor of rain. I did all I could to keep from bursting into a full-blown hysterical cry.

You did baby. You did see me.

Thank you for all the ways you communicated to me Mom. I knew I wasn't seeing things. I didn't know if anyone was looking at me. All I could see was you.

I was so happy to see you and experience all the things we were experiencing together. I wanted you to know in your heart and soul I was there with you the whole time. I still am.

I Just wish I…

No baby. No regrets.

Pontini finally came over to me. He had tears in his eyes too. His smile remained as his hands gently wiped my wet face. After some time, the boat taxi honked its horn and we were reminded that I had a train to catch. Day became night so fast.

We took the boat back to the main island. Pontini and I ran to my Pensione as we both scurried to gather my things to make the next boat taxi that would take me to the train. Just before I boarded, he held me in his arms and said the words I so longed to hear from you. He said…

I said, "You are my daughter. You will always be my daughter."

More tears accompanied with gasps of air in-between overcame me.

Kristin, you are my daughter. You will always be my daughter.

Not even death can separate us.

That's right.

This was, by far, the most memorable and important part of my travels.

Mine too.

Pontini and I exchanged addresses and even wrote to each other when I got home but when I began the next chapter of my life, we lost contact.

Thank you.

For what?

For letting me take you around Venice. I had so much fun. I loved meeting Pontini, his wife and all his friends.

I hope I didn't cut our trip too short. Should we have stayed longer?

No. The glass makers were the perfect way to leave Venice. Besides, we had another place to visit that - another place you've wanted to see for a long, long time.

PARIS, FRANCE

Parisian Bridge

L'Arc De Triomphe

Oh Paris!

Oh, Paris is right!

There is something about Paris, like Italy, that made me feel like I'd been there before. As soon as I got off the train, I felt a familiarity that eased the homesickness that was setting in. Paris is so...

Romantic.

Well, it's a cliché but yes, very romantic and not just for lovers but even for singles, like myself. Even though I was alone in Paris I didn't feel lonely. With the other countries I traveled too, whether with people or not, I felt a loneliness that only went away when I was in Italy and now Paris. There was a sense of peace that lingered in the air. The language was spoken like a never-ending love song - so fluid and easy.

I noticed you were able to speak your French with the Parisians.

I hope so after seven years of French in high school. The French really appreciated that too. I'm not as fluent as I used to be but I'm trying to get back into it. Europeans speak so many different languages. I guess because of the proximity of each country.

So, let's recap the first thing you did when you got there.

The first thing I did was settle in at a place called The Young and Happy Youth Hostel located in the section of Paris known as the Latin Quarter. It was a great place to stay because it was close to everything, i.e. shops, cafés and clubs. I wasn't into clubbing, but I definitely loved the shops and waking to the smell of freshly made crêpes. I couldn't resist the chocolate crêpes. They were yummy! That hostel is still there by the way.

After all this time it's still there?

Yeah, can you believe it? Of course, now they have computers and what not but back in the eighties they didn't. Things have really changed. I mean with the introduction of the internet the world took a drastic turn. People navigate from one place to the next with phones that are minicomputers, digital recorders, etc. Back then we used two forms of navigation, no offense to anyone, but one was our heads and the other was maps!

Those are the day I remember. So, after you checked in you…

I started my day with a few touristy things I wanted to see.

Such as?

Oh, for starters L'Arc de Triomphe (The Arc of Triomphe). You'll never guess how I found it?

I know but tell me. It's a funny story.

Right, well I took the train to the stop that would lead me to the exact spot where the Arc was. When I got off, I looked around and didn't see it. So, I asked someone. The person pointed up!

Ah ha, yes! I know what happened.

The L'Arc de Triomphe is so big that when I got off the train and was searching for it. I didn't realize I was standing only a few feet from it! I was just a touch embarrassed.

How funny you are.

Yeah. Again, the things I'd read about in books were definitely a lot different in person. I bought a baguette and cheese along with a "Gini," and sat under The Arc for a while basking in its enormity.

What's a Gini?

It's a local Parisian drink, similar to a flavored soda.

Ahh, and then what?

After that I went to my first museum known as the Petits Palais Musée built in 1902 and designed by architect Charles Girault.[11]

What kind of museum was this?

It houses the city's finest murals and sculptures created between 1903 and 1925. It was really interesting and amazing to walk through. I have such an appreciation for historic art as opposed to modern art. I think modern art lacks depth and creativity and for me, there is no relevance to it. A lot of it is abstract and communicates nothing about history or what was happening in the time it was created; whereas art from the turn of the 20th century is just the opposite. Everything I saw in the Petits Palais communicated the struggles of the people and times as well as their everyday life and celebrated joys.

Who knew? I could barely get you out of the house and you were doing all these things all by yourself.

When I would stop and take a breath, I sometimes wondered who I was, you know? I would say to myself, "I'm in Paris," or "I'm in Florence" and the fact that I was visiting these places by myself felt surreal, yet it was all real and I took it all in, moment by moment.

Yes, you did. You took on so much at home why would you think you couldn't make it on your own and travel?

I don't know. It was a different kind of responsibility. You were always a motivation for me to be responsible. Now, I had to be enough for myself, you know?

Mmm, hmm.

Traveling presented so many challenges and sometimes it was like meandering my way through an obstacle course. I was curious to see if and how well I could make it on my own. So far, I was doing it.

I was just thinking that very same thing and yes, you were. You could have done anything with the money I left you kids. I was so glad you used it to see the beautiful places and people the world has to offer. So, what else, after, how do you say it? Use your French accent. I love it when you use that accent. You sound so natural.

Okay, The Petits Palais. From there, The Palais opens into the Champs Elyseés gardens. Oh my gosh the flowers were unlike anything I'd ever seen. It was rows of gorgeous colors and flowers of all sorts. I thought if I ever had a garden, I'd want it to be as colorful, soft, aromatic and beautiful as the Champs Elyseés gardens. I could have stayed there all day. Instead I took a long stroll down this street, what was the name again? Oh yeah, The Champs Elyseés! That was neat because it's a long, busy road lined with trees on either side, filled with various trendy shops and expensive restaurants. I wanted to walk all the way down it, but it turned out to be about a mile long and I had another spot I wanted to get too.

Which was?

Yes, this one was also funny because here is a little-known fact about this landmark. Even though you can see it from a distance that doesn't mean you can walk to it. The landmark is the Eiffel Tower and I found this out when I saw it from my hostel. I said, "Oh, it's right over there." Meanwhile, you can probably see the Eiffel Tower from several towns away. It's several times taller the The L'Arc de Triomphe. So, unbeknownst as to how far I actually was from the Eiffel Tower, I started my walk early in the morning thinking I'd get there in an hour or so. Then, gosh, I don't know, hours went by and I finally asked someone how close I was to the Eiffel Tower. They said if I continued to walk, I'd be there by morning, the next day! So, realizing my error I got smart and hopped the metro. When I arrived, I had an hour left before they closed. I had just enough time to get to the top. Pretty amazing views but I didn't stay too long.

Why not silly?

You know why, my terrible fear of heights! The higher I climbed the more vertigo I felt kicking in. It was a hard for me to appreciate the beauty when the world was spinning.

Oh, Kristin!

I couldn't help it. Looking down at the entire city like that. I felt like I was going to fall off the top. It was scary!

Did you at least get pictures?

Of course, I did. I took as many as I could in the span of ten minutes and then got the heck out of there!

Kristin, you're too much. I always wanted to go to Paris and do what you did, visit amazing places, sit at the cafés drinking coffee and people watch. You did a lot of people watching honey. Rarely do you talk to people unless they speak to you first. I would have been talking with everyone.

I know. I liked to take things in and not get too rustled. You, on the other hand, were friendly, engaging, gregarious and funny. People liked talking to you. Your open energy drew them in.

People like talking to you. You're friendly.

I think so but I'll admit only up to a certain point. I don't have the patience for people the way I do animals. Seeing and experiencing all that I have has made me less fond of humans. I was always surprised that with all that you experienced you remained so genuine in your good feelings toward people, but that is what made you so special.

Well the people you met on your travels found you engaging.

I hope so. One of the things I realized while traveling was that for some places, the experience was all about the place itself. While other places the most memorable part of the experience were the people. In Paris, it was both. I met a really nice woman at the hostel I was staying at. Her name was Penny. She was a cellist from Stockholm, Sweden and very beautiful. She looked like she could have been a model with her tall statuesque physique, soft blond hair and baby blue eyes. Penny was the kind of person who became more attractive the more I talked with her. She was genuine, friendly and non-judgmental. There was an openness and sweetness about her that I took to right away.

She sounds lovely. What did you two do?

Well, we started our day at The Centre George Pompidou.

What's that?

I didn't know what it was either nor did I ever hear of it until Penny told me about it.

Oh. What was in there?

The Centre George Pompidou is a modern complex designed in the style of high-tech architecture. It's this massive steel structure supported by concrete floors. It's not particularly aesthetically pleasing, not to me anyway, but its structure is interesting. It houses the Musée National d'Art Moderne, the largest Museum of Modern Art in Europe as well as the Center for Music and Acoustic Research. Penny wanted to go there because of her love of music. I was happy to go along. Afterward we got a bite to eat and relaxed for a while before heading back to the hostel to drop some things off. When we got back, I met up with another friend, Mike from Australia, whom I met in Switzerland. Mike was one of the few really nice guys I met while traveling. We're still in contact to this day. He's back in Australia, married, kids and all that.

That's great and Penny sounds like a good connection too.

She was. It was hard to meet just plain nice guys that weren't looking to get laid but to actually make friends. Mike was nice, respectful, funny and just had a great outgoing personality all around. He was the kind of guy that got along with everyone. He was traveling for the same reasons I was, to experience different people in different parts of the world, meet new people and hopefully make lifelong friendships along the way. I definitely did with Mike. Penny liked him right away too. Together we all headed to the Louvre.

Oooh, The Louvre.

The only way I can describe The Louvre is massive. It looks like three connected Palaces that take the shape of a square missing one side. In the center is a large pyramid shaped, glass and metal architecture known as The Louvre Pyramid. The Louvre is completely overwhelming with art upon sculpture upon painting. We couldn't believe how much there was to see. It's a never-ending experience but definitely worthwhile to visit again and again. It's huge and would take a lifetime to see all the art it holds. You can spend hours in once section and go to another section and do the same. It holds an intense amount of history too. You were never a big museum buff.

No. I mean I liked to learn about different things, but the Museums were never my first choice of things to do.

I know. Me either but I definitely appreciated places like The Louvre and The Petits Palais because of the history and their beautiful structure. Plus, I was with people that I was so happy to have met and they made the experiences that much more enjoyable.

Yeah, good people can make so-so experiences great. Did you get to relax at all while you were there?

Sort of. While at The Louvre Mike, Penny and I met another girl by the name of Parker. She was from Jersey of all places. So, we all decided to have an adventure and took the train to Vernon,

France which is just north of Paris. There we rented bikes and rode throughout the countryside to Giverny, France to visit Claude Monet's house and gardens.

Now that's fun and interesting.

It was and riding bikes made me feel less like a tourist. Monet's house is a big, beautiful brick home covered with Vines surrounded by trees, and his famous well-kept garden which were almost as beautiful as the ones at the Champs Elysées. There weren't too many people there which made them quieter and easy to relax in. There were trees, flowers, streams with little bridges and Lily Pads floating throughout which is where Monet got his inspiration to paint one of his most famous painting, The Lily Pad. It was peaceful at Monet's house. Being a lover of the countryside, I could see myself having a home like that.

Monet's house was peaceful. I wish I had a garden like his.

I know, me too.

Paris and Italy seem like they were your favorites.

They were.

Yet they're so different.

Italy speaks to my Sicilian/Italian roots while Paris speaks to the aesthetic in me.

Do you still keep in contact with Penny?

No. We exchanged info but we lost contact.

That's too bad.

Yeah, still I was glad to have met her at all as well as Mike and Parker. Paris and the people I met there were memorable.

I was so happy you were having these experiences and meeting such interesting people. You were long overdue for some firsthand culture in your life. So, after Paris was another interesting place.

Yes, and this place had the best waffles in all of Europe!

BRUGES (BRUGGE), BELGIUM

Countryside

City life

You went to Belgium and all you can remember was the waffles!

Is that the name of the country? I thought it was "The best waffles in the world!" I'm just teasing. Those waffles were the bomb!

I'm sure they were...

They were sweet, moist, warm and chewy on the inside with a slightly sweet crunch on the outside. Oh my gosh, I think I may have dreamt about them a few times. Is that weird?

You're weird. They do sound delicious. So, describe Belgium.

It reminded me a little of Amsterdam. Brugge, the city I went too, is filled with old buildings of exquisite architecture, lots of cobblestone streets, intimate shops and bakeries and down to earth people. I really liked it.

I did too. It felt old world but not archaic if you know what I mean.

I do.

And where did you stay?

I stayed in a hostel and met a gentleman from England by the name of Chris. We walked the side streets and less touristy spots in Brugge. Then he took me to this club in the evening which I didn't like at all.

Why not?

Again, I'm not a club person. Clubs are pretty much the same wherever you go. It was crowded and the music wasn't the kind of music I listen to. It was this hard, in your face metal head music and they played it super loud.

I gather you didn't stay long.

No.

Was your friend Chris nice?

He was. We talked a lot.

About what?

Oh, our families, school, what we liked to do, politics, the places we'd been to, all kinds of things. He was really smart and interesting to talk with. After spending some time with him I decided to take a bike to the countryside. This is where I would finally get another rest I needed.

Yes, you did.

Yeah, so with that I packed a lunch and rode a bike to the countryside. I rode for a couple of hours and then settled in the long, thick green grass next to a half-finished barn. Across the way was a picturesque pasture with horses and a beautiful country home. It was like a dream. It looked like the perfect place to live. The grass was so green. The sky was baby blue, and the sun was shining. It couldn't have been a better day. All I did was sit and think - one of my favorite things to do.

What did you think about?

A lot of things. I thought about you and us. I thought about the gazillion talks we had over the years about everything under the sun. How lucky I was to have a mother I could go to for anything and did. All these memories flooded my head but your crossing over still didn't sink in. It felt like you were "away." I felt like I was "away" too. I mean I was physically, but I didn't feel truly present in my body or spirit. I distanced myself from my feelings of your crossing over. I could only feel so much before I had to shut down. I likened myself to a faucet. As soon as the feelings became too much, I would turn the faucet off and do something else.

I nestled myself in the grass and pulled out the camembert cheese and bread I brought with me. I thought about all the days you took me to the park, or an outside concert and we'd bring our lunch and make a day of it. I thought about how vivacious, vocal and strong you were before you got sick and how you changed afterward. I know you didn't want too.

No, I didn't. I wanted to get stronger and more vocal about all the things that were important to me like women's rights, civil rights, politics and spirituality but my mind and body went the other direction. Cancer sucked the life out of me.

Not at first Mom. You fought it harder than anyone I've ever met. You gave cancer a run for its money so to speak.

Really? I always thought it was the other way around.

No, maybe it felt that way because, as you've said, cancer backed you into some places and circumstances you probably wouldn't have been in had you not been ill. You sacrificed so much for us Mom. You made decisions based on what would serve your children best as you battled a life-threatening illness. I don't think some of the decisions you made while you were ill were ones you would have made otherwise if you remained healthy.

Like what?

Like going back to Buffalo. I know how much you love your family but at the time you got sick you'd already spent the 70's embarking on a path of alternative healing and progressive thinking that challenged your old thoughts, behaviors and patterns. This way of being helped you see your self-worth and instilled some sense of self-respect in you that wasn't present when you were married. Am I right?

Wow. You pretty much nailed it, but I was no saint honey. I made my share of mistakes too. I sure did enjoy having a good time whenever I could, that's for sure.

Don't do that Mom, please?

Do what?

Put yourself down or minimize your accomplishments. That's what other people did to you. You're human and as you say, "Everyone makes mistakes." Yet none of that affected your desire to learn, grow and be a better, stronger woman did it?

No, it didn't. Thank you for acknowledging that.

Yeah, absolutely Mom. I feel like your sisters and a few others made you feel bad and/or guilty for being human and enjoying yourself and that's bullshit. I'm your child and I know what an amazing mother you are. I'm glad you had a good time here and there. You deserved it for crying out loud.

You used to get upset any time I went out without you. That's why I always took you with me. I didn't have a choice. This would explain why you liked the company of grown-ups as opposed to kids your own age.

I know, sorry. I believe after Dad's absence I developed separation anxiety from you. Plus, I just loved being around you, so did everyone else.

I'm just kidding. Don't apologize. I liked having you with me. I'm glad you loved being around me. It made me feel good. You were a well-behaved kid and I was so impressed when you would take part in discussions Mom had with her friends. You were really learning to think for yourself at a very early age. You had interesting things to say and were developing a real sense of independence in you that I, too, was striving for. I almost got there.

You did get there, Mom. You did!

I think I did through you. Your way more independent than I ever was and you've been through quite a bit yourself honey. Give yourself credit where credit is due.

I will if you will, deal.

Deal. So what other things were going through that busy little mind of yours in the Brugge countryside.

Sophie, of course and how much I hated leaving her while I traveled. Do anything for myself made me feel selfish.

I know, which is why you needed too.

I missed her so much. My Euro rail pass would soon expire so I knew I had to make some decisions about what I was going to do.

What do you mean?

Do you know I actually pondered sending for Sophie and staying in Europe?

You did? I didn't know that. Tell me more.

All these thoughts were racing through my head. I didn't want to go back to Buffalo. You know how much I hated it there. It held so many negative memories for me and I wasn't about to get caught up with the negative thought patterns of your family. I couldn't take them. I felt so free without their voices in my head of, "You should do this," or "Why don't you do that," and "Why are you this way," and "Why don't you be that way," and "You should find a man and get married." Ugh. No. I saw myself free settling down in a countryside that looked like Belgium or going back to Paris or Italy but definitely in the countryside. City life is too much hustle and bustle for me. I need calm, serene surroundings.

I know you do, and you've always been a little on the introverted side. I think you would have done just fine if you stayed in Europe. Why didn't you?

Fear, I guess. Fear of the "What ifs." What if I don't find a job? What if I don't make friends or create some sort of supportive environment and most important of all. What if something happens to me? That was my biggest fear and concern. I'd be all alone with my little Sophie and I just, I don't know. Living abroad felt too unstable for me at the time. The thing is I didn't have much more stability at home. The reality was Sophie was my only stability.

I was just going to say you didn't have a stable life there anymore and you could have built a new life for you and Sophie in Europe learning different languages, meeting different people and building a support system there. Who knows how different your life could/would have been?

I know. I wonder if all the things that happened to me here would have happened at all if I stayed abroad.

Some things would have and some not. There are some things that happen in our lives we just have no control of no matter where we are.

True.

What else did you think about?

After fantasizing about living abroad I returned my thoughts to the reality that I needed to get my little Sophie.

You two were inseparable. I know she must have missed you something awful while you were away.

I missed her that's for sure. She was my touchstone. All I knew was that I wanted to be as good a parent to her as you were to me. I wanted to provide a stable home for both of us and while it killed me, it temporarily had to be in Buffalo until I could figure out what city I wanted to settle. I figured when I got back, I'd take a few months and figure out the best place for me and the little Sophers.

For now, I had another couple of weeks in Europe. I had one last place I wanted to see. I'd read about it in a book that I can't, for the life of me, remember but I couldn't get the place out of my head. I had to go there.

COPENHAGEN, DENMARK

Royal Danish Theater

Town Circle

Denmark! You went all the way up to Denmark! Way to go baby girl!

I sure did. From Brugge I shot up to Denmark and the place I needed to see is called "Christiana," or "Freetown Christiania." I was excited to go. I wasn't sure if I'd ever get the chance to visit Copenhagen or Europe, for that matter, again. So, Christiania gave me a good reason to make the leap from Belgium to Denmark.

That's some leap!

It was but so worth it. As soon as I arrived in Copenhagen, I immediately noticed how dark and cloudy it was. It was kind of depressing. The clouds looked so close too. I felt like I could touch them. I checked into a hostel and then started out around Copenhagen. I went to the Royal Danish Theater, which was absolutely beautiful, elegant and huge. From the outside it looked like a Palace. Then I headed to the town circle hoping to meet a local who might be able to steer me in the direction of Christiania. I met up with a drummer and dancer from Gambia. They were playing at the fountain in the center of town. The drummer invited me to play with him. I had a lot of fun. The dancer wasn't too bad either. I noticed a gentleman was watching me play. After I was done, he sat next to me and introduced himself. His name was Raphael. He was originally from Italy and had been living in Copenhagen with his wife whom he recently divorced from. Guess where they were living?

I'll take a wild guess, ummmm, "Christiania!"

Bingo. Can you believe it? Every now and again it felt like I was destined to meet and visit certain people and places.

Amazing. So, let's talk about this Christiania or Freetown.

It's one of the places I told you about earlier that I wanted to see. The one I read about in book, whose name I can't recall, that was about the Rainbow Gatherings. Freetown actually began as a social experiment by the Danish government in 1971. It's a gated community/park where people live and do as they please without interference from the Danish government. The residents use make-shift sheds for homes and live without electricity, rather everything is lit by candles and lanterns and there is very little to no use for money there. They use the barter system where they trade with each other for goods, food and household items. They were also free with drugs too. When I was there things seemed okay, but I was only there for a day. In the past few years Freetown has received a bad rap. I think the drug use has gotten a bit out of control. However, Raphael was very kind to take me there which was good because you can't get in unless you live there or know someone who has or does live there. Freetown was as close to outdoor communal, hippie living as you could get. It is an interesting place.

Sounds like it.

There were some drawbacks.

In a place where you need little to no money? What drawbacks?

Well, Raphael failed to tell me this and I didn't learn it until I went to pee. I was enlightened to the fact that there was only one bathroom and it was used by EVERYONE, women, men and children which was fine but…

But what?

It was open. There were no doors for the toilets or showers.

Oh, my, surprise!

Yeah, surprise is right. Imagine my shock when I went to pee, and someone walked in only to see me with my naked bottom peeing and that person wasn't embarrassed or anything.

Knowing you, you must have been floored.

Well, not floored but a wee bit embarrassed. I had to lose any and all inhibitions, quickly. I'm not used to peeing in front of others. When I came out Raphael was laughing. Apparently, he thought it was funny. Real funny! Afterward he took me to little bar in Freetown. It was lit by candles and lanterns and filled with smoke. Everyone was smoking pot and hashish. Raphael disclosed that he was a recovering alcoholic, so we ordered sodas and sat and talked for a couple of hours. He told me his parents had passed away. He also told me of a beautiful dream he had of his father shortly after he passed. I told him of your crossing over and the dream I had of you.

Which one?

The one where you were in the coffin and woke up. You climbed out, hugged me so tight, took my hand and said to me, "C'mon baby, let's go." Then we had the day together I was so wishing for. Gosh I love that dream. I can recall it today as if I just had it last night. As soon as I told Raphael he said the same thing you did. He said, "That was not a dream," then smiled this perfect smile.

You see.

I always felt it was real. It was just nice to have someone objective affirm that for me.

I used to dream of my father all the time. Sometimes that brought me comfort.

Sometimes?

Depending on the dream, yes, sometimes. Sometimes when I would dream of him, I would wake up feeling very alone but that was just my own issues making their way into my dreams. Did you ever feel that way when dreaming of me?

I've always felt just the opposite. If I dream of you, I wake up feel like you've been hugging me all night long. I will say that I have had dreams where I woke up and thought you were angry with me for something.

That's not possible. I could never be angry with you for anything you do. Freetown and Raphael sound very interesting and exciting. You didn't do too much else there right?

Yeah, that was pretty much it. I only stayed in Copenhagen for a few days and then headed back down to Amsterdam. I thought it would be best that I begin and end my trip in Amsterdam. It seemed the most logical don't you think.

Sure, in a purple sensei logical kind of way☺.

Exactly, although I did do more than just smoke.

I know. I'm just teasing you. What else did you do?

I went to the Van Gogh museum and relaxed in this beautiful park. I also took great pains to make sure I didn't have any near fatal trolley incidents as well.

Thank goodness for that. Well my little minute. After traveling throughout Europe for two months what stood out to you the most about your travels and what do you think you learned about yourself.

There isn't one thing that stood the most. I do remember the air.

The air?

Yeah, it smelled different.

How different?

Just different, new. There were all these new smells, i.e. food, flavors, plants of all kinds and nature from the ground I walked on from city to city to the air I breathed. Everything was so new and…

Different.

Yeah. Each country/city has its own unique flavor, feel and scent. My gratitude and constant amazement that I was able to journey to such beautiful, interesting, sometimes painful but always exciting places traveled with me from one place to the next. I felt awake and alive as though I'd been sleeping all the years before this and my travels opened me up, woke me up.

It makes me so happy to hear you say that because that's exactly how Mom felt on her travels. That's why I wanted you to go. If anyone needed to be awakened to the fact that a whole world was out there for her to experience, it was you. So, what about the second part of my question. What did you learn about yourself?

That I could move forward after you crossed over and make this life on my own. That was a painful realization because I already felt this intense, lingering loneliness without you. Knowing that feeling would be there the rest of my life was something I could only allow myself to feel in increments.

You're stronger than you realize Kristin.

How's that?

You, at the very least, acknowledged the pain and even had the courage to feel it.

You taught me to always be true to myself and pay attention to my feelings. After you crossed over, I felt this burning desire to throw myself into the abyss just to see what I would make of it. My travels changed me for the better forever. They tested my survival skills, expanded my mind and opened me up to people and places I would have never met had I not traveled. Until this day, whenever I feel sad, I look at the pictures of my travels and instantly feel good. I looked so young. More importantly, I WAS young.

You're still young baby. You have a ways to go before you get old.

I guess but it doesn't feel that way.

How was your trip home?

Ooh yes, the trip home. The plane ride was fine. I couldn't wait to see Sophie and plop on my bed and cuddle with her. However, Andrea pulled yet another stunt on me.

Which was?

Yes, well she apparently had run through her inheritance so in order to make rent she decided, without telling me, to rent out my room. She let me know this when she picked me up from the airport. I was furious because I was so tired and all I wanted to do was go home and cuddle with my little girl in my bedroom, on my bed and feel safe again. Not to mention the only personal space I had in that house was gone. Instead Andrea and I started yelling and screaming at each other and this lasted the entire ride home. As soon as I got home, I greeted my little girl, hugged her and then…

And then…

I burst into my room, told the renter to get out while I searched for my stuff. Andrea was trying to stop me because she didn't want me to disturb the renter. Can you believe that! I couldn't believe she said that because I gave her my share of the rent for two months, the amount of time I knew I'd be gone prior to my leaving. It was my room! I couldn't find any of my things. I felt so violated and disregarded.

Where was your brother?

He decided to move to the west coast, so it was just Andrea, me and one paying border (that I knew of anyway) living in our house. Other people would come and go. It was like a free for all. Our home was a disgusting mess. It was never the same after you crossed. Andrea never could handle any kind of responsibility.

When I asked her why in the world, she do something so blatantly hurtful and wrong as rent out my room when I already gave her rent money; as well as completely disregarding my feelings and space she gave me some bullshit story about how she needed money. I asked her why she didn't just get a job?

What was her response?

She evaded the question just like she evaded responsibility overall by trying to turn her error around on me. She had the nerve to scream at me for being upset and not being more understanding. Then she tried to make me feel bad for leaving Sophie with her while I traveled. With you not around she took things to a whole new level. Oh my gosh I wanted to punch her in face. I really did!

Breathe and take your time.

I never felt so disregarded by her in my life. I would never do anything like that to her, never. I mean the thought would never have crossed my mind, yet she found it so easy to hurt me. I didn't know what to make of her actions and to know that poor Sophie was living in such an unstable environment made me so angry with her. The fact that she couldn't understand that made me see how self-involved she really was. She told me she wasn't happy watching Sophie while I traveled. This I didn't get because she said she was fine with taking care of Sophie for the time I was away. She had no plans to go anywhere and not because I made plans to travel but just because she had no plans.

Maybe that's what upset her, that you had plans and she didn't.

Then she should have said something because I would have definitely found someone to watch Sophie or I wouldn't have gone.

I'm sorry your sister did that. That was an awful thing for her to do.

That night I couldn't even look at her. I grabbed Sophie, whatever things I could find, all my mail that piled up and stayed at Carolyn's. I didn't want to but, not having a car, she was the closest house I could walk to.

I've told you of the fights I've had with my sisters.

Yeah, ya know I asked Carolyn, that night as a matter of fact, if you guys ever fought like Andrea and I and she said, "Oh no, not like that, never like you two." Is that true? Why are you laughing?

I'm laughing because my sister was lying through her teeth and she knows that. We've had some knock-down, drag out fights, believe you me. The more we talk the more I remember the things that were happening with me and you and all the ugliness that was surrounding us. For some of us, family relationships are the hardest relationships to maintain.

I was beginning to understand that. I have to say you were good at it. Your sisters and their respective families were lucky to have you, lucky.

I know that what your sister did was downright terrible, but you also came home to a blessing right - something in the mail perhaps?

Yes. I told you before that something told me to start applying to graduate schools while I was still a senior. So, thank goodness, I did. I really liked the Dance/Movement Therapy course I took in my last year. So, I figured, why not? I'll apply to graduate schools with a Dance/Movement Therapy program "just in case," always that "just in case" right?

Right.

The blessing was that in the pile of mail was an acceptance letter to the Dance/Movement Therapy/Counseling Psychology Masters Program at Antioch New England Graduate School in Keene, NH. I was over the moon.

So was I!

I accepted right away. I couldn't wait to get away from Buffalo, your family and most of all, my sister. When I told Andrea the news do you know what her response was?

Oh no, what?

"Why would you want to go to Graduate School?" As if this was a bad thing. I ignored the comment. All I saw was me and Sophie in the mountains. This gave me incredible hope and peace for a new life. I kept in contact with Spencer who offered to drive the U-Haul truck with me to Keene. I was so glad because I thought, "This is great. I'll start this next portion of my life on a positive note and leave all the garbage with Andrea and the family in the past. It'll be just me, Sophie and Spencer. You can imagine my utter disappointment when Spencer, who drove from Syracuse to Buffalo to help me with the drive, announced she wanted company for the ride back. That company would be Andrea. I told her what happened between us and that I didn't want my sister coming with us because I knew all we would do was argue but she insisted. I couldn't say no because she already made the trip from Syracuse to Buffalo, but I was not happy, and Andrea knew it. The ride from Buffalo to Keene was long and painful. Andrea and I argued about everything from past to present and so on. At some points during the ride we were yelling and screaming so loud Spencer had to stop the truck. She regretted having Andrea come along. I told her, "I told you it wasn't a good idea for her to come."

Serves her right; she knew how you kids could get. She probably wanted to jump out of the truck.

I know I did. Now the memories of my journey to Graduate School are filled with negativity and anger. Whenever I did something good for myself Andrea criticized it to the point where she hoped I wouldn't do it. I ignored her.

I knew I was a responsible person and a loving daughter who, for years, took excellent care of her mother and no one could ever make me think or feel otherwise.

Do you feel like someone did?

All I heard from your family was, "While you were at school your sister had to do…" Andrea would reinforce the same thing. Yet everyone seemed to have this memory lapse of the person that cared for you all the years before. Your sisters and my sister didn't actually step in until my last year of college when you were really sick. All the years prior to that they visited, had lunches and dinners with you, parties but as far as real help they couldn't be bothered. They had their own dysfunctional lives and families they concerned themselves with. I was the one with you every day, doctors' appointments, meetings, support groups, everything and I loved every minute of it. They always made comments that they were glad I was there because they couldn't be. Yet when you crossed none of them could remember this. In fact, they gushed how THEY did this and that for you. Every time I heard them talk, I felt sick.

Kristin, I know who was there for me. I remember the wonderful care you took of me. You shouldn't pay any mind to them or their lies and that's exactly what they are, and they know it.

Yeah, they loved you so much they patronized you when you could barely communicate what you wanted. That's when you're supposed to have those you trust around you to be able to make sure your wishes are followed. No, what do they do? They ignored your wishes and disregarded you - characterizing you as being "unable to make decisions for yourself." They catered your caretaking around their needs and what was convenient for them and called that "caretaking." Then bad mouthed me in the process.

It's very sad for me to hear that the people I trusted with my last wishes and my children's hearts were turning out to be so untrustworthy, hurtful and careless. I don't care if they agreed with you, liked you, loved you or what not. You are my child and if they loved me then they should have respected my child. Or they should have left you alone to make the decisions I asked for and let you deal with your pain, not add to it.

Yeah, and this was just the beginning.

You're a woman without fear. Well, at least you were away from them. Let's talk about school. I was so proud of you Kristin, so very proud. I saw was the woman in you unfolding in a beautiful way.

HIGHER LEARNING
ANTIOCH NEW ENGLAND GRADUATE SCHOOL, KEENE, NH

1992-1995

What about my lost day?
What about my lost hours?
My thoughts have gone to places where nightmares begin.
On my knees I've pleaded to God, that I cannot see,
feel, touch, hold or let in.

It's Monday morning.
I look in the mirror and see nothing.
It's Saturday in the afternoon.
I look in the mirror and see the most
beautiful woman I've ever laid my eyes upon.

My thoughts are scrambled.
One stone after another cast to the water.
The knife is sharply placed against the inside of my belly -
careful not to move, mindful not to breath.
I'm the woman I once hated.
The butterfly I've spent years creating.

I defy self-degradation and shove your harsh words
so far down your throat you choke on them, little by little.
Light cigarette with smile.

Today I will meet friends for dinner,
share laughter, hear the music of my soul,
and dance like Isadora while I release years prior.

I am the wind.
I am the sea.
I am fire
Let knowledge and wisdom surpass the heat of these words!

Kristin A. Crage ©1993

So, what was Keene like?

Keene is beautiful. It's a small college town surrounded by green mountains and only a short drive to beautiful Mt. Monadnock. I couldn't wait for me and Sophie to begin this next chapter of our lives. I loved having Sophie with me wherever I went. We were growing up together and my relationship with my dog was paramount. Sophie came before anything and anyone else. We were surrounded by green grass, mountains and fresh open air. Sophie was so happy to be in such a serene place. So was I.

I'll bet.

I asked my older cousin Stan to hold onto my piano while I was in New Hampshire.

That was nice of him.

Yeah, it was.

So how did the financial aid work out with graduate school?

It didn't. I didn't have any financial aid. I had to take out $40,000 in student loans. Now-a-days that's considered cheap but back then it was very expensive. Especially since I owed only a few thousand dollars from undergraduate. The thing is, when I was getting these loans for school it never occurred to me to think about the day, I would have to pay them back you know?

Oh boy

The government sent me a huge check for tuition and any other miscellaneous things and that's all I thought about, just paying for school and getting by.

Yes, and you hate to be in debt. You spent years worrying about my finances. Something tells me you didn't think about paying it back because of the stress that would cause you.

Exactly. I had to get out of Buffalo, and I was willing to do it at whatever cost necessary.

Well, an education is a worthwhile investment and you live...

And learn, I know.

Did you at least have an apartment lined up before you got there?

Well…

Oh Kristin!

Mom, I was under all this pressure with time constraints. By the time I got back from traveling I didn't have time to find one. I don't remember the internet being available at that time but even if it was, I didn't have a computer. I had to rely on calling realtors and requesting real estate pamphlets to be mailed to me which I didn't have time to do. I had to get to school and register for classes. So, I winged it.

You winged it! That's not like you at all.

I know. It was Spencer's idea. It was hard. She was the only help I had, and things were just a mess. I just needed to get out of Buffalo, fast. Spencer wanted to drive there on a weekend, rent a motel for the three of us and find me an apartment before the weekend was up. I told Spencer we needed to think this through more thoroughly, but she wanted to do it her way and you know how militant and dogmatic she can be. I didn't want to deal with that. I just figured, "Fine, whatever, let's just get there and find me a place."

How did that go, or should I not ask?

Oh, my lord. The tension of the three of us sharing a motel was yet another incentive enough for me to find something, anything and fast. I didn't want to settle but with the beginning of the semester and everyone going back to school and not just at Antioch. Keene State College also had their share of students coming back so there weren't a lot of places available. Those that were didn't allow dogs. We got the local paper and started looking for rooms for rent that would allow dogs. There was only one room for rent that would take Sophie.

One, are you serious!

I know. I couldn't believe it either, but this was my introduction to small town life. Without any other options available I checked it out. A gentleman by the name of Barry, who was recently divorced, was renting one of the bedrooms in his modest two-bedroom apartment. The room was very small, but I had use of the kitchen, living room, washer, dryer and phone. It was also within walking distance to school. Not having a car made the room doable until I could find something better. Most importantly, he didn't mind Sophie and it was either this place or a motel and I couldn't afford a motel for the whole semester. This tiny bedroom with a man I didn't know was the only option I had.

Oh honey. You must have been so scared to live with someone you didn't know.

I didn't feel scared, but I did have an eerie feeling about Barry.

If I were there, I would have never allowed you to live alone with a strange, single man. Never and Spencer knew that. I can't believe she let you live there.

I didn't like it either but like I said, I didn't have a choice. Spencer had to get back to work and get the truck back. Let me just say this. I always trust my gut and my gut is never wrong.

You see. It was a bad move, right?

The place was fine. It was Barry.

I knew it. He didn't hurt you, did he?

No, no nothing like that. Well, first let me tell you about school.

Okay, but I want to hear about Barry. Don't forget.

I won't, trust me and you'll see why.

Okay. So, how was graduate school? What an accomplishment!

It sure felt like it. I was enrolled in the Dance/Movement Therapy Master of Science (MS) Program with a minor in Counseling Psychology.

What exactly is Dance/Movement Therapy?

In the simplest terms, Dance Movement Therapy is a form of psychotherapy that utilizes both verbal and body movement to uncover unresolved issues and begin the journey of healing. The MS Program at Antioch also incorporated some art therapy classes as well. I learned a lot about myself as a person, a young woman and potential therapist. Traveling helped me realize I had the will, intelligence, creativity, drive and potential to do anything I wanted and was bound by nothing, except me. However, all these things were realized in my head, intellectually. Emotionally I felt stuck - like I wasn't growing or moving but stuck in my grief. Another thing cancer taught me is coping mechanisms, and how to mask my pain well. You know how it is when you have to keep going and you don't want others to know how much you're hurting because they don't or can't understand. So not only did we have cancer to deal with but other peoples' un-comfortableness surrounding cancer. It's a lot of pressure.

It is. Having cancer was a lot of pressure for Mom. I had the weight of my impending mortality, the worry of my children and my family over me. Sometimes I just wanted to run away. I didn't care where. I just wanted out of my life, not away from you kids, just out of the misery that cancer brought into our lives. I understand your need to break free and get away from the family and the city that held so many painful memories for you.

There was never a moment I didn't think of you and all the things we went through, sort of. I could only let myself feel so much, think of so much before I would get this feeling in me.

What feeling?

Actually, it was more like the fear I described earlier - of breaking into tiny pieces and not being able to piece myself back together; that humpy dumpty effect. I never had that fear until you crossed over. I had to stay afloat and keep my head above water. I didn't have time to full feel my grief. I had a lot to do and many things I wanted to accomplish.

I know you did honey.

School kept me preoccupied. What I liked about Antioch is that they're predominantly experiential based - that is they believe students learn best through experience, which is great for me because, as we know, I learn best by doing things.

Right.

They didn't wait a semester to start you in an internship as with other programs. Internships started our first semester under the guidance and supervision of our Professors. That was kind of scary at first, but I got used to it. I had to.

Wow, they didn't waste, any time, did they?

No but it was good. It's like saying, "Be courageous and dive into the unknown." I asked myself, "How can I gently bring people(s) to that place of courage to begin to heal if I don't go there and experience it myself?"

That was very wise of you Kristin, considering what you were feeling.

Yeah, I mean that was the intellectual in me speaking. I've often found I'm good at helping others, especially in emergency situations. At the same time, I'm very much a loner in many ways and here I was studying to help others on their inner journeys', yet I was barely able to go through my own journey. That was my paradox. However, I still try to do better, be better and feel better in anything and everything I do. Yet no matter how hard I try; I feel like I always miss the mark. Do you know what I mean?

I do and it's frustrating, I know.

I tried to be like you and not think about if, and, or when things don't work out. So, unfortunately, when they don't, it tends to be a very big disappointment for me because I've already filled myself with hope that they would. So much for positive thinking.

I know. I know exactly what you're talking about. I do. I used to feel like that all the time like, "Why should I have hope about this or that?" My hope inevitably was crushed time and again. I always wanted you to think positive because I truly felt that if you think that way then positivity will come to you, but that's unrealistic because it may or may not. Like we've talked about before, sometimes things happen and it has nothing to do with our thought pattern. I think the lesson here it to keep thinking positive but just always know in the back of your mind that there's a chance things won't go the way you're hoping or working toward, that's all. I think that given what we went through it's not as much of a paradox as you think. You always had to be "on" and "ready" for me. "On" in the sense of keeping up with school work, dance, keeping the house in order, helping me maintain my meds that even I sometimes forgot or didn't want to take, and "ready" in the sense that we had many doctor and hospital visits, planned and unplanned to be prepared for. You spent so many years helping me and doing so little for yourself. You became adept at helping me and others but didn't spend much time on doing for you. Did you do anything for yourself in New Hampshire?

I spent my nights reading and writing papers while simultaneously listening to any one of your favorites like Michael Franks, The Art of Tea, or any one of Anita Baker's albums or Lee Ritenour. Those things were for me and felt good to me. I also danced, exercised and started playing drum again. I played a little in college, but I needed more of it. I really wanted to play djembe. I responded more to the sound because of my west African dance background but I couldn't find anyone that played djembe in my area, so I played conga. I have memories of being in Syracuse when I was very little, going with you around the Syracuse University Campus and hearing the drums, any drum someone might be playing on the hill or wherever. I was so pulled to the sound of the drum and its rhythms. It called to me in the same way dance did and still does. I could envision myself being in a forest, hearing the drums and feeling so connected to them that I knew where they were and how to get to them without hesitation, fear or losing my way.

The way you did coming down from that mountain in the Swiss Alps.

Exactly.

I loved taking you with me to different places and exposing you to all different kinds of people, thoughts, things to see and do; art, music and dance. I loved having my little companion to explore new things with.

Yeah, I can still feel my little hand in yours and wondering, "Where are we going next? What new person, place or thing will we meet or do next?" When I was with you, I felt like I was on an adventure where anything was possible. When you crossed over, I felt all my hope for anything good in my life melt away. Sophie, drumming and dance were the only things that made me smile and feel like I had some sense of life and passion in me. They kept me going more than anything else. This was also when I decided to go back into therapy.

I'm glad you did.

Me too. I mean I should have gone back because I needed too but the precipitating factor was that the program "strongly suggested" everyone be in therapy to work on their issues in order to be the most effective therapist possible without transferring your issues onto your patient, which is another reason why I loved this program so much. They designed their program well so that when you graduate, you're truly prepared and good at what you do for your patients, which is how it should be. Some people become a therapist, and not only do they suck at it but they're in it for the money. "Let me listen to you for forty-five minutes, put you in a diagnosis code and get you out because I have a two-story condo I need to go and look at." That kind of thinking, you know.

I do and have seen a couple of those so-called therapists. They were terrible experiences.

You see. I know. So, have I. It's hard enough for people to go to therapy and allow themselves to be so vulnerable. Therapists need to be empathic and compassionate with their patients.

That's right.

The challenge for me was that lost doesn't begin to describe how I felt after you crossed over. For as long as I could remember my thoughts and everything, I did in my life centered around you and what would be best and easiest for you. I didn't know what to do without that way of life anymore.

Isn't that what a good mother does for her child and yet this is what my child did for her mother.

Yeah. So, guess where one of my internships was?

Where?

It was at the local hospital on the Psychiatric Unit where I met a woman about the same age as me with a very interesting story.

Oh yes. I know this story. Let's talk about her. Why do I all of a sudden have your trip to Amsterdam on my mind?

I know, I know. So, this young woman had a neuropsychological and physiological condition. In layman terms, she had brain and nerve damage.

From…

She traveled Europe after college like me. While in Amsterdam she was hit by a Trolley, like I almost was.

You see Kristin. Do you understand now why I was so upset that you were so careless that time in Amsterdam?

I know Mom but it was one isolate incident and…

It was one isolated incident that could have caused you permanent damage!

I understand. I was never careless before and I never was again. Actually, meeting this young woman really shook me into reality. You're right. I had the very same thought you did, had I been just a little more careless in Amsterdam, and that wasn't hard to do, that could have been me.

I just want you to always know that you have me and God's angels watching over you.

I remember being so stoned out of my mind and just walking around Amsterdam without any regard for oncoming cars or people or anything and hearing the Trolley horn. The next thing I remember is feeling a man's hand on my arm as he pulled me out of harm's way. All he kept saying was, "Miss, Miss please watch out. You're okay Miss. Please sit. You're okay. It's okay." Even after I was pulled out of harm's way, I was so stoned I didn't grasp the full extent of what could have happened to me. I was fortunate, very fortunate and had great empathy for this young woman I was chosen to work with.

It's no accident you were chosen to work with her.

I agree. I liked working with her. We talked a lot about our travels. She said when she remembers her travels throughout Europe, even though she had this horrible thing happen to her in Amsterdam, they still make her smile and lift her spirits, and she never regretted going. She was a real fighter.

Like you.

Yeah. I tried to get the same internship the next semester, but my professors encouraged me to work with a different population to get as much experience as I could. I felt an immediate kinship with her and never forgot her.

Something tells me she never forgot you either.

Certain people touch me Mom, even if our meeting is brief, they do, and I hope I touch them in as positive way as they do me.

I think you touch more people more positively than you think.

I hope so. The other part the program was based on writing papers which I liked. I've never been very good with tests, as you know.

Goodness, you used to get so nervous. I still can't get over the fact that you failed your Lerner's Permit test three times and…

Okay I think we covered that. Thank you.

I'm just saying.

Any who, my professors were so were supportive. They provided safe boundaries for us students as we explored ourselves from the earliest stages of life, i.e. utero, all the way through the adult stage. Each class was like being in therapy. My professors were quite good at maintaining a very important boundary.

What was that?

They reminded us that although, at times, it might feel like it we were in therapy during class, we weren't. That's why they wanted us to see therapists outside of school. We were studying to be therapists with movement as the modality. That boundary was an important distinction made and enforced. I liked being in a place that had boundaries. I needed them. My professors stressed that we work on ourselves, resolve whatever is unresolved and know that if we didn't do the latter. It would creep into the therapist/patient relationship. They were right. Resolving the unresolved would be one of my greatest challenges while in graduate school.

I think your actual challenge has always been knowing, I mean really knowing your self-worth without ever wondering consciously or subconsciously whether or not you deserve a good life. It's only when we know the value of our true self can we then go on to help others. I know you wonder if you deserve a good life and I understand why you feel this way, but I can, without hesitation, tell you the answer is YES! You're going to be okay honey. We have some more work to do but you're going to be okay.

What makes so sure?

You are my daughter. Your blood and bones were born of me. That's how I know. Now tell me more about this program.

It wasn't an easy program by any sense. It required me to have the tenacity to delve deep, the strength to work on what I found and sustain the healing that would take place or was supposed to take place.

I'm glad you were there. You needed a safe environment at this point in your life.

The fact that you made it there at all is amazing to me, especially when I tell you of the rather startling thing that happened to me while I was there.

Really, what was that?

As I began to write my papers my professors would call me on things, little things such as spelling and punctuation. This was before I got into the habit of using the spellcheck. I never made anything of it. Until one of my professors called me into her office after I'd turned in one of my papers.

And?

She told me she liked my paper and that my theories were excellent, even ones to think about writing my thesis on. Then she pointed out some major spelling errors, lack of punctuation and half sentences. With each error she pointed out my heart raced, and I became sick to my stomach that I was so careless with my writing, something I loved to do. She then asked me something that just about threw me into shock.

What did she ask you?

She asked me if I had a learning disability. Can you imagine how awful I felt? How humiliating that was for me to hear? I didn't know what to say. I felt so small, so stupid and in my head, I could hear myself responding with, "Are you serious!" Rather I responded with the only answer I knew of.

Which was?

"No," of course. After that I had to go through my papers two and three times before I turned them in. I still did well in school, but I had to focus super hard, to the point of exhaustion to make sure my writing made sense. I still do. It's kind of weird that I have to focus so hard isn't it? Mom?

Yes, it is. Let's talk about this later. Now isn't the time.

Why not?

I don't know. I thought we were talking in chronological order.

Mom? What the hell is wrong with me? I mean between the reading struggles I had in grammar school and now college?

There's nothing wrong with you honey. You're a smart, capable, intelligent woman who can do anything she sets her mind too.

So, you've told me.

Can we talk about this a little bit later, please?

No! I want to talk about this now Mom.

Please, honey please. I promise you we'll get to this, just not right this second. There are some things that are hard from Mom too, you know.

Okay. Where was I?

Sophie.

Um, I think I was talking about writing versus taking tests, but I've said all I need to say there.

Okay.

Since you brought up my little girl, I was glad I had her with me. I turned to her for strength many a times when I felt myself sinking too deep into my sadness. Whether it was taking a walk in the forest. Or, playing or just snuggling together and listening to music. Sophie was my comfort and my home. With her, I felt like I still had a piece of you with me.

You did. I wished you didn't need Sophie to feel that. You will always have me for as long as you need me. So how did you do in your classes?

I did well on paper, but I had some distractions, hence my living situation. As my first year progressed, I discovered a couple of things about my new roommate.

Oh no. Am I going to get upset?

Probably. I know I did.

I'm ready. Let me hear it.

Barry liked to take baths.

Okay, and?

Barry liked to take baths with the door open and his porn magazines all spread out on the floor. To top that off he would fall asleep in the tub with everything hanging out, and I mean EVERYTHING. I was in shock when I first saw that. I couldn't believe it.

Oh my gosh. That's disgusting.

Yeah. I asked him if would be so kind as to keep his bathing habits private, but he maintained that I was just a border and he could do what he wanted. He was right but I was hoping he would have some self-respect or decency about him and respect for me. After all, I may have been JUST a border, but I was JUST a border who was paying rent and I sure as hell didn't want to pay rent to see his junk hanging out all over the place.

Exactly. What if you wanted to bring a friend home? That would have been so embarrassing.

I know.

So, did he respect the space you two were sharing and close his damn door?

No and since I was getting buried with practicum's and papers, I didn't have the time to find a new place to live. I had to finish out my first year of school and then find an apartment. In that time, I discovered Barry had another habit.

Oh dear, do I want to hear this?

No, but I'm going to tell you anyway. Barry started having an affair with his ex-wife's sister.

His sister-in-law?

Yes, and they enjoyed having sex on the living room floor. At night Sophie and I would hear them panting, heavy breathing and moaning. That was my cue that I couldn't come out of my shoebox of a room. Sometimes, at night, I would have to go to the bathroom so bad and I would have to hold it until these two jerks finished doing their thing. I politely asked him if he would do his personal business in his room, but he still refused. This guy really made me miserable and I was paying him rent! I was so mad. So, I took action.

Oh, this I can't wait to hear.

Since it was his phone I was using, every time I found him naked in the tub or heard him with his sister-in-law, the next day,

I'd make a long-distance phone call, to any one of my friends from childhood that I still kept in contact with. I would stay on the phone for hours. I called everyone and anyone I could and stayed on that damn phone for as long as possible.

Good.

I also withheld my rent for two months so I could save up for an apartment. I believe I left him with about a $500 phone bill. He was pissed and I felt justice had been served.

Serves him right.

What can I say Mom? "Doormat" would never be a word to describe me.

Neither would "quiet."

I can only take that as a compliment.

It is a compliment and you're welcome. Ugh! Barry sounds like a real pervert! I'm glad you got out of there. Did he say anything to you about the rent?

He did. He asked why I hadn't paid the rent. I told him that under New Hampshire Real Estate Law I was paying rent to occupy space in a safe environment (Warranty of Habitability), inclusive of the Right to Privacy. I reminded him that he violated both clauses set in my lease when he decided to purposely and without regard expose himself as well as subject me to his sexual behaviors. Who knows what kind of secretions were on his floor which my poor dog was laying on. YUCK! Then I told him he was lucky I didn't call file a lawsuit.

Are those real New Hampshire Laws?

They're actually general clauses in most landlord/tenant lease agreements.

How did you know that?

From when you were renting our house out. I looked up a lot of the clauses you had in your lease agreement. I wanted to make sure I understood the conversations you had with our tenants when we'd check up on things. Especially when there was a problem, to ensure you weren't getting screwed over which you, sometimes, were.

Boy Kristin. You really picked up more than I ever thought.

I did. I learned a lot from you. So, I was thrilled when I finally found another place, so was Sophie.

How was your new apartment?

I loved it. I had to get a car because it was further from school and, unfortunately, in order to do that I had to take a large chunk out of my CD, which is where my money was. I didn't care. I was just happy to be out of there. I had the downstairs apartment in a two-family house. It was a little more expensive than the room I was renting but I was able to get a job at the local convenient store and make ends meet. Another single guy had the upstairs apartment, but he was nice. I was so busy with school, my internships and work that I barely had time to do anything. I made some connections in my classes but mostly kept to myself outside of class. Ethan came to visit me.

He did? How was that?

It was good. I thought about us from time to time - the way we were before things got bad and a few other things.

Like what?

Like the time he took me to his parent's cabin. I have fond memories from those two days. I don't know. We just couldn't come together on anything. The arguing was too much, for both of us. I always thought when you love someone it's through thick and thin, but we wanted such different things. He wanted this square life - you know where two people have their jobs, their children, a home. They go to work, they come home, have a vacation here and there, visit with friends, that kind of thing but that's not me. When we first met things were good. However, as time went on and with some of the things he did, our relationship began to feel more confined to me. Then there was also the fact that I was grieving, still and forever and Ethan didn't understand that. I needed space to go through what I was going through and I didn't know how long that would take. You know, grief has no timeline.

That's for sure.

The fact that he didn't love animals as I did was also a major factor for me. I could never be with anyone that didn't LOVE animals and want to help them as I do. We just couldn't find common ground. We couldn't give each other what the other needed and had to move on. However, his visit was fun. We climbed Mt. Monadnock, laughed, joked around, went around town and it really felt like old times with him. He was definitely supportive of my going to graduate school that's for sure. I appreciated that.

I always liked Ethan and you know honey. I think you nailed it when you say you two were couldn't find common ground. You did the right thing by honoring your need to have space to grieve, and you're right. Grief has no timeline. I know how much the grief of losing your parent can affect every area of your life, especially when you're as close to your parent as you and I are. My Dad and I weren't as close, but I think that was the problem. I wanted to be close to him, but he was a hard man to get close too. Still, I loved him just as much.

I know. When I think about my time in Keene, I feel good because I know Sophie was happy there and that made me happy. You know how she loved her car rides.

Oh yes. All you had to do was say the magic words, "Go for a ride?" and she would get all excited.

I know. That whine she had combined with barking was funny. That's all she did was whine and bark. Sometimes she whined so loud the neighbors thought there was something wrong with her.

I know. She was a silly little girl.

We went for a lot of car rides down long country roads. She loved it! I did too, especially with her. Seeing her happy made my heart explode with joy. It really did. Whenever we'd go for a ride, she would stick her head out the window and let those Beagle/Bassett ears of hers flap in the breeze. We had a lot of fun. We were kids together doing as much as we could and having as much fun as possible. I had this big back yard and we'd play chase, or we'd run around the apartment and went on hikes through the forest almost every day.

On one of our excursions we found this peak. It was a combination of rock and soil. We'd sit for hours, sometimes until the sun went down. When we'd come home, Sophie would have her dinner and pass out for the night. We also had another special place. It was this pond that had a picturesque view of Mt. Monadnock directly behind it. We went there a lot. Sophie liked dipping her paws in the water. She wasn't much of a swimmer, but she sure enjoyed relaxing by the water for hours. It was so peaceful. That's us by the pond. The picture is a little blurry, but it was taken with the manual timer on the 35mm camera that your friend, Aron, gave me. I took all my photos with that camera.

Me and Sophie with the backdrop of Mt. Monadnock
Keene, New Hampshire, 1993

I love this photo. It captures the special bond between you and Sophie.

Me too.

What did you love most about New Hampshire?

The forests and being so close to nature - the gentle shuffling of orange, red and yellow leaves that covered the forest paths in fall. The quiet stillness that winter's snowfall brought and how the clean, white snow illuminated the small town, especially at night. The white dusting of winter's snow under the moon instilled calmness in me I so needed. By the time May made its way around you could see how anxious everyone was for spring as the layers of clothing started to slowly peel away and the fresh scent of blooming flowers began to fill the air. Only to ease into the warm, long summer days accompanied by the chirping of all the birds that have made their way back from the south after a long winter. The summer not only brought the birds but ignited a skip in everyone's step and lightness to their being. Sophie and I couldn't get enough of the mountains we so came to know and love.

You needed to be in a place like this babe, bad.

I did and I'm glad I was there. I didn't care that the winters were long and cold. I was used to long, cold winters. Besides, the beauty of spring, summer and fall made up for it. Since Vermont was just a few short minutes away Sophie and I took A LOT of road trips to Brattleboro. I wish I would have gone to school in Vermont, but I don't think they had any DMT Programs, or at least I wasn't aware of them.

Vermont would have been the perfect place for you to do your graduate work, but I think that Antioch was a good place for you to be as well.

I guess. I fell in love with Vermont after my first visit. When Sophie and I didn't go to Vermont I'd take her on one of our long hikes. Sometimes I'd take my reading materials into the mountains and stay there for hours. I feel safe and at home with nature and animals. Before going to New Hampshire, I felt like I'd been holding my breath for years and now, being in the mountains I was feeling so light and free. I could breathe. There's just something about God's land that calls me to her, like the drums do. In the country there's space, untouched, open landscapes that go on for miles and the changing of the seasons were breathtaking. A stillness entered me that I looked forward to every day. Our trips to Vermont during the fall foliage were absolutely beautiful and my favorite part about living in New England. The leaves on the trees looked like a painted canvas adorned with earthy oranges, reds, yellows, greens and browns. Sophie was in her bliss.

And you?

Yeah, I mean…

For someone who was so happy in nature you don't sound to convincing.

I was working hard. Being at graduate school and doing well was validation to me that I was more than the angry person your family labeled me as.

Kristin you were then and are now more than anger. I wish you wouldn't have let them affect you.

I could say the same to you, couldn't I?

Okay, you got me. They weren't easy to fight off, but I realized something about my sisters and that whole clan.

What's that?

That all the emotional baggage they dumped on me was what they couldn't handle themselves. That helped put things into prospective.

I didn't see that then, but I do now. I put forth this strong, capable, intelligent woman who could do anything façade. Inside I had layers of grief and sadness that I didn't have the time or energy to work through and that's exactly what I was supposed to be doing, per my professors. I had so many unresolved feelings about your crossing over and my life. This was not the best time for me to be in graduate school but I'm glad I went. I needed to be around caring, supportive, warm people and that's exactly what I got. Being so far from your family was good for me. I needed the support I got at school because I couldn't shake all the years of hospital stays, your pain, the meds, doctor appointments, etc. that we went through. After all that you didn't make it and you were supposed to. I knew how hard you worked to stay here. I just thought the Universe would have been kinder to us - given us a better ending.

Yet here we are sweet baby girl. The ending turned into a beautiful beginning.

Not for me. You transitioned to a place of peace while I was dealing with all this shit.

Such as?

Such as all that I've been talking about - a manipulative, controlling extended family I wish I never had along with this feeling of being so emotionally fragile, I thought I would "lose it" at any second. I was so afraid of that because I thought, "Who is going to care for Sophie if I don't keep it together?" Unfortunately, my grief and intense despair was getting stronger and becoming impossible to swallow or hide. In addition to therapy I went to a bereavement support group but the emptiness in me only grew. The pain became so deep I felt like I was being sucked into a bottomless black hole. I spent my days going to class, studying, attending internships I felt shaky in and coming home to lie flat on my back on my living room floor. I felt like I was bearing the weight of the world on my shoulders.

You were and long before I crossed over too.

I didn't connect it then but thinking back now I'm reminded of the exercise I was asked to do in my first Dance/Movement Therapy class as an undergrad.

I know the one, where your father is above, and your mother is below, and you have to do the authentic movement around those two entities.

Exactly. I'm surprised I was able to get up at all. I just wanted to lay on the floor and be with my mother. While I loved being in the mountains, I was lonely, very lonely for you, for family, not your family but people that truly loved and accepted me for me. The way you did. Not to mention I had two car accidents that didn't help matters. The first one Sophie was with me. We were on our way to Brattleboro and my car was rammed off the road by some kid speeding and making a left-hand turn into oncoming traffic. I was the oncoming traffic. My car was totaled. Thank goodness Sophie wasn't hurt. The second time I was at a stop light and my car was hit from behind, by a lawyer no less. Both times I walked away without ever going to the hospital or being checked out.

I told you to go to the hospital just to get checked out and make sure you were okay.

I heard you but I was sick of hospitals! Whether I was comfortable there or not I didn't want to step back into another hospital for the rest of my life. I wanted a life without hospitals for as long as possible if not forever.

A visit to the hospital would have changed your life.

Don't you think I know that! Don't you think I replay those accidents over and over in my head like a movie? Each time I feel my regret for not doing what my mother told me too. Who knows how different my life would have been had I just gone to the fucking doctor!

Okay, I'm sorry. I didn't mean to bring you back to your regret.

It's too late! I have regrets all over the damn place.

Don't do that to yourself anymore. What's done is done Kristin. You can't change the past. When you focus on your regrets it's like torturing yourself on experiences that hurt you that you can't change, and you've been through enough.

Still, I stayed in school - partly because I really did want to succeed and do something important with my life but mostly because I had nowhere else to go. Pretty sad huh?

No, that's not sad, honey. The fact that you had nowhere else to go took you to the best place possible.

True.

Sweetheart, you didn't need a master's degree for me to be as proud of you as I already was and always will be.

In the back of my mind I knew that.

Perhaps it wasn't so much that you needed me to be proud of you but more that you needed to be proud of yourself. What do you think?

I think you're right. All this time in school I could barely breathe. Sometimes I would feel sick or dizzy before my internships. Especially if I was working with abuse survivors. Or, a lump the size of a large gumball would gather in my throat during class, or a mock therapy session. It was so bad I'd have to excuse myself. That's not a good thing when you're in the midst of a therapy session and you're the intern therapist.

You were starting to have, what do they call that, psycho…

Psychosomatic responses to the abuse survivors I was working with. I was identifying with them well, too well, to the point where I could no longer distinguish the line between intern therapist and patient. I was having physical reactions while listening to their stories. My body sometimes shook, or I'd break out into a sweat and my heart would begin to palpitate. I'd get nauseous before and during my internships, yet I hid it well - too well. My Professors were so supportive. They took all this extra time with me. I felt fortunate to even have the opportunity to study for my master's and I didn't want to blow it. Yet going from one moment to the next became excruciating. I wanted so much for the things that Cody did to me to not affect me. I didn't want to give him that power, but my body was remembering a lot more than my mind wanted too, you know.

I do.

I was never comfortable with men, not ever.

I know you…

Remember that really nice young couple you were able to get to watch me after school when you and Dad first separated? I think I was around 7 years old or so.

No.

Well, you did, and they were really nice. Unfortunately, because of the things Cody was doing to me I started to develop this fear and uncomfortable feeling around men. This couple was so nice, and I really liked them, but the more Cody was touching and hitting me the more frightened I became of the man, and he did nothing to me to make me scared of him. I was getting so beaten and abused so young the fear was overwhelming to me. I remember I told you I didn't want to go over there anymore, and you asked me why? I started to cry. Then you asked me if the man had done anything to me or if he touched me in my private areas. I assured you he didn't. You were so scared he molested me, but I made sure you knew that he didn't. I wanted to tell you then who was molesting and hurting me, but I couldn't. I just couldn't because, at the time, I thought I was doing something to make my brother do the things he was to me.

Oh baby, this was my fault. Looking back, I'm sure I saw the fear you had of men, but my blind eyes didn't want to know why. I'm so sorry honey.

So, you've said. When I was with Paul, we hardly did anything but kiss and fondle each other a little. With Ethan, we were so stoned all the time I don't feel like I was truly present in my body and mind as much I thought I was. Couple that with grief and I needed to smoke a lot in order to get through the day.

I know you did and honey. Feeling the pain someone so ruthlessly caused you doesn't mean you're giving them power. It means you're human - your kind, compassionate and care about yourself and others, something your brother wasn't to you.

I started to dread my classes and any interactions with people at all. I'd been in Keene for two and years. I hung on as long as I could Mom. I swear I did. In fact, that's all I felt like I was doing was hanging on – by a thread.

I know. I know baby. You were doing great. Your little heart was breaking and there was no one to help you heal it. I know how important it is for us to heal ourselves but it's equally important to have a good support system in place while we do the inner work. You had no support system. As wonderful as the Program was it wasn't a support system. Like you said, they had boundaries and stuck to them. Having no support is a huge stress and burden to bear when you're grieving.

My therapist had, for some time, offered to prescribe me anti-depressants. At the time Prozac was still new but the most widely used. For a long time, I told her no. I was always against using drugs to treat depression and still am, for me. If others choose to do so I hold no judgment but for me, I wanted to walk through the journey of self-discovery drugless. I wanted to uncover the layers, deal with things, be strong for myself and not have any interference from any meds. Yet things became so unbearable that I finally told her I would give the Prozac a shot. I think it was within weeks when I started to feel like things weren't getting better, rather I was feeling worse.

Did you tell your therapist this?

No. I was only on them for a couple of weeks. I didn't think it was enough time to make a decision as to whether or not they were working.

Do you think that was the reason for what happened?

Partly, yes. I absolutely take responsibility for attempting to take my own life but, at the same time, since then I've never gotten to the point where I'm feeling so low that I actually take the next step and attempt my life.

Right.

I mean I was depressed but once I started the Prozac, the black hole I felt like I was sinking in was no longer just a thought. It was a tangible place, feeling and state of mind I fell into and I couldn't, for the life of me, get out from. I could feel my hands and nails grasping at the earth's dirt and getting sucked deeper and deeper into the blackness of my own grave.

Do you want to talk about it?

Not really.

I knew you'd say that, but it may help. I may help.

Okay, catch me if I fall.

My arms and heart are wide open and ready to receive.

Um, I bought a bottle of wine. Knowing how low my tolerance level is I knew that between the two boxes of the over the counter sleeping pills and the wine there was a pretty good chance I'd cross over soon. I downed everything, laid down and went to sleep. I was hoping for good but at the same time, I wanted to wake up and have everything we'd been through to be a nightmare. I wanted to wake up to hear your voice calling me from a different room. I wanted to wake up to my mother, still alive and cancer free. I wanted to wake up to a life we never got the chance to experience or I didn't want to wake up at all. I thought of Sophie, but I couldn't hang on Mom. I couldn't breathe. I felt like someone's hands were around my throat all the time. I was so lonely without you. It's hard to put into words the depth of pain I was in.

You don't have to. You have nothing to be ashamed of. Whether the Prozac initiated it or not, there is nothing for you to be ashamed of.

I used to feel ashamed. Not anymore. Lots of people try, at some point in their lives, to kill themselves and in various ways but…

But what?

Something happened while I was out.

What?

I was walking down this long tunnel. On my way there I felt nothing but lightness and as though everything was okay. I felt good. I had no anger or sadness. I felt so free and full of love. I could see this beautiful bright white light at what looked like the end, or the beginning. I couldn't quite make out which one. Then I saw you. Your arms were outstretched to me. You were smiling. I started to run toward you and in an instant, you took your index finger and moved it side to side as if to say…

Not yet. Then I shook my head no.

I wanted to be with you. I never had the zest for life you did. If anyone should be here it's you, not me. Why did you send me back here?

I didn't. As much as I want you with me it wasn't your time yet.

What do you mean it wasn't my time yet? What kind of explanation is that?

It's not an explanation. It's the reason. Do you remember anything else about that night?

Yeah, it didn't work. I woke up and was choking. I had something in my throat.

Your stomach was pumped.

How did I get to the hospital?

You.

Me? I feel like I'm in the twilight zone. How me?

You dragged yourself to the phone and dialed 911. You didn't say anything. You just left the phone off the receiver. EMS came and took you to the hospital.

What in the world was I thinking? Why would I call 911? I could have been out of this god-for-saken place.

I think you know why Kristin.

I don't.

I gave you one thought that helped me get you back. Do you remember what that was?

No.

It was very simple but powerful. The thought was, "What if tomorrow things get better and you miss them?" You're a fighter and quitting isn't your style, regardless of how sad you are. If you're going down, it's not going to be without the fight of your life. Although it felt like it, you still had yet to put up the fight of your life. YOUR life was just beginning. You and I already did my life.

Mom, I…

I understand you and what you were feeling better than you think.

You?

Yes. I'm not proud of an attempted suicide but, yes. Your mother tried to kill herself.

How?

Same as you, pills. You had Sophie to worry about, but I had three children and I tried to take my life. Talk about feeling guilty. I understand the depth of your despair Kristin. You're very succinct in the way you describe it. It isn't LIKE falling into a bottomless black hole. You do fall into a bottomless black hole and you're so spent you don't have the strength to pull yourself out. All the while you know you have people depending on you. It's an awful, scary place to be.

I remember visiting you once in the hospital. This was before your cancer. Spencer told me you were sick, but I knew something wasn't right. When you're sick, the doctors don't have you attend "creative group" classes where you make things like key holders, crochet, knit, draw and talk with other people about your feelings. That's what one of the nurses, who was watching us for a moment while Spencer spoke with your doctor, told me when I asked her, "What else does my mom do besides make key holders?" She probably assumed Spencer told me the truth about where you were.

You were an astute little girl. Nothing got by you. You see honey, we're all human, beautiful and not so beautiful, perfect and imperfect.

Yeah well, my imperfections landed me on the same Psychiatric Unit as the one I interned on not too long before. How embarrassing. After I awoke from a suicide attempt, I wanted to die, again! I'm being facetious but you know what I mean.

Oh honey, I do.

I had fellow students there that were doing their internships. Oh my gosh I just wanted to hole up in my room but eventually had to partake in group sessions and creative arts therapy. I was considered a "special case." The staff made sure I wouldn't intersect with my fellow students. I really didn't like being there.

I know you didn't. I didn't like that you were there either. But at least you were safe and alive. That was a better alternative for me than you having crossed over before your time.

Even as an intern I didn't like the hospital's philosophy and the way they approached individuals with depression. It was all about behavior modification and changing your behavior to suit their paradigms. They didn't really explore the root of problems, only the symptoms and that does nothing. It felt superficial to me. There was more to what I was going through than my behavior. For me, my behavior, whatever it was, was only the symptom of my underlying grief, sadness and anger at the abuse I endured and our separation. I feel like I pushed a lot of the anger and sadness I had of the abuse Cody put me through down, way down.

I know you did, until you crashed so to speak.

I crashed while going full speed ahead. The hardest part was that I didn't make the kind of friendships I was hoping to make while in school. Out of fear of being hurt or misunderstood I went inward and kept to myself most of the time, although I still offered to help people if they needed something, anything. I explained to my professors and fellow students that I was grieving the loss of my mother. I let them know if I seemed introverted, I was doing the best I could with the feelings I was working through. The program was hard enough, and my professors encouraged us to try to be as good a support system to each other as possible. That didn't happen. Some of fellow students judge me but I think I judged myself more than anyone else.

Yes, yes you did, and you didn't deserve that. You were going through enough. Being as hard as you are on yourself is partly what got you in that hospital in the first-place babe. With regard to the other students, suicide is a scary thing for people. It reminds us of how fragile we all are. For some it makes them think, "That could have been me or someone I love."

Understanding behavior doesn't always lessen the hurt, sometimes but not always. I felt like a leper to my fellow students.

I think if you'd had a good support system - family, friends' things would have been different for you, better.

My therapist came to see me at the hospital. I remember her apologizing to me and telling me, "I'm so sorry Kristin. I'm so sorry. I should have seen the signs."

And what was your response.

That she had nothing to apologize for because I hid whatever signs there were as far away from both of us as possible. I had to in order to get through the day. I told her I was worried about Sophie. I didn't want to talk with any of the other graduate students. I was too embarrassed. However, there was one student whom I let live with me when she broke up with her boyfriend. I asked my therapist if she would contact her, on my behalf, to see if she would stay with Sophie for a few days until I figured something else out. I offered to pay her, but she said it was no problem but that she could only do it for a couple of days. I was going to be in the hospital longer than I realized. I had to swallow my pride and do the unthinkable.

Let me guess. You called your sister.

She was the very last of any and all last resorts and I regret it until this day, yet I had no other option.

There was no one else for you to call?

No. I came to graduate school with someone that I was friends with at Brockport. We would hang out every now and again after you crossed over, and even choreographed a dance together in our senior year.

That's wonderful honey. Why didn't you ask her?

You know, it's hard to explain for me sometimes.

What is?

The breakdown of a friendship and/or relationship. It's painful for me and I don't like to recall them, but it is good to talk about all this.

I'm glad. I knew it would be and I understand. Take your time.

You know that once I feel betrayed my back is turned to that person and I never look back.

I know. What did she do?

They. She and the student that I let live with me and was watching Sophie, found out where I was and what I was going through.

How did they find out? It wasn't your therapist was it?

No, my therapist was a wonderful, caring, nurturing person who really cared about me and did whatever she could, within her ethical boundary, to help me. So, no, she, thankfully, never disclosed where I was to anyone. My therapist only stated that I was going through something and that it was private. They found out because they were either interning on the same unit or knew of other students that were and they disclosed I was there.

Oh boy, okay, so what happened?

So, rather than respect me and our friendship and come to me with any concern or uncomfortableness they felt, they went behind my back and disclosed this whole nightmare to all of my professors making me look incompetent, which I wasn't.

Oh my gosh! Oh my gosh! Why in the world did they do that? And after you helped one of them! What goes through peoples' heads? I don't get it.

I don't know and I don't care. They should have talked to me. Actually, as I said before, I didn't want to see any of my fellow students because I was embarrassed and ashamed. Two stigmas that should never be assigned to grief and suicide, attempted or otherwise. Either way, the decision as to whom to disclose what I was going through was mine, not theirs. What they should have done was mind their business, plain and simple. My therapist let the person know that was watching Sophie that it was only for a couple of days and that I was handling things. They had no business doing what they did.

Yeah, absolutely.

The fact remains that the way they handled this was to treat me like I was a person without a brain, unable to make my own decisions. I felt voiceless and robbed me of my ability to make decisions about my life, which I was more than capable of doing. I was going through severe depression and grief. I often felt like someone had their hands on my heart and was squeezing the life out of me.

Oh honey.

Yeah, that's how I felt but I still deserved the same respect they would have wanted. I wasn't someone lacking her faculties yet that's how they treated me. I felt so betrayed. I would have never done this to them. I understand what it's like to sink so far into a black hole within yourself and try to climb out, and just not be able to get yourself out. That's where I was and they, in their selfish, stupid, thoughtless minds, poured salt in my wounds. This all happened over Christmas break and I was going to speak to my professors but that was for me to do, not them. I just needed to get through what was happening at the moment. I was really hurt by them Mom, really hurt and angry.

I don't blame you. What they did was inexcusable, and they were studying to be therapists? That's scary.

Yeah. Antioch was a good place for me to be up until this point.

So that's why you had to call your sister?

Yeah.

What did she say?

One of the first things I asked her was to keep the reason for my being in the hospital private. At the time I felt ashamed and like a complete failure. I think, for her, it was more like an, "Ah ha! Now Kristin is the fuck-up! Not me!" She used the painful place I fell so deep into to make herself look good and I just –I was feeling so low and she added to it.

I gather she didn't keep you stay in the hospital private.

No. She said she needed support. When I asked her for what she said, "You attempted a suicide. I may need to talk to someone about this." I told her if I could have called anyone else, I would have. I asked if she could to talk to a friend or go to a support group. There were support groups for families right at the hospital. I reiterated how awful I felt about where I was and that it was important that it be kept private. Instead, she informed your sisters. They, in turn, told everyone else in the family the reason for my hospital stay. News, especially news like this, spread like wildfire in your family. If she had to tell them anything she could have just said, "My sister is going through something and I need to be there for her" and left it at that. That's what I would have done.

Yeah, she didn't need to do that.

I felt betrayed. For the sake of Sophie and getting out of that hospital I, again, swallowed the hurt. I couldn't afford to alienate her. If my sister wanted something kept secret, I kept it a secret. Protecting her, respecting her privacy, giving her my loyalty and support was my love for my sister. I didn't get that from her.

You know, at the root of your pain there was something, or shall I say, someone else.

I know but I realized, a long time ago that, Dad. I wasn't about to share anything with him. He was a stranger to me. I mean, the man really felt that because he couldn't support us or be there for us that we were all supposed to just understand and accept that.

Well, we know that's a crock of shit.

Yeah, or he would turn things around on me. He would say that I was being, dramatic, over emotional or deny everything.

He was the same way with me. When we were together and I tried to confront him about any of our issues, and we had A LOT of issues, I would get similar responses. "Mary, you're being ridiculous," or "Stop being so dramatic," or "You don't know what you're talking about." Or he would tell me I was being paranoid and making things up in my head. Then I would cry and get hysterical and he would tell me I was being too emotional, and he couldn't talk to me anymore. That used to drive me crazy! Then he would leave, sometimes for days.

Yeah, I wasn't going to let him do that to me. I had enough of him and the emotional bullshit he dealt us. I knew a long time ago that whatever I had to work out with regard to my father I'd have to do on my own. I just needed to be a little gentler with myself in the process, that's all.

That's true and very smart of you to realize. So, what happened next?

Andrea agreed to help with Sophie but...

I don't think I want to hear this.

Oh no, you do. She would come if I paid for her and her girlfriend's entire trip there and their spending money. She said she didn't have any money. The remainder of my inheritance went toward buying a new car after my accidents. I didn't have any money either but what could I do? Again, I said nothing and gave her my credit card which she racked up and didn't even offer or bother to pay back. From the time I was in the hospital Andrea took on this "I take care of my sister" act which wasn't true, at all. This is why I didn't want to call her. Whether things were good or bad I was taking care of and handling my own life. So, what if I had this set back. That didn't mean I was any less independent. Then she made another unsettling comment.

More?

When I asked her why it was necessary for her girlfriend to come, that I was already in debt she said, "I need her with me. Besides, who else are you going to call if I don't come?" She also said, "See, I told you that graduate school wasn't a good idea. Look where it got you, in a mental hospital." My heart sank upon hearing her words. Oh my gosh, you don't know how much I despised her at this time. Both trips were put on my credit card. It was no surprise that this visit was the only visit my sister made the entire time I was in New Hampshire. While I lived in New Hampshire, if I wanted to see my sister I had to drive with Sophie, which is exactly what we did, a couple of times.

Oh boy, she really knew how to stick it to you.

Yes, she did, and it never got easier to take.

What was your response to all this?

I corrected her and told her it was a psychiatric unit in a hospital, not a mental hospital. Andrea was good at making herself look like the supportive sister. The reality was that she was manipulating, lying about me behind my back to others, over-critical and discouraging of the decisions I made which were MY decisions, not hers. This was a truly low point in my life and my sister was adding salt to all my wounds. I now had more expenses on my credit card in addition to whatever thousands was being racked up in hospital bills because I had no insurance. All I wanted to do was stay focused on getting home to Sophie. This is where I started to wonder if I was worthy of a good life or not. Here I was trying for just that and failing.

You weren't failing Kristin. You were having a hard time. I'm sorry your sister put you through so much and made you feel otherwise but you're stronger and smarter than that.

At the time I was feeling flimsy and shaky inside. These were the times when I thought of you and how much you had to swallow in order to get help from Dad and the man still didn't help you. The emotional toll Andrea put me through added to what I was already dealing with. Her cold hearted, self-centered, narcissistic actions were more out of control than I ever realized. Everything was about her, her, her and how much attention she could get even if she had to get it at the expense of someone else's pain, meaning my pain. She just wanted people to see her as the poor little savior, yours when you were sick and now mine and she wasn't for either of us, but she sure did make herself out to be that way.

Honey, it pains me to say this but, you're right, your sister wasn't very good at handling responsibility or any kind of emergency situation. I didn't want to say this before but that's why I went to stay with Trudi when I was getting my last chemo treatment. Remember that and how upset you were that I was there?

Yeah?

Your sister had a terrible time helping me and she couldn't take being in the hospital. She herself was suicidal. One of the nurses told me. They offered her support groups to attend for people living with cancer –

like the ones you attended. They also offered her low-cost counseling, but she refused.

Are you serious?

Yes. She was so ill-equipped to handle my caretaking let alone the hospital stays and that didn't help me. You were always calm, confident and making sure whatever I had to get done was done, and I was treated with respect and compassion. Your sister was unable to get a grip, like my sisters.

So that's why you were at Trudi's.

Yes. When I wasn't at Trudi's my sisters were over a lot more when you were at school, a lot more, as you know. They were seeing, in more detail, what you and I were dealing with and they were no better at handling the stress of it all than your sister was. When they weren't there your sister wasn't all that pleasant to be around.

What do you mean?

She was moody and impatient. I got to the point where I didn't feel comfortable asking her for anything.

That fucking asshole, and here she was bragging about how well she cared for you.

She needed a lot of attention and she wanted it at whatever cost. This time it was you.

You were right about not having a positive, strong support system and this was the time I needed it and didn't have it. Instead, I had a self-serving, narcissistic sister I had to stomach until I could get home.

I know exactly what you're feeling honey, I do. It's discouraging to try and not succeed and feel the "I told you so's" of people who could barely care for themselves all around you.

That's exactly it. I could see this huge mountain I had to climb in order to be healthy in mind and body and I had no energy to climb it. All I knew was that I wanted to get out of the hospital and back home to Sophie. I basically followed the hospital rules, did what they told me to do and when I realized I signed myself in. It occurred to me; I could sign myself out. That's exactly what I did. Andrea wanted me to go back to Buffalo but the thought made the hospital seem like a retreat. I had only one more class, and my thesis to go. I really wanted to complete my master's. It was important to me. Andrea wasn't happy. Sophie and I were happy.

This is what I don't get about your sister. You were trying so she should have been happy and supportive of you.

Yeah, should of is the word.

Well, there is one positive to all of this.

What in the world would that be?

If there is any place, I wanted you going through all that you were, Keene, NH was the place - certainly not Buffalo, NY that's for sure.

That's a good point and I agree. I finished out my last semester and felt proud. I felt like I was redeeming myself for myself, not for the approval of others but for me. Yet the loneliness in me remained and ultimately became unbearable again. Between the hospital bills, my credit card bills, student loans that I knew I was going to have to pay back I was way over my head in debt.

What a minute – credit cards? You said, "Credit Cards," plural. How many credit cards did you have?

Oh, that's right. There was the credit card my sister maxed out at around $4,000. Along with that was the credit card my father, the one you so wanted me to forgive that I hadn't spoken with since my college graduation, decided to take out, in my name and also max out and not pay one dime of. That amount was somewhere around $8,000.

That son-of-a-bitch! Oh honey. You were getting screwed from the very people that were supposed to love and be there for you.

Yeah, it hurt Mom. I had so much hurt from so many different places. I had to choose the deepest ones and start from there, you know?

I do.

Yet I could barely do that. My finances went from well managed to out of control in a matter of months. I didn't' have the money to pay my bills and was getting hounded by creditors. I couldn't handle the debt that was hanging over my head. With much regret, at the age of 23, feeling financially backed against a wall I made the decision to file bankruptcy.

Honey. Remember, it's only money.

Yeah, money that would affect me for the rest of my life. I couldn't believe the things that were happening to me. I went from caring for you and having everything organized and meticulously managed. Then you crossed and I completely lost hold of my bearings. My safety net was pulled out from underneath me and everything was spinning out of control. I think the only reason I did well in school was because by this time schoolwork became automatic, almost robotic to me. It was easy for me to read a lot of material, synthesize it in my head and paraphrase it on paper. Are you disappointed in me for filing for bankruptcy?

Disappointed? How could I be disappointed? I'm sad you had to do that. Spencer wasn't helping you kids manage your funds?

We had a falling out. I don't even remember over what, but we never spoke again after it.

How long ago was that?

Oh, geez, 1994, I think. Somewhere around there.

I believe it. I do know how Spencer can be. We've had our share of doozies. If you remember she and I stopped speaking for a long time too.

I remember.

Well, it's done and over with now and you move on.

Yeah, that's how I feel. It's all for the best. I have no regrets with Spencer. I mean I'm sad we fought but sometimes things happen and like you say, you have to move on. I had more important things to deal with.

That's right.

I was so unprepared for the things that were happening in my life. I never thought I would ever attempt a suicide or file bankruptcy, but I did, and they were grave setbacks. You know these are the times when kids go back and forth to their parents. At least that's what my cousins did. I didn't have that. I just...

You took too much on.

Yes, and I didn't want to end up in the hospital again. I would talk to Ethan from time to time and he wanted me to come to New York to be with him. He said his parents wouldn't mind if I stayed with them while I worked and found a place of my own.

After completing that semester, I spoke with my professors and made a difficult decision but only because I was told it would be okay to do so by the school.

I know. You left school and went back to Buffalo.

I just needed a break but obviously, wasn't thinking clearly going back to Buffalo. I had that choking feeling again - like I was being strangled and couldn't take the loneliness. I felt like someone shoved me into this box and I needed to get out - fast. I really wanted to finish my degree I just felt so isolated and - I don't know, so...

Alone?

Yes, I don't know how else to put it into words. Intellectually, I knew I should finish my degree. I just - my head felt like it was going to explode. I think what made this decision even more hard was Marion.

Marion? Who's Marion?

Prior to working with teens, I had an internship working with the elderly. I was interning at a nursing home and had a couple of patients I worked while focusing on the counseling aspect of my degree. Marion was a 95-year-old woman who really touched me. We would meet twice a week and I was supposed to be working on my "counseling" skills but really, all I did was listen to Marion tell me her life story. She was fascinating and inspiring. Marion's memory was completely intact. It was her body, including her sight, that was taking its toll. We both looked forward to each other's visits. I looked forward to learning about her life and a world that existed before I was born, and seeing her whole body perk up at the sound of my voice. She looked forward to having a break from the pain of having had to leave her home and the independence she had. We both empathized with each other; how it felt to lose our home and the life we once knew and bonded from there. Marion was kind, funny and very strong minded. I loved that about her. I would take her for walks around the grounds while she told me stories of her and her husband, their son and life in New Hampshire. She was extremely intelligent. I learned so much about how things used to be in her day (the 1930's and on up). How she lived life through simple means and was taught to value education. Yet she was sad and rightfully so. She missed her independence and being able to do what she wanted when she wanted. She hated having to live under the constraints of the home which, weren't bad, but when you go from being free to living under someone else's rules. It feels like agony. That's how Marion felt. Her son lived in the south, so I took her out for brunch on Mother's Day and it was so nice Mom. It was so nice to have someone to take out for Mother's Day again. I looked forward and enjoy my visits with Marion just as much she did.

Honey you are so kind and loving. I remember when I took you kids to the elderly home one Christmas Day. You must have been about 9 or 10 years old. You bonded with everyone you talked to, and they loved you Kristin. They loved you because you saw beyond their age or disability and talked to them like people, with true respect and interest in who they were. Many of them hadn't had that. And like your friend Marion, they too, didn't have families for the holidays. What a beautiful friendship you had with Marion. Why didn't you mention her before?

I don't know. I guess I still harbor some guilt for leaving her. That's what I felt like I did but I wouldn't have Mom, if I really felt like I could've stayed. Even after my internship at the nursing home ended, I still went to visit Marion. Right up until my difficult decision to leave. Even with Marion, I was choking on loneliness and this gut-wrenching emotional pain from grief and a childhood of abuse. I talked with Marion about how I felt. I didn't tell her the details of what I was going through, just that I had some personal challenges I really needed to address.

What was her response?

She was sad for me to go but she understood. I was sad to go too. I wished I wasn't so lost so I could find my way in my life, somewhere and stay put, you know?

I do honey.

I thought of Marion often and found out she crossed over a few years later. I have many regrets in my life. Leaving school to go back to Buffalo and saying goodbye to Marion are definitely at the top.

I understand baby. I had regrets too. We all do. I think the painful situations that were thrust upon you led you to make some decisions that weren't in your best interest. What do you think?

I think you're right. However, again, I only left because I was told, by the DMT Dept. heads, that I could finish up the following year. I just needed to breathe. I was trying to find a home, my home and along the way I was fumbling, falling and running into brick walls. Some of those walls were put up by others and some I put up myself. I was turning left when I should have been turning right, going backward when I needed to go forward and so on. I needed you. I needed my touchstone and was...

Lost, I know. I know. I wish I could have helped you through all these times the way you needed me. That hurt me too.

Yeah, it was hard for me to tell Ethan I was going back to Buffalo. He couldn't understand why I was leaving school and going back there either knowing all the discord I had with your family.

Well sure, he was trying to help you. You would have been all set in New York City, and you chose Buffalo. You went back to the one place you hated. That doesn't make any sense.

I don't know, I just wanted...

What? What in the world made you go back there?

Andrea begged me incessantly to come back. She said she didn't want to be alone there with the family. I, too, was so lonely. I missed you. I missed you so much. I was so angry we didn't have the house in Syracuse. We could have been renting it and I could have gone back there but now I was stuck. I didn't know where I wanted to be. What can I say Mom? I didn't know which way to turn or where to go. I just felt so lost and it was a weird feeling because I'd never been in that place before. When you were physically here, I knew who I was and what my role and purpose in life was; you. I was Mary's daughter born to care for her. My life was changing in ways I didn't understand, and I was making decisions based on loneliness and fear as opposed to what I wanted and knew would be good for me. That, too, was new for me.

I understand baby. I do. You will always be my daughter and my friend and this inner growth beginning with, "Who am I without my mother?" while painful, is also something you needed.

Exactly. Boy, I had no clue what I was in for, none at all.

No one does babe. You just have to go along as best you can.

I know that you always wanted me to remain as independent as I was. I wanted that too. What scared me about going to NYC was that Ethan wanted us to try and be together again. My fear was that if I went back with him, because I was feeling so fragile, I'd lose whatever sense of self I had and become dependent on him and remain sad. More importantly, I wasn't in love with him. Here I was supposed to be healing myself and I was doing everything that went against that.

Kristin, at least you would have been in New York City, not Buffalo. The one place you hated and then returned to. That was your big mistake along with selling your piano.

Mom, don't you think I know how bad that decision was. Until this day I kick myself for selling my piano but because I was in so much debt that was part of the money, I was using to get me back to Buffalo. Besides, I didn't want Stan to keep it anymore.

Why?

He and his wife lost all my piano books that I kept in the bench or maybe Andrea did. I don't know which one.

Oh no.

Yes. I forgot they were in there when he took the piano. I was in Keene when they sold it and I don't know that they ever looked in the bench before they sold it, but even if they didn't, I'm sure the people that bought it would have said something.

Well I hope they would have anyway. Oh, honey, you're beautiful piano and books.

Yeah, I never got over losing the books. They held a lot of memory of you and me sitting at the piano while I practiced.

I know, me too. If it's any consolation I was proud of you baby. You practiced so hard and with such determination. You were the same way with dance and pretty much anything you did. You never did anything half-assed. Everything you did was 110% and more - my little perfectionist.

Thanks. I'm sorry I sold the piano Mom. You worked so hard to get it for me.

Listen, they're all just things, material things that, at the end of the day, don't matter. It's you, your life and heart and mind that matter.

Both of which were completely out of whack.

Well, again, I know that feeling and sometimes we have to let go. If something is no longer in your life, it's important to let it go. "Letting go" isn't your strong suit.

I'm aware of that. Thank you for reminding me.

Sorry. So *how did you find a place?*

Andrea assured me she would find me a good apartment with the money I made from the piano.

Did she?

She did what Andrea would do.

Which is?

She found me exactly what I didn't want, a hole in the wall.

Oh boy.

After I got settled, every day for months I'd go to our old house and park in front of it. I'd watch you come out, walk to the end of the driveway, wave to me and motion for me to come in. Or I'd look for you in the front window, watering the plants or fixing something in the front room. The sound of your voice calling me seemed so close, so real. All I wanted was for us to run errands, watch movies, bicker, laugh, hug or cry.

I'm sorry baby. I'm sorry I wasn't there for you the way you were used to but remember what I told you when we were talking about your travels?

What?

I've never left your side, not once, ever and I won't.

Thank you. Not too long after I got settled Andrea and her girlfriend fell on hard times and needed a place to stay. They asked if they could stay with me. I said no problem. Again, here I am opening my heart and door to help her AND her girlfriend, who by the way, was cheating on her all over the place. I helped her without question or needing to blab the help I was giving her to the rest of your family so they could give me praise, which is what Andrea did. That's why she was pissed I didn't come back to Buffalo with her right away after I got out of the hospital. My going back to school pretty much blew the "I take care of my sister" act out of the water. She wanted everyone to give her praise for "saving" her sister's life. She made me sick when she did that.

Why didn't your sister stay with one of my sister's and why did they need to stay with you in the first place? Wasn't she working?

I don't know Mom. They were working but I guess got evicted for something and needed a place to stay. So, rather than ask one of your sisters, she asked me. It never crossed my mind not to help her. So, you know how neat I am and how completely disorganized and messy Andrea is.

Right.

In my house everything has its place. Andrea had the audacity to complain about my being so neat. She would throw everything all over the house. She made a mess in every room she went too and had no respect for the fact that she was living in MY apartment. I found myself being the same mother hen I was when I was little to my big sister.

Honey, you were kind to your sister and she, without a doubt, should have been more respectful of your space. Neat or not she was lucky you opened your door to her, and her girlfriend given the hell she put you through.

Yeah, right?

You were too much. I never could find anything in our house because you were always putting things away here and there. I couldn't leave a piece of paper on the counter for two seconds without you putting it in a pile. Every piece of paper I had was put into a pile according to the categories you gave them, and I could never remember what they were.

I knew what they were and that's all that mattered. Everything was organized which enabled me to tend to matters, quickly.

What matters?

Our insurance paperwork, bills, me and Cody's financial aid stuff for school, food coupons and miscellaneous documents.

What went under miscellaneous documents?

Unnecessary papers and junk mail Mary J. Crage refused to look at or throw out. I put them in manila folders with labels on them. I tried to make it easy for you.

I see. Thank you.

Sure. Still, it never failed. Every time I would ask you if I could throw something you didn't need out you would bark back, "No. Leave it. I'll get to it when I get to it." Ugh! That response was so frustrating. It's so open ended. The least you could have done was give me a date as to when you would be getting to it. I could have filed it that way.

You're a control freak.

You say this like it's a bad thing. I have a secret. Want me to tell you what it is?

Okay. Do we have to whisper?

Yes. So as to keep the manila folder of "miscellaneous" items manageable I took matters into my own hands and threw the junk mail out without asking you. Ha!

Kristin! How do you know you didn't throw something important out?

I knew what was junk and what wasn't Mom.

You little sneak.

Getting back to Andrea and our living situation. The other thing was that I paid for all the food when Andrea and her girlfriend lived with me.

Did your sister pay some rent?

A little bit.

Good. So how long did your sister stay with you?

It seemed like forever, but it was a few months. I was so glad to get my space back when they found their own place.

You don't know how much I wanted you out of Buffalo Kristin. I really did.

That makes two of us. I didn't want to be there either, but I felt like such a failure Mom. I went to graduate school to better myself and ran full speed into a brick wall. I wanted so much to make you proud and felt like I failed not only you, but myself as well. That was the worst part.

Kristin, you could never fail me.

I wasn't sure what to do or where to go. Nowhere and no one felt safe to me. I thought, "What if I did go to New York and failed, again?" Look who I would have to turn to, my sister, your family? I couldn't bear the thought. Your family didn't remember that I busted my but balancing school, internships and a full-time job. They only commented on the fact that I attempted a suicide. Your sisters and their kids said over and over, "It was bound to happen Kristin".

"It" being the suicide attempt.

What else? The underlying message your family gave me was do what we want, live and believe what we do, and we'll be there for you.

And boy do I know what happens when you don't.

Thank you. I'm not the only one who knows that you become the outcast, the black sheep, the hated one. I think this is truer for the women in our family. The men have always been free to do, be and say as they wish. Even the slightest mishap earned me comments such as "What did you expect going off to a different state on your own like that? We all have dreams but it's time to wake up and live in the real world." Being in their presence without me made me feel like I was choking on the denial and anger they had for their own lives. I felt the weight of their words. The more I was around them the stronger my thoughts of you grew. I mean I was always thinking about you but when I was in Buffalo it was different. It was as though someone shined light on this small portion of my life which I was about to change in a big way.

You were always stronger than all of your family put together. I remembered the look on your face when we had to move back to Buffalo from Syracuse. I knew if I stayed in Buffalo I, too, would watch my dreams fade into the background of my life only to, should have, would have, could have and what if all over myself. Returning to Buffalo was wrong and I knew that. I just didn't know where else to go in my loneliness. I didn't have to go back to Buffalo, or anyplace else for that matter, to find you. We're a part of each other, now and forever. Yes, we had some good times here and there in Buffalo, but it was the place you lost the life you strived so hard to have and never got. It was also the place where we physically separated, and I didn't need to be there. All I wanted to do was make you proud. I needed to do and be more than what I was. Perhaps I needed to go back to Buffalo, even if it was brief, to figure all this out.

That's right baby. It's like you say, sometimes you need to return to the place where the trauma happened, even for a short time, to see what it is you need or don't need or both and you're no quitter.

That's right. I may have moments where I get down, but they pass, and I've never been on medication for depression again.

You see that. Maybe it was the Prozac?

Well, I did learn that one of the side effects was, guess what?

No!

Yup, thoughts of suicide and suicide attempts.

Kristin you could have died!

I know.

You should have sued!

I didn't find this out until years later. I'm not going to lie, some days are harder than others, but I persevere because there wasn't a day in my life where I saw my mother give up or quit on anything - not her children, herself or the hope that her cancer would be cured.

Thank you for seeing that in me.

I know you got down too. Things were sometimes so hard they felt unbearable, yet you kept going. Do you know what an amazing gift you gave me?

What?

Hope. You gave me the gift of hope and while it may waiver from time to time, it is ever present in me since the day I was born.

You are my hope. I know it's hard for you, more so because I'm not physically there to help you through the hard times but you have to keep trying in life, never ever give up on the things or life you want, regardless of what obstacles lay ahead. That hope is what made you make your next decision isn't it?

Yes. I couldn't shake the feeling that I had this whole life ahead of me with so much to see and do.

You did.

It's like I was stumbling around until I could get my bearings, but I finally did. It wasn't more than eight months when one afternoon while hanging out with Sophie I said to her. "Sophie, we're going to try one more time. This time, we're going to New York City." I always wanted to, and I thought, "What do I have to lose? I traveled Europe by myself and made it home just fine. I can do New York City." I thought, "If I fail, I fail. At least I'll fail on my terms."

That's my girl.

Kieran made the move from the South to New York City. He encouraged me to come down so that meant I wouldn't be alone. Ethan and I continued to talk. He, too, still wanted me to come to New York. He said the offer to stay with his parents was still on the table. So, I thought, "Why not?" I assured him I would pay room and board as well as food and would only need two months. Unfortunately, since I was staying with Ethan's parents that meant I, once again, would have to leave Sophie with Andrea. This part made my heart sink, again. I hated having to leave her, but I knew if I didn't go, we'd never have a life away from the family and that's all I wanted. I killed me to do it, but being without any other option, I asked Andrea to watch Sophie, one more time and didn't care if she had a problem with it. At least she wasn't in a house filled with drug addicts this time.

No one else in the family offered to help with Sophie?

Right, Mom. Like that was really going to happen.

Right. Sorry.

At least with Andrea I knew Sophie would be loved and it was temporary. She tried to give me a guilt trip I had no qualms about reminding her of the nightmare she put me through in Keene and that I was the sole caretaker of Sophie. Yes, by choice but still, I bought her food, paid for any doctor bills and gave her all the love and care in the world. I never asked my brother or sister for a dime for anything. I had no guilt whatsoever about asking my sister to watch Sophie one last time and it was, the last time.

Good for you that you stood your ground. Your sister wasn't too happy I'm sure.

I didn't care. As I was beginning my young womanhood, I was also beginning to understand you more as a woman and some of the decisions you needed to make in your life, which were always for the good of your children.

Like what?

Your travels to Hawaii and India. I know it was hard for you to leave us and especially me on my 16th Birthday but now I was getting it. You had to. You were trying to bring healing, light, love and positive energy into your life and what better gifts to give your family.

Thank you honey. I always hoped you would understand and forgive me for leaving you on your special day. I think it's true that as we grow older and have to make certain decisions for the good of ourselves and our families, we begin to understand our parents more as people.

You're right and there is nothing to forgive Mom. I'm glad you got to travel. I'm so proud that you didn't let anyone stop you, not even your sisters.

Me too. So, your sister watched Sophie and you were on your way.

Yup. I brought my car from New Hampshire to Buffalo so I could easily drive down.

I have to say when you do things it's all or nothing. How did the family react to your spur of the moment decision?

You know, as the years went by, I noticed they had these rituals.

What rituals?

They would get together, whether it was family dinners or some other gathering and gossip as one big collective group. Then, they would separate and call each other on the same topics and gossip individually. I was the recipient of some of those calls which included more comments regarding my departure such as, "When are you going learn you can't always get what you want or have the life you want?" "Just stop all this fuss, get married, have kids like your cousins and be happy." They were made with such distaste you'd think that leaving Buffalo was a crime. I let them say what they wanted. I wasn't going to let them stop me. All I thought about was what you taught me, which was to live my life to the fullest, to never let anyone stop me from doing what I wanted to do, and to strive for what I wanted in life and not settle. I can't believe they were stupid enough to think I'd listen to them over you.

Me too but that's just because they wanted you to be miserable like they were. They said similar things to me while we were in Syracuse, and the pressure and level of guilt to come back to Buffalo was there.

I remember. The thing is I really wasn't sure what I was doing. I only knew I couldn't live in the cage I felt like I was being shoved into. Buffalo wasn't my home. You and my siblings were all born and lived there. I was born in Maryland, raised in Syracuse and spent a couple of years in Buffalo during high school. I never liked it there. I just wanted a better life for me and Sophie. There was nothing wrong with that. I so needed and missed your support. I knew you'd stand by me.

You bet I would have. I loved their last comment.

Oh yes, "Just stop all this fuss, get married, have kids like your cousins and be happy." Now there was something to look forward to because most of my cousins were divorced, in dysfunctional relationships and still relying on their parents for emotional and financial support in their 30's and 40's. Your sisters were no better. I wanted to dance again, like I used too. I weighed all of this against my fear of failure and dove into the unknown!

NEW YORK CITY

1995 – 1998

I am my mother's daughter,
a child having grown into a woman whose
strength and fierce determination have been passed to me -
soul to spirit and blood and bones.
I reach for the arms that once engulfed me,
if only to be reminded, one more time, that perseverance and love
are tenets to live by throughout years to come.

When I was small, I stood at the bottom of a mountain
looking up at the climb of my life.
I began the journey so many lifetimes ago.
There were days my legs cramped with a pain so unbearable
I didn't think another step were possible.

There were moments of blood
as my hands dug deep into the soil to keep me
from slipping into the blackness of the abyss
and losing a life I knew was mine.

It was she that taught me to lick my wounds clean and heal my
soul amidst the gushing winds of life that dance betwixt and
between my sun-drenched mornings and moon-lit nights.

I once dreamt that I reached the plateau of the mountain.
I looked down to see all that I was,
feel all that I am and dream of all that I hope to become.

A dove flew to my shoulder,
her eyes filled with wisdom, love and longing.
She understood me as no one else had.
Together we stood on the mountain's top,

breathing deep, feeling courageous and knowing –
I've got time to feel the earthy colors of fall transform into the depth of winter.

I'm my mother's daughter, having grown into a woman.
I've got time to watch spring gardens bloom
and feel the softness of warm summer breezes.

Kristin A. Crage ©1996

I saved $500 and packed whatever I could into my 1980 Ford Mustang and made the 8 ½ hour drive from Buffalo to Yonkers where Ethan's parents lived.

That's a long drive to make by yourself.

You're telling me. Being a smoker helped pass the time. Can you believe I started smoking while I was in grad school? I'll never forget how.

No, I can't believe it. You always hated the smell of smoke. It's very upsetting to me that you even started. It reminds me of my smoking days. Remember those?

Oh yes. You never even looked like a smoker.

What do you mean? What does a smoker look like?

With some people a cigarette looks natural in their hands but not you.

Yeah well not you either.

I still shake my head when I think of the way I started.

How was that?

One night I was studying in my apartment with one of the women from class who just happened to be a smoker. She was smoking Natural American Spirits and said, "You've got to try one of these. They're 'all natural' and not as bad for you as regular commercial cigarettes." Yeah right. I hesitated but was curious, so I tried it. I thought, "One cigarette won't hurt." I was so naïve. Ten years later I was smacking myself on the head over and over going, "Why did I try that cigarette? Why?"

That was your mother smacking you on your head!

Thank you. I appreciate that.

You're welcome. That's what I'm here for.

Quitting smoking is hard. It's a relaxing habit. It's almost Zen like the way you breathe in and out with a repetition that carries the ability to calm your nerves.

I don't think so. There's nothing Zen like about inhaling harmful toxins such as nicotine which causes cancer.

So does stress, caffeine and white bread. What else is new? Let's get back to my car. Wasn't it a classic?

I don't want to talk about your car. I'm still upset you were a smoker.

What a great car.

Kristin! Don't ignore me when I'm talking to you.

Even without its power steering it was still a beauty, and it's not possible to ignore you. You're still as loud as ever, even from the other side!

Ha ha and funny funny SMOKER!

Alright Mom. I'm sorry I smoked. It's been years since I quit, and I won't be smoking again.

Your darn right you won't. How was living with Ethan's parents?

They were terrific. They helped me a lot just by letting me stay there. Don't worry, I was respectful of their home and rules.

I know you were.

New York was massive to me. I took the express bus into the city which ran down 5th Avenue. Coming back, it ran all the way up Madison Avenue. One thing I quickly learned about the city is this - if you walk west, you're on the west side of the city. If you walk east, you're on the east side of the city, pretty simple right?

Not if you're unaware of how big the city is which I'm sure most tourists aren't.

Exactly. Paris is similar with its east and west banks. You think you can go here on the east bank or there on the west bank until you start walking and realize how long you've been walking and the size of the city, you're walking in. For the first few months I looked like a tourist in New York City. I got lost all the time and took the subways in all the wrong directions. I had to ask for directions all the time. Thank goodness people were always nice and patient. One thing about New Yorkers, we know how big this city is to those unfamiliar to it and will go out of our way to help you get to your destination safely and in the quickest time possible. I've seen an entire subway car help a family of tourists get to where they had to go. It was touching. I think I cried.

I found New Yorkers to be helpful every time I visited there too.

The world finally opened up for me Mom. Anything and everything felt possible from my dreams to my fantasies to anything I could think of. "It" whatever "it" was felt like it could happen in New York City.

You had that same excitement when I took you all those years before. New York City, just the words alone made you giddy. What is it exactly about the city that makes you so happy?

I just really needed the time to be completely and totally carefree and I was. My only responsibility was going to work and making as much money as possible to get Sophie as fast as possible. That was all I thought about and that was enough. The city is so alive and there's so much culture. There's so much to see and do that if you live here all your life, you still won't have seen nor done everything. I love the everyday city life such as the coffee shops, corner falafel stands, the parks, and people watching. People walk so fast and I've wondered, "Why do we all walk so fast?"

Good question. Why do New Yorkers walk so fast?

We cram a lot into one day and the day still never seems to be long enough. In Keene, if I got home at 5:30 or 6:00pm that felt late. Now, in the city, that's early. People have dinner at 9:00 or 10:00pm here and start their evening from there. That's city life and why New York City is known as the "City that never sleeps." New York City and its people are continuously moving and progressing. It's often been said "If you can make it here [New York City] you can make it anywhere." I think it's harder to make it in the smaller towns of rural America.

Why do you say that?

New York City is filled with one opportunity after another. Whether it be work, or for those out of work, a plethora of organizations from government services to community and privately-run charities, New York has it all to help you if you fall down on your luck. In addition, we have the best public transportation in the country. No matter what time it is the subways always have people on them and not just a few but a lot of them. The 4, 5 and 6 trains known as the Lexington lines are always full. It's amazing. I've often found it odd when people tell me they live in the city and have a car. You pay an exorbitant amount in parking, particularly parking garages for those that live in Manhattan, and the insurance is outrageous!

This is true.

It didn't take long for me to get my bearings. Getting Sophie back with me was my incentive. Within the first week I found a job as a receptionist on 23rd Street and Broadway. Of course, I would have rather been dancing in an off or on Broadway play, but the receptionist gig was fine. I kept telling myself it was only temporary. I reminded myself of what you used to say to me. "If you work hard enough, you'll get what you want." That's all I did was work hard and within two months I saved enough money to get a one-bedroom apartment for $650.00/month on 46th Street in Astoria, Queens. I was two blocks away from the N and R trains. It took me 20 minutes to get to work. I loved it. It was the easiest commute ever.

You did all that in such a short time? Wow, you really were motivated.

Yes, I was. You were the same way when you needed or wanted to be.

Sometimes.

I thanked Ethan's parents for being so kind to me, dashed back up to Buffalo to get Sophie and headed back down to Queens, NY for us to begin this next chapter in our lives. I couldn't wait to be reunited with my best friend!

How did Sophie handle city life? She must have been shell shocked?

It was a change. In New Hampshire we had a huge yard, took long walks in the forests and lived a quiet, peaceful life. Now, we were surrounded by the sounds of car horns, ambulance and fire truck sirens, and screaming voices due to the paper-thin walls in our very small railroad apartment. Sophie wasn't the only one that needed to get used to being in such a big city.

Well that's understandable. You were in a new city and feeling like a fish out of water. What's a railroad apartment?

Railroad apartments are where the rooms are all in a straight line, one after the other. Not to mention that not too long after I got to Queens the transmission on my classic baby died. I was so upset. I didn't have the money to fix it, so I sold it, very, very cheaply to the mechanic that was working on it. I'll bet it would have been worth a fortune had I kept it. No more long car rides in the country or anywhere else for me and Sophie.

Little Sophie must have missed her car rides. She loved them when we had my car too but the fact that it broke down when you got to Queens sounds like fate. As you said, car insurance is outrageous.

I guess it was all for the best. It was stressful to think of how I was going to afford car insurance and sometimes I would have to drive several blocks from my apartment just to find a parking space. So, I said goodbye to the last tie, aside from my student loans, to New Hampshire and sent my car on her way, hopefully to a better place.

I was so young and wide eyed.

Yes, you were baby!

Yeah. I obtained a bank account and started my journey of writing and bouncing checks like it was a normal thing. Thank goodness I was in the overdraft protection program which covered me if I should bounce a check.

Kristin. That's not like you at all.

I know. This was another part of my life that was really weird for me, and you're right, very unlike me. I was always so careful with your money.

Yeah, you always had my checkbook completely balanced.

Every time I wrote a check, I'd get nervous, my hands would shake and then the numbers would get all blurred. I kept inverting my numbers. 59 became 95, 46 became 64 and so on. At first, I laughed about it but then, the more it kept happening even when I tried not to, the more concerned I got. Then, after bouncing so many checks, my bank called me and dropped me from the overdraft protection program. I was mortified. Who gets dropped from their overdraft program?

Honey, you just needed to calm down and remember that you can do anything you set your mind too.

That's what I kept telling myself. I finally did some self-talk every time I wrote my checks and doubled checked them to make sure the amounts were correct. I mean I had to really focus every time I wrote a check. At first it was annoying but then I got better at it and eventually stopped bouncing my checks. That's what I mean when I say it's weird that after years of being so responsible and taking care of you that I would do that isn't it? I was always so responsible. I was really flabbergasted by the whole thing. Mom? Do you have anything you want to add here Mom because I think you do.

One thing at a time, okay?

Oh brother, again with the one thing at a time.

Did you and Kieran spend time together while you were in the city?

Not too much. I enjoyed being in the city, but I wasn't a bar/club person. Being the social butterfly that he is, he made a lot of friends.

How about Ethan? How were things there?

We were okay. We made the stupid mistake of giving our relationship one more try. I say stupid because it was. All we did is what we did before, argue.

Why didn't you guys just stay friends?

I guess because there was the temptation for us to try and rekindle things. For a while I forgot what it was that drew me to Ethan, until I saw him and remembered.

What was it?

In the beginning, I felt safe. He was gentle and genuine in every way. I feared closeness with most men but not Ethan. He saw all of me and loved me just the same. That's what made me love him so much despite all our ups and downs.

One day soon someone else will see all of you just the way Ethan did and love you just the same, more.

Maybe, I don't know. I'm older now and more stuck in my ways.

Or, maybe someone will come along, and you'll feel such a connection with that person that you won't remember the ways you're stuck. They call that love.

Maybe.

You and Ethan did the right thing. I've known many couples to stay together for all the wrong reasons and before you know it a huge chunk of their lives is gone, and they find themselves stuck in the same old miserable rut. As painful as my separation was with Dad, it was better we didn't stay together, for the sake of you kids. You three had seen enough. Like you and Ethan, we wanted different things, believed different things and didn't feel the love we had when we first met. I often wondered if it was ever truly there in the first place. There was a lot of pressure for men and women to fit into the roles that were carved out for us back then. I think if you convince yourself long enough, you'll squeeze yourself into any role, even if you don't fit, but that doesn't last long. Pretty soon you find yourself trying to break free from the cage, like I did.

That's how I felt.

It's like we talked about. Sometimes you need to revisit certain people and places, a few times maybe, in order to realize if they're right for you. Or, at the very least how they were wrong for you. Some people spend years with someone or in a place feeling miserable and stuck.

Don't I know it.

Babe, you're not miserable and you're not stuck.

I feel like I am, both.

I know but honey, you're not. You truly aren't and please don't let the circumstances of your life make you feel that way.

This, of course, is coming from the woman who moved her entire family to be in a city she didn't want to be in near a family she had more peace living away from.

Okay, you got me there. I just…

I know Mom. You don't want me to feel like you did; like your back was against a wall.

Yes.

Too late because I've already been in that place but I'm a fighter, like you.

I know you are babe.

At the time, I still couldn't get passed the darkness I felt from your crossing over.

You needed to give yourself time, be gentler with yourself. You're such a driven person that you forget you need to slow down sometimes and let yourself process what's present in you. Remember Corfu and how you felt there.

I tried but the city is so fast. I wished you were with me. You would have loved it. I know you would have. You would have made so many friends, gone to all these support groups, shopped for everything under the sun because everything was within walking distance from my apartment. Most of all, you would have had access to the best cancer hospitals in the country.

You know how much I loved New York City. I was thrilled you even got there. I remember when you used to tell me you were going to take me there to live and take care of me. So, tell me, since you didn't like the bars/clubs what other kinds of things did you do?

I took dance classes on 46th Street and Broadway. I continued drumming and I also contacted school to try and finish my degree.

Good! How did that go?

Not good. They reneged and told me I had to do the entire program over again. It was only a year later. I completed 54 of a 65-credit program. The last credits were a class and my thesis which I was working on.

No, Kristin. You're kidding me?

No. I tried to get work as a counselor but because I didn't have my degree I couldn't. I continued to call them to get them to honor their assurance that I could finish, and still do but I get stonewalled every time.

Oh honey. Those bastards.

Yeah, all that work for fucking nothing. The thing is, had they not told me I could finish later I would have sucked it up and stayed. I would have never thrown my degree away like that. They said I could take the break I needed so I did. I get sick and angry when I think about it so, I don't want to talk about it anymore if you don't mind. At least not right now.

Honey, are you sure?

Yeah, anyway…

I love you Kristin. You're a good person honey and a hard worker who bears the weight of the world on her shoulders.

Yup.

Come here. Let those tears fall babe. I'm here.

So, what were we talking about? Oh yeah, what else I did as a New Yorker? I had late night dinners with co-workers. I strolled the east and west villages, went to hear some jazz and saw dance concerts. Sometimes Kieran and I would get together and go to dinner. We didn't work too far from each other, so we had lunch here and there. We also went to Jones beach a few times. If we went all the way to the end of the beach there was a place there, I could sunbathe topless. I loved it!

You sunbathed topless?

I did. Ever since I sunbathed topless in Europe, I got hooked on it. I even went in the water without a top. How about that!

Well, do I dare say my little minute was loosening up?

Hey, I can let go when I want to. I felt so uninhibited when I was topless. I liked that feeling.

I guess so.

My body was tight and muscular from dance. I never even owned a bra until my thirties. Dancing made my whole-body firm and strong. There was no need for a bra. What was I going to put in it?

That's true. From the time you were little you had a dancer's body, so fit and trim. In addition to your dance you loved to exercise too so that made you double fit and trim. You were so young when you started to do sit ups, pushups and use weights. I was impressed by that. I always wanted a body like yours. You took after your father's side of the family, tiny and lean. I had the "Territo body".

Do I dare ask what the "Territo body" is?

Plump.

You had a beautiful body Mom, hence all the women and men who followed it.

This is true. Thank you!

No problem. Let's see, what else? I took Sophie to the nearest park from our apartment all the time. It wasn't that big, but she enjoyed it. In the summer I'd take her to Central Park via the subway.

Sophie went on the subway! I didn't know they let dogs on the subway. How was she?

Yup, the little Sophers went on the subway. They didn't actually "let" dogs on the subway, but they also didn't tell you to get off if they saw them on there. Sophie was great. I couldn't believe it. She was really calm. I took her everywhere I could. Sometimes it was Washington Square Park in the summer so she could frolic in the water fountain that sits right in the center. Other times I would take her walking through the east and west villages. You know what great a personality she had. I mean she was a whiner, but she got along with everyone, people, dogs, cats...

Except kids. Sophie didn't like kids too much.

That's right, except kids but we didn't spend time with any kids so that was okay. I know Sophie missed the country, but I think she liked the excitement of the city too, for a little while anyway. As long as Sophie and I were together we were both calm. I wished I could have taken her to work with me. It would have made my day much more bearable. I did not like the corporate world, at all. In fact, I hated it. I still can't, until this day, believe that I even had to have a desk job. I always envisioned myself doing something artistic, not sitting at a desk all day.

I know, another reality we didn't get too.

Oh my gosh and I so wish we did because in my mind, things were supposed to work out if I worked hard. Here I was working hard but I didn't have direction. I wanted to dance yet I didn't know if I wanted to be a full-time dancer because of the travel, you know. So, I just took an office job to pay the bills.

Like many, if not all, artists do.

Right but I wasn't supposed to be in it for so long. At least I didn't think I would be. I didn't like the way people spoke to me, like I was an idiot or a slave. I never took it and always stood up for myself as well as others if I saw someone being mistreated, which happens all the time in the corporate world.

I'm glad you did. What did you do?

Why do you ask?

When I was working, degrading or condescending women was part of the workday. I had a number of experiences where I was sexually harassed. My gut reaction would be to walk out but I couldn't. I had three children to feed and a shit ex-husband and my male bosses knew that. They took advantage of my being a single mother as was common practice for most women during the 70's and 80's. It was hard to work with the inappropriate, demeaning behavior of grown men who wouldn't conduct themselves in a respectful and professional manner toward women, but I stood up for myself. The Women's Movement was still so new so there were no laws that protected women back then like they do now. If you were sexually harassed in the 70's and 80's you either had to take it and smile pretty or leave your job or you would lose your job. Our town was small and there were only so many jobs. I always felt if I'm going to smile pretty it's going to be because I feel the smile from the inside out.

That's right.

When I would stand up for myself, my boss would make my job very difficult by finding fault with everything I did, speaking to me or yelling at me like a was a child in front of others, even customers, giving me grueling workloads and asking me to do things he knew I couldn't right from the start.

Like what?

Like staying late knowing I had kids to get home too. "She's not going to let me fuck with her so she's outta here!" That kind of thing.

Fucker!

When I told him, I couldn't stay he told me he needed someone that could and I, inevitably, lost my job. All because I stood up to him although that's not the reason, he gave me. He needed someone to stay late, of course.

Of course.

Spencer used to tell me to just keep my mouth shut but I couldn't. I kept my mouth shut about too many things for too many years. I didn't know what was worse, the consequence of job loss by saying something or the consequence of loss of self-esteem by not saying something. I wanted to teach you girls to always stand up for yourselves, have self-respect and never let a man intimidate or dominate you, not even in the workplace.

That's awful and scary, especially because you had us kids to worry about.

That's right.

If I could have seen into my future, I would have asked you to teach me one other thing.

What's that?

That standing up for yourself, more times often than not, would mean standing alone.

I'm sorry baby. I should have. Sometimes my idealistic way of thinking left out the realistic details my children would need to know about the realities of life, love and the workplace.

I was learning this, one painful lesson after another. The laws that are supposed to protect women are just words. Without hard evidence nothing can be done if a woman has been violated, sexually harassed and/or mistreated in the workplace. Employers, especially male employers, manipulate and lie their way out of situations to ensure there is no evidence. Some just blatantly disregard the law and somehow or another, get away with their inappropriate actions. Thus, women still get sexually harassed, coerced, bullied and discriminated against in some very ugly ways. Some might argue that because women hold higher positions, we're treated better; given more respect. I wouldn't.

For me, when I found myself mistreated by a higher up, I would privately speak to that person and respectfully request that he not treat me in the disrespectful manner. What I also learned is that even when you respectfully approach your higher up about the mistreatment, there still could be negative consequences. The fact that you're calling your higher up on their actions, which they feel entitled to, is a no-no. From that point on, you're a target, their target and their goal are to get you, the "troublemaker," out.

It can be a no-win situation.

It can be but I'm a strong woman whose tolerance for bullshit is zero and one that doesn't back down, ever. The loss of a job is a huge risk, but I'd rather lose a job than self-respect and let some weak, chauvinist corporate fuck diminish my self-esteem. No way.

I'm proud of you. You are a force to reckon with little girl.

I am who I am Mom. I don't try to be this way. I AM this way and it doesn't go over well in the corporate world. Every corporate job in America has some policy and procedure manual that advocates equal opportunity. They say they don't tolerate sexual harassment or harassment in general in the workplace and encourage you to speak up on such behaviors. Yet the manuals are just words and in place for companies to be politically correct. The reality is if you speak up and/or so much as cause what they view as even the tiniest wave. They'll do what they have to and go to whatever lengths necessary to get you out and that is the ugly reality. Hence the reason I hopped from one job to another. This is where I would think of you and the situations you were describing earlier.

How do you mean?

I don't know how you did it because I can't swallow how disrespectful, manipulating, cruel, backstabbing and gossipy people are in the workplace. I would think how fortunate I was that I didn't have children. If I had to change jobs it wasn't too detrimental for me. I mean money would be tight, but it was just Sophie and me. I thought, "What if I had human children?" and "How did my mother handle being mistreated on the job and leave with no money or have to stay because of lack of money." Like you said, your male bosses knew your vulnerability, which was your children, and used that to their advantage.

They did and not just me but my other female co-workers as well. Sometimes I felt like someone tied my hands behind my back and I was being pinned against a wall. It was an awful, helpless feeling and clashed with the independent, feminist I was striving to become. Not a good feeling at all.

I love you Mom. Thank you for all that you sacrificed for us.

You're welcome but I sacrificed nothing. I gave willingly and freely to the three beautiful children I chose to bring into this world.

The corporate world is a hell on earth and nothing like the spiritual world you raised me in or the artist world I came from.

I'll bet. I was shocked you ended up there too. There are some places I could see you in, even if temporarily. The corporate world is not one of them.

No, you're right, but I needed the money to get my apartment. I had every intention on getting out as soon as I could. I danced. I played drums but I didn't really audition as I should have in order to get work as a dancer.

Why not?

I mean I love to dance, wanted to dance and went on a few auditions here and there but the process of auditioning and then the toll traveling takes on you when you're in a company is tough. I knew that from the company I was in in college. I liked being in a company but the traveling that goes along with it wasn't for me. I don't like to travel or be uprooted in anyway. When I got home from Europe, I was so happy to not be traveling anymore. I'm a homebody. That's where my heart is and where I feel happiest. Most importantly, I had my little girl and my motto was, "If Sophie can't come, I'm not going."

Yeah, but not all the companies require you to travel do they?

All the ones where you make a living do. The local companies were better but there wasn't much pay there, if at all, so I still would have had to keep my day job. I wanted to perform but I also liked choreographing. For the time being I had to be content taking classes until I could figure out what I wanted to do as a career. College was great because all I had to do was take class, dance and hold a menial job. I was used to that life, the simple life. If I could have lived that way for a long time I would have.

Yes, but how would you afford your rent, maybe buy a house, take a vacation, all that stuff?

I know.

Oh, the realities of adulthood.

I know. All I wanted to do was hang out, relax, enjoy life and have no agenda for a little while.

Me too except I had these three little people that kept calling me "Mom." What a buzz kill.

That is a buzz kill. Really, I thought I had time to figure things out.

Honey, many people make the mistake of thinking they have time and why not? We don't know what the future has planned for us. We can only live in the moment. I have to say you were at least living in the moment as opposed to the future which is what you had to do when I was there. We always had to plan for this doctor or hospital visit or that support group meeting and on and on. You were finally living in the moment and that's good.

I guess but at least, with you, I had direction. I could anticipate this or that because I knew what my days were going to be like ahead of time. This living in the moment shit wasn't for me. I really needed and wanted to know what I was going to do for the rest of my life, and I felt no calling anywhere. The only calling, loyalty, joy, incentive or direction I had was with you. I literally could not see my future without you. Everything was a blur. I was just floating, waiting for something or someone to say, "Here we go, this way. Your future is over here." It was really uncomfortable for me to not have direction.

Honey listen to me. You were no different than any other graduate. I mean there are some kids that know what they want to do right away but many don't, and they do exactly what you did; float until the direction they feel comfortable and happy in presents itself.

That's what I was hoping. In the meantime, about a year or so of being in Queens I got a call from Cody. He was traveling around and said he wanted to come and visit New York City.

What did you say?

I really didn't want him to, but I thought about you and what you wanted for us kids - to get along and be there for each other. Cody and I talked on the phone once in a great while but it was superficial stuff and the conversations were quick, just the way I wanted them to be. I put up a wall between me and Cody. It went up when I was little, it had to so I could protect myself, and it stayed there.

Honey…

I try Mom. Lord knows I've tried to be a forgiving person but that is one of my shortcomings. I'm not as forgiving as you were or as I'd like to be about those that have hurt me. I try but it's hard and my brother's despicable actions are unforgiveable to me.

I understand and I would feel the same way you do. For the record, forgiving was hard for me too. A part of me thought if I didn't make a big deal of things they would go away. It hurt me that your brother was so angry. It hurt me even more that I couldn't do anything to help his pain or yours.

I know and I understand. I see where things were hard for you, but I also see the places you turned a cheek for the sake of your sanity. Those are the places I got hurt the most.

I didn't want to see what was happening between you two until it was too late. That's my fault. I love you honey. I can't apologize enough for not doing something about the pain your brother was causing you.

I know you did the best you could with the little you had but Cody is someone who doesn't see or accept that what he did was wrong. I've confronted him before, not before this visit but afterward, and he actually denies it ever happened. He'll never change, and I don't deserve his anger and I won't take it either. Even as an adult I felt like I still had to watch what I said, or his anger would surface.

When you're young you're like unset cement. If someone etches their footprint in you, good or bad, the cement hardens, and the footprint stays with you. I lost count how many times people, even you, have told me to let it go. I've learned to let the pain Cody caused me go, until I hear a man raise his voice to a woman, and I cringe inside. Or if I know a woman is being abused. My gut instinct is to get her out of that situation, save her and show her she does have choices, that she's not a victim and worth a good life that doesn't include being emotionally or physically abused.

The way you've saved yourself.

Yes. It was hard for me. "It" being, the fear of the, "Oh no here comes the rage," feeling got to be too much to carry.

I understand.

Do you remember when we lived in Cobblestone Apartments in Syracuse?

Yes, what about it?

Remember how I sometimes got scared in the middle of the night?

Yes. Sometimes?

Okay, a lot. Remember how you and I shared the double bed, but you often slept on the couch because I had all my animals in the bed too.

Oh my gosh. You and those stuffed animals.

I always told you that you could have moved them.

Honey, after a long day with three children and no husband I had no energy to move 25 stuffed animals.

Sorry about that.

Yeah sure! That's okay. What made you think of this?

I remember several times when Cody's rage was so unbearable for you, you'd either go into the bedroom and cry or sit in the closet you, me and Andrea shared. That was also hard to see Mom. We never knew what was going to set him off. You not only turned the other cheek on me but on yourself as well. I was glad when you sent him to live with Carolyn.

You're right. Honey?

Yeah?

I turned other cheek because I couldn't face the fact that my son was picking up the same abusive patterns as my ex-husband and taking things even further and...

Molesting me Mom.

Oh God, when you say that word my spirit feels like it's falling off a cliff. Yes, molesting you. So as to not have to see my son for the monster he was becoming, what I'd remember were the times when you were real little, before you could even walk, he was so protective of you. I would set you in his arms and he would get this big smile on his face, laugh and giggle and say, "baby, baby." He held you like you were glass and kissed you. You were his baby sister. And every once in a great while you two had these tender older brother/younger sister moments that made my heart melt. I would think to myself, "Look at them. How bad can things really be?" Your father and I used to have tender moments as well, but we still argued, viciously. It's possible to have moments of closeness with someone that's also hurting you. You want to make everything okay. You forgive again and again hoping things will get better…

Yes, but for me they didn't, and I was too young to remember those tender older brother/younger sister moments. I remember everything else; the ugliness. The only time I felt bad about Cody going to live with Carolyn is when he came back. That's the truth Mom. I mean I felt bad that you were hurting because he was gone but only to a certain extent. I was torn between guilt because you were hurting and relief because I no longer had to live in fear. You don't know how good it felt to come home knowing I had nothing and no one to be afraid of and I wouldn't be hit. That's freedom.

I know. I often felt the same way with Dad. As your brother got older, he just didn't know how to harness and creatively express his anger and rage. What are you thinking about?

Those times, what we went through.

Some of them were tough, tougher than others. On a happier note it's good to know your stuffed animals had the double bed to themselves.

Does someone resent my furry friends?

Who me? Noooooo.

That was funny.

So, getting back to your brother's visit, how did it go?

We hadn't seen each other in a while and anytime we were around each other there was this uncomfortable tension between us. I wanted to resolve the pain he caused me on my own because he wasn't willing to acknowledge how he hurt me. Like I said, I didn't want him to stay with me for even one second. The thought of him anywhere near me made me cringe but no one knew the things he did to me. I thought, what would Andrea or your family, for that matter, think of me if I turned my own brother away? I wasn't about to tell them the truth. Firstly, it was none of their business. Secondly, I knew no one would believe me and third I felt and still do feel disgusted by what he did to me. I truly do.

I can't even imagine sweetheart. It must be so hard to reconcile that pain and then to be around him out of fear and guilt of being ostracized by your own family. That must have been excruciating.

It was. What was more excruciating was that he actually ended up staying with me for a couple of months, which was unbearable. I felt like a kid again, walking on eggshells, trying to make sure not to upset him and it was my home for Christ sakes!

Oh boy. This is where you did what I used to do - not say anything in order to "keep the peace."

Exactly and I couldn't take it, at all.

How did that happen that he stayed so long?

He was traveling around, and he needed a place to stay. He had nowhere else to go. Every day he was there I wanted to crawl out of my skin.

Honey, can I ask you something without you getting upset?

Yes?

How were you able to let him stay with you for a couple of months, or even a couple of days for that matter, with all that he did to you, particularly the molestation? And please don't take that as my questioning any of the horrible things he did to you because I'm not. I just need to understand…

No, that's a good question and I'm not upset. I used a technique I'd been using all my life.

What technique?

I pretended the abuse happened to someone else. I had to. I learned it's not uncommon for abuse survivors to stay in contact with their abusers if there is a connection that keeps them connected. For me, it was your family and my sister. I stuffed all those hurt feelings, the horrible memories down - way down. I compartmentalized it all and, in a way, the abuse did happen to someone else - another Kristin A. Crage who looks exactly like me. Has lived the exact same life as me in the exact same places as me. Only, that Kristin was never abused. She could live her life looking like a free person but inside, bound by pain, constantly fighting off horrible memories of abuse.

Oh god Kristin. You must have felt like you were suffocating.

Killing the best part of me is more like it but I fought that feeling. I didn't want to let him win, ever. I worked hard to keep whatever in me is good so that I'd never become like him, evil because that's what he is.

And I'm sure it would have been too painful to try and talk with him again about any of the things from the past?

No way! Why would I do that if he denied it the other times, I brought it up?

Right, I know.

He wasn't interested in working anything out from our past. He couldn't.

What do you mean?

Cody brought some baggage with him in the form of a heroin addiction. I found his stash around the third month he was staying with me and told him, flat out, that shit will not be in my home. It's time for you to go. With that, he left.

Please tell me he stopped using.

I don't know and I don't care how long he kept using. I have no empathy for him. My feeling was, "How dare you disrespect me by bringing that shit into my home when all I've done is help you out after all the bullshit you caused me you, lousy fuck." Users like Cody and your sister with her alcohol and pill popping don't care about anyone but themselves. They try to get others to feel sorry for them with their excuses of drinking and drugging by saying, "I went through this and I went through that and…" blah, blah, blah. Your sister drinks and Cody were or still is (who knows about that one) a drug addict because they're weak and can't handle their shit, that's why. You went through a terrible marriage, hardships with your shit son, a nine-year battle with breast cancer and never succumbed to addiction. Cody and Louisa are good at manipulating people, but they ultimately bring trouble to themselves and the people around them. I wasn't going to let that happen to me.

I understand why you feel that way but then again, everyone deals with their hardships in their own way, even if that way is destructive.

True but Cody and Louisa were assholes prior to their addictions. Their addictions just made them that much meaner and more destructive. I wanted to keep them and anyone like them as far away from me as possible. Your family thinks of no one but themselves. Selfishness, self-centeredness and indifference are family traits that I never could accept and one of the many reasons I disliked being around them. I didn't care if Cody destroyed himself. That was my home and I wasn't going to allow him to disrespect me or the positive energy I put into what little I had.

You're right. I felt the same as you did. You always have a choice. I begged my sister to get help and always told her she was choosing to be an alcoholic. I tried to help her see she had more power over her feelings of sadness and whatever else than she exercised. She gave in to her depression which led to her drinking and pill popping because of all that was going on in her life, like your father.

Yeah, no wonder they got along.

Between the two of them they sure could put away a lot of liquor.

I believe it.

I'm glad your brother didn't stay long. If he hadn't changed and wasn't willing to even make amends then, you're right, his leaving was for the better for you. I want you to remember a positive male person that was in your life. A man I introduced to you specifically so you could see that not all men were abusive or would leave.

Aaron!

You got it.

I didn't even have to think twice about that one.

No, you didn't and look at that big smile on your face.

For someone who preferred women you certainly had some very strong feelings for Aaron and him for you. I could tell by the way he looked at you. He treated you like a Queen. What was he to you, if you don't mind me asking?

We enjoyed each other's company. Whenever he came to town on his business trips, we'd have dinner and talk for hours.

I think you two had something much stronger than dinner and conversation Mom.

I loved him. Aaron was a good man and a good friend to me. He was kind to me and my daughter. He made me feel like a beautiful, strong woman.

You were a beautiful, strong woman, always, even when you were down.

Thank you but sometimes it's nice to feel that way with someone other than you daughter. Catch my drift.

Yeah. I liked him because he was good to you. Whenever you two were together, you were smiling, both of you. Anyone that made you happy made me happy. Was there ever anything more to you two than friendship?

We gave each other the warmth we needed and weren't getting at the time. How's that for an answer?

Is that a yes or a no?

That's a "none of your business."

Okay, I get it. I feel silly now, you know.

No, I don't know. What do you mean?

Well, when he would come to town, I used to ask you to let me come with you when you guys went for dinner. I should have let you two be alone. I'm sorry. I really liked Aaron and just wanted to be around you when you were happy, and Aaron made you happy. It was a nice change of pace.

Honey don't feel bad. If you recall sometimes, I told you no. I thought it would be good for you to be around Aaron. He was a special man. He liked it when I brought you with me on our visits.

He did?

Sure. He said you were more mature than your age and asked such interesting and deep questions for a teenager. I remember in one of our phone conversations I told him you were taking photography in school and loving it. Do you remember what he gave you the next time you saw him?

He gave me a manual single lens reflex 35mm camera which I love and still use until this day. I was so taken back, ecstatic, and honored he gave me such a special gift. When I take it around, people ask me, "Is that a real 35mm camera?" I tell them yes and they say, "That's a classic."

Having mainly women in my life I wanted you to know that not all men would exhibit anger and/or violence. That's why I say, he was good to my daughter who needed some goodness in her life too.

I definitely got that from Aaron. He was as gentle as could be. Aaron reiterated the things you taught me about men but wasn't quite seeing yet; to never allow a man to hurt me, to always make sure a man treated me with gentleness, respect, love, affection, warmth and kindness. That's how he was with you.

He was a real gentleman. You see. I'm glad to know you got all this from him.

I don't know if I ever said thank you for allowing me to spend time with you and Aaron but if I didn't, thank you.

You did say thank you, but you don't have to. We were glad to have you with us. I knew you needed to see a different side of men. So, did your sister ever come to see you while you were in Queens?

Once, with her girlfriend but, again, anytime we saw each other it was me that rented a car and traveled with Sophie to see her. I felt like our sisterhood was one way. I was making the effort and Andrea was on the recipient end.

I used to feel like that too sometimes with my sisters. How many times did I pack all you kids in the car to go to Buffalo when we lived in Syracuse versus the number of times my sisters came with their kids? It was more for us, right?

Yeah, that's for sure.

People are like that honey. Sometimes you give more than you take. The important thing is to keep on giving to those that are kind and grateful. How did the visit go?

We bickered about everything Mom, from my move to New York, to the jobs I held and on and on. That never changed. Andrea had her own control issues too, via guilt trips, which I never fell for.

Did you pick on her for anything?

I used to get on her about not saving money for a rainy day and to stop getting on me. We couldn't even enjoy each other's company without arguing. Our relationship was exhausting.

Did you two have any fun?

We did. We went to the farmer's market, walked around the village and talked about the family - who was doing what and getting married to whom that kind of stuff. The truth is we weren't as close as others thought us to be, as Andrea led others to believe.

I know. Even when you were little you girls fought constantly. I hoped as the years passed and you got older you would stop bickering, but the bickering turned into arguing. You two remained at each other's throats.

I felt that since Andrea was the only sister, I had that I should let things go to, again, "keep the peace." Yet little instances where I found myself saying, "Oh she didn't mean to do this," or "She didn't mean to say that" were starting to add up in my head and heart. My relationship with my siblings was always strained. I liked living far from them.

That was very hard for me. I wished my kids would be close since you were all each other had.

No Mom, no. For years I felt like I'd be better off without them. I only stayed in contact with them because I know how much you wanted us too, but they were way too destructive, selfish, indifferent and irresponsible amongst a number of other things.

Had I not been sick and able to stay I would have never let you kids hurt each other as you have. I don't mean to blame myself. I only mean to say that my sisters and I had our mother as do your cousins. When a mother loves her children as much as I love you kids and physical separation happens, that makes a difference in the lives of siblings especially since you three were still so young. All three of you were in the midst of this terrible angst and I couldn't talk to you, help you or hold you. For years I was sick and tired. Then after all that I crossed over. My illness and physical absence made a painful and permanent difference in the lives of my children. One that cost them more than I ever thought it would.

It's not your fault Mom.

I want to see you move through the molasses of heartbreak you're in Kristin, for your sake. It blocks your road to forgiveness. I love you.

I love you too.

Where were we?

Cody going back to the west coast.

Okay, are you okay?

Yes. Are you?

Always. I love that we talk like this.

Me too. After Cody left it was Kieran's turn. He just broke up with his boyfriend and needed a place to stay so I offered him to stay with me. He and his cat, Sam (Sammy), moved in.

That was nice of you. Boy, everyone was coming to you.

Yeah, as unstable as I felt inside, I was still stable on the outside, taking care of bills, working hard and all that.

I know. That part of you has never wavered.

And it won't either. Not if I can help it. Filing bankruptcy was an eye opener for me. It taught me to never financially deplete myself again. I was living my life on my terms and I wanted it to stay that way. The thought of depending on anyone for anything scares me. I took great pains to not let myself get into such a vulnerable position.

Is that because of what I went through with Dad?

Yes, and not having money in general put you in a constant state of vulnerability that was unfair to you. I particularly didn't like the way you had to beg for money from Dad and the long cries you had when he didn't pay, which was all the time. It made me sad for you and one of the reasons I was so angry at him. What was unfortunate about that is that we had to rely on the kindness of strangers. Thankfully you met a lot of wonderful people but if they couldn't help and you had to ask your family for help. It was more bullshit you had to go through. If they said yes it was preceded by them making you feel bad about yourself by reminding you of decisions, you made in your life they disagreed with.

Such as traveling.

That and the herbs you bought or the healing alternatives you tried or whatever. I was so angry at them for making you feel so bad about yourself when they had so little to feel good about. Your sisters and their children never had to worry about money. They always had spousal support and could never relate to the day-to-day financial struggles you had, ever.

This is true. I'm sorry you saw me go through so much.

It's fine. I'm fine about it. I'm sorry you had to go through so much.

You're not fine about it but you will be.

I don't know why you have so much faith in me especially when I feel that, if I haven't already, I'll let you down.

Why do you say that?

I don't know. I didn't turn out to be anything special and I really wanted to be, for you.

Kristin, your special to me and you can't let me down baby. You can let yourself down but not me and certainly not God. My hope is that one day soon, you see just how truly special you are. Tell me more about living with Kieran. You two must have had so much fun.

Sometimes, yes.

What do you mean?

Kieran put himself out there more than I did. I liked having the option of going to the village or seeing live jazz but after my first year in New York I rarely did anything unless Kieran invited me someplace, which wasn't often. He had his own group of friends and because he rarely invited me out with him, I got the feeling he didn't want me hanging around him. I was trying to find a space and place in my life where I fit in and I couldn't. I felt like an outcast everywhere I went and I'm not pushy. If I'm not invited someplace, I don't ask, you know?

No, I do, and you shouldn't have too. Why do you think Kieran didn't invite you out?

Maybe he just wanted his own friends apart from me and that's okay. I was happy to hang out with him here and there. He didn't feel the same. Sometimes he would tell me, "You need to get your own friends." That really hurt because I thought he was my friend, you know. I opened my home to him after he broke up with his boyfriend. For him to say that was un-necessary. I know I'm not the most outgoing person. I felt like I could accept my outgoing friend, but my outgoing friend wasn't very accepting of me.

Right.

I was a good sister to Andrea, but I didn't get that same effort back. I didn't like the pattern that I saw playing out in my life. Anyway, I was more content at home with my little girl. Kieran and I had a few good moments here and there

Like what?

We used to get really high then spend an hour laughing our faces off as we tried to record an "out" message for the answering machine.

Now that I would have loved to see.

Oh my gosh. You would have been laughing with us. The second we'd push the "play" button we'd start laughing hysterically. Or, the first night he moved in. It was around 12:30 a.m. after we got all his stuff in and he said, "Let's get a cup of coffee and go sit by the water in Battery Park."

How exciting and spur of the moment.

It was. The best part was the two of us sharing this fun, sentimental moment and all of a sudden, a police boat whizzes by. Just as a joke Kieran yelled out, "What are you guys looking for dead bodies?" The cop yelled back, "Yeah. Let us know if you see anything suspicious." We looked at each other and high tailed it out of the park. It was really funny. I don't know if the cop was serious or not, but it didn't matter. We were out.

How funny. I'll bet he was serious.

Probably. Lord only knows how many bodies are dumped in the Hudson River. Then there was the night we decided to go for Bagels, again, it must have been around 1 a.m. or so. He introduced me to H&H Bagels in the village. This is one of New York City's best bagel places. When you get the bagels fresh like we did, they're soft, warm and the creamy melted butter makes it mmm, mmm heaven!

How sweet. I'm surprised you stayed up that late. You've always gone to bed early and been an early riser.

I'm still that way. I make an exception every now and again. We also saw Mickey Hart of the Grateful Dead at the Hammerstein Ballroom in the village. That was a lot of fun. We danced, laughed and had a great time. Sophie and his cat Sammy were funny together too.

Funny how?

Well, by this time the little Sophers was getting older. She was 14 years old. All she wanted to do was relax. Kieran's little guy was young and all he wanted to do was play. Sometimes he would hide behind a wall and as soon as he heard Sophie coming, he would jump out and scare the bageebees out of her. Sophie's stunned face was hilarious. Then she would look at me as if to say, "When is he leaving?" Other times Sammy would sit next to Sophie's bowl and stare at her while she ate. He was such an antagonist. They actually loved each other but Sammy did have a way of annoying my little Sophie.

Poor Sophie. Did she ever do anything?

No, you know Sophie. She was so easy going she just let him do his thing and she did hers. They were entertainment for Kieran and me that's for sure.

Sophie and Sammy, Queens, NY, 1994

How cute they are.

Aren't they funny there? See how Sammy sits over Sophie. He just antagonized her.

I see. I'm sorry you guys weren't as close as you hoped but it sounds like you had some good times.

Yeah, we did, here and there. All those times were spread over a number of years, but I try to remember those more than anything else.

That's right. Is that a tear in the arm of your couch in that picture?

Yes, it's a tear in the arm of my couch. It was free. Someone from work gave it to me so I took it until I could afford to buy a new one. Hence the tapestry cover.

You made sure it was covered if someone came over, didn't you? Because it doesn't look like it's covered well.

The cover came off a little bit but yes. It was normally fully covered.

Good. You have some papers lying around there too. You picked those up, didn't you?

Yes Mother, I picked the papers up.

Just checking. You're right. You can see Sophie's age in that picture.

I know. I should have seen how tired she was getting. I mean I saw it, but I didn't want to, you know.

Yes.

I have another funny memory of Kieran and me.

Oh yeah, let's hear it.

After about a year Kieran moved out and into Hell's Kitchen which was around 47th Street and 11th Avenue in the city. Otherwise known as "Hell's Kitchen." One Thanksgiving he invited me for dinner at his new boyfriend's sister's place. I decided to make something simple to bring so I made a Quiche.

Oh, that sounds good.

It sure does. So, while cooking I was also smoking a joint, dancing around the kitchen and being happy with Sophie as I cooked.

Oh boy. I can't wait to hear this.

While I was making the Quiche, I was also preparing a bowl of moist dog food for Sophie for her Thanksgiving dinner. She was coming with me, of course.

Of course.

So, I was preparing the food and...

Oh Kristin, please don't tell me…

I know. I can't believe I'm admitting this but it's just one of those classic memories I have to share. Ready?

Go ahead, share away.

At one point, without realizing it, I accidentally used the same spoon I was using to prepare Sophie's wet food and then….

And then…

I started mixing the Quiche and forgot to change spoons and there was moist dog food all over the spoon!

Oh no! That's something I would do!

I know. I felt awful but I'd put so much work into my Quiche already and I didn't have time to start a new one. So, I...

You didn't…

Baked them, brought them with me and…

Don't tell me…

Served them! Yuck! Hey, everyone loved them. I think it's because I used the moist food as opposed to the dry kibble.

You are a trip. Did you have any?

No, I wasn't really "in the mood for Quiche."

Hmm, I can't imagine why. What was the flavor of Sophie's food?

Chicken, her favorite. Every time someone complimented my Quiche, I gave a humble "Thank you" but it was hard to keep from laughing. I told Kieran years later. He wasn't very happy with me.

I'll bet.

Kieran stayed with me for almost a year and then found a place of his own, I stayed in the city a little while longer before deciding it was time for me and Sophie to make a move to more serene surroundings. I'd had my experience in the city and now it was time to go!

That didn't take long. How long were you in Queens?

Uh, I moved there in 1995 and left in the beginning of 1999 so, four years. I wanted my little girl to be comfortable in her elderly stage of life. Another contributing factor was the mice that infested my apartment.

Oh no! Are you serious?

Yup, they were everywhere, between the radiators, in the closet, my bed you name it. At night I would wake to the sounds of them squeaking in my ear and jump out of my bed. Or they would jump over Sophie and me. No matter how much I cleaned there was mouse poop everywhere. It was so disgusting.

Yuck! How did they get in there in the first place?

The mice have access to all New York apartments under $1,000 per month and I think those over $1,000 as well. For those over $1,000 they have to make arrangements with the owner as to when they can have access and which rooms, they can go in.

Very funny.

It's NYC. Half of NYC's residents are mice! No, there were cracks between the floor and the wall and holes in the closet. I told my Landlord, but they never did anything. Really though, the biggest reason I moved was for Sophie. The hustle and bustle that she'd only known for a short time was taking its toll on her spirits. Being raised in the suburbs, it didn't take too long for me to get tired of city life too. It began to feel claustrophobic to me. One day I was enjoying Queens and the next everything felt so close, too close. Everywhere I went I felt like everything and everyone was on top of me and essentially, that's how it is. The city and its boroughs are built upward and in close proximity to each other. So, we all live and work on top of each other. I wanted and had every intention of going to Vermont or someplace else more serene but...

But?

It seemed like such a big move. With the mice problem I felt the pressure to get out of the apartment fast. Also, I didn't feel finished in New York, not yet. I wanted more space and peaceful surroundings, so I found myself a one-bedroom apartment in Westchester County, not too far from the Bronx.

Well, Westchester is nice isn't it?

Yeah, it is, especially if you go a little further north than me. You're still not too far from the city but you're in the country but it's expensive because of its proximity to the city.

Yeah, I can see that.

Kieran came to my new place and helped me clean and paint the entire apartment. He really helped make it look beautiful.

It is nice here, very homey, like you.

Thanks. It's spacious compared to my Queens apartment. I also like the fact that it has a kitchen and a kitchenette, a big living room and my bathroom has a big tub too. The only drawback is that it's on the third floor and it's a walk-up but it's doable, for now.

Well, it's perfect for a single person like yourself. If you're meant to be in Vermont or any other place, you'll find a way to get there. I know you. You lucked out with your apartment that's for sure.

I did. When I moved in back in 1999 the rent was the same as my apartment in Queens, $650/month. Since its rent stabilized the rent can only go up $20 every two years. Having been here now for 20 years my rent is still $1,000/month while the others around me are going for $1,500-$1,800/month. So, I'm fortunate in that regard.

I can't believe you've been in this apartment so long. That's the longest you've lived anywhere, including Syracuse!

I know.

Was Sophie happy here?

Yeah, she was. Moving from the city to the suburbs was a breath of fresh air for both of us. She had grass, trees, the air is a little thinner and best of all, no mice! It's good.

You see. The move was good.

Yes, but it's not...

I know. It's not the countryside - one day baby, one day.

FOR THE LOVE OF SOPHIE

The first day I met you
it was love at first sight.
I knew we were going to be inseparable, and we were.
We began as little girls.
I couldn't wait to come home from school.
Seeing your face while you watched for me
through the living room window,
as the bus pulled up to the corner of our street
was the highlight of my day.
It all seems like a lifetime ago.
I made sure never to leave you alone too long.
I knew how it felt to be lonely.
I also knew sadness and anger and
was determined to bring us both toward the sun
where laughter and joy reside; and I did!
I love you little girl.
From the earth to the sun and moon and back again.
I love you.
Your friendship, unconditional love and devotion
carried us through one dark spot after another.
Thank you.
You are my sister, friend and child.
Neither of these is no less exalted because you wore fur.
Everything I did, every decision I made was
for the love of you, Sophie.
We began as little girls.
We grew into women, together, always together.

Kristin A. Crage ©1999

It wasn't Vermont or the countryside, but I sure did meet a very special man that distracted me from wanting to be in Vermont.

Finally!

Okay, okay calm yourself there Mary. His name is Devon. I always hoped I'd meet a tall, dark and handsome man and that's exactly what Devon is. He's 6'2, African American and very handsome gentleman born in Brooklyn and raised in the Bronx.

I love him already. How did you two meet?

It seems fate had a hand in this. Although I was living in Westchester I kept working in the city. I also did volunteer work on the weekends for an Animal Welfare Organization doing administrative things like typing up lists of companies that don't test on animals to be mailed out, stuffing hundreds of envelopes, running errands to the post office. That kind of stuff. It was in the west village. Devon was studying to be an actor, taking classes, also in the west village.

An actor? Uh oh.

He was not your stereotypical actor. Devon was one of the most unselfish, caring people I'd ever met.

How sweet that you two met in the west village.

We didn't actually. This is where fate stepped in. We met on our way back from the west village on the bus. I took the express bus from 23rd Street and Madison back to Westchester and one night I saw Devon at the stop. He also took the same bus and sat behind me. I was so tired and, of course, Devon started talking to me. I can't remember what he was talking about. I just remember him talking and talking and finally he said, "Hey do you mind if I sit next to you?" Without waiting for me to answer he sat next to me and continued to talk. He likes to talk which was good because I like to listen. He was sweet and the more he talked the more handsome he was to me. As we neared Westchester, he asked me what my stop was. I told him and he said, "Really? That's my stop." I thought he was joking but in turns out, he wasn't. "Hey," he said, "Do you live in that area?" I told him yes and the street I lived on. Then he said, "Are you serious! I live on that street." Then he asked me what number and he said, "That's where I live!" It turned out we lived in the same building! He lived on the floor above me one apartment over. Can you believe it?

You two were destined to meet. There is no doubt about that?

We were. I know people say never date anyone that lives in the same building as you and I actually feel that way too, but we were opposites attracted. Devon loved to go out and play Pool. Boy did he love Pool. I liked to stay in and hang with Sophie. Devon wasn't much of an animal person, but he said he gained a real appreciation for animals the more time he spent with me. He even liked my vegetarian cooking. More importantly, he was caring and loving toward Sophie which meant the world to me. You know me, if you don't like animals and particularly my animals - it's not going to work.

Oh, that's a given.

It was hard for us to not want to be around each other. I really enjoyed his company.

What did you two do together?

He took me to see the off-Broadway play, Chicago which was awesome! Sometimes we visited with his friends and we had dinner with Kieran and his boyfriend. Or we'd go to the city and hang out anyplace he could play Pool while I relaxed and watched him in action. He was really good.

You sound like you complemented each other well.

We did. Devon was super friendly, polite, easy-going and hard not to like. He was funny, generous, had a warm, inviting spirit and an abundance of patience. I felt blessed having him in my life. He saw my strength, humor, and even found humor in my flaws and accepted me for who I was. Devon was someone that I admired and respected because of his goodness toward others, his inner strength and his ability to remain dignified under any circumstance. Devon was, without a doubt, a man to be admired and respected.

I'm glad. You deserve that and I'm sure you accepted him the same?

That goes without saying. Once, Devon did a scene from the movie, "The Verdict," for me. At first, I was nervous. You know, what if he wasn't very good and so on. I wouldn't tell him that but then I'd have to lie. All these scenarios were running through my head.

That's a hard one. How'd the scene turn out?

I couldn't believe how good he was. Devon's the kind of actor that acted for the love of acting, not because he wanted to see his name in lights or get some aware. When he was in character it was hard to see Devon, which means he was talented, very talented.

Phew!

Yeah. He met Cody, once.

He did. How did that happen?

He was doing some more traveling and asked to visit me. Louisa's son was living in Long Island so I told him he could visit but he had to stay with his cousin because I didn't want him staying with me.

That was a good move.

This was 1999. I wouldn't see or speak to my brother until the incident. That was almost twenty years later.

I know. We're going to talk about that later.

Yeah, we need to. I take things for as long as I can and when enough is enough that's it for me.

You're done.

Exactly. I think he could see it in my face and the boundaries I established that I really didn't want him in my life anymore. I know Devon could. I never told Devon what Cody did to me. I only told him he was violent to me all throughout my childhood and I'd had enough of him, period. Devon actually said that he could see Cody getting angry because, like I said, he never changed. Any little thing he'd get impatient about from traffic to a drawer getting jammed, you name it. He flew off the handle. So, I was more than happy to be done with him. As we've said, sometimes you need to revisit a person or place a few times to close the chapter. In this case, after this visit, Cody didn't call me, and I didn't call him. There was no need and no love on my part to do so. I was actually relieved. Not having him in my life felt like a huge weight lifted off me. I have peace without Cody in my life. I wouldn't change this for anything. Mom?

Yeah honey.

I know you wanted more for us, from us but the struggle to get to a place we couldn't reach was exhausting. I never wanted to have to defend myself against someone I loved and that's what it boiled down to with your son. I didn't deserve what he did to me. Neither did you.

No, you didn't, and you're right. I didn't either. I have a mountain of regrets in how I handled or didn't handle your brother's rage. I was just always concerned that you not be alone. Your brother and sister made friends easier than you but at least, now, you had Devon.

I did. I was in my first relationship in years and enjoying every minute of it. Devon was respectful, caring and protective of me. He did little things for me that meant a lot. He opened doors, or if I was sitting on a sofa whether we were home or out he would prop a pillow behind me to make sure I was comfortable. If we were walking on the sidewalk, he made sure I was walking on the inside and he was on the outside closest to the street to protect me from any harm. I appreciated all the things he did for me.

He sounds sweet. What did you do for him?

I was supportive of anything he did. I cooked for him as often as I could, and you know how much I hate to cook.

I was just going to say, you cook! Wow! Although, you made some things for Mom here and there. I mean we mostly ate boxed or canned stuff, but you found a way to spruce it up.

I did. I tried. Cooking never appealed to me but seeing how happy it made Devon, made me want to cook for him. I felt that way with you too. I just didn't have the energy to make things from scratch, but I tried.

I know you did babe and we ate well and healthy at that.

Yeah, that was important. I wanted to see Devon happy and I liked making him laugh. We both shared a similar dry sense of humor. We had fun. We were light, breezy and at the center of us was Sophie. Devon delighted in caring for her as much as I did and was protective of her. We had this wonderful first year together but soon after, things got bad, real bad.

Sophie, now 16, developed terrible arthritis and her kidneys were failing as well. Sometimes she was in so much pain she'd cry these loud, howling, gut wrenching screams. Other times she would take off running down the street as if she was running from the pain. Our vet prescribed different anti-inflammatories and pain killers while I researched homeopathic remedies, but nothing was working. The medications back then weren't nearly as effective as they are now.

At the same time, I developed severe neck pain, headaches and migraines. When I lived in Queens, I heard a little popping in my neck from time to time but never felt any pain. I didn't make anything of it or more accurately, I would tell myself, "I'm okay. I'm okay. It's nothing."

You denied it. This is what I was afraid of. It's important to have a good support network in your life in case things go wrong, not just one person. You had no one else but Devon. That wasn't fair to either of you.

I know Mom! Don't you think I know that! I don't need to be reminded of what I didn't have. I just need you to listen, please.

Okay. I'm sorry. I'm sorry honey. I'm listening.

No, I'm sorry. I don't mean to blow up at you. I just didn't know what was happening to my body. I needed you to hold me and tell me everything would be okay, that we'd get through this together. I didn't want Devon to see me the way I was. I wanted him to see me healthy, strong and fit. I told myself, "It's nothing" until the pain became so bad it took over my body and way of being. It truly destroyed the best part of me. I could barely get to my job. The pain was so gripping I could hardly have a conversation. All I wanted to do was hole up in my apartment. I'd never been through anything like this and it was awful. The more time went on the more the pain increased. The pain was so intense it felt like hands were wrapped around my neck and all I wanted to do was scream, cry and beg God to let me die just so I wouldn't feel the pain. I know it sounds dramatic but that's how it felt. Words don't scratch the surface of what I was going through. I'd rather die than have to feel that kind of pain again. It changed me and not for the better. I felt like one day I was healthy, strong, dancing and exercising. Sophie was her happy, healthy self and the next thing I know we're in the midst of a nightmare. One morning I woke up and couldn't get my head off the pillow or move my neck. My neck muscles went into a state of atrophy and didn't want to work. I literally had to put my hand behind my head to lift my neck off the pillow. I freaked and out of fear and panic started to hyperventilate. I couldn't breathe. I didn't know what to do. I was so scared.

The pain affected every area of my life including my relationship. I wanted Devon and I to be light and free as we were in the beginning but there was this heavy energy around me and Sophie. The pain made it hard for me to be around. I don't deny that. Everything, including simple conversations, took so much effort and exhausted me. Physical pain really puts a downer on your personality.

I understand babe. I really do

I know you do which made it all the more difficult that you weren't here. I missed you so much that it hurt. This physical change that set upon my spine shifted me 360° the other direction. I lost my sense of humor. I was miserable, irritable and short tempered. I didn't think I was going to go through something like this after I spent most of my life dancing. I thought I was going to be healthy and strong the rest of my life. I thought I'd been through the worst in my life with cancer and your crossing over. As delusional as this might sound, I thought I was going to have smooth sailings for the rest of my life.

It's not being delusional. It's being hopeful. I felt that way too many times in my life.

When?

Oh goodness, when my father died, when your father left, with you kids, after I was diagnosed. After each one of these instances I thought, "God, you gave me enough. I can't take anymore. I'm at my limit," and then another thing would hit me. I felt like as soon as I got up from being knocked down, I got knocked down again, and again, and again.

That's exactly how I was feeling. Sophie and I went back and forth to doctors having tests done, trying this medication, that medication. I had spinal injections in my neck, MRIs', CAT scans, x-rays, and electrophysiologic testing. That's where they put these tiny needles in the affected area that send impulses to each nerve to see if there was nerve damage in the extremities (arms or legs). I also tried physical therapy, but it didn't help. The pain got worse. I was unable sit up for long periods of time which made sitting at a desk hard to do.

Oh my gosh Kristin, and you were just starting something good in your life.

I know and it was so short lived.

Did you have nerve damage in your neck?

No, thank God.

How did you work and get around and all that?

I just did it. I had to. I had rent to pay, bills and my little girl needed caring for. My pain took a back seat to Sophie. You know I never took any pills, but the pain was like a sharp knife cutting me from the inside. It was unbearable and I needed something to stop it right away. I vacillated between Motrin, Norflex, Relafen, Naprosyn, (anti-inflammatories) and Flexeril and Cyclobenzaprine (muscle relaxers) and finally alternating Percocet's with Oxycodone (pain killers). Those medications each came with their own set of fun side effects such as mood swings, irritability and general agitation not to mention addiction. I was quick to temper as soon as the pills wore off and aware of it, so I'd have to take another one right away to nip the pain in the butt before it got bad. I tried so hard to control the mood swings but sometimes I wasn't able to. If I didn't take my pill in time the pain kicked in. I'd lose it at the slightest thing such as forgetting something at the grocery store or dropping something. I would get upset with Devon over little things and we, absolutely, weren't having fun anymore. Part of the reason I was so miserable wasn't just the pain and the side effects of the meds but the fact that I needed the pills because the pain was so intense. It wasn't something that yoga, exercises or homeopathic remedies would help. I couldn't believe I was taking pain pills at all. I steered clear from having to take any medicine since you crossed over. I felt like I was in a twilight zone episode. At the time, I was still a smoker which didn't help and please, please don't lecture me. I know I should have never started smoking in the first place.

Honey, I'm listening. I'm not saying a thing. I know how hard it is to quit smoking.

The less I could dance or exercise the more I smoked. I went from being a healthy, artistic and fitness-oriented person to someone that counted the minutes to when she could take her next pain pill. The worst part was the not knowing. Finally, after months of testing and seeing three different doctors I received my diagnosis.

Inter-County Imaging
955 Yonkers Avenue
Yonkers, New York 10704

"Date:	May 10, 1999
Patient:	Kristin A. Crage
Examination:	MRI of the Cervical Spine
Conclusion:	Central herniation without compressing the cord or nerve roots at C4-5. Straightening of the curvature of the spine suggestive of muscle spasm."[12]

****

You had a herniated disc in your neck of all places.

Which explained the headaches and migraines I was getting, and it wasn't like the slipped disc in my back that slipped to where it needed to and then stopped causing me that nagging pain. This slipped disc went to a place that was unbearable. I was blown away by this diagnosis but at least I had a better understanding of what was happening to me. Thankfully I didn't have any nerve damage, but it was a double-edged sword. Since there was no nerve damage, I was being told the same thing by different doctors, "You just have to live with the pain. There's nothing more you can do." I never accepted such statements when they were made to you and I wasn't going to accept them being made to me, mostly because the pain was unbearable. The rest of my body was compensating for the pain and loss of range of motion in my neck. My erect, perfectly center aligned, dancer posture changed into constantly shrugged, tense shoulders and curving or "hunching over" of my spine when I sat or stood. The slightest bump anywhere to my body caused an immediate radiation of pain to my neck making it stiff and tender. I could barely turn my neck from side to side. It was hard to sleep and even harder to wake up. Daily activities such as lifting a plate or reaching for a cup in the cupboard were challenging because I couldn't lift my neck to see what I was doing, and the constant muscle spasm caused weakness to my arms which made them shake whenever I exerted them. I just couldn't believe this was happening to me Mom. I really couldn't. No one should have to live like this if something can be done about it. When you know your body like I know my body and you feel something is "off" go with what you know and don't let anyone tell you otherwise.

That's right.

I knew there had to be a solution somewhere and I was going to find it. Unfortunately, the solution, whatever that was, had to be put on hold. At the time, I couldn't focus on me. Sophie was dealing with a similar routine of x-rays and taking anti-inflammatories. I was also working full time in the city too. I kept on with the anti-inflammatories and pain meds for as long as I could.

Oh babe, you're right. No one should have to live with that kind of pain. I certainly never would. You had a lot going on.

I did but I was more concerned for Sophie. When I would take her out, I'd have to hold her back legs up because she couldn't walk on her own. My neighbors would comment that they went through the same thing with their elderly dog intimating the end of her life, but I disregarded their comments with a polite smile. If my neck was in too much pain Devon would carry Sophie up and down the steps. He was so sweet and gentle with her. Between the pain I was feeling and Sophie there was tension between us. He tried to prepare me for the inevitable with Sophie, but I had a hard time accepting it. This made us argue more, so much so that one night we had a fight and stopped speaking for a little while.

You pushed him away. You really had those blinders on tight when it came to little Sophie.

I didn't mean to. They became a coping mechanism to yet another painful situation I wasn't ready to confront. Sophie and I had been together since I was 11. I was now 29. I wanted more time with her. She was my touchstone and the last connection to you and the life we had together. When I looked at Sophia, I saw what I wanted and needed to see in that moment. She didn't look old anymore, but as young as the day we first met. There was nothing in me that was prepared to let go of Sophie.

I know honey. Talk to me more about your experience with Sophie.

I wrote a lot of it down.

Why don't you do both. Read me what you wrote and talk to me. I think it'll help, a lot.

In the months to follow I watched my little girl struggle, but still didn't see what was staring me in the eye. I couldn't help Sophie as she lingered somewhere between our lives and her physical deterioration and transition to the other side. I'd never been in this place before; one where I was struggling so hard with issues of morality and "right" and "wrong." If this was someone else and it was me on the outside looking in, as was the case with Devon, I'd say, "Yes, definitely, it's time to end your companion's suffering." However, I was the one on the inside and I couldn't see my life without my dog. The pain and loneliness I knew I'd feel was too much to bear. I thought, "If Sophie is meant to cross over, she will," like you did. I didn't want the decision left in my hands. I didn't know what to do with it.

The problem was Sophia didn't cross over. Instead, she became more sickly, tired and despondent. She couldn't defecate without my holding her up and walking became increasingly painful, almost impossible for her. Sometimes in the middle of the night Sophia would let out these long howls. I didn't know from what, pain maybe? I wasn't sure. In those moments I would hold her but that didn't seem to help. My body cringed at the thought of her being in any kind of pain. Unable to walk without my help she couldn't get to her wee wee pads so sometimes she would urinate on herself in bed. Every morning I bathed Sophia in a tub of warm water to wipe clean the urine on her body from the night before. Many times, I whispered in her soft, fragile ears. "It's okay Sophie.

We'll be alright, I promise. We're going to make it through this one." My timing, however, was off and Sophia remained frail as ever. The medicine had outlived its use. Devon was right. Sophia's body was rapidly shutting down. Still, I prayed night after night for the natural process of crossing over to occur. Yet Sophia remained my devoted, loyal and loving friend. She wasn't letting go and neither was I. One could definitely say I was being selfish. On the other hand, I'm a person who merely loved her friend and family and neither of us knew how to say goodbye. In that love rest my sadness of a life to be lived without the companionship of my dog that had been with me since childhood.

I continued to have hope and faith in the natural process of life and death and waited for that process to occur. It didn't. The life in Sophia's eyes faded. Her energy and fervor turned to listlessness. There were moments when Sophia didn't know who I was, where she was or what was happening to her. She was miserable, tired, sick and struggling with all-consuming frustration.

The delusion of Sophia recovering faded in the form of empty pill bottles and lost hope which acted as a mirror held to my face. I saw the truth of me and Sophie. We began as two little girls. We grew into women together, always together. Sophie was my lifelong friend. I couldn't bear to see her in pain. This is to say that now the blinders were off, and I could finally, for the sake of my friend, see.

She heard you all the times you begged her not to leave. She listened and she left this part of the journey in your hands. She had to honey.

Sometimes even the obvious gets lost in the oblivion. The unselfishness of Sophia's nature and the selfishness of mine brought me to my knees.

Sophia passed her breaking point and I couldn't bear to let her go any further. There was no cure and there were no more medicines to give. There was no more time to borrow, no more arguments or bargains to wage. There was nothing left to do, nothing left to say. My love, my selfish love was not saving Sophie from anything. At the end of the day, I was only prolonging her suffering. I always said I would do everything I could to not let Sophie suffer when the time came. While it's easier to say to someone else, "Don't let your friend suffer." The decision to euthanize is a gut wrenching one and it felt impossible for me to bring myself to. My fear of living without her was clouding my ability to do the right and humane thing. Even as it stared me clear as day right in the face. I had to make a decision, for Sophia.

One fateful night I awoke to the sounds of Sophia's frightful screams combined with howling that reverberated throughout our apartment. I jumped out of bed in a panic. I rushed over to her, carried her into the bathroom, carefully placed her in a tub of warm water and gently wiped the urine from her body. I glided the warm washcloth over her face and spoke to her in a weakened voice.

"Please help me Sophia. You and I have never been in this place before. What do you want me to do Sophie? I'll do anything. If you want me to let you pass from this world on your own, I will. If you want me to help you, I will. I love you my little friend. You've been the best friend and family I could have ever asked for. Please don't stay for me because I can't bear to see you in this pain anymore. I'm here for you. I'm not going anywhere. It's always been just you and me. We've been here for each other, always. All the days you'd wait for me in the window as I got off the school bus. I couldn't wait to see you. Our walks and talks in the woods, all the beautiful time we spent together is our cherished, unbreakable bond. My love will go wherever you go. Thank you for being the best part of my life. Talk to me little girl, I'm listening. Tell me what you need me to do. I'll give you the world."

Sophia laid her head on my shoulder. Her belly tightened up from her soft whimpering and moans. Then, she moved her head back, the most sudden move she made in months and her whimpering stopped. She laid her forehead against mine. There we sat, forehead to forehead and soul-to-soul as the minutes went by. We gave each other support. We listened to each other breathe.

She nudged her head alongside my face and I, in the weakest moment of my life and having relinquished all control, finally heard the voice of my friend. For the love of Sophie, I knew what I had to do. I spoke to her from the deepest part of me.

"Sophie, I'm not taking your life, but giving it back to you. You deserve to run and not be in pain. Thank you for helping me figure things out. Thank you for not being angry if I took too long. You are my best friend. Don't forget me Sophie because I'm never going to forget you. Wherever you go, that's where I'll be, always."

Andrea already knew Sophie was sick and she let Cody know. Finally coming to terms with the journey Sophie and I needed to take. I called Andrea to let her know that I was helping Sophie to cross over.

Did either of them offer to help you through this?

Andrea offered but I told her I had things under control.

Why? No, wait, I know why.

Yeah, I wasn't up for the arguing, which is pretty much what her visit would have mounted to. We still weren't talking but I called Devon anyway to see if he wanted to say goodbye to Sophie. He was eager to come down. I didn't ask him to be with me on our journey and he didn't offer, not out of spite or anything negative. Saying goodbye to Sophie was difficult for him too. He'd grown attached to her quickly. Sophie was easy to love. Instead, I called Kieran and he came to be with Sophie and me.

On the way there Sophie shivered and urinated in my shaking arms. She knew what was about to happen. While I'd already made arrangements with our vet we arrived late and he'd already gone home for the evening, knowing we were coming. I was devastated but nothing was going to be as devastating as what we were about to experience. I had to have the emergency vet help us through the journey. I couldn't very well put Sophie through one more day of her agony because of some piece of shit vet.

I held her tight as she lay whimpering in the blankets, I bundled her in. Kieran asked if I wanted him to go in the room with us. He seemed relieved when I thanked him and said no.

This was something Sophie and I had to do together, always together. I cradled my little girl's tiny body in my arms. Neither of us could wait any longer. It was time.

In one last unforgettable moment Sophia took every ounce of strength she had to lift her head and give me one kiss to my face. She nestled her head against mine. Her eyes were heavy and weak yet looked soulful. I could see heaven in them. I knew then there was nothing more that could be done that would make this experience any easier. We knew how much we loved each other and would miss each other.

I hated this moment, this day, this room, this town, this state and my life with every breath.

I know you did honey.

From the corner of Sophia's eye, a tear formed and gently fell to my wrist. Then, another tear fell.

"It's okay, Sophie." I assured her as I sheltered her in my arms. "I'm right here. Don't be afraid little girl. I'm right here."

I kissed the tears from Sophia's face and rest my lips on her nose while the first injection entered her bloodstream. Her eyes slowly closed as she breathed into me. Her body relinquished its weight into mine as my face remained pressed against her fur. I wanted her to know that I was with her every moment of her journey wherever she was going.

Then it was time for the second injection; the one that would gently stop her heart. I watched the green fluid rush through the I.V. drip. My arms trembled with fear and my body broke out into a massive sweat. In an instant, Sophia took one breath and just like that, her body froze in my arms, immediately becoming hard just like yours did when you crossed. In that life altering moment I felt everything in me that was once alive, died. I couldn't breathe. I was overcome with panic and began to hyperventilate as I felt myself slowly come apart from the core of my being. Once again, I felt my heart being squeezed until the pain seeped through my chest. My lips were still pressed against Sophia. Our tears mingled into one. I whispered to my lifelong, irreplaceable, cherished friend, "Run Sophie, run to Mommy. I'm with you. Can you see me? I'm right here little girl. I'm right here for you, always." It was June 11, 1999. Mom! Oh my gosh, Mom! I love her so much. I love my little girl so much! You don't know what letting go to Sophie did to me. I had everything I needed with you and now with Sophie. The second I felt her spirit leave her body I felt hollowed out. Oh my gosh Mom! Mom! I had nothing without you both, nothing.

No baby, you had you. You just couldn't see it then. Let it out. I've got you.

My body was overcome with the vibrations of my palpitating heart. The realization that Sophia would never breathe again sent me into an uncontrollable state of fresh grief piling ever so high on top of the grief I held for you. I was slammed by a torrential down pour of tears. Until that moment, Sophia's crossing was merely a thought. Now it was real.

I sat with Sophie and watched her bodily fluids empty themselves. Death is peaceful and gruesome within moments of each other. The air became thick from the scent of death. I needed more time with my friend; a lot more. I wanted to vomit my decision and the injections that came with it. I wanted Sophia back. I wanted my life as it was with Sophia back.

There I sat, shivering, crying as I held sixteen years of my life with my most cherished friend. As I held Sophie my mind traveled back, way back, just after her second birthday. That was the day Sophia, still a baby herself was in heat and got impregnated by your friend's dog. You couldn't keep all the babies and we, sadly, had to give them away. I could only imagine how difficult Sophia's separation from her children must have been. I could tell because Sophia looked for her babies all over the house for weeks afterward. Had it been up to me, I would have kept them and raised them all. I remembered the one baby girl. She was the smallest of all her children, the last to be born and the one pup who didn't make it. The two looked exactly the same. I thought about the nights Sophia and I stayed up trying to get those little ones to nurse. Sophia, in the prime of her youth, didn't have the patience to nurse her babies yet she'd still play with them. She was so cute the way she'd flip and lick them, play chase and run with them and stick her nose up their butts. They were a beautiful family.

I moved a few years beyond and remembered the times Sophia would be staring out our living room window waiting for me to return from school. I'd run home because I was so happy to see her, always. She, in return, would greet me at the door with an abundance of energy. Every day on my way home from school I looked for Sophia in the window. I looked forward to her excitement and love and came to depend on it.

"There are a lot of things I'm not going to be able to do without you, Sophia." I said to her. "The first is separating you from my arms in this very moment."

Sophia made me feel like I wasn't alone in the world through her presence and years of consistent love and friendship.

I didn't know who I was without you and now her. You and Sophie's crossing over, turned my world upside down and inside out.

I continued to talk to her. "I'm still here Sophia. Can you see me?" I whispered to her. "Can still feel my arms wrapped around you?"

Hours went by until the vet informed me, they were closing. He carefully eased Sophie from my arms and prepared her for cremation. Mom, the pain of leaving Sophie was as deep as it was to leave you. Kieran took me home. I needed to be alone, with Sophie. I felt a vulnerability and weakness come over me that was unbearable.

I fell to my knees, releasing pain and anguish in the form of belted screams that were primal, deep and roaring from the bottom of my gut. I laid in Sophie's bed crying inconsolably for her, you and the life I no longer had as you and Sophie's family. I realized there would be no more whining or moaning, no more urine to wipe clean, no holding Sophia up, no more holding her in my arms and smelling her fur. There would be no more sunrises and sunsets for us to watch, no more walks together, no more Sophie and Kristin, Kristin and Sophie. That's how everyone knew us. I was now alone and still had no clue how to say goodbye to my friend. My sense of direction and way of being in the world was up for grabs. I was despondent and unbelievably lonely without my friend and family with whom I identified myself with practically my whole life. The gap Sophia's crossing over left in me was as big as my love for her. The river that streamed from my swollen eyes was bottomless. My heart had been hollowed out. Life lasts such a long time and crossing over, takes a millimeter of a second for it to happen and is so final. Perhaps this is why I agonized over the decision to send her to you and God.

I felt lost without you and Sophie. I didn't know what to do. I knew what I was looking at with Sophie but acknowledging my physical separation with her would have meant acknowledging the same with you. I felt the Universe was asking too much of me.

Sometimes it's hard to see the things that are before us when we know how much pain they're going to bring us.

The very next morning after Sophie crossed, I felt the same way as I did when you crossed. I wanted the day to be nothing more than a nightmare. I wanted Sophie to come running toward me to play and go for a walk. I wanted you to send me for more cookies. Do you know how long I still wished and looked for your letters at school? Or, every time the phone rang, I prayed it was you? I don't make friends easily. I've always been much better with animals than people so where does that leave me?

Someplace between you and God. Sophie's okay honey, we both are. She's with me. She loves you and knows you will never forget her and she's never going to forget you. One day you two will be reunited, we all will. You captured your experience with Sophie beautifully and so vivid. Your writing, my sweet angel, is going to take you to the other side of your anger - where love resides.

Sophia Loren Crage
(6/28/83 - 6/11/99)

MONTE

1999

Little man, little man.
No one knew more than me
What it feels like to have your home taken from you,
your life turned upside down, inside out
and everything become unfamiliar.
You were sad but I knew that together, we could change that.
And guess what? We did.
Welcome Home Monte.

Kristin A. Crage ©1999

All I did after Sophie crossed was go to work and come home and cry. I was so lonely without her. I missed my Sophie like you wouldn't believe. I felt like I couldn't remember my life prior to Sophie we'd been together so long.

Honey, your whole life was wrapped up in me and Sophie. Like you said, every decision you made centered around what was best for her and before that, me. It was time for you to focus on you.

I should have but I couldn't. I just couldn't Mom. That wasn't my style, and it still isn't. I feel selfish when I don't have an animal companion to care for. I'd never been without an animal companion, ever. We always had a dog for as long as I can remember.

I know it. I saw how happy a dog made you kids, especially you. It was easy for me to have a dog in the house. When you were little they were like your little sisters and you were always so nurturing toward them. I didn't have to do anything.

I felt afraid and completely vulnerable without an animal companion in my life. My apartment held an eerie silence that I couldn't get used to. I'm a caretaker. I need to take care of something or someone. That's my thing and I'm good at it. Devon and I reconciled but I could tell the loss of Sophie affected him too.

I'm sure. She was a good girl. She loves you honey, and that love will always be with you. I know you dreamt of her often.

I did. I missed her so much it hurt. I cried every day for Sophie. In one dream I was unhappy and couldn't figure out why. Then I realized it was because Sophie wasn't with me. She was staying with someone and wanted me to come and get her. I could feel the longing between the two of us. I ran to tell Devon that if I could get Sophia and bring her back home then I would be happy. I realized the person she was staying with was God and that she would never be coming home. I woke up crying.

I had another dream that I went to sleep with Sophie in my arms. We were in Grandma's old apartment. I looked up for a second and when I looked back down Sophie was gone, but I could still feel her presence. Yet I was afraid to be alone. The fear forced me to get up and check the front door to make sure it was locked.

It wasn't but the chain was on. I remained afraid and wanted Sophia. I woke up crying, again. In another dream, we were living in the apartment above Carolyn. There's a Catholic School across the street but in the dream, it was an open field. In the dream Sophie and I were in the field, playing like we used too. She was happy and running free. I was watching her and feeling happy too.

I used to pray and ask Sophie to please somehow let me know she was okay. Then I had a poignant dream of Sophie. She came to my bedside, sat next to me and was wagging her tail. She just looked at me as if to say, "I'm alright. Thank you. I love you." It was like the weight of the world had been lifted from her. Then she went away. I woke up and I was so happy I cried because I could feel she was alright, for sure.

That wasn't a dream sweetheart.

That's what I thought. I told Devon about it and he said the same thing.

You had all these beautiful dreams of Sophie. Some I think held your guilt. Would you say that's true?

I often felt like, and sometimes still feel like I wasn't a good enough mother to her. I regretted the times I left her to travel and then to find a place to live before I brought her back down to New York.

Honey, you needed to do those things and she understood that. She knew you'd come back for her.

How do you know?

I know because your goodbye was never final with her and she felt that.

You know I was still so young myself and trying figure things out. It was hard. I had no sounding board, no one to go to for advice or even argue with. I missed having you tell me what was best or not. Even if I disagreed. At least I had a starting point. I felt like I was winging everything, and I hate that feeling.

I know. You like everything planned out nice and neat.

I really tried to the best parent I could to Sophie. She was my whole world. Every decision I made centered around one question, "Is this going to be the best thing for Sophie?"

Kristin you were a wonderful mother to her. Those aren't just my feelings but Sophie's feelings too. Was I the best parent to you kids?

I think you were the best parent, yes.

Thank you, sweetheart, but I do remember several instances where I lost my cool. You three drove me up the wall! Sometimes I just wanted to throw you kids out of the house, just for the day.

Uh, you did Mom☺.

You see! Parenting, whether your child is an animal or human, is hard. You need a lot of patience and sometimes, depending on the day, you might not have it. Don't beat yourself up Kristin. You kept little Sophie when my sisters told you to give her away and your siblings just didn't have it in them to care for her. That's your strength and devotion as a sister, friend and parent to Sophie. She knows how much she was loved by you. She knows honey. Don't ever doubt that. She was glad you took her with you on all your journeys' together. Some she liked, some she didn't but all she wanted was to be with you, all the time. As long as she had you, she felt safe and secure. Just like you.

Thank you.

You're welcome.

A few months after Sophie passed Kieran asked Devon and I for a favor.

What was that?

Him and his boyfriend were taking a trip and couldn't take Sammy with them. Kieran asked if Devon and I would stay in his apartment for the weekend and watch Sammy.

What did you guys say?

Are you kidding? We rarely got to do anything fun, so we jumped at the chance to spend a weekend smack dab in the middle of the city. Even though I was working in the city I didn't get to enjoy it as I would have liked. Mainly because I wanted to be home for Sophie but it's also hard when you work in the city. I was always too tired because I got home so late.

Yeah, especially since your commute was so long right?

Yeah, I don't live far from the city, but we still have to take a bus and then the subway to get there. It's a hassle and takes a lot longer than if you drive. If I didn't have to take the bus and train,

I'd be there in a half hour. Sometimes it takes me two hours to get into the city because of bus and/or train traffic.

Wow, that's a long time!

I know. This time, however, Devon and I took the express bus. It's a little more expensive but it's faster and shoots you right into the center of the city.

That sounds like fun.

It was fun but as most vacations, even stay-cations go, it started as a fiasco.

What happened?

Kieran gave me a set of his keys before he left. When we arrived at his apartment, I searched through all my bags and as organized as I am, I did something completely out of character.

Let me guess. You left the keys back at your apartment.

Can you even imagine! I was so excited to get out of my apartment for the weekend I left Kieran's set of keys sitting on the kitchen table ready to go. I was so mad. Devon laughed. He knew how upset I was. This is what I mean when I say he saw humor in me. Thank goodness because he brought light to a not so pleasant situation.

To say the least. That's something your mother would do.

I think you've left your keys as well as other items in different places, a few times.

This is true.

Devon was an angel. All he said was, "What do you want me to do?" I apologized and said, "Nothing, this is my mistake. I'll make the trip back and get the keys." I felt horrible because it was the summer and New York City summers can get in the upper 90's sometime to 100° with high humidity. Being in a city with 11 million other people and high humidity can get pretty sticky. There was a bar on the corner. I told Devon I would be as fast as I could and meet him at the bar as soon as I got back. At least they had A/C. When I got back, a few hours later, he was laughing at me, again. I asked him what he was laughing at and he said, "I heard you and so did the rest of the neighborhood." I knew what he was talking about and laughed too.

What did he hear?

Let's just say when I got to the sidewalk, I attempted to murder one of the empty garbage cans on the street.

I didn't know it was possible to murder garbage cans.

Ha, ha, ha. That's one of the things I love about New York City.

That you can murder inanimate objects?

No, that no matter how off the wall you are. People don't stop to make a fuss of you. They just get out of your way and keep going. Some don't even stop their conversations. They just nonchalantly move off the sidewalk you're on or to the other side of the street.

Well you sure are a fun date.

Yeah, I'm a real catch. Still, we ended up having a good time. Kieran had a roof top apartment, so we made meals in the apartment and ate on the roof top which had an amazing view of the City. It was good to be around Sammy again too. He reminded me of all the good times with Sophie.

I'm glad Devon made you laugh at yourself. You needed that.

You're right.

What's wrong sweetheart. Your energy just got heavy.

Talking about Kieran and watching Sammy made me think.

About what?

Nothing, it happened a long time ago.

What? C'mon, tell Mom.

I don' t know. I mean it's in the past, but it does still weigh on me.

I can see that. Whatever it is it'll help to talk about it. C'mon. Don't hold your feelings in.

Something that happened between us.

Who? You and Devon.

No, me and Kieran.

What happened?

It's a sore subject for Kieran and me but it was about a year before Sophie passed. I had to go away one weekend. Darlene was getting married and I had to go back to Buffalo but couldn't take

Sophie with me. I hated leaving her home since she wasn't feeling well but I had to go to the wedding because I was in it. I don't even believe in institutionalized marriage. I especially didn't like having to attend the wedding of someone who I never got along with.

Let me guess. You didn't want to tell her you wouldn't go because of the trouble the family would have caused you?

Exactly, anyway, I asked Kieran to stay with Sophie in my apartment and to not go out as he usually did because she was sick, that she needed someone with her as much as possible. He said he would. When I came back my upstairs neighbor came to my apartment and told me that Sophie had been crying and howling so much, she was going to call the police. She thought Sophie had been abandoned in my apartment. I was so mad. I never said anything to Kieran at the time. It just came to my mind as were talking about the time I watched Sammy, and this wasn't the first. When we lived together and even when Kieran moved out, he used to leave Sammy with me all the time because he traveled for work. I was happy to watch Sammy. I loved him as if he were my own kitty. Still, I couldn't help but think to myself, "Sophie wouldn't howl and cry if Kieran had been there?"

Did you talk to him about it?

I tried. We were on the phone one day and he was talking about some things he needed to buy for his apartment. As the conversation progressed, he asked me which store I preferred, the Pottery barn or Crate and Barrel. I thought, "who gives a shit!" All I was thinking at the moment was him leaving my baby girl. I told him I didn't care about any of that stuff. That I had more important issues on my mind such as the pain I was still dealing with in with my neck. He got upset and a snowball effect happened. All of a sudden, we were yelling at each other about things that happened in the past. One of them was this time I'm talking about now, when he said he watched Sophie, then other things came out too.

What other things?

Just stuff, you know. One of the things I was never totally honest with Kieran about was you.

Me, what about me?

In the last year or two of your life Kieran was gone. He moved to the South for school. While he was down there you crossed over and he never attended your wake, not that I even wanted to attend your wake, but you know what I mean.

Right, you wanted the support.

Exactly and Kieran used the distance as the reason for not coming to visit. Yet he'd travel long distances to see friends, but not to attend the wake of his long-time friend's mother whom I know he loved very much. At the time, I told him it was fine because I was going through so much inner turmoil from your crossing over but truthfully, I was angry with him for not showing up. I wanted to tell him, but Kieran isn't the easiest person to talk to, you know. He gets silent when feelings are uncomfortable for him.

Maybe if you had let him know how you really felt he would have come up?

I don't think so Mom. I wanted him there because he wanted to be there for you and me. Not because I had to ask him to be there. I really missed and needed him. Without you I felt so outnumbered when it came to your family. It would have been nice to have someone in my corner. I never had any qualms about being there for him whenever he needed me and you were always there for him - so kind, loving and embracing toward him. Especially during some of his hardest times. He couldn't possibly know how I felt because he wasn't there. Sometimes you have to get over yourself so you can be supportive to the people you love.

It sounds like he didn't feel strong enough to be there for you and couldn't tell you that.

Let's just say for the who-ha of it you're right but think about this. There were times I didn't think I would be able to help you through some of your rough patches. The point is helping someone you love isn't about what you can or can't handle. When you love someone, and they need your support it shouldn't be an effort to be there for that person and help them through a difficult time(s). It's not the time to take your "stuff" out on them and hurt them in the process by being absent. I don't even remember him sending a card.

I understand what you're saying.

For me, if the shoe were on the other foot, I would have been there for him. Yet he, for whatever reason, couldn't find it in him to be there for me when I needed him most. That was a huge let down.

I won't argue with you there. I would feel the same way.

Mom?

What honey?

I don't think you realize how much your presence affected so many people in nothing but positive ways. Your crossing over was a huge loss for a lot of people. What I'm saying is; I just want you to know how much you were and always will be loved, not just by your children but by all the friends whose lives you let in, touched and helped heal.

I know baby, I know. I was fortunate.

You were. So was I, and still am.

What happened with the argument?

Things came to a head and I asked him if he really came and cared for Sophie while I was away the way I asked him too.

What did he say?

He didn't say anything. He was silent. I was devastated because the only conclusion I could deduce from his silence was that he wasn't there for Sophie as I asked him to be; as I was for Sammy.

Hmm. It sounds like this has really been weighing on you.

It has. I loved and cared for Sammy like he was my baby when he was with me. I hoped Kieran would have done the same. At the time, he was in his party mode and being with his boyfriend. Nothing got in the way of his partying. My sense, from what my neighbor told me, is that he walked, fed her, maybe stayed for a short while and then left to go and be with his friends for the rest of the night. When, in fact, he was supposed to stay with her the whole night and as much as possible when he got home. It was only for a weekend. Sophie was sick and needed someone with her all the time. He hung up and I hung up. We didn't speak for almost ten years.

Honey, I'm sorry. I really am. You were getting sandbagged by unreliable and pretty downright hurtful people (excluding Kieran) and you didn't deserve it. This was just another added thing.

Yeah, exactly. Years later we reconnected and talked about it again. He assured me he was with Sophie, but I didn't then and still don't believe him. What stays in my mind is that if Kieran was there for Sophie as much as I was there for Sammy, she would have had no reason to cry and howl as she did. I mean she had her moments where she would howl but, according to my neighbor, this was all day and all night. Also, it would have been Kieran that told me how Sophia was crying and howling, not my neighbor. You know how loud she was. You couldn't sleep or do anything if she cried or howled like that. I trusted my family with him, and he broke that trust. I've never felt Kieran was honest with himself about what happened and thus, he'll never be honest with me about it. My heart aches at how lonely and frightened my little girl must have been. Another experience comes to mind.

What's that.

One night, when Sophia first showed signs of getting sick, Kieran was over, and we were listening to music. Sophia was lying in the living room. All of a sudden, she started howling and crying. I immediately turned the music down and went over to her. Even with me holding her she kept howling and crying and do you know what Kieran did?

What?

He turned the music back and up; told me I worry too much and tried to get me to dance with him. I mean she was crying at the top of her lungs for crying out loud.

My poor baby Sophie. What did you do?

I turned the music off and said, "I know you hear her crying! What's wrong with you? Sophie is obviously in pain!" I called a cab and took her to the vet right away. I was so upset that he could shut her out like that. I just held my little girl as I waited for the cab to come.

Devon couldn't watch her this particular time.

I can't remember if he was doing something or away. Otherwise he would have. I love Kieran. I do but even before this incident with Sophie, things were changing with us. As we got older, if I opened up about something I was going through, Kieran would actually try and make things my fault.

How?

He would say things like, "What did you do?" or "Are you sure you're not misinterpreting…?" Whereas with him, whenever we'd talk or whatever he disclosed to me I immediately supported and even reminded him not to let whatever experience he was going through to negatively affect him or get him down. I'd then follow that with positive things to say about him. I don't feel like he's given me the same unconditional support over the years. Or the space to feel comfortable enough to talk to him about anything I'm going through, past or present. He either changes the subject or makes the conversation short, mitigating what's important to me. There have been a few times where I've hung up from conversations with Kieran about painful things that happened to me in the past, feeling like I just got slammed with judgment and/or blame with the statements I mentioned before.

Why don't you talk to him about this? Oh, right, you don't feel comfortable.

Exactly and now, it's been so many years. There's no need to rehash this. I just needed to get these feelings out.

I know. I understand.

That's why I say that sometimes I have to work things out on my own and not hash out the past. Particularly if the person that I feel hurt by is unable to acknowledge that.

Honey, what did you need to hear from Kieran?

The truth. "I'm sorry I hurt you and Sophie. I should have stayed with her. You were always there for me and Sammy. You loved Sammy and I know I could always trust him with you." That doesn't seem too hard.

No, but honey, not everyone is like you. When you say you're going to do something you do it. When you say you're going to be there for someone you're there. You are a person of her word and a loyal, trustworthy friend. You have very high principles and standards. I also think you hold people to those same high standards, perhaps too high, and when they don't measure up. You're left disappointed, very disappointed and hurt.

So, what are you saying?

What I'm saying is that people are going to fall short of what you hope for in them and who knows my sweet. I'm sure you've fallen short a few times for people as well.

I understand and I, at the very least, own up to where I fall short if it's pointed out to me. How can I know if someone doesn't tell me, you know?

I know and you did point that out with Kieran. You just didn't get the reaction you were hoping for. What? What'd I say? I said something wrong.

Mom...

I hear you babe. I really do. What I can offer here is that you have to decide if you can accept that he may never be the supportive friend you need. I know that's not what you want to hear but it's the way things are and that's hard. I know, believe me, I know. I've had friends like that. We were still friends but more for dinner and a "light" chat or something. The other thing to do is just take it day by day, let the things of the past go see how things progress, or not, with you two.

Like I said, it's hard for me to let past painful situations go when the person(s) I feel hurt by can't/won't apologize. Unfortunately, most times it leaves me not wanting to have anything to do with that person and rightfully so. Who would?

I agree.

I never forget.

I know.

I mean that's not the case with Kieran. I love him Mom. I really do but, you're right. There's this limitation there. We don't talk the way we did when we were younger. I remember we used to laugh, cry, talk about what was happening in each other's lives and were there for each other. That all changed as we grew into adults. I guess you could say we grew apart. Our conversations are few and far between. When we do speak, it's light and quick.

Friendships change sweetheart. You go through good times and bad times. Not all your friendships will survive the ups and downs. That's what separates the good friends from the not so good ones.

I guess I've never wholeheartedly forgiven him for what happened with Sophie. My animals are my life and that really hurt.

I know. Sounds like there's a few things you haven't wholeheartedly forgiven him for. Perhaps you should start there and like you say, that doesn't necessarily mean you have to be in connection with him to forgive but forgive within you for you. Okay, so now that you've expressed yourself and gotten all these feelings out. Why don't you express what you really feel? What's at the heart of all this.

Oh, and what's that? What do I really feel?

That you miss him. You miss your friend and the friendship you two shared.

I do. I miss the friend I had in him.

I know.

I think the person I'm having the hardest time forgiving is me.

You? For what?

For not taking Sophie with me and for leaving her, yet again. I have this mountain of regret for the times I had to leave my little girl. I really do Mom. I feel like in those times I was the selfish one and that's on me.

Honey, you were doing the best that you could.

I can honestly say I really was doing just that. The thing is I had no one else to watch her at the time and with that, I should have taken her with me. I did all the other times I went to Buffalo.

Why didn't you?

I didn't have a car and was getting a ride with Darlene's brother and he didn't want her in his car. Then with the wedding, the dinners, rehearsal and all that crap I would have had to rely on someone to take me back and forth and your family sure as hell wouldn't have helped me. Andrea didn't want the hassle of driving back and forth either, even if it was for Sophie. Oh Mom, if I had it to do over, I would have never left Sophie. The regret weighs on me.

I know babe. That's why you are the way you are with the animals in your life now huh?

What do you mean?

You never leave your animals' side honey, ever. You don't travel anywhere without them.

I learned my lesson. As I said, I was selfish when I was younger and floundering around in grief. I made the mistake of leaving the only being in this world that mattered to me, aside from you, one too many times and with the wrong people.

Kristin, you weren't selfish, and Sophie forgives you. Actually, there's little to forgive honey. You cared for and loved her more than anyone in our whole entire family and she knows that. Don't you think I regret leaving you kids when I had to, be it to go to school at night, or for a weekend retreat. I hated leaving you with Spencer when I went to my EST retreat, but I needed too. I knew how upset you were. It's no different with Sophie. Sometimes parents have to make hard decisions, but you were there for Sophie all the time honey and she knew that. You nailed it when you said you two started as kids and grew into your young adulthood and Sophie's elderly years. You are a wonderful caretaker honey. I've never known one better.

She'll always be my best friend, family and my little girl. Every time I think of Sophie, I think of her running free or watching her bask in the sun and I smile.

That's it honey. Think of all the wonderful times you two had. You had many more happy times than you did hard ones. Don't beat yourself up about this trip you had to make for Darlene's wedding. I know how hard the family can make things for you.

Yes, they do. Oh gosh Mom, you had to see this wedding.

Why, what, tell me.

Well, I think it's accurate to say that her sleeves and entire dress were so poufy she looked like a stuffed mushroom. Rather than tell her the same thing everyone else was telling her which was how beautiful she looked. I politely smiled and said nothing as I silently thought, "You manipulative, ignorant, heartless asshole."

I think you should say what you really think dear.

Well she is. All her sorority sisters were there giving fake kisses on each other's cheeks and acting like the stupid, caddy girls they are. Then, at the reception, her husband body dived into the crowd onto the dance floor. I so regretted going to that wedding.

He body dived into the crowd? Were there elderly people on the floor?

I'm pretty sure they got out of the way. At least I hope they did.

What would make him do a stupid thing like that at a wedding, his wedding no less?

Your guess is as good as mine. All I thought about at that moment was, "Oh my gosh, these two people are going to procreate. Great, just what this world needs, more fucked up people."

He doesn't sound very smart but very much like the boys your cousin dated, not too classy. Her mother was the same way.

Well, I'm sure Louisa couldn't be more proud of her daughter.

What does Darlene's husband do?

He's a pharmacist - perfect for your druggie/alcoholic sister.

Oh, you've got to be kidding.

Nope.

My sister must have jumped for joy when she heard that.

I'm sure and I bet she's got her son-in-law writing "just one more" script after another.

I hope not.

Truth be told. I didn't want to go to her wedding not just because of having to be around your family but because I didn't want to be reminded of what I'd never have - my mother by my side at any portion of my life - milestone or not.

Sweetheart come here.

All my cousins have no idea how fortunate they are to have their parents for as long as they have. They've never had to worry about anything, money, a place to stay, nothing. As I was going through all this stuff with Sophia all I kept thinking was, "I have no family. What if something happens to me? Sophia and I have no one."

I won't even ask about your sister.

I couldn't count on Andrea for anything, I mean nothing. She came to visit me only once when I moved downstate. All the other times Devon and I rented a car and drove to her. The phone calls between us were getting further and further apart. During one of our visits I asked her if I could hold your ashes.

What made you ask for my ashes?

It was time for them to stop fulfilling their wishes and for yours to finally be fulfilled. This time, no one was going to stop me. Your sisters had your ashes then Andrea had them. Many times, I told Andrea and Cody we needed to release your ashes because you never wanted to be sealed shut in an urn. Once again, they said no, completely disregarding your wishes, and insisted on keeping them. It made me sick the way you were being passed around like some inanimate object. I wasn't going to let that happen anymore. Your ashes were coming back with me and I wasn't taking "no" for an answer. The two against one thing was starting to get on my nerves, big time.

With Cody out of my life and the distance growing between me and Andrea, I felt pulled because if anything did happen to me the only person, I had in my life was Devon. I didn't want to rely on him.

It sounds like you really wanted to be rid of the family and these "what if's" prevented you from totally separating from them. Or, more accurately, your fear of being alone prevented you from being free.

Yes, and yet I was alone, even with them in the peripheral of my life.

That's right and you're so independent honey.

It's one thing to be independent. It's another to be independent and alone. That's like walking a tightrope without a net. I was used to walking the rope just not without my net; that would be you.

I know honey. I felt the same way. I was so scared to be alone. Why do you think we went to Buffalo? It wasn't just because of cancer. I was plagued with "what ifs." Having children, I couldn't take the risk of any "what if." Yet the Universe has an uncanny way of helping us get exactly what we need, not always what we want but definitely what we need, even if the journey is painful. If it's something where growth is assured the pain is worth it.

Really?

Really.

Thankfully, at the time, all I had on my mind was how lonely I was without an animal companion. I wanted to give another life the best life I could. I found myself looking to adopt a cat. Even though I've never had a cat I'm happy whether I have a dog or cat as long as I'm saving a life. I didn't even have the cat, but I already put up a kitty window perch. I think it's safe to say my heart was set on a cat and I was preparing, or as they say, "nesting."

How funny you are. Did you clean too? Cleaning your house is also part of the "nesting" process.

Of course, I did. I searched and searched and finally caught the eye of one mesmerizing little man on Petfinder.com. His name was Monte and he was a 10-year-old beautiful tabby boy.

How sweet. Did Devon like cats?

He never had a cat either. I think he was just glad I was bringing another animal companion into my life. I'd been so sad without Sophie. All he wanted was for me to be happy. He saw how my face lit up when I talked about Monte and his story.

What was his story?

His human parent was a vet who recently crossed over from cancer. His foster mom said everyone was passing him by because he was older but there was something about him that made me want to and meet him. The only problem was that he was being fostered all the way out in New Jersey, a town about two hours from me by public transportation. When I called his foster Mom, Liana, to ask her if she would meet me halfway, I liked her response.

What'd she say?

"No."

She said "no", and you liked that?

There was more to it that I absolutely agree with. She explained she wasn't trying to be rude, but she'd had many experiences where she was overly accommodating to potential adopters in order to get the cats into homes. However, it was wearing her down because people weren't making much of an effort. At the end of the day she would go through all this trouble to make it as easy as possible for others and they would end up not adopting the cat for one reason or another, or they brought the cat back or gave her/him up for adoption again. In short, they weren't as vested in the relationship when she made it easy for them. She said she felt if people truly wanted to bring an animal into their lives, they'll make the effort because caring for an animal is effort and she's right. While it was a hassle for me it's a bold statement to make and one that weeds out the loving, permanent homes from those that aren't. Adopting an animal is a lifelong commitment.

That is exactly right.

You have to care for her/him forever, even in the face of adversity or tragedy, i.e. if you're evicted for some reason or lose your home. You have an animal companion to think about as part of your family. You can't just discard your companion, yet many do. It's simple to intellectually understand that cruelty to animals needs to end. However, for those that can barely be kind to other human beings it's apparently a difficult thought to embrace, and an even more difficult task to execute. Yet I still remain hopeful, for the animals.

My animal companions are with me through thick and thin. That's it and that's how it should be. Once we're together we're not separating for any reason. Maybe I have separation anxiety.

I was just going to say that. It doesn't matter. Your devotion is admirable, and your animal companions are lucky to have you. So, what happened? How did you get all the way out to New Jersey without a car?

Considering my neck wasn't in good shape. I was hoping and praying things would work out when I got directions and discovered I would be taking two buses and three trains.

Wow!

Yeah, it was a long ride but something in me told me to go. I had a good feeling about this little one. When I spoke to Liana, she advised me to bring a carrier just in case.

Good suggestion.

Yes, because traveling that far, you never know how things will go. Maybe it'll be a good fit, maybe not but it's good to be prepared. She also keyed me in on one other little detail.

What was that?

That Monte was hissing at all the potential adopters that came to meet him. I appreciated Liana's candor about Monte, but it didn't stop me from wanting to meet him. I remained excited and couldn't wait to meet him. Again, I had a feeling there was a reason behind his hissing. Animals aren't defensive unless they're being mistreated or they're unhappy about something, i.e. they're living situation or their health, etc. I listen to the animals when they talk to me. I was about to hear what Monte had to say.

Now I can't wait to hear what he had to say.

Liana had a big, beautiful house with a lovely backyard. Inside the house, she was fostering fifteen cats, some were young, and some were old and very sick but don't worry. She wasn't a hoarder. Her house was big enough for all of them.

That's a lot of cats to care for.

It is and she was busy cleaning litter boxes and little messes here and there the entire time I was there. Liana was really nice, and she truly appreciated that I made the trip to see Monte. I set my carrier down in the living room and left the door open. We sat in the kitchen and spoke for a little while. She asked me questions about why I wanted a cat, what would I do if I fell on hard times and what would happen to Monte? You know all the questions that should be asked of a potential adopter in order to ensure the animal is going to a permanent, loving home.

Sounds good so far.

Then she gave me a four-page questionnaire to fill out which I did. Then, it was time to meet Monte. Liana led me upstairs where Monte's hiding spot was. She explained he spent all his time in this one spot.

Where was that?

In their bedroom, in the closet, in a clothes basket underneath the clothes. Now mind you, all the other cats were roaming about relaxing out in the open. Some were playing with each other. Some were simply too sick to do anything. Those cats weren't up for adoption but being permanently cared for by Liana. If I had a house like hers, I'd be doing the same thing. Liana left me alone with Monte to get to know him. I sat next to him and put my hand out for him to sniff. He hissed so I just gave him some space and started to talk about Sophie, having lost her not too long ago, what she was like, the things we did and so on. After about a half hour I let him sniff my hand again. This time he didn't hiss or growl. In fact, he seemed okay. Then I went to gently pet him, and I got another hiss and this time he topped it with a growl.

Uh oh. Growl? I didn't know cats could growl.

It' more like a snarl growl, not quite as deep as a dog but enough to get their message across.

What do you think Monte's message was?

As I was sitting next to him, I thought about what he went through. Here was this beautiful boy who lost his Mom and was now thrust into a home with strange people and cats he didn't know, some of which were close to dying. Even though Liana and her husband were wonderful caretakers Monte wasn't getting the kind of love and attention he had before. He wasn't happy and wanted to go home. You know? I understood that. His life as he knew it was ripped out from underneath him. No one could relate to that more than me.

You're so good with animals Kristin.

I feel like I am.

What happened after Monte hissed and growled?

I took my hand away because I realized that was too much for him and stayed by his side while still giving him space so as to be as non-threatening as possible. We sat next to each other for another hour. I was getting tired and you can't force an animal to do something or go someplace they don't want to any more than you can force a human. I said to Monte, "Monte. I know you're not happy here. I understand how you feel. I do. I know what it's like to miss your parent and the life you once had so much it hurts and makes you angry and sad. And people just see your anger and sadness and nothing else." He kept staring at me with his big green eyes and never took them off me. I continued, "Monte, I have a one-bedroom apartment with plenty of space for the two of us. I think you'd really like it and I have a wonderful boyfriend that's excited to meet you. If you come with me, I'll love you and care for you until the day you cross over. We'll be best friends forever, you and me. We'll be there for each other through thick and thin. I put a window perch up so you can stare out the window, or cuddle with me on the couch, whatever you like. I want you as my family Monte if you want me. If you can let me know somehow, someway that would be great." He just sat there. I let him know I was going downstairs for a few minutes to use the restroom and that we could talk more when I came back. I'd been sitting on a hardwood floor talking with Monte for almost two hours. I thought it would be a good idea to give my but a rest.

Oh, that was so intuitive of you to take so much time with Monte.

Here comes the best part. When I came out of the restroom, I spoke with Liana a bit more before going back up to Monte. Wouldn't you know Liana said to me, "Look behind you but be casual." I looked behind me and Monte was standing behind me and began to rub against my leg. She said Monte hadn't been downstairs in weeks. I was overcome with happiness. What happened next is a testament that Animals know goodness and gravitate toward it.

That's for sure. What happened?

Right after Monte rubbed against my leg. He looked at me with those beautiful soulful eyes and very slowly walked over to my carrier, got in and stayed there until it was time for "us" to go.

No, he didn't!

Yes, he did. Liana and I both started to cry. We were so happy. Liana said, "I guess Monte finally found his new Mom." "He sure has." I replied. Liana later confided that she didn't think Monte would be adopted because of his hissing but I knew something was happening underneath. Poor guy just wanted out of that house. I know with his first mom he lived with another dog and cat but that's very different from fifteen other cats. He just wanted some peace.

Kristin that is a beautiful story. Animals communicate in ways that are so easy for people to hear. I think you're right. Too often they get ignored. So, you two made the two-hour journey back home.

Actually, Liana was kind enough to give us a ride home. I guess I earned it☺.

I'd say so.

Devon was happy for both of us. He liked Monte right away. He thought he was a "cool cat." He was too. As soon as he got into my apartment his hissing, snarling demeanor turned into the sweet, loving and affectionate cat I knew he was. The second he got in my apartment he hopped on the couch and looked at me as if to say, "Thank you!" He loved me right away and I loved him the same. He followed me everywhere I went, just like Sophie used to. He also found a comfortable place to sleep at night.

Oh yeah. Where was that?

On top of my chest☺. I just loved that. It gave both of us a feeling of safety, as though we weren't alone in the world and we weren't. We were together now, me and Monte, Monte and me. The fact that he was 10 had no bearing on him or me. He still had all this life and energy in him but mainly, he liked to "chill." Having Monte filled the loneliness I'd been feeling without Sophie. More importantly, Monte and I became the family both of us longed for.

Monte, 1999

You're right. He is beautiful and he looks peaceful too.

He was. We both were. I was so glad to have him. Every day I came home from work Monte would rush to the door as if he were a dog. Having him there brought life to me again. Devon was glad because I was happier and cried less. Without the ability to dance and exercise because of my neck I needed an outlet. I took the advice you gave me in one of your letters and started writing.

Good for you. What did you start writing?

I wasn't sure what to write about. I had a few ideas in my head, but nothing stood out. Until one day, while reading the Sunday paper I saw an article and the title, in big, bold letters read, "SUFFER THE ANIMALS." It was about our local animal shelter and the terrible shape it was in. The article inspired me so much so that I began to write in the hopes of one day helping the shelter. I wanted to write a story that dealt with animal welfare. Since animal welfare is a pretty broad topic, I decided to hone in on three specific areas. I also knew that if I wanted to educate readers on animal welfare, which included some pretty gruesome details, I would need to insert something in-between. So, I made my characters quirky with a lot of humorous dialogue between them.

That was good thinking on your part.

Yeah because even for me, when I read something and it's all heavy material it's hard to keep reading. I wanted to write something that would engage my readers and keep them coming back. Once I started writing the story began to unfold and slowly but surely the characters emerged. I love my characters too. They're all endearing and relatable in their own special way.

That's great! Was the book fiction?

It was both. It was fiction in terms of the characters and story line but all of the information regarding animal welfare was non-fiction. Monte would sit by my side as I wrote, often for hours on end. I was determined. I wanted to help the animals at the shelter and many more if I could.

How exciting honey! So, what is the book about?

The book is about a quick witted, temperamental former pro-basketball player with a big heart, by the name of Leinad ("Lee") Reed who gets hurt in a game and rendered unable to play ball again. Rather than becoming the stereotypical sportscaster he turns to his other passions which are writing and animal welfare. Through his college buddy he lands a job as a columnist in New York City. The column, entitled "ASWFI" short for "<u>Animal Sphere - Words from the Inside</u>," is interactive in that Lee poses a question regarding a specific area in animal welfare and invites readers to respond, positive or negative.

How creative.

I thought so. In his personal life Lee has his best friend and animal companion, Sophie, of course.

Of course.

His human best friend since childhood is Dr. Myra Hillman who, to the dismay of her conservative Republican parents, became a veterinarian rather than a surgeon. Leinad is also close with his second Mom, Sheila (his mother's girlfriend and yes, his mother is a Lesbian) and his sister, Sunray. His biological mother crossed over from breast cancer. His father was a jazz musician, a drinker and a dead-beat dad who only briefly made it into the book.

This story sounds awfully familiar in some ways. I wonder why?

Can't imagine. Hey, when you write about what you know the writing flows and that was the case for me. Once I started, I couldn't stop. Through Leinad's column, he meets a woman whose husband is the Senator of Vermont. Together, the Senator and Leinad work to introduce and put into effect three laws which focus on specific areas of animal welfare.

Kristin, this sounds great! What were the laws?

The first is banning animal testing. The second dealt with banning puppy mills and stopping animal breeders holding specific breeding licenses. Since animal breeding and the subsequent treatment of animals as commodities go hand-in-hand, this bill was amended to also prevent all animals from being sold in retail. The third dealt with increasing annual funding for county animal shelters nationwide.

Wow. That's a mouthful. Wait a minute, what happened to the woman, the Senator's wife?

That I won't say but they're all connected in one way or another?

I see. Sort of, tell me a little more.

For starters, animal testing is cruel, outdated and inaccurate. Secondly, animals that are no longer considered "useful" for breeding are sold to laboratories for experiments. If we stop breeders and these horrific puppy mills, then more will be adopted from local shelters. This would considerably cut down on the number of unwanted animals in shelters with the goal being that no animal would ever suffer in a laboratory, pet shop or puppy mill again, and shelters would be comfortable and plentiful while animals await their loving, permanent homes.

Oh my gosh! I knew it! You see, I always knew your writing would be out of this world if you let go and let it take its course and you did.

Yes, I did.

I'm impressed. You're really creative and smart honey.

Thank you.

I'm not shocked though. This is right up your alley. You like politics and you love animals so to combine the two was smart on your part.

Thanks. It was a natural progression. I'd been active with animal welfare and keeping up to date on domestic and international politics for years. Whenever I wrote everything flowed together perfectly. I loved getting lost in the book.

So, what happened?

With what?

The book silly.

Oh, right, well the Senator and Leinad work together to get these laws introduced, passed and enforced. In the process, Leinad, Myra and Sophie encounter some sticky situations. Someone gets shot and in-between there are lots of very funny as well as positive things that happen too.

Unbelievable. What did you call it?

Between Humans and Animals.

That's a perfect title.

Thank you. Things were good, for a little while.

How was your neck and the medications holding up?

That's what I was referring to. They weren't. It had been a year since my diagnosis and my neck wasn't getting better. Exhausting all treatment possibilities there was one other option presented to me by yet another doctor I was seeing. He informed me the results of being pain free were about 60%-70%.

Those aren't very good numbers.

No but the other option was to live with the pain which was consuming 100% of my mind and body and I couldn't do it anymore. I wanted to be myself again, without pain. I was eating anti-inflammatories, muscle relaxers and pain killers like candy. My doctor said he'd done this many times before and most people responded well to the treatment and were pain free. I weighed the pros and cons of the option presented to me. The pros outweighed the cons and vice versa if I didn't go for this next course of treatment.

You must have been so scared.

The pain I was in outweighed my fear. I was at the point where I said, "Let me do whatever I have to do to get some relief." I just wanted this next phase over with. I was more nervous than anything else. It's like standing on a train track and seeing the train barrel down the track from a distance, a long distance, and you're doing everything you can not to get hit. Then you look away for a split second only to turn around and BOOM!

THE DANCE

2000-2002

I am as light as can be
Soaring high above the clouds, overlooking the sea.
I am as light as can be
Living inside, dreaming of the outside.
Through the cold and snow, sun and rain
I'm feeling you in all of me.
Releasing old skins that must be set free.

I am as light as can be
A serpent in the water, beautiful as the sky.
Accepting, denouncing and working all that's left of me.

I am as light as can be
Resting and floating one wave at a time.
I'm living this nightmare that no one can see.
I'm feeling this nightmare take hold of the best part of me.
I'm seeing this nightmare erase all that I once was.
No longer alive but dead without cause.

I am as light as can be
Connecting with the sun, moon, stars and sky;
Bathing in love, hate, passion and fate.

I am as light as can be.
Mourning the eviction from my life of
Freedom and independence
Too heavy to arrive wherever I'm meant to be.

I am as light as can be
Struggling, to once again, be free.

Kristin A. Crage ©2003

Phelps Memorial Hospital Center
701 North Broadway
Sleepy Hollow, New York 10501

"Admission Date: 08/31/00

Patient: Kristin A. Crage

Preoperative Diagnosis: Cervical spine degenerative disc disease C4/5. Cervical C4/5 with intractable neck pain. Mild Cervical degenerative disc disease C3/4.

Postoperative Diagnosis: Same."[13]

****

I decided to go with surgery. I had to Mom.

I know and you don't have to tell me about pain. I completely understand.

I knew you would. You're one of the few people that does. A small incision was made in the front of my neck. The corroded disc was replaced with bone graft. My neck was fused at C4 and C5 and a titanium plate was inserted at the fusion site. My doctor said as soon as he opened me up the disc was so corroded it literally fell out and almost landed on the floor.

Oh boy. This sounds painful.

Before the surgery, yes, but after the surgery I felt like a thousand-pound weight had been lifted from my neck. My doctor sent me home with this hard, plastic two-piece neck brace called a Bone Growth Stimulator that had to be secured from front to back with Velcro straps. It essentially stimulated my bone to grow and helped with the healing process. The downside was that it had to be worn every day for three hours. It was the ugliest thing I ever saw and worse than that it was battery operated. It beeped after the three hours was up and when the battery was low.

Oooh, that doesn't sound fun.

It wasn't but you won't believe what happened on the way home from the hospital.

What?

Devon and I took a cab home and we got into an accident because the cab driver was drunk.

Oh, you've got to be kidding.

Nope. We didn't notice he was drunk until after we got in the car.

What was he doing that led you to believe he was drunk?

He was talking to himself and his words were slurred.

Oh geez.

We were going to call a different cab, but we were in between towns with no phone access, and I needed to get home. Devon and I were so mad. We made it home, but I told Devon not to pay the guy. Rather, I told the cab driver to wait downstairs while we got our money. Instead, we called the cops.

Did they do anything?

Oh sure. One of the cops threatened to arrest me because I refused to pay the cab driver that almost killed us!

That's crazy! Why did he do that?

The cab driver saw the cops first and told them I stiffed him which wasn't the case. We were just waiting for them to show up so they could arrest this guy for driving while intoxicated. Instead of even giving the cabbie a breathalyzer the cops stormed up to my apartment and started threatening me and telling me to "shut up" because I was trying to explain what happened. So, I said to the cop, "Who are you to talk to me like that when I'm trying to report a crime." The cop responded with, "You better shut your mouth before I take you in. I don't care if you got out of the hospital or not." Devon and I were furious.

I would be too. What assholes these officers were.

Yes, they were. So, with the cops threatening to arrest me, Devon stepped in and had me go inside while he smooth talked them down, which was good because I was in no condition to deal with this nonsense.

So, what was the end result?

Thankfully, I didn't get arrested, but we still had to pay the cab driver and I ended up having to go back into the hospital to get checked again and they still didn't give that guy a breathalyzer or do anything to him. I mean how nuts is all of that?

It's like a movie! Oh honey. I just don't know what to say sometimes. You go through some of the hardest stuff yet you're never a victim.

I despise even the through of being a victim. I want my cab fare back!

I know. I don't blame you. Let's see if we can find the man and break his legs if he doesn't pay.

That sounds like so much fun!

I figured you'd say that. Well, how about work? How was it there? Hopefully better than your cab ride.

It was fine.

What job were you working in at the time?

I was a Legal/Administrative Assistant to the in-house attorney and three of the principal investors in a real estate office in Westchester. They bought and sold buildings in Manhattan. It was a crazy office to work in. I still couldn't believe I was in an office atmosphere. It all seemed like a bad dream.

I'm sure. What do you mean by "crazy"?

It wasn't uncommon for investors to have screaming matches with people on the phone or with each other if a deal was about to bust or did bust. One guy threw a phone across the room.

For what?

I guess he was mad about something.

Did he hit anyone?

Thankfully, no.

That's ridiculous! Did anyone do anything about him?

Yes. We all ducked.

Are you serious?

Yes, it's true. There are some whacked out people in the world and many of them are in the corporate world. Don't let the attire fool you. I have many stories that would sound completely unbelievable to someone who hasn't had any experience in the corporate world, particularly in a metropolis like NYC. In the city, people are very aggressive, quick tempered and they spend their day in a rush - rush to get to work, rush to get this and that done, rush to eat lunch and rush to get home. Trust me when I say that when you enter the corporate world, hope for the best and prepare for the crazies!

I believe you. There are good companies to work for but they're few and far between. I know. I've worked for some real characters myself in my day too. Were you out of work for long?

I used whatever vacation and personal time I had and went on short term disability. I was out for about a month.

How did they handle you being out?

They weren't happy about it but what could they do? I had to have this surgery. When I returned to work, I still had to wear the Bone Growth Stimulator. I was in this thing for four months. It was so annoying.

You wore that huge thing on your neck for four months!

Every day, three hours a day for four months, yes.

Oh, my goodness. Now that's discipline.

The challenging part was that I had to wear it during work hours and that brought some unpleasant experiences.

You couldn't wear it at night when you got home?

Not really. My doctor said it would be better if I wore it during the day when my body wasn't so tired from the day.

What happened that was so unpleasant?

Whenever I had to wear the neck brace no one would look at me or talk to me which was kind of nice for me because I got a lot of work done. All people really did anyway was gossip, which I don't partake in. What bothered me was that one time when I went to the kitchen to get some coffee. Just before entering I could hear some of the other assistants making fun of my neck brace. They were saying things like, "Did you see that thing? Oh my god it's huge and it beeps!" Another woman made fun of the beeping noises by mocking the sound the brace made when it beeped. Another person said I looked like the cousin of Frankenstein. I couldn't believe they were even bothering themselves with such hurtful comments. Those same individuals would walk by my desk (in pairs of course) stare and laugh at me like children. When I see someone going through something painful or if I know they've come back from surgery I want to help them and be supportive. They made my return so uncomfortable.

What jerks. That must have been awful and stressful for you. Did you say anything to the Human Resources Dept. or office manager?

I couldn't. One of the women commenter's was the HR/Office Manager.

Oh, nice.

I'm sure I could have said something to her, but I don't think I would have been very calm, and I didn't want to jeopardize my job. Besides, she wouldn't have cared about anything I had to say but she would care about what our bosses had to say. So, I let my higher ups know she and a couple of the other assistants were making inappropriate comments about my neck brace in common areas where others could hear them and asked if they would speak to her.

Did they and did she close her big mouth?

She did, at least in public areas and that's all that mattered to me. People can be so insensitive and unprofessional in the workplace. I mean you're there to do a job so just do your job. Unfortunately, gossipy, aggressive, mean and twisted behavior is rampant in the corporate world. I got through it but then left that job.

Because of what was being said about you?

Partly. I didn't want to be in such ugly company. The other reason was that the company moved offices to the next town over and it was too far a commute for me. I was glad to get out of there and move on and I did. I found another job in the same type of office, again working for an attorney and the owner's daughter of a real estate office. The daughter ran the office. Her father was semi-retired.

I'm glad you got out of that job. Was this new one any better?

In the beginning, it was fine. The owner's daughter liked me, and she was really nice to me too. We got along well.

That's good.

Yeah, I'm a hard worker and go the extra mile, even when the job is tough. I was pleasantly surprised when, after a few months of my working there, she took everyone out to a Mets game which also happened to be on my birthday.

How nice of her.

It was. I really appreciated it. It was good to get out for the day. You'll never guess what she did?

What?

You know those big tv screens they have where you can see everything twenty times larger and sometimes the camera pans on the audience?

Yeah.

Well they also do messages that people want to send out to someone. I'm sure it costs a lot of money to do that, but my boss knew someone, which is how she got the tickets. There was a message put on the screen and they only stay up for a few minutes. I was focused on looking at the field, the people and what not until I heard everyone calling my name, "Kristin, look up! Hurry!" I looked up and there were three words, all lit up in bright lights with letters as big as myself.

What were they?

"HAPPY BIRTHDAY KRISTIN!"

Oh my gosh how nice of her. What a surprise!

It was. I couldn't believe it. I thought it was amazing she did that. I was really touched.

Well, she must have really liked you to do that.

I guess so. It was very special to me. The first and only time my name was in lights. It was a great moment and a great game.

Who won?

I can't remember. I only remember my name in lights.

I bet. So, you said things were good in the beginning. What happened?

Well, because of this wonderful thing my supervisor did for me I stuck out a rather uncomfortable situation for a long time.

What was it?

I, again, worked for the in-house attorney. This guy was a piece of work, to say the least.

How so?

He was so old school which was fine until his old school ways started to infringe on my personal space.

Oh no. What did he do?

He refused to use a dictation tape for letters and lengthy documents. You know the kind where he talks into it, hands me the tape and I transcribe whatever he's said.

Right, so how did you get your typing done?

The guy insisted on sitting behind me and dictating his every word. Sometimes he would reach over my shoulder and point to where he saw a mistake and wouldn't continue until I fixed it. Sometimes the documents were long too. He'd be sitting behind me for hours talking and changing what he wrote. Working with him was so stressful and aggravating. I tried to get him to use a dictation tape, but he wouldn't.

Oh my gosh. What did supervisor say? Being the owner's daughter, couldn't she do anything about this?

No, she didn't care. She just wanted to make, collect and spend money. So, I had to deal with it. I was biding my time while I worked to try and find another job. I couldn't just leave. I needed the insurance.

Of course. Wow, that's borderline harassing isn't it?

It sure felt like it. Imagine having someone over your shoulder, literally, while you're working. I mean he would actually pull up a chair, sit behind me for hours and dictate, correct my mistakes and get impatient with me. Ugh. It was a nightmare.

Oh boy, it sure sounds like it. I'm surprised you stayed. I mean that's some discipline you have to stay at a place that's making you so miserable because you know you have too for insurance and money.

I know you know what that's like.

Yes, I do. It's like having your every nerve being tested to the very core of your being.

Yes, it is. Sometimes I wanted to turn around and scream to him, "Get the fuck away from me and go in your own office your fucking freak!"

Honey, I completely understand.

Thank you. Whew, that felt good to get that out.

Good.

Of course, my sister didn't make things any better for me.

Why, what did she do?

While I was recovering, she asked to borrow money from me.

Are you serious?

Yup.

Did you?

Yes, she's my sister, right? We're supposed to help each other in times of need, right? So, I lent her whatever savings I had.

Kristin, you were recovering from neck surgery.

I know.

Did she know this?

Yes. She waited until I was out of the hospital and back to work before asking me. I told her I gave her what I had and that I would need her to pay me back.

Did she come visit you or help you at all during the time you were in the hospital or afterward?

No.

Didn't you need that money to help you while you were recovering?

Yes, I did but I was back to work, and she said she needed the money, so I gave it to her. That's what sisters do. They help each other, or so I thought.

What the heck was going through your sister's head? First, she uses your credit card to have her and her girlfriend come to New Hampshire to be there for you when you attempted a suicide, and didn't you say she racked up your card?

I mean, I really don't like being reminded of such a painful time Mom but, Yes.

I'm sorry but now, she's pulling this stunt and she only came to see you once since you'd been in NYC?

Yes.

Your sister had a funny way of helping you.

That's what I've been telling you mother. I'm glad you're finally seeing this.

I have seen it, trust me. I know how irresponsible and self-involved your sister can be. I think my sisters tend to see her through rose-colored glasses, the same rose-colored glasses they accused you of seeing me through, and only because she partied with them that's all.

What brought that up?

Ah, just hearing you talk about these things is taking me back to when she was supposed to be helping me. She was the same way, unable to handle responsibility and I love her with all that I am, but she couldn't handle stressful situations, at all. She panicked but never mind. We talked about this earlier.

I can't tell you how affirming it is to hear you be honest about how Andrea was with you.

She tried. I know she did and so did I. I tried for years to get her to be more responsible, compassionate and empathic but so many things just went right over her head.

Thank you.

For what?

Your honesty.

Oh honey, I'll always be honest, regardless of what others may think. You can count on that.

I'll always be honest too.

So how do you think the surgery went overall?

I thought it went well. After I was done wearing the Bone Growth Stimulator the pain improved. I even started to decrease my meds although I still had to take Darvocet for pain.

That has some serious side effects doesn't it?

It had your basic constipation, itching, drowsiness, sore throat, impaired alertness, confusion and serious or fatal heart rhythms, yes. It was taken off the market in 2010 because of heart side effects.[14]

Did you have any of those side effects?

I was experiencing some drowsiness but by this time my body was developing a tolerance for pain killers. It felt like the cloud that was hovering over me had gone elsewhere. I made a point to speak to your family as little as possible and completely stopped speaking with Trudi, which eased the stress and I, absolutely, never asked them for help and they never offered. Not even a "Hey don't let this get you down. Keep going. You're going to be okay."

Why did you speak to them at all if you didn't want them in your life?

I felt like I had too because Andrea was still in touch with them and if I wasn't then there would be all this negative backlash, "Why doesn't Kristin call us? Does she think she's better than us?" You know, that kind of shit. Usually I would leave a message when they weren't home just so that they could never say, "Hey, how come you never call us?"

Yeah, but you know they'd say that anyway whether you call them or not. I know how they are. I shouldn't have even asked that. I think I know why you didn't call Trudi, but you tell me.

She was cold and distant on the few times we spoke after I moved away. She had this bitter tone to her voice about everything and turned the conversation into something negative. She hated this and wished this person would do that. She didn't care to hear anything about me or what was happening in my life. In fact, the conversations lasted all of about ten minutes of which she complained about all the things she felt were bad in her life. Then she would hang up abruptly and with the same cold tone she started with. I dreaded speaking with her, so I didn't.

My sister was never a very happy person. She takes after our mother in that respect. I don't need to ask why you didn't ask the family for help.

No, you know how they are. I know it's hard to help family or friends when there's physical distance between you but there's always something you can do, i.e., send a card or make a phone call. You taught me that. I never got a call back from any of the messages I left.

This is very disheartening to hear.

No. A few times I actually got a hold of someone, but I'd get nothing but excuses as to why they didn't call but that's how they are. They wanted me to make all the effort, yet they also wanted to complain about me too, and they did to Andrea.

They did right.

Yeah.

What did they say?

The same old shit, "Your sister is so angry. She's so depressed. I just can't talk to her." Meanwhile, months would go by before anyone would ever return my call and I never spoke to them in a depressed or sad tone. I didn't want their complaining to come back to me, yet it still did. No matter what I said, or did they found fault with me, so I had to just let them, for my own peace of mind.

That's right Kristin. You can't control what they're going to say or do even if it is bullshit and it was. They criticize in order to make themselves look good to others and justify the fact that they really weren't there for you. The worse they make you look, the better they think they look.

I knew that and so they thought. I also knew that whatever recovery I had to do would be on my own. I mean I had Devon by my side but when it came right down to it, I was the one that had to push through the pain and get my body going again. Sitting around wasn't an option for me. I was never like that and I wasn't going to start. I asked my doctor for a Physical Therapy script and started that twice a week. In addition to Physical Therapy I began to do my own exercises, slowly.

You had to ask your doctor for a Physical Therapy referral? He didn't automatically send you?

No.

What if you didn't know to ask for a Physical Therapy referral? Then what would you do?

I probably would have remained in more pain than necessary which, sadly, many patients do. I go by one rule of thumb, the same I used with you in fact.

What rule of thumb is that?

Doctors know ailments but we know our bodies. That's an important distinction to make. I don't let a doctor tell me how NOT to care for my body. I am the ruler of my body, not them. I have a list of questions to ask my doctors and things I want to do versus what I can do. While I couldn't dance the way, I used to I was, at least, able to do the stretching and strengthening exercises I used to do on the ballet bar. That felt good. I never let my body be down for too long. I strongly feel that exercise and getting your body moving, if you can, after trauma/surgery is extremely important. It enhances your recovery process and increases your progress, a lot because you need to get that oxygen to your blood to help you heal and that's what movement does, even if the movement is small. It's still better than nothing.

That's exactly right. I remember how you would give me very small exercises to do with my arm after my surgeries. You were so good like that. Then Trudi would tell me not to move my arm.

Oh, she used to upset me so much when she'd say that. That's when we'd argue because I'd tell her, "Don't tell my mother not to exercise. She needs to get the blood flowing in her arm. The doctor said it's healthy for her to do little exercises."

Then you two would fight and I'd pass out from the myriad of medications I was on. We were a close family.

Yeah, real tight. I know Dance is what helped me through my surgery. Once you start dancing as young as I did, the movement, rhythms, combinations, counts and discipline are in your blood forever. Dance was one of the positive footprints etched in me while I was still wet concrete. It never fades.

That's true. Dance has been your greatest survival technique. Devon sounds like he was very supportive of you.

He was great through it all. He was truly concerned about me, definitely supportive, caring and he helped me with anything I needed. I couldn't have asked for a better partner in life. I mean it. I felt fortunate to have met Devon.

He was fortunate to have met you. Well, it sounds like the surgery went well. How do you feel talking about this? It's been a long time since you've talked about this hasn't it?

Yes, I feel, okay. I mean I wasn't prepared for a herniated disc in my neck, but it happened, I got through it and moved on. I focused on writing as an alternative to dance. It wasn't nearly as fulfilling but when I write I feel the same things I felt when I was dancing.

Which are?

Hope, possibility and purpose. In addition to the book I thought about Vermont. I envisioned myself in a country house with two cats and two dogs and the green mountains as my backyard.

You used to say you wanted four kids.

Yup, I was thinking about adopting another dog but wasn't quite ready. I wanted to save some money and be in better physical shape. I was exercising and getting better every day, but I wanted to make sure I was strong enough to care for a canine companion.

Sometimes the Universe knows exactly what you need before you do.

I agree although sometimes the Universe's timing is a little off.

I'll go with that.

One night, maybe a few months after my surgery I came out of our corner grocery store and saw the sweetest, cutest most adorable American Cocker Spaniel. She was tied to a pole in front of the store. She was so little and trembled in a cowering position. I smiled and said hello to her. Then I kneeled to her level and let her approach me. She cautiously moved toward me and sniffed my hands which I held palm side down. When she realized I was friendly she nudged me to pet her. She was sweet but very skinny and looked malnourished. She shivered not because she was cold. It was the middle of summer. She was scared. You could tell by her pulled back ears and squinty eyes, as if she were waiting to pull back out of fear of being struck. Her fur, although a beautiful tan/golden color, was matted in different corners of her body, and there were two hair clips tightly placed on her ears which caused red, bloody irritation marks. I took the ear clips off and went inside the store to see if anyone knew her. Someone that worked at the store said she belonged to a woman who would go into the store and then shop in other stores on the same block leaving this little girl tied to the pole, sometimes for hours. I tried to find her human Mom but no luck. I asked the store employee if he wouldn't mind keeping an eye on her for a few minutes while I dropped my groceries off at home so I could come back and get her. He was happy to do so. He was concerned for her too. He said she'd been there for a long time.

What were you going to do when you got her?

My plan was to put up flyers, let area shelters know I had her and do what I could to find her human. In the meantime, I was going to keep her with me.

Would you have given her back to her human if you did find her?

I would have had no choice, but I definitely would have gone to great lengths to make sure she was in good hands. I got the sense, just from talking with the gentleman at the store and from the physical appearance of this little dog, that this woman wasn't caring for this little girl as she needed to be. Although I didn't have to think any further on this because when I went back to get her, which wasn't more than five minutes later, she was gone. In a way, I was relieved but still concerned. I was relieved because she was no longer alone but concerned about the type of people she was in the hands of. For the time being I had to let it go. Yet all I could think about was this trembling, little dog and wondered if she was okay.

Stories like this make me sad. That's why I couldn't listen to all the details whenever you would tell me about the inhumane treatment of animals. It was hard for me to hear.

I know. I figured that out. Sometimes you would do other things while I was talking to you about puppy mills or laboratories that were experimenting on animals. I understood. You were still supportive of me and the positive changes I wanted to make for the animal world. That's all that mattered.

I was always supportive and proud of you for that. You have a big heart and you're generous to no end when it comes to animals and people you care about.

Thank you. Well, I hoped that the little dog was okay and continued to go about my day and write. One night, while I was writing I heard these screams that sounded almost childlike and echoed throughout our four story, 30-unit apartment building. I burst out of the bedroom and said to Devon, "Did you hear that?" He replied yes and was as concerned as I was. The sounds vacillated between high pitched whines/cries, then there would be a pause and then there would be a bark or two in-between. It sounded like an animal was being tortured. Devon knew by the look on my face I was about to find out where this cry was coming from. He insisted on following me to make sure I was okay. We followed the cries to an apartment on the other side of our building. The closer we got the more gut wrenching it was to hear. Once we located the apartment the cries were coming from, we knocked on the door. That's when we heard the whining, clawing and sniffing from the other side of the door. We knocked for a long time, but no one answered. I called the police to see if they would either try to find the person(s) that lived there or break down the door so we could make sure the dog was okay. I thought maybe she/he was caught under something.

What did they do?

Nothing. They came. They listened to the whining and cries and said there was nothing they could do and left.

That's nice. You didn't just leave, did you?

No, I called a few animal welfare organizations and my local shelter. At the time the animal protection laws weren't enforced like they are now. Now-a-days if you're suspicious of animal abuse anywhere and you report it to the police, an animal welfare organization and/or the Humane Law Enforcement and they'll break the door down to help the animal. Since there was no suspicion of fire or animal fighting no one did anything. I could hear the dog pacing and jumping in the apartment. At least I knew she/he wasn't caught under something and was able to leave and come back to the door. I tried to calm the dog down by talking to her/him. A neighbor heard me and said, "That won't do any good. She's out probably for the day." I asked who "she" was? The neighbor replied, "The woman that lives in the apartment." I asked her when she would be back? She said that the woman wasn't out of the apartment. She was actually in the apartment but "out," meaning, "strung out." The neighbor also said that the woman rarely walked the dog and sometimes would leave for a few days leaving the dog alone. I asked her why she didn't call the police. She just shrugged her shoulders. I wanted to smack the neighbor and the woman inside the apartment. Devon just shook his head in disbelief.

What did you do?

I left a note on the door leaving her my phone number and apartment number asking her to call and/or stop by. I offered to help her by walking her dog or dog-sitting. I even offered to pay for vet visits if she needed it.

Where were you going to get the money for vet visits after having lent your savings out?

I don't' know. I would have found it. The woman never responded so I left two more notes until she finally came to my apartment. Guess who the dog was?

The little one from the store?

You got it and I didn't have to be told she was a junkie. She didn't even bother to hide the track marks on her arm. This little dog was a ball of pent up energy. The woman said she'd just given birth.

The woman just gave birth?

No, the dog. I was shocked because she couldn't have been more than a year old. The woman said she couldn't keep her and asked if I would take her. I told her absolutely. I asked her to give me a day to get some dog supplies and to bring me whatever paperwork she had and any leashes or dog food, so I knew what she was eating. Do you know as soon as I told her I would take her dog she came back with her boyfriend or whoever he was almost immediately?

Oh know.

In terms of paperwork all they had was the certificate of her breed which read her date of birth and their names. The food they had was a can of Alpo they just purchased and a thin rope he called a leash. I was so glad to get this little dog out of their hands. I asked them about the puppies and told them I wanted to help find homes for them. They said they already sold them. It turned out this little dog was being bred for drug money.

Bastards. How did Devon feel about you taking the dog in?

He was glad but he was also concerned. I was still healing from my surgery and he didn't want me to overexert myself. I understood that but this little one needed me, or as you say, "Sometimes the Universe knows exactly what you need before you do."

That's right. Oh my gosh. I can't believe that people can be so cruel to defenseless animals. It's sickening.

It is.

Well, this little one was lucky you found her. What did you name this sweet girl?

I named her Lillicoy and affectionately referred to her as "Lilli" or Miss Lilli." I thought it was the name of a Greek goddess or something. It turns out Lillicoy is a Hawaiian fruit.

Oh, how cute.

The first night Lilli was with me she whined, cried and shook all night. At one point I could see tears forming in her eyes. She didn't know where she was, if we were going to hurt her, where her puppies were. She was an emotional wreck and separated from her puppies to soon. They didn't let them wean long enough so she still had milk dripping from her. This is where she developed severe separation anxiety. She was traumatized first by being bred for money, then by having her babies taken away before the weaning process was complete and now, she was being dumped in a stranger's apartment. I wanted to punch these fuckers in the face. I really did. I also think they physically abused her because anytime I lifted my hand to get something, brush my hair, etc. she would cower. Whatever abuse she suffered while in the hands of those two losers left an emotional mark on her. Physically she was emaciated. The matted fur caused her pain because anytime she tried to itch herself her paw got caught in the fur.

Whenever we went for a walk, she would hide behind me if another person came toward us. If another animal, even the little ones, came near her she'd start barking at them as if she was being attacked, or she would lunge for them if they tried to know her through sniffing. She was in full on defense mode, "I'll hurt before I get hurt." Lilli was in bad shape, but I saw hope, life and love in her eyes. I knew I could help her, but I wanted to get some guidance too. I'd never dealt with an abused animal one on one. So, I sought professional help for her.

Poor honey. What kind of help did you get her?

I found a dog therapist.

A dog therapist? I didn't know such a therapist existed. We could have got one for Sophie.

Sophie didn't need a dog therapist. I'll tell you Mom; Lilli was at the complete opposite end of the spectrum from Sophie. We adopted Sophie when she was a baby. Her only history was going from a playpen to our home. Lilli went through a lot and who knows what else they put her through. My heart ached for her. I was determined to show her the good side of life; one where love, gentleness, warmth, kindness, toys and treats existed.

You were her angel.

Devon paid for the dog therapist who came only once and showed us what we would need to do on a regular basis to help Lilli learn how to trust us. A dog therapist basically works with humans to help you better understand and positively change your dog's behavior through positive and repetitive reinforcement exercises. I worked with Lilli every day for a year and a half re-enforcing positive interactions with me, Devon and other people. I could tell Lilli was trying too, she really was. She wanted to please me, but she had these intense fears of being hurt. So intense that sometimes if I gently but firmly disciplined her for something like urinating on the rug or something like that she would get aggressive and even lunge at me. She wouldn't hurt me, but it was, again, automatic defensive mode for her. This, I understood. I had to focus on positive reinforcement and not negative discipline. So, I didn't acknowledge her peeing on the rug. Instead, I praised her when she urinated outside or on her wee-wee pads and gave her treats when she "played nice," these kinds of things. I walked her every day at the same time, three times a day, and purposely stopped her when a neighbor or someone would pass by to let them say hello so she would get used to people and know that not everyone would hurt her. When I felt we developed enough trust together I took us to another level. Lilli's fur grew very thick all year round which meant she needed a haircut every six weeks or so. Her previous humans failed to groom her which is why she had all those mats on her. I bought a dog grooming kit, watched a video and taught myself how to shave Lilli so I wouldn't have to spend $100 on a groomer every six weeks. This was also a good trust exercise for her as well. She was wary at first but once she realized that being groomed equaled feeling cooler and not all tangled up, she let me shave her.

Oh my gosh honey, this is amazing! How did you get Lilli used to the shaver?

I turned it on and let her listen to the sound. Then I'd turn it off. I did this a few times. Then I turned it on and gently let it vibrate next to her so she would know what it does and that it wasn't something that was going to hurt her. She got so used to it she would fall asleep during her grooming and I would simply roll her from one side to the other as I shaved her fur from head to toe, literally. She was so happy when I was done. She'd run from one end of the apartment to the other, bark, jump in my lap and be silly Lilli. She was all mangled up when she came to live with me but after a few months of love and care she gradually started to understand that not all humans would hurt her.

Little Lilli

That's her when she was just a baby.

Oh my gosh she is adorable! How sweet. She looks like the little dog from the movie, Lady and the Tramp.

I know. Everyone used to say that.

You saved her Kristin. Who knows what would have happened to her if you didn't take her?

We saved each other.

That's true.

I often wonder what happened to her children. I couldn't save them, and I know Lilli longed for them. She guarded anything that was "hers." I hurt for her because of this. It took a long time but the more I worked with Lilli the less she guarded her food and toys and became what she truly is; a loving, loyal, warm, funny, sweet, devoted little girl but she always remained fiercely protective of me and Devon. People that saw us walking every day would comment because whereas she was hiding behind me before. She would now stop, sit and wait for the passerby to pet her. She was so cute.

Oh, how beautiful, and did they pet her?

Most did. She was hard to resist. I mean, if you see a dog walking toward you and you're the only person walking toward him/her and they sit and wait for you to pet them even before you get to them, that's a precious moment waiting to happen. For those that were in a hurry and didn't she would still stop, and then look at me as if to say, "Hey, that human didn't pet me. What's going on?"

A sweet little girl rescued by a sweet person.

Lilli took her pain and helped others stop, take a moment and pet a once hurt dog now on her way to healing and experiencing nothing but love.

She was giving them what you were giving her.

Yeah?

Yeah.

Hmm, I never saw it like that, but I'll take it.

Kristin don't get upset with me for saying this but a career with animals would have been perfect for you.

I'm not upset and you're right. When I was little, I used to toy around with the idea of being a veterinarian.

I know. I remember. What happened with that?

I'm terrible at math and science; two of the main courses you need to succeed as a vet. I also thought about working or running a sanctuary, something like that.

That would have been great too!

Oh well.

Honey, your dreams can still come true.

Na, not that one. I'm a realist about my body and the limitations I have now but it doesn't crush my love for animals or prevent me from helping them whenever I can. Do you like the Mohawk I gave Lilli?

I love it and I hope you still keep your dreams alive in that realist head of yours because you never know babe. You never know.

I do.

So, did you ever see those people again?

Do you know I did? I saw the boyfriend at the bodega by my house. He recognized me and stopped me to say hello.

What did you say? Oh boy, this should be interesting.

Firstly, I couldn't believe he had the nerve to even stop but as soon as I saw him, I thought about what my poor Lilli went through, and I wanted to strangle him. I started out pleasant but as I went on to inform him of what he put MY dog through by abandoning her as he did, I got upset. I found myself telling him that if he ever came near Lilli, or if I heard of him or his crack head girlfriend buying or adopting another animal, any animal, I would call the Humane Law Enforcement on them. Then I would call the human police and have them raid their home just to see if they would find anything interesting. When he started to say something, I cut him off and said, "Say one word, just one and I'll call the police right now!"

Oh, my goodness you didn't say that Kristin.

Oh yes, I did. I remember those losers like it was yesterday.

Well, be careful. I don't want you getting yourself hurt.

They're not going to hurt me. They're too stupid.

How was Monte with Lilli? Did they get along?

Oh boy, Monte wasn't too thrilled to have a sister. When I first brought Lilli home, I kept the two of them separated by a gate while I was out because I wasn't sure how they would relate to each other. This lasted only a couple of days. One day I came home only to find that Monte had climbed over the gate to be with Lilli. I found them sleeping on the bed together so there was no more need for the gate. They were so cute. This, however, didn't last too long. Monte was older and wanted to relax. Lilli was a baby and brought a sense of chaos mixed with excitement to the house. Still, with him being the older sibling he managed to establish his dominance over Ms. Lilli. His previous human declawed him which I don't believe in. When I first came to New York I worked in a vet office and the procedure is extremely painful for cats. I've lost a toenail and thought it was excruciating. I couldn't imagine if I lost all ten at a time especially since the cut at the joint.

Oh yeah, that does sound horrible. Why did she declaw him?

Probably for the same reason most other people do; they don't want their furniture ruined or get scratched. The thing is, when you declaw a cat or any animal, they can't walk, scratch themselves or go to the bathroom without feeling this incredible pain. It's terrible. They have to be on all painkillers and it really affects their personalities. Some get lethargic, in part from the meds, but also because of depression from being in such pain for so long. After they've healed and hopefully without complications, they have no defense mechanism. Some might argue that indoor cats don't need it, but I would then argue the pain factor. You don't need to cause un-necessary pain to your feline companion. The remedy to keeping your furniture nice and keeping yourself from being scratched is to get a cat tree and/or scratching posts and get your kitty's nails trimmed regularly.

Is that what you did?

Yes. I could and would never declaw a kitty. Thank goodness some states are now banning it which is good. I bring it up because with Monte's little cotton ball like paws, if Lilli got on his nerves, he would swap her face three times in a row until she stopped. It didn't hurt her, but she got Monte's message of "leave me alone." It was funny because Lilli would squint her eyes and wait until he was done. Yet she had this look on her face as if to say, "Yeah, go ahead, smack away cat. I'll get you," and she would. Lilli would see Monte sleeping and quietly go up to him, bark as loud as she could in his ear and scare the bageebees out of him.

That's funny.

They didn't fight but they definitely had a typical love/hate relationship. Monte was the happy boss and Lilli was the unwilling submissive kid. The following picture pretty much sums up their relationship.

Monte and Lilli

Oh, my goodness. Check out the look on Lilli's face.

Yeah, she was pretty funny. Lilli was looking at me as if to say, "Get rid of the cat or I'll torch this place!"

And Monte looks like a happy go lucky camper. What a pair! They could have had their own comedy show. The Adventures of Lilli and Monte!

Exactly. When I was home, they would race to see who would get on me or Devon's lap first. The two of them had this thing if they were lying next to each other which they often did. They would begin this staring contest. I don't know what conversation was happening between them, but I know it was something very interesting because I could see their stares building up to this big burst of energy where one would all of a sudden get up, and start chasing the other to an adjacent room.

They sound hilarious. What do you think they were saying?

Who knows but whatever it was, it was enough to light a fire under one of them. If they didn't hear me walk in the apartment when I got home from work, it never failed that I would find them curled up on the bed together.

That's sweet. So, aside from Lilli's puss face they did love each other?

Oh yeah. They really loved each other. They never fought. They just teased each other. They were quite a pair and a lot of entertainment for Devon and me. So that was that. I was on my journey with Monte, Lilli and Devon.

How are you?

I'm okay.

I'm glad you had these three because you were still going through a lot.

Yeah.

Do you want to talk about what else you were experiencing?

Not really. I feel like I'm going back to dark, ugly places in my life. I just want to let them go and leave them behind me.

Sometimes, in order to work through those dark, ugly places we have to revisit them in order to better understand the events and ultimately, ourselves. Once you understand them better, you'll be more apt to let them go. I want you to talk more about what was going on with you because you haven't fully let it all go.

I know. It's just so exhausting.

Well, take your time. We're not in any hurry.

Here I was in my new job going about my life and boom! I get hit with the neck pain again worse than before. This time it was more severe on my right side, which is my dominant side. It went between my shoulder blades and trickled down my arm as though I had pins and needles in it. I was trying to get off the pain pills and now found myself taking more again. I was also back on the muscle relaxers. I was only thirty when I had the first surgery. I was going on thirty-two and all I wanted to do was enjoy my life, my animals and my boyfriend and this pain was screwing all that up. I was more limited than before, way more. Before, every day activities were challenging. Now, they were impossible. I couldn't lift a plate like I normally did with one hand to put it in the cupboard. I had to use both hands and keep my elbows close to my body for support. When I took the bus, I had to put a towel underneath me. Since these big city buses have very little shock support, every teeny tiny bump sent pain that radiated from my head, to my neck, down to my arms and the low part of my back. When I would lay my head on my pillow for the night, I would get these spasms on the right side of neck that would jolt me forward so fast that I would pull the already fragile muscles in my neck. Then I would get nervous wondering what further damage I may have caused to myself and start to cry because I just didn't understand why this was happening to me or how to help myself. With all the pain I was in it was hard to know what the right choice was for anything. All the things like even light exercise and stretching became harder for me because they added to the pain, I was already in. I couldn't hold the phone to my ear for too long because the pain from my neck was causing weakness in my arm. I couldn't walk very far because it placed stress on my neck from having to hold it up for so long without being able to relax the rest of my body. You'd be surprised how much you use your neck. You don't really know until you take most of its strength and endurance away and you're left with the rest of your body. What's holding it up? Everything stems from the bone, muscles and joints in your head and neck and from there trickles downward, from pain to pleasure.

That's true. I remember when Mom had her whiplash and how painful that was for me. Not just in my neck but everywhere. You're right. Your whole body gets affected.

It does because the rest of your body is compensating for those parts that are in pain and/or not working as they should. Along with the physical challenges I was facing I also faced some intense emotional challenges too.

Depression?

That and along that same line, body image. I was putting on weight. All my muscle turned to flab and I lost almost all of the strength I acquired and retained through dance. I felt like a big weak, floppy, mess. I wore big clothing to hide my body. Part of my angst was that I couldn't dance or exercise. I had all this pent-up energy and no way of expressing it.

I was just going to say that. You danced and exercised your whole life and now all that was at a standstill. You must have been going out of your mind with energy that needed to be released, in a healthy way.

I was. I walked but it wasn't enough. Sometimes I would pace my apartment just trying to get the energy going but nothing helped. I hated the way I felt inside and out. Even though I wasn't in as much contact with your family they still gave me grief. I didn't even know that was possible.

How so?

I couldn't travel for a long time. At first it was because of the surgery and recovery process. Now I was feeling the pain again only a year and a half later. They were quick to get mad at me for not attending a family function or a cousin's wedding. Every time I tried to explain what was happening with me, they didn't want to hear it. They thought I was exaggerating or making excuses. Between having to explain my every detail of neck pain and its subsequent damage to my life to your family that had little empathy to begin with, and my job I was feeling overwhelmed. I could only take so much. Your family was so negative. I would still leave a message with them to say hello, just to shut them up. I dreaded making those phone calls. I used to have to pretend I was a different person; a character and feign a happy voice so I wouldn't get their negative feedback but that didn't help. If I had the bad luck of someone picking up, I tried to sound in good spirits and even tried to make whomever I was talking to laugh, yet they would pin me back to their negative perspective of me.

What do you mean? How? Actually, I think I know how. I've been there but tell me.

They would ask me how things were going with my neck, doctor and what not. As soon as I expressed any frustration I was feeling about my doctor or what I was going through they would shut down and/or end the conversation abruptly. In the next phone conversation, they'd accuse me of being angry and depressed and Mom, I was neither nor to them or anyone else. I always made a point to keep my feelings confined to my home and not take them out on anyone. The only one who could ever say the above would be Devon. Since we spent so much time together, he's the only one who saw my anger, frustration and depression. No one else did. No one else was around.

I understand. Sometimes I would get a similar reaction.

You would?

Oh yes.

How? Please tell me so I don't feel like this horrible person they tried to make me out to be.

First of all, you're not and I've told you many times, even while I was physically present, to not let them get to you like that.

It was easier when you were here to stand up for me. This is where the "without a net" feeling came in.

I know.

So how did you get a similar reaction?

Oh, my sisters used to tell me how they thought I should see a therapist for the depression I was feeling, as if they didn't need a therapist themselves. When I told them about my cancer support groups, they thought it was a great idea I was going. When I asked if they'd come with me everyone was busy. You were the only one who came with Mom to her support groups.

I liked going with you. I could see a glimmer of hope in you that brightened up every time we went.

I did have hope honey. I truly did. So, what else was going on with the family that should not have been had I been there?

They acted like what I was going through wasn't happening or as though it wasn't that bad. The only person out of all your family that, at the very least, knew I was going through something bad was Carolyn. I did my best to not let the things they said or the way they were get to me, but they did. My cousins were fortunate to have their mothers buffer their words. Your sisters used to say I talked back to them, but I was no worse than my cousins, some of whom were way more disrespectful than I. In the few conversations I had with anyone in your family I felt like someone was punching me in the gut. The conversations always ended the same way, with me feeling small. They judged me based on what a spinal injury was doing to me. That part hurt me immensely because what I was going through wasn't my fault. I missed you so much. I used to hug that stupid urn and pretend you were hugging me back.

I tried to get you to hear or feel me, but your energy blocked us. You had all these negative voices in your head telling you, you were nothing and not worth anything. None of that was true sweetheart. Those pills separated us even further. I was hugging you little girl, every day of every minute that pain entered your body I was hugging you, loving you and kissing your pain away. It just wouldn't go away.

I know, I know. I wish I wasn't so blocked.

It's okay. You had a lot going on, physically, emotionally and mentally.

I showed my strength, will and determination but when I was alone, I'd curl up into a ball and cry, often letting these primal screams into my pillow. I begged God or the Universe to help me through this constant pain that altered my life for the worse.

I'm sorry you were going through this honey. I'm sorry the family wasn't more supportive, but I want you to know something.

What?

It's not you. They could be the same with me too, give me that same harsh judgmental talk and behavior but you know what got me through my toughest times?

What?

You. When they'd talk it was easier for me to take their words with a grain of salt because I had my daughter to smooth out those rough edges. I know for you it was harder. You had your animals and Devon, but you didn't need, nor did you deserve all that extra negativity the family was putting on you. Did Devon ever have anything to say about your feelings about the family?

Devon met them once. This was before I was having neck problems. One summer Devon and I visited Andrea and she invited your family over for a barbecue. When you meet your family in a family gathering setting as Devon did, they come off as fun, jovial people. You don't see the betrayals, cruel, backstabbing behaviors that are their true colors. He thought I was exaggerating or misinterpreting things. He found out, later on, that wasn't the case.

I can see that. Our family, if nothing else, loved to party. Your older cousins all grew up in the 60's and you kids are of the 70's. I think you were the only one out of all our family that wasn't a partier. That's probably why you got teased so much. Your head was in the books and your feet were on the dance floor. The only thing in-between was me and Sophie. How were you able to get through the workday with your plate stacked so full?

I was taking a lot of pain killers. I mean a lot. If I knew I had to call the family because it had been a while or so I'd take a pain pill a few minutes before the call. That often helped. What? Why are you laughing?

I used to do the same thing with my sisters. They were easier to take that way. How many pills were you taking a day Kris?

I think I was up to anywhere from 10 – 12 Percocet's a day plus the muscle relaxers and Celebrex, the anti-inflammatory.

Kristin, that's a pain pill almost every two or three hours. I'm surprised you didn't OD!

Mother, when I tell you the pain was unbearable it was. You know the kind of pain I'm talking about, right?

I do.

It was that teeth grinding, heart racing, sweat inducing, screaming, agonizing, "let me die" pain. Devon told me that he could literally see when the pain medication was wearing off on me because my face would tighten up and I'd go from being okay to being short fused in a split second.

I know that feeling all too well. It's hard when you want to do things, but your body won't let you. It's like being imprisoned by your own body and others can't imagine what you're feeling, and our family isn't the most compassionate bunch!

You can say that again and again. Others can suggest this or that but man when that pain would hit. That's all I could focus on was the pain and how to get rid of it as fast as possible. I don't know how to put it into words except to say that it was like someone was taking a knife to the inside of my neck and cutting.

What did your doctor say about all this pain you were feeling?

He sent me for an MRI and CAT scan which showed I had a spinal stress fracture in the same area as my previous surgery. Combine that with cumulative little traumas from repetitive daily activity and you have the makings of Cervical Spondylosis.

Oh, baby girl.

I found the clinical definition of Cervical Spondylosis.

What is it? Let me hear.

Cervical Spondylosis, "also known as cervical osteoarthritis or neck arthritis, is a common, age-related condition that affects the joints and discs in your neck. It develops from wear and tear of the cartilage and bones found in your cervical spine, which is in your neck. While it's largely due to age, it can be caused by other factors as well."[15]

So, this probably started while you were dancing.

Probably, my doctor said Cervical Spondylosis can begin when you're young and may not show symptoms until many years later as was the case for me. What was happening was that a portion of my neck bone slipped forward. Due to the Spondylosis I developed what's called cervical foraminal stenosis at my C3-4 and C4-5. This is where osteophytes or bony protrusions or bone spurs as they're often referred to, developed on the back of my neck at C3-4. What happens is that the foramen (the opening through which the nerve root exits) narrows.

Why did you develop bone spurs?

Bone spurs develop as a "result of the body trying to grow extra bone to make the spine stronger. However, the extra bone can press on delicate areas of the spine, such as the spinal cord and nerves, resulting in pain."[16]

So, your body was trying to grow extra bone?

It viewed the neck surgery as "trauma" and reacted by trying to protect it. In doing so, rather than growing just enough bone to fuse it grew too much bone. The only upside here is that my body loves me. It was trying to protect itself from any perceived trauma. That was nice of it.

Oh sweetheart, come here. So, the bone spurs are what caused the Cervical Spondylosis?

Yes, and thus all the pain in my neck and the feeling of pins and needles down my arm, as well as instability at my C3-4. All of this meant one thing.

AN ENCORE PERFORMANCE

2002

"Dance is a delicate balance between perfection and freedom.
Dance is life at its most glorious moment.
The dance –
it is the rhythm of all that dies in order to live again;
it is the eternal rising of the sun."

Kenneth Grooms

St. John's Riverside Hospital
967 North Broadway
Yonkers, New York 10701

"Date of Operation:	01/09/02
Patient:	Kristin A. Crage
Operation:	Bilateral posterior cervical foraminotomy, C3-4, C4-5, with foraminal decompression; posterolateral fusion, C3-4 and 4-5; microsurgical dissection; posterior cervical segmental fixation system with 3.5 x 12mm screws, bilateral C3-4-5; utilization of allograft for fusion (Graft-on).
Preoperative Diagnosis:	Cervical spondylolysis, C3-4-5; bilateral foraminal stenosis, C3-4 and D4-5; cervical instability, C3-4; status post anterior cervical fusion, C4-5; intractable neck pain.
Postoperative Diagnosis:	The same."[17]

****

A foraminotomy.

Sweetheart.

My surgeon decided to start his own practice and I went with him. It actually wasn't much of a choice that I stay with him. Once a surgeon operates on you it's hard to find another surgeon who will operate on you in the same area if the first outcome wasn't successful. They don't like doing that out of fear of liability should something else go wrong. This time I would be at St. John's Riverside Hospital in Yonkers, NY. When my doctor explained the procedure to me, I froze with a fear that I quickly had to shake if I wanted out of the pain. He flat out said to me, "Kristin, this is going to be some serious pain. I have to go into your cervical spine (neck) through the back and shave off some of the bone off with a drill." The procedure entailed my doctor making an incision through the back of my neck, moving the muscle around and out of the way to reveal the bone underneath and cut a hole in the vertebrae. From there he would drill off the bone spurs to allow fluid to pass through so it wouldn't build up and cause more swelling and pain. When bone spurs grow, they take up space preventing fluid from passing through your cervical spine. Then he would extend my fusion to keep my neck stabilized and realign that portion that was protruding forward caused by the Spondylolysis. So, my first fusion was from C4-C5. This time the fusion was extended upward from C3-4 and C4-5. My neck would be secured with titanium screws and plates.

Oh my gosh Kristin. I don't even know what to say.

That made two of us. I couldn't quantify how much pain I would be in afterward since the pain I was in was already unbearable. I didn't think about the fact that my doctor would be moving muscle and tendons around so that a drill could be taken to the bone to remove it. I didn't think about what a hard, heavy, fast vibrating tool would do to my neck. I didn't think about it because I couldn't. I just wanted out of the pain. Also, I asked all the questions I could think of but after that I was at a loss and doctors only tell you so much. They don't want to scare the hell out of you. I'm surprised my doctor was as forthright as he was and told me I'd be in pain. I'm glad he did. The hard thing about surgery, recovery and the challenges you may or may not face afterward is that you don't know what questions to ask because you don't know how you'll be affected, not really. Since doctors disseminate only so much information about your procedure it's hard to know what types of questions to ask. Yet I learned a lot from being with you and your journey through cancer as we maneuvered our way through doctors, nurses and one procedure after another. As I did with my previous procedure, I came up with a list of questions that started with the things I love to do. My questions began with, "Can I still do…?" Whatever my doctor told me I couldn't do led me to what can I do and what can't I do. From there I devised my exercise, strengthening and stretching plan. Now, when my doctor said pain, I thought he meant the kind where I could take a pain pill and it would work. I was about to venture to a very different kind of pain and, again, not having ever experienced it, was hard to envision or prepare for.

Oh boy.

Aside from the surgery I was also nervous about what my job would say. I was trying to manage the pain and work but here I was back in the same position of having to explain to my new job that I had to go for neck surgery.

I know but this was not your fault.

I know that and you know that, but the corporate world is unsympathetic to your health plight because all they see is, "Who is going to pick up the slack of this person while she's out?"

I know.

I just started this new job and now I had to take time off. I would be out of work again. I felt like I was in a pattern of one step ahead and two steps backward. I applied for the short-term disability and called my sister for the money she owed me.

Did she give it back to you?

No.

What was her excuse?

She said she didn't have it. I told her what I was going through and she said, "Well, what do you want me to do? I don't have it."

Did she offer to come and help you, be with you during the surgery?

No. She kept asking me all these questions, "Why do you have to have these surgeries?" "Why don't you find another doctor?" "Did you get a second opinion?" On and on like I was stupid, and the questions wouldn't stop. They were really to try and distract me from the fact that she flat out refused to help me.

She could have like I helped her, but she chose not to. I told her I'd done all those things and reminded her that I was more than familiar with how to navigate myself around the healthcare industry. When I would assert myself and tell her it was my body and I was making the best decisions based on what I was experiencing and conversations with my doctor she'd get upset.

Why?

Anytime I disagreed with my sister she didn't like it. My feeling was tough shit. Honestly Mom, I didn't have the energy to deal with her. I also didn't like her questioning my judgment and the decisions I was making about MY body. My feeling is that if you can't be supportive to the people you say you love and their decisions regarding their health, even if you don't agree, then you should stay away because you'll do more harm than good.

I agree.

If that were me, I'd be at her bedside, but that's me.

I know babe. It would have been nice for her to come and help you.

Yeah, it really would have. I remember talking with Carolyn prior to the surgery. When I told her of the procedure, I was about to have she went silent. I thought I was getting the cold shoulder. I was super surprised when she said, "I'm coming down." What surprised me even more was that I didn't tell her "no" which was my first instinct. I don't know. Devon seemed pretty nervous about this procedure. My doctor put some serious fear into both of us about what this particular procedure would entail. The only reason I agreed to her visit was that I thought Devon could use the support. A lot was falling on him too you know. He would help me post-surgery with things around my apartment because I couldn't bend over, reaching for things I couldn't reach because I was also told not to stand on a stool for anything just in case I slipped. You know little things like that that meant a great deal to me.

I am so glad that you had him. I really am.

Me too. Carolyn said she couldn't make it down until a couple of days after my procedure, but the interesting part was her insistence on coming down in the first place. Her voice sounded worried, almost scared.

This was one of the few times my sister actually heard me. I had a feeling you were going to need help. I wanted her to help you, for me. I didn't want you alone especially since Devon was working.

I had no idea what I was getting into. I could only hope for the best and prepare for the worst, but nothing prepared me for this. When I awoke from the procedure, I was unable to lift my head off the pillow and I couldn't move my neck. I went to rub my head and felt all this cakey stuff on my scalp and in my hair. When I pulled some of it out, I freaked. Then the nurse reminded me that my head was in a retractable device during the surgery, which took almost four hours, to keep it still. That cakey stuff was dried blood. My neck was all bandaged up, but I could still feel the huge bump the size of a mini baseball on the back from the swelling. There are no words to describe the pain except to say it felt like a boulder hit me in the back of my neck and split it open. I immediately started to cry and began pushing the morphine button over and over. Even that didn't help. I could hardly talk and had a hard time breathing. The nurses kept telling me to stay calm so as to not let the fear and anxiety cause me to hyperventilate. Devon was by my side with a look of concern and fear on his face that scared me. My doctor came in and said, "I told you this was going to be painful." Then, after checking me over he said the words that broke my heart. "You can forget about ever dancing again. Those days are over. Try to get used to that." My doctor might as well have killed me right then and there.

Oh, that lousy bastard. Nice bedside manner. He sounds like some of the doctors I had.

When he said that my heart broke into tiny pieces. My ability to move and be free as I once was, was over and I was forever attached to a body that I didn't know and didn't want to know. As soon as my doctor uttered those ugly words Devon quickly changed his demeanor from fear to hope. He moved the doctor out of the way, smiled, put his hand in mine and squeezed it as if to say, "Hang in there. It's going to be okay."

"What happened to me?" I asked him. "What do I look like?" He tried to calm me down, told me to keep breathing slowly and assured me I was going to be okay. I asked him not to leave me. He didn't. He took off work so he could stay with me for the three days I was in the hospital and for the days I was home until Carolyn arrived. I was scared and clung to Devon. He was amazingly supportive. He never argued with me about the things I knew were best for myself i.e., if a pain med wasn't working or if the nurses were rude which they often were. One nurse couldn't find my vein, so she kept jabbing me in the hand with the needle. I cried out to make her stop but she kept jabbing away. Even as weak and vulnerable as I was, I asked Devon to call the Patient Advocate to my room and asked for a new nurse to be assigned to me. Some nurses can be rude, controlling and completely insensitive. I was dealing with enough.

They can be. We certainly had our share of dealing with them with me, didn't we?

Yes. With you, the hard part back then was that I was too young, and it was hard to get anyone to listen to me when I spoke on your behalf. Now it was hard because I had to do all this advocating for myself and I'm the patient! Devon is more on the reserved side and wasn't as comfortable asking for a patient advocate, but he definitely supported me when she came. Patients shouldn't have to do any advocating for themselves. Every patient should be treated with sensitivity and compassion and given excellent care. That's rarely the case.

That's for sure.

When it came to my discharge my doctor told me complete bed rest for at least two weeks and sent me home with a script for Oxycontin, more pain medication, which Devon filled. That first night was scary. Neither Devon nor I knew what to do with me; how to help me sleep, go to the bathroom or eat. I had to sleep sitting up for the first few days. Any pressure on my neck was excruciating and I couldn't sleep on either of my sides and definitely not my stomach with my neck turned. My neck was too sensitive and couldn't be moved until it healed. When Carolyn arrived and saw the baseball on my neck, she put her arms out and held me ever so gently. My body was still trembling from the trauma of the surgery. She started to cry. "Something told me to come." She said. "I don't know what it was, but something told me I had to be here."

I'm glad she heard me.

Me too. I was right to not tell her "no" to coming. I could tell Devon was relieved she was there. One instance, in particular, sticks out in my mind.

Oh, which one?

My doctor and anyone at the hospital neglected to give or tell me to take stool softeners because of all the pain meds I was on. As you know, those pain meds, especially the morphine, cause severe constipation.

Why do you think I lived on Dulcolax [stool softener]?

Yup, so without a stool softener or laxative my stool hardened up like a rock. When I tried to pass it, I bled from my rectum. Every time I tried to push it through it felt like something hard with sharp edges was stuck and scraping the inside of my rectum. Each push put pressure on my neck forcing my already trembling body to shake and drip with sweat and caused me even more pain. Carolyn came into the bathroom, held both my hands while I screamed, cried and bled as I tried to pass this stool. Finally, Carolyn said, "Honey, take a breath and no more pushing." We decided it would be best for me to let it temporarily let it stay where it was, and she had Devon get some suppositories. I've never used them, but I remember when you used to. I cleaned myself off and laid on my bed and Carolyn put the suppository in. I wasn't ashamed or belittled or anything like that. I cried for you. I needed you to tell me this was just a setback and that I was going to be okay and hold me like you always did.

Baby I was there. I would never leave you. I was there holding you, loving you and…

You weren't there and you never would be. I needed to be able to call you and say, "Mom, I'm not doing well. I need to come home and stay with you until I get back on my feet." I was grateful for Carolyn's help but when she went home, I was left alone. I had Devon but he was so stressed out from seeing me go through all this agony and working full time. He was at a loss. He didn't know what to do, how to help me and he really hurt for me. Imagine seeing someone you love going through so much. I knew exactly how he felt. I watched you cry for years, as I was. I lost the healthy life and body I once knew and had no idea what to do or how to handle this new damaged body and the pain that came along with it. Mom, I…

I know honey. I know. I wish I could have helped you through this the way you needed. I truly do. It's hard to prepare for the traumas that occur in our life because we don't know what they are and when they hit. It's like getting hit with a bulldozer.

That's how I felt. The use of my upper body was slowly deteriorating. Without being able to express my feelings through movement my world turned dark. My thoughts and my dreams were all dark. I had nightmares about being killed and cut into tiny pieces. When I took the Oxycontin it gave me hallucinations and enhanced my already bloody dreams. My doctor switched me back to the Percocet which I took every hour and half. I wasn't supposed to, but I didn't care. Sometimes I hoped I would overdose, "by accident." I felt terrible for my animals. I adopted them to give them a good life and now I was going through all this ugliness. Lilli and Monte heard me cry all the time. When I would lay down Lilli would go to the back of my neck, sniff my wound and try to lick it. She sat next to me and never left my side. I felt terrible for Devon too because I wasn't much of a partner. We couldn't go anywhere or do anything. Having sex was the furthest thing from my mind. Devon didn't go to his acting classes anymore because he was afraid to leave me alone even though I kept telling him to. I wanted one of us to keep living and doing. I had no friends because I didn't have time, energy or the wherewithal to make friends. My life felt like it was over, and I wanted it over. This was different from being suicidal. I mean things were just awful, truly awful Mom.

I know. You didn't want to die. You just wanted all the ugliness to end. I'm here.

Yes, exactly. One night I was in the bathroom crying. Devon heard me and knocked on the door. I let him in. He asked me what was wrong, and I couldn't hold back the cries and tears that came from the bottom of my gut. I cried for the loss of my strong body that I used to challenge every day with exercise and dance but was now stationary from agonizing pain. I cried for the loss of the relationship I had with you. I cried from the pain that wouldn't go away. I told Devon all these things and then I uttered words that shook fear into him and peace into me. I'm sorry. I'm going on and on and not letting you say anything.

I'm listening. I want you to keep talking and get this out of you. Keep going.

I asked Devon to hold me while I swallowed a bottle of pills. I wanted to die but I didn't want to die alone. How selfish is that? I couldn't take anymore. This was not the life I wanted for myself or my animals. I had no quality of life, at all. Devon sat behind me and wrapped his huge arms around me as the river of tears continued. I gasped for air and felt saliva trickling down the sides of my mouth. My nose clogged and I couldn't catch my breath through the crying. Devon held me and said, "C'mon now Kristin. You just hang in there. You just hang in there. This isn't the Kristin I know. Where's the fighter? Where's that angry woman that doesn't take shit?" I begged him to let me go because it was the only way out of the pain, I was in. I loved him and my animals so much. Call it self-pity I don't care but I didn't want him to see me like this. I felt like I was no good to him or my animals. All I wanted was for me and him to have our lives back.

Kristin? Honey? What else? What are you thinking?

That I didn't think this was going to happen to me. I didn't factor this into the plans I had for my life. I had no idea how to handle the magnitude of this pain and the loss of the full use of my upper body. I was back in that big, plastic annoying, beeping neck brace. I couldn't carry groceries or take the garbage down for the longest time. I couldn't carry laundry. If I wanted to pick anything up it had to be less than 1lb. and I had to keep my elbows close to my body in order to utilize my lower body as well. If I held my arms out and you put something in my hand like a glass or dish, I would drop it. I couldn't think about socializing or enjoying my life. I relied on Devon for everything including walking Lilli. He never complained. He just helped me, but I was miserable and with all the wonderful help Devon gave me, so was he. It was hard to for him to see me going through so much and not be able to take the pain away. He saw me go from a gregarious, funny, fit person that wanted to go and do, to someone who could just barely lift a plate and counted the minutes to her next pain pill. Our relationship was characterized by doctor visits, tests, x-rays and prescription refills. It was stressful. I didn't want Devon always staying with me in my apartment. I was the one going through all this shit, not him. I knew that Devon wanted to do his own thing. I used to tell him to go out and not to feel bad because I couldn't, that I would enjoy the time alone and even missed having my alone time. He would play pool from time to time, but I know he wanted a partner in life he could do and experience things with. I felt like if I weren't going through so much, we would have been happier.

I don't know about that although I do understand. I felt like that too when I was going through my cancer. Had I not been going through this this person would have stayed and loved me, on and on. Illness is a challenging road for the person going through it and for those around her/him.

It is and often, people around you don't know or understand how it's affecting you, emotionally. So, they place judgment on your behavior that's not really you but a symptom of your illness/ailment. Thankfully, Devon wasn't one of those that judged me. Once, in the midst of all this ugliness, Devon did something that, for a brief moment, made me feel I was worth something.

You are worth something honey.

I didn't feel that way. I felt like I was being lowered into a well of darkness. I was sinking deeper into my already existing depression that at its foundation was a lack of self -worth and feeling as though I must have deserved what I was going through, as some sort of payback from my prior life.

Kristin, there was nothing you did in this life or any other life for these very painful occurrences to have happened in your life. I know you want more of an explanation but honey, bad things happen and often there is no explanation. It's what we do with them that counts and, for me, as long as you weren't hurting yourself or anyone else, which you weren't. You were doing just fine, better than most as a matter of fact, but feeling altogether the opposite. I know. You don't know how much I wanted to reach out to you and make everything all better. I could see you sinking so low and I couldn't help you. You went from one extreme to the other. You were this fiery, strong young woman ready to tackle anything to someone whose pain and depression became the center of her life.

I know and while I'm sure it was hard for Devon to watch. It was even harder to feel. I wanted to get well but my body just wouldn't cooperate.

I know. What did Devon do for you that made you feel worthy?

Devon always knew of any doctor appointments or tests I was having. This one time I had to go for a CAT scan, and I was waiting on the corner for the bus. I was watching for the bus when I saw Devon. When he came up to me, I asked him, "What are you doing?" He replied, "I'm going to the hospital." I said, "For what?" He replied, "Your CAT scan." Just then a cab pulled up, Devon stood on the curb and like a prince motioned for me to get in. I felt like a princess. Maybe some women dream of being whisked away to a beautiful home or castle or some fantasy like that but not me. I was happy being whisked away to the hospital for my scheduled CAT scan with a wonderful man who truly cared about me amidst my ailment and all that it brought me.

You see honey. You were loved more than you realized.

I was and feeling so bad about myself I couldn't see it.

Why?

Mainly because of all the things I could no longer do. I felt like the best parts of me were stripped away and I was left with the things I didn't like about myself.

Such as?

Being a dormant person in chronic pain that lost full use of her body and was left with no drive, ambition or goals. I didn't like who I became. The worst part was that after this surgery and its subsequent nightmare there was only slight improvement from the pain. When I was finally able to return to work, I could only carry the basics. My bag consisted of my lunch, my wallet and my keys and even that felt like too much. I didn't carry a purse. The day was hard too because of that attorney I was working with. He continued to sit behind me and dictate. My natural reaction was to try and look behind me for clarification of what he said. Each attempted turn of my neck felt like every muscle was being ripped apart, tear by excruciating tear.

He couldn't move so you wouldn't have to turn or your neck or use that machine to dictate?

Apparently not. Other people were just as unsympathetic. Some gave me the cold shoulder. Some were rude as if I'd been out shopping as opposed to having neck surgery. Then there were these little things that happened?

What little things?

Oh, just little things. Once I was walking down the concrete steps in our apartment building. It was winter and the stairs were slippery with people having tracked in wet snow. I slipped and fell and had to be rushed to the hospital to make sure my neck was okay and none of the equipment moved. Another time someone bumped into from behind as I was getting off the bus and I fell to the ground. Again, I had to be taken to the emergency room to have everything checked out. Or, if I slept on my neck wrong, the next day my muscles would be as strained as if I'd fallen. Each instance was enough to cause the persistent pain to be even more intense. Thus, I'd have to increase the number of Percocet's I took just so I could be functional enough to work. It was those little things that, before my injury surfaced were mere nothings, now were major setbacks that took months to recover from. What scared me was that it was getting harder for me to take care of my kids. Walking Lilli was a challenge. I could barely hold the leash because I was never able to train her not to pull. I was in the process of teaching her to walk by my side before my surgeries, but we never got there. Everyday things in my life, i.e., doing dishes, cleaning my apartment and laundry were also still difficult. These are the things Devon helped me with. Again, I became short tempered, more so than before. As time went on Devon and I felt more strain on our relationship. We were no longer intimate. It was more like him helping me with all the things I needed help with and me trying to make it through the day without crying or getting upset from chronic pain, which was rare. I tried to do things to show him my gratitude for all that he did for me like cook or buy him gifts here and there. Still, I could tell he was unhappy, and you know what?

What?

So was I. Devon always said he loved me, but I knew he stayed with me more out of guilt than anything else.

I don't think that's guilt Kristin. Devon could have left. He stayed out of love. He fell in love with you, the person. I know you were trying to be the fun-loving girlfriend he fell in love with but, unfortunately, you got rerouted to unfamiliar territory. I don't think anyone can say they would have been any better in your situation. I can't. As we've said, pain changes a person. It makes you miserable, snappy, short fused, angry, sad, lonely and depressed because you've lost your ability to enjoy life as it should be enjoyed.

That's how I felt. Like there was a dark cloud hovering over me and as though I were carrying 1,000 lbs. That darkness left me feeling lonely, pathetic and bleak at the prospect of having any kind of positive life ahead of me. I never went into detail with your family about my spine and what I was going through, and I don't know how much or how little Carolyn may or may not have shared about my neck. The truth is they didn't want to know if I was doing bad or good. The times I did make the effort to speak with anyone of them they complained I didn't call them, and I'd get this surge of negative energy, but no one called me either, no one and I'm not the type to push where I'm not wanted. That's how I felt, like they didn't want anything to do with me, so I only spoke to them as little as possible. It was a no-win situation with them and one that caused me more stress than I could bare. I was already dealing with enough. I also hated that pity sound in their voices.

What pity sound?

The conversation would start with them bragging about this person having this baby, getting that job and how happy they were. Then their tone would drop, and they'd ask in a voice as if I were half dead, "And, how are you?" I would just respond with, "Everything's good. I'm fine." Then change the subject with an easy statement like, "So tell me more about..." If I put the conversation back on them, I was spared from having to talk about myself.

It's hard when you're going through something that others can't really relate to. They often don't know what to say or end up saying the wrong thing or just plain being insensitive.

With your family it was the latter, that's for sure. Everyone around me was moving forward, including my sister, whom I spoke to only occasionally. I felt stuck in the rut I was in. The pain never got to the point of being bearable. In fact, it got worse. Unfortunately, as my body healed it also grew more bone spurs bringing with them more pain that was stronger than the pain pills I wanted off of. Thus, began yet another journey.

Oh my gosh Kristin. Are you serious?

Yes.

THE DANCER IN ME

2003-2004

"Dancing is the loftiest, the most moving,
the most beautiful of the arts because
it is not mere translation or abstraction from life.
It is life."

Kenneth Grooms

St. John's Riverside Hospital
976 North Broadway
Yonkers, New York 10701

"Date of Operation:	05/28/03
Patient:	Kristin A. Crage
Operation:	Exploration of previous fusion C4-5. Removal all anterior cervical instrumentation C4-5 (Blackstone Titanium System). Preoperative placement and postoperative removal of cranial traction tong. Anterior cervical microdiscectomy C3-4. Anterior cervical partial corpectomies C3 and C4. Anterior cervical interbody fusion C3-4 and C4-5. Anterior cervical instrumentation placement from C3 to C5 with Spinetech Trinica Titanium System (34 MM Titanium plate and 12 mm titanium screws). Utilization intervertebral prosthetic device. Microsurgical dissection. Intraoperative fluoroscopy.
Preoperative Diagnosis:	Status post anterior cervical fusion C4-5. Status post posterior cervical fusion and decompression C3 to C5.

Progressive cervical degenerative disc disease C3-4. Osteoarthritis.
Anterior cervical Spondylosis C3-4.

<u>Postoperative Diagnosis:</u> same."[18]

****

All I wanted to do was Grand Jéte (leap) across a hardwood dance floor and feel sweat dripping down my back. I wanted to rehearse for hours for upcoming performances of any dance I could be in. I wanted to jog, workout, turn, twist, jump, fall, roll, extend, bend, leap and pirouette myself to exhaustion as I used to in college. It was 2003. I was 32 and rather than squeeze myself into a leotard my head was being squeezed into a retraction device so I could undergo my third cervical fusion. Everyday a part of me died Mom. I could feel myself gripping onto to every last bit of delusional hope that I would dance again. Yet with each doctor visit that hope diminished until there was nothing left. While I didn't want to dance as a career I still wanted to just dance whenever I could and at least exercise, you know?

I do know.

I felt like my life was over without dance. Dance is how I defined myself as a person and as a woman. The movement I created was executed with such joy in my heart that nothing, and I mean absolutely nothing could touch or change until now.

You were beyond devastated. I know and there was nothing I could do to make you feel better. Even if I were there, I wouldn't have been able to ease your pain.

Not true. Your presence would have eased my pain. You always did with your reassurance and unconditional love.

Oh sweetheart, c'mon. You're saying that now because of how much you want me there but even when I was physically with you there were times when I couldn't ease your pain.

Yes, but I always knew I had your love to heal me.

You still do but now you have to learn how to heal yourself.

I'm too far gone and way too old.

Not true. Not true at all. What was this procedure for?

I was diagnosed with degenerative disc disease and Osteoarthritis which I already knew about. I also had a recurrence of Spondylosis, all in my cervical spine but the rest of my spine was being affected too. Basically, it was the same thing that happened in the second surgery. More bone spurs grew that had to be drilled off.

Okay, and the rest of your spine was affected because it was compensating for the weaker parts?

Exactly. This procedure was to remove the existing hardware and replace it with thicker, stronger hardware to help keep my neck aligned and not curve or protrude forward from the Spondylosis. Once again, my doctor removed the bone spurs and put in the new hardware. With each procedure I felt like my neck was being hacked into pieces only to be somewhat pieced back together again. I, again, awoke with dried blood caked in my hair and on my head from the retraction device they used to keep my head still during surgery. My saving grace was that the incision was made through the front of my neck instead of the back which meant a little less pain post-op. At the end of the day, on an x-ray, my neck looks like Frankenstein. Here it is.

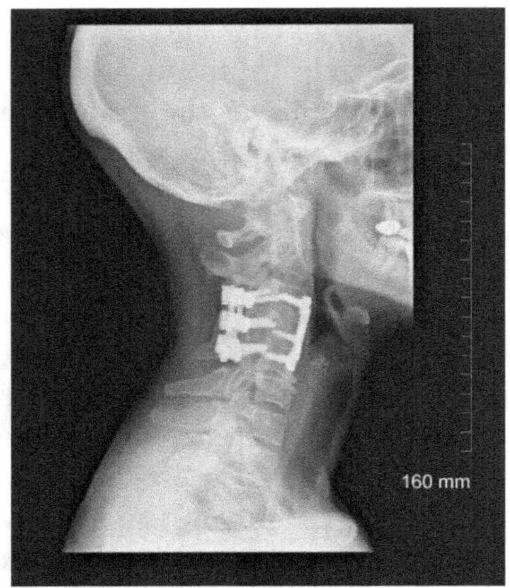

Cervical Spine, lateral view

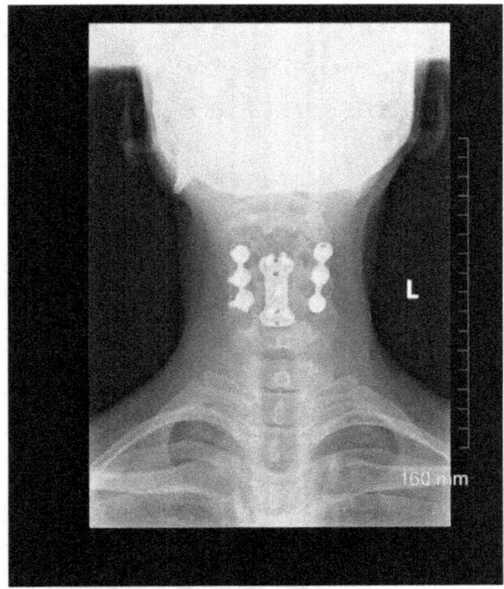

Cervical Spine, back view

Oh, my sweet girl, come here. Let me hold you.

It did but it's getting better and certainly not like it did then.

Wow, that looks like it hurts, a lot. Does it?

I'd use two mirrors and stare at the long scar in the back of my neck that goes from the base of my skull to the bottom on my neck. Then I'd stare at the scar that lay horizontally across my throat and kept asking, "Why is this happening to me?" I didn't understand what I did. I didn't care if I was feeling sorry for myself or not, on the pity pot or not I just wanted all this ugliness to end.

What is it about hard times that make us beg the question: "What did I do?" I know for me having a reason and/or an answer as to why I was going through such hard times would have given me finality. I would have been able to see a beginning and try to figure out an end just by having more information, which I never had. Things always felt undone for me because there were never any answers to why this or that was happening to me. There were material and physical things left undone when I crossed over but, more important, were the emotional things left undone. I don't want that for you. If there was an answer to any of the questions above, what would they do for you?

I feel the same way. Having more answers would have provided me with a starting point to understand more about what I was going through and a place to begin to heal. Just having an answer to the "why" is comfort for me, even if the "why" isn't what I want to hear. It's still a place to begin in order to bring about an end to difficult times. Having the answers to all of my "why's" would give me rationale and closure where there was none. When there's no answer for the hard times I go through it's like hanging in limbo. It's a constant uncomfortable feeling of angst. Even though you say sometimes bad things happen without reason I still wanted one, you know. Something, anything.

I do know, yes. Yet when good things happen, as humans, we just accept them as they are and go about our lives, no closure necessary☺.

That's right. Good things are acceptable because they're good and they bring about good feelings that make me want more of them. Good times never need closure because there's no strife involved.

Without the hard times we'd never know how to appreciate the good would we?

True but at the time of this surgery I was feeling inundated. Again, I was out of work and in more neck braces, pain meds and told no activity while I healed. Then, you'll never guess what I did not too long after this procedure.

What?

I sprained the right side of fucking my neck.

You did what?

Yup.

Are you serious?

Oh yes. I know. Can you believe it?

How in the world did you do that?

Well, firstly my neck, inclusive of all its muscles, was so fragile. It was hard for me to get used to. Sometimes I'd forget about the limitations I now had and would try to do something on my own and hurt myself. I was used to doing everything on my own. Now I had to wait for Devon to help me with everything, even little things like putting laundry in a bag because I couldn't bend over or reach. Anything that utilized my neck muscles (and you'd be surprised how much you use your neck muscles) increased my pain or there was the potential to pull or stain something which is what happened here. Most times I was careful but this one time I was impatient. I hated always having to bother Devon and/or wait for his help. I should have waited for him because in the end I hurt myself.

So, what were you doing that you sprained your neck?

I was trying to move my coffee table.

Oh, Kristin.

I know I know. Since I couldn't use my upper body, I tried an alternate route.

Which was?

I laid on the floor and attempted to use my legs to try and push it to the spot I wanted it in. For a split second, which is exactly how long it takes to sprain something, I forgot about the fragility of my neck. I got frustrated because it wasn't moving, and I went to pull it toward me and boom! I had an instant sprain. I actually felt the muscle rip across my neck and my whole right side, including my shoulder, the back of my shoulder and my right side underneath my arm swelled up instantly. This lasted for months. It still flares up from time to time if I overexert myself. Combined with the weakness I already had from my surgeries, this injury left the right side of my neck and shoulder permanently weaker than my left.

So now you have an injury on top of an already three times cervical fusion. I can't believe that's even possible.

Trust me, it is. This is what I mean about feeling inundated. I was in and out of the emergency room more times than I can count trying to get my pain under control. I increased my pain pills and stuck Lidoderm patches all over the swelled areas so I could at least function during the day.

Lidoderm patches. Those are for pain, aren't they?

Yeah, they're big patches that stick on you and temporarily numb the area, but you have to be careful not to overexert when you're wearing them. Otherwise, when you take them off its double the pain. I looked so silly with all these patches on me. I used to try to hide them with my hair. All this didn't just affect me and Devon. Animals sense every unhappy and unsettling emotion there is and act accordingly. This is true for positive emotions as well. Animals definitely react to their surroundings.

How were your babies doing through all of this?

Poor Lilli would get so nervous and protective of me when the EMS people would come. It must have been scary for her. I was taken to each ER visit by Ambulance. Each time they'd come they'd arrive with all this equipment and strap her mommy on this huge stretcher and take me away for a day or two. She and Monte didn't know where I was or when I was coming back, if I was coming back. It was awful for them and, of course, for Devon. I was grateful I had him. He was affected too. He'd be at the hospital with me for hours until I was seen or was sent to a room if that was the case. Then he'd come home late and have to deal with two traumatized animals and get up early the next day for work. I would come home with yet another pain medication to refill and this just went on and on. The stress factor was high, very high. I wondered if I was ever going to have any kind of life at all. I have to count my blessing and acknowledge how grateful I was that I had insurance which allowed me to even have these procedures and aftercare, but money was tight when I was out of work. The doctor appointments, co-pays, prescriptions, ER visits, MRI's, CAT scan's, blood draws, etc. in addition to everyday life seemed never ending. It was all just too much, way too much for me. Still, I handled it. Every time I was in the hospital for whatever reason I was kicked into "emergency/survival mode."

Just like you were with me.

You got it. It's like a reflex in me. Prior to my procedures I was off and running taking care of whatever had to be taken care of for the three months or however long I'd be out of work afterward. This way I could do what I was supposed to and rest and relax. Although I'm not very good at staying put. I like to keep busy.

That little girl who likes to keep busy, clean and organize was saving the woman in you.

Yes.

I think, too, the fact that you took on so much because of the help I needed while I was going through my cancer also helped you when it came to your surgeries and aftermath.

It did.

You were prepared very early for emergency situations. As hard as our past was it gave you something positive; the means to survive on your own.

I definitely did the best I could and handled whatever came up on any given day. I never missed an appointment. Whenever I went to the ER, as soon as I was out, I picked myself up and went about whatever I had to tend to even if I had to stay still. I'd do whatever I could from the couch, make phone calls, deal with insurance issues of which there was many. Sometimes my doctor would incorrectly code the procedure and the insurance company would send me a letter stating they weren't paying. I, in turn, would have to call my doctor and make sure he got the same letter and sent the proper information. Sometimes I'd go back and forth with one phone call after another. Then there were Monte's doctor visits, trying to work with Lilli's hyperactive energy and get her to relax. I felt like she was more affected than Monte. Lilli already had separation anxiety issues.

Did she do any damage to your apartment when the EMS people would come and take you away because that's pretty traumatizing for a dog with separation anxiety?

Surprisingly no and probably because Devon came back. She could be possessive with me at times.

How so?

I told you how Monte would be on my lap and if Lilli came over, he'd give three or four successive pats in her face as if to say, "It's my turn to be on Mommy's lap."

Right?

As time went on Miss Lilli got a little bolder and every now and again, if Monte was on my lap, she would go right up to his face and bark at him to scare him off so she could plop on my lap.

Did he get off?

No, he just ignored her. Those two were a trip. Barking was another challenge Lilli and I worked on. It took a long time for me to help her control her barking due to all the stress I was under and the energy that took in me.

I'm sure. What would she do?

If there was a knock on the door she'd bark incessantly and run back and forth. Still, I continued to work with her as much as I could. She got a little better as time went on. Unfortunately, with all these health issues going on I went further and further into debt with each procedure I had. It was like this huge, heavy, dark financial cloud constantly hanging over my head. Bill collectors were calling me, credit card bills and hospital balances that the insurance wasn't covering were coming to my mail daily. I had to put my ever-mounting debt to the back of my mind. All I kept telling myself was, "They'll have to wait." I always paid my bills but for the time being they had to wait until I was back on my feet. Bills are a huge stressor.

Don't I know it! I'm glad you put it into the context you did though because you're right. What else could you do.? You were doing as much as you could and you're only one person. That's what I used to tell myself.

I'm glad I don't like to drink. I hate to think of how much alcohol I could have consumed if I did.

And you certainly didn't need any drugs. You were on enough.

Yup. I was good to go.

You could only take it day by day honey and that's what you were doing. What's upsetting for me is that your only support system was Devon and that's not much for you and a lot of pressure for him.

That's how I felt. I used to tell him to take a vacation, but he felt guilty leaving me. I told him I would have managed just fine, but he insisted on staying. We made do the best we could. Sometimes Devon would treat us to pizza.

You two didn't go out to dinner or anything like that?

Every now and again but not often. He was so tired at the end of the day. Going out to dinner seemed like a chore.

That's sad that something like going out, which is supposed to be fun and help relieve stress, seemed like a chore but I can understand that.

I know. You said it was fate, that Devon and I met, and I think you're right. It's no coincidence that I met a man right when I was about to go through the worst times of my life and I was basically alone, you know? I just wish our relationship saw better times.

I think it was fate, but you also willed him into your life too.

What do you mean?

You knew exactly the kind of man you wanted in your life and asked for him every night. Don't think I don't know about the list you kept under your pillow of the kind of man you wanted. It was rather long sweetheart, but God knows what you need and so do you, and that's exactly who you got.

Oh yeah, my list. I wrote down all the characteristics I wanted in a life partner and put it under my pillow.

Yup and in walked Devon with all those characteristics and more.

I was fortunate.

So was he. You two loved each other for who you are, not something you thought the other could be. Your love was honest and pure. It was also tested very early on.

Yeah, I think we'd only been together a year when all this started to happen with my neck. It took us both off guard.

I know.

When I was finally able to return to work my boss and some of the other assistants gave me a hard time.

Because of your neck?

Yes. People would tell me how ugly the neck brace I had to wear was and how uncomfortable it looked. I would tell them to mind their business. They, in turn, would tell me I was being short with them and I should have stayed home longer.

They don't sound like very compassionate or even nice people.

They weren't. I tried to keep to myself as much as possible. Say my "good mornings and good nights" and leave it at that. The owner and his daughter were also giving me a hard time because I wouldn't do what the owner's daughter wanted me too.

What was that?

Remember I was working for the lawyer in a Real Estate office? The one where the daughter took us all to a Mets Game and it was my birthday and she had my name put on the big scroll tv.

Yes, yes, I remember.

This was also the place where the lawyer I was working with would sit behind me and dictate.

Right?

Well I was also responsible for collecting fees from the tenants in the myriad of office buildings the company owned. The tenants liked me and depended on me for clarification if they had questions on the bills sent to them. Some sent me little gifts at Christmas time.

Well that was nice of them.

I really appreciated their kind gestures. Just as an aside, this company made millions of dollars annually on the buildings they owned so they weren't hurting for money by any means.

Okay.

Some of the fees ranged from "common areas" also known as the lobby areas or any area in the building that all the tenants used and paid for in order to keep that area neat and clean. Another fee was for the parking garage but there was one fee that the daughter labeled as "miscellaneous." It was pretty substantial to the tune of hundreds of dollars. That's a lot for some people.

I sure as heck would never pay any fee labeled "miscellaneous" small or large.

Me too. The "miscellaneous fees" weren't stipulated in the tenants' rent agreements. I know because I edited the documents. So, when the tenants asked me about the "miscellaneous fees" I asked the daughter. I kind of had a feeling of what she was doing but I wanted to hear her response. She had no shame in telling me. "Kristin," she said in a matter-of-fact voice. "My father has done this for years. How else are we supposed to make money on these buildings?"

What were they?

The daughter was plumping up the rent rolls so she could get more money from the tenants. They were nothing fees; just her wanting more money and putting it in the category of "miscellaneous" in order to justify it. I told her the tenants were asking me what the fees were. She responded with, "Tell them they are just what they say, 'miscellaneous.'" When I told her that wasn't good enough for them, she followed with, "Just tell them they need to pay the fee." I told her I didn't feel comfortable doing that. I felt like the next thing she was going to ask me to do was ask me to "knock" some people off for not paying. Instead she said, "Other assistants never had a problem with this, and you won't either if you want to keep your job." I couldn't believe what I just heard from her. You know most people might say, "Just don't say anything and do your job." Or, "Mind your business and do your job" but I can't look away when an injustice, regardless of how big or small, is staring me right in the face. It's not in me to let hard working people get screwed over like that. I wouldn't be able to sleep at night. You raised me with the morals, ethics and principles to know what's right and wrong. I'm proud of that. Fight for what you believe, stand up for what's unjust in this world and never let anyone silence your voice. That's what you taught me and that's what I do.

It is but sweetheart I hope you're not going to be upset when I tell you that you live by those right and wrong principles more so than I ever did☺.

I'm not upset, and I know.

What happened with your boss?

I reiterated that I didn't feel comfortable lying to the tenants and telling them they had to pay fees that didn't exist and weren't required of them. I respectfully let her know that I would transfer calls from tenants to her regarding questions on the "miscellaneous fees." I established good rapport with the tenants, and they trusted me to help them with any questions or concerns they had. As the tenants called in, prior to transferring the calls to my boss, I suggested they ask the landlord (my boss) to itemize all the fees as opposed to labeling anything "miscellaneous." I also told them they should ask for the itemization of all their previous "miscellaneous fees" as well. This way they would know exactly what they were paying for. If I ever got a bill from my landlord with a "miscellaneous fee" to the tune of $700 or more, you bet I'm going to call and ask for an itemization of said fee and dispute it. They had a right to that information.

Good for you. Did your boss know you told the tenants this?

I don't know but they may have had a wee bit of a suspicion when the tenants started to ask for all their bills to be itemized. I couldn't sit back while hard working people were getting robbed each month. I didn't want any part of that.

I'm so proud of you.

I was too.

They weren't happy with you though.

No and too bad. I'm not one to turn the other cheek when it comes to a blatant wrong that I can do something about. The other part is that I was naïve to the ways of the corporate world. I was just coming to learn that the much of the corporate world is run by dissociative, underhanded, backstabbing, heartless, thieves who thrive and would sacrifice their own families in order to preserve the illegal practices of their companies. Screwing people over becomes an addiction to some people; a high they can't get enough of. Corporations are filled with crooks that hide under aliases like "LLC" and "LLP."

You were learning the dark side of the corporate world.

This next part was just a scratch of the surface. A couple of months went by when the father came over to my desk, pulled a chair beside mine and said, "Kristin, we need to talk."

Oh know.

Yeah, that's what I said. I knew what was coming next. He continued, "My daughter doesn't feel you're the right fit for this job. Unfortunately, we have to let you go." I was still healing from my surgery and on expensive medications, but they didn't care. I exposed their little scam and that's it. I was out of there. The lights my name was in at a Mets game only a short while ago went out and I was without a job and insurance.

I know. I couldn't believe you were being compounded like this. What they did to their tenants was wrong. There is no doubt about that. Letting you go was their way of covering their asses so they could keep on robbing people.

I know but at least people were aware now and my former bosses couldn't get away with what they were doing anymore. I don't regret my decision. At the very least I made people question something they had every right to question and hopefully do something about.

You know honey, many times I didn't always preach what I taught you but I'm glad you stuck to your guns. I'm sorry this happened to you. I know the loss of income and insurance caused you another huge hassle.

It did but like I said. I take responsibility for my actions and don't regret it. I just wished I was more prepared for the outcome.

I kept getting hit with these surgeries and their respective healing time, the hospital bills I incurred along with the myriad co-payments I was paying out, as well as having to take time off work. Also, around this time Monte got sick with a thyroid problem so that was another very big expense. I felt like I couldn't get out from under and had no time or money to put anything away for emergency situations, like being fired from your job for standing up to a bunch of corporate crooks. This is where the real ugliness began. I had to figure out how I was going to pay for my medications. I only had my insurance for one more month. Just before I was let go, I sent my prescriptions through the mail to the insurance company. They would refill the scripts for up to three months, which my doctor approved.

What about Social Services? You went there right?

I did and it was such a hassle, you know?

I do know.

I know you do. I had to provide this document and that document. Proof of this and proof of not getting that. It was demeaning as well. Having to provide all this documentation about my health was such a violation of my privacy.

I know babe. Unfortunately, you have to take the bad for the good.

I can't believe healthcare still isn't provided to every US citizen by the government. You know we're the only country that still doesn't provide healthcare. Still, I was both grateful but also sick of struggling. I had a childhood filled with Social Services and now I was an adult on Social Services. This wasn't what I wanted for myself you know?

I know but you have to do what you have to do sometimes. You were surviving.

I wanted to do better than survive. I wanted to live and be happy. I hated being down in that office. It reminded me of when I was little, and I'd go with you.

I know. I hated going to Social Services too, boy did I hate it. It took the whole day and then I'd have to come back and bring this piece of paper and that piece of paper. I never made a habit out of being on food stamps, but many do. I used to always tell you that Social Services should be a last resort and only for temporary help. You pay into it but that doesn't mean use it as a crutch like some people do.

Tell me about it. You wouldn't believe some of the things I saw down there. I felt like a loser.

Oh, yes, I would and being on Food Stamps or Medicaid or any other type of public assistance doesn't make you a loser. If that were the case, I'd be a loser too and I'm not. We're not. We're people that truly needed and for you, need help. Don't let this get you down honey.

I tried not to. It really helped with my medications, but I so wanted to get off them. My doctor offered no hope about my getting well. He just kept writing prescription after prescription. I had to ask him several times for a script for physical therapy. Each time he would respond with, "What's physical therapy going to do for you? You still won't be able to dance."

Nice guy.

Yeah, real nice. When he said that I wanted to punch him in his face.

You should have. What did he say when you asked him to help get you off the pills?

He'd respond with, "Well, if you don't want them then let me know." I told him that that's exactly what I was telling him, that I didn't want them or to be on them but that I was sure I would need to go off them slowly. I even suggested that he refer me to a nutritionist or herbalist or someone like that so I could replace them with healthy things for my body. Not synthetic medications that were causing me serious side effects and had long term and potentially fatal effects to my other organs.

What did he say to that?

Nothing. He shrugged his shoulders and told me to stay on the meds until I had a plan which is exactly what I was asking his help with. He didn't know anything but scalpels and medications. I hated being on all those pills. I really did. I couldn't function normally. I was tired all the time and my body was becoming tolerant but also addicted to them. I could feel it if I went more than a couple of hours without a pain pill or anti-inflammatory.

What did you feel?

Agitated, very agitated and restless. Then I would get snappy from the pain as soon as the medication wore off. I looked for work while I was on unemployment but couldn't find a job. Then, the unemployment ran out and I was without a net.

Oh no. You were left with nothing?

Yup, I had no income, insurance and my body was still very sensitive from the surgery. It was taking a long time to heal. I wondered if it would heal at all. I was scared for myself and what the future held for me.

I know you were.

I never called your family for help because I knew, number one, they wouldn't have. Number two, if they did it wouldn't be before they picked apart and needed to know every detail of my life. They have this way of making you feel small when you're going through a hard time. I was going through enough and for three years now.

Did they know about this last surgery?

They knew because I was still in contact with Carolyn and Louisa and you know how they are.

When one knows everyone knows.

Yes. I scrambled to find money to make rent, care for Monte, pay for my utilities and medications. I called different organizations for help. One organization wouldn't help me because I wasn't paralyzed. Another gentleman at a different organization told me I would have to leave my apartment and apply for Section 8 housing. Do you have any idea how long it can take to get Section 8 housing and what those housing sites are like?

I'm guessing by the tone of your voice not too pretty.

Not by any stretch of the imagination and I have animals too. Not many places allow animals. I lucked out with the apartment I'm in now. Everyone here has animals. Besides, why should I or anyone have to leave their home because of something that isn't our fault? That guy really scared me. He offered me no hope. In fact, he took whatever hope I had of getting out from under, away. As I was scrambling for money and my landlord was hounding me for the rent. I figured I had to be creative and find a way to back her off while I figured things out, and creative I was. I didn't tell her about my situation because it was none of her business anyway. I just withheld my rent in accordance with my lease.

What do you mean? Why would you be able to do that?

The tenant's heater above me leaked so badly it caused a hole right through my bedroom ceiling. It was so big that I could actually see into her bedroom. Before that, there was a fire in the tenant's apartment beneath me which caused major smoke damage in my apartment. In addition, when the fire department came to my apartment to get me out, they had to knock out a portion of my wall. The landlord also never fixed this. It was covered by plastic only. So, I withheld my rent because my landlord wasn't providing "safe housing" which was a violation of my lease. While these things were an aggravating pain to live with, they bought me about five months which is how long it took for them to be fixed. During that time, I prayed for the Universe to help me help myself and figure out the rest. I tried to think of different ways to make money. I was getting desperate because there was absolutely no income coming into my life. At this point, my relationship with Devon was more like a friendship and truthfully, my mind wasn't on being in a relationship anymore. I was in survival mode. Devon did whatever he could to help me. For a fleeting moment, and I mean fleeting, I actually thought about becoming an escort.

What!

Yeah, here I am a feminist and one night I found myself online browsing at what "escorts" do, what they don't do and so on. Devon caught me and asked me what I was doing. When I told him my fleeting thought he got scared. "No, you're not doing that Kristin." He said. I told him I wouldn't have sex with anyone but stipulate to just be someone's date for an evening. He got very upset. He reminded me that I was just at a very low point and not thinking clearly. He was right.

I ended up feeling worse about myself than I already did. Here I am an educated person and I couldn't get a damn job for anything and I applied everywhere I could, and I'm looking at escort ads while I'm still healing from my third spinal fusion. Really?

Honey, like I said. You were in survival mode.

After talking with Devon, I wondered how many women in my predicament ever felt the same way. Not so much having an ailment, or maybe I don't know, but being jobless, or having kids and being jobless and having to swallow your pride in order to do what you have to do to survive. Nothing prepares you for when you're kicked to your lowest time and again and the things you need to do to survive. I just didn't know what to do Mom and my mind was everywhere.

I don't ever want you to feel bad about yourself for having these thoughts. You're not going any place many other women haven't gone, including myself, when you're at your lowest. I had those very same thoughts you did, being someone's escort or a full out prostitute.

You did?

Of course! Like you I had plans for my life. I wanted to be in a partnership made up of two equals that loved each other and my children unconditionally. My mother reared her daughters to be "taken care of" by a man like she was by my father, but my parents were miserable. They were stuck with each other. I'm glad I learned how to take care of myself but it, too, was out of survival for my children. I didn't think nor was I prepared to be a single mother who came out only to become a cancer patient gravely ill for the rest of my life which ended way too early. While it's good to have a plan more times often than not life turns out much differently and in ways we're just ill prepared for. That's when the scrambling to survive begins. All kinds of thoughts go through your head. You start thinking of things to do to make money that you would have never thought of before had you not been so backed against a wall. You were fortunate you didn't have children, very fortunate.

Thank you! Thank for validating my feelings. You just summed up exactly what I was going through. I think about that a lot.

What?

The "What if's?" "What if I had children? Where would my life have gone? What turn what I have had to make in order to survive and provide for my children the way my mother did?" With all that we went through I always felt cared for, I mean emotionally. You were so loving, caring, forgiving and patient with us. Somehow you always found a way for us to have what we needed and more. Mom?

Yeah babe?

I wouldn't have become an escort. I would never do that.

I know you wouldn't have. I know you better than that.

It was just a thought I had as I struggled to think of different ways to get myself out of the horrible situation, I was in. I really tried to find a job. I would have worked at a grocery store if that were the case. If they were hiring, I applied. I put applications into places like MacDonald's, CVS Pharmacy, the corner grocery store, everywhere. I wasn't ashamed and I went for my masters. I needed a job and that's all I thought about.

Did you get any call backs?

No. Jobs were scarce, very scarce and I didn't even put how much education I had on those applications. Nothing was panning out. Devon was scared for me because he was also struggling to help me but made very little money himself. The "what if's" were getting stronger and more plausible than overcoming my obstacles. "What if I don't find a job? What if I don't' get better?" These questions scrambled through both our minds. I asked Andrea for help, but she would get silent before she would tell me she couldn't. The reason was always the same.

Which was?

"I need to be focusing on me..." blah, blah, blah. She wasn't supportive. In fact, we barely spoke. I would call her, but she never called back. I finally stopped calling. I won't pursue a relationship that's coming to an end and that's what was happening with me Andrea and me.

Like your relationship was coming to an end?

Yes. I didn't need nor did I want the aggravation of our relationship. Anytime I encountered anything challenging her only response was that I should move back to Buffalo or go and live with her. She had moved down to North Carolina by now and was seeing a new woman.

Oh, well that was nice of her to say that to you.

Yeah, right. My sister's feeling was that having these spine challenges meant that I should forfeit my right or desire to live on my own. She said to me more than once, "You can't have everything your way." I told her my ailment wasn't about having things my way but more about the right to live an independent life, if possible, amidst a physical challenge.

Sounds like she didn't want to be bothered.

I got that. When I would stand my ground and tell her I'd built a life where I'm at she'd respond with, "What life? Look at you? You can barely do anything with your neck. What life do you have?" As if a life in Buffalo with your family or with her was any better. I wasn't going to take my sister making me feel like a failure because of a spine injury that she knew nothing about, as if the way she was behaving would make me want to go and live with her. Yeah right!

Yeah right is right! Why would you want to go and live with someone that was making you feel bad about yourself?

Yeah well, I wouldn't. I was willing to try the odds and stay where I am. Compassion, empathy and understanding were never Andrea's strong suits. Still, I felt awful after this conversation because she made me think.

About what?

About what I didn't want to think about.

What was that?

That the fact was, whatever life I'd built, was crumbling.

That was harsh for her to say those things because you did and do have a life. It may not be the life you hoped for but it's your life, the one that Kristin built. She should have been more supportive, but she wasn't and all you could do was hold onto the good things in your life like Devon and your animals.

I did. I wasn't going to waste my time thinking about her when I had important things to figure out. I wracked my brain to try and figure out what seemed like an impossible situation. Then Devon did something that made me feel like I'd just been flushed down a sewer. He didn't do it on purpose but out of fear of the unknown for me. Devon didn't know them like I do. At this point he still thought of them as "family," people that will help you when in need. He was about to see their true colors; the ones you and I know.

Oh know. Don't tell me he called the family?

He called Carolyn and told her all that I was going through. She, in turn, not having any money contacted another family member and that person called another person and so on and so on. This wouldn't have been a bad thing had they been people that wanted to help but these were people that were barely helpful to themselves, let alone each other. They weren't about goodness. They were and still are all about instilling shame and guilt if you fall on hard times, as if you brought it on yourself.

I know that feeling. If I didn't do exactly what the doctors told me I should do and I had pain or had to go back to the hospital I felt that same shame and guilt with questions like, why didn't you do this or that? Or, "You heard what the doctor said..." I didn't always agree with the doctors. I absolutely didn't like all the meds I was on either, but in the end, I inevitably did what my made my sisters feel better, not me, for the sake of argument.

I know. They exhausted you. There is no doubt about that and that upset me a lot. Their initial response to me after Devon went to them was, "Why aren't you and Devon getting married?" Or, "Will you and Devon marry soon so that all this can be over for you. You can be on his insurance plan." I couldn't believe they were suggesting such a thing, as if Marriage was nothing but a contract. I think it is for them. I could never bring myself to be with someone for anything other than love and companionship. I don't even believe in the conventional/legal aspect of marriage anyway. If I ever met someone, I wanted to spend the rest of my life with I'd celebrate by having a small ceremony with friends and lots of vegan food. Like a commitment ceremony. This way it's about love and not contracts.

Right, to them marriage is about security and being "taken care of", not love and companionship. I wish I would have forgone all the legal stuff with your father. This is the part where I get to say, "Had I known then what I know now…"

Exactly☺.

I'm glad you stood your ground. Good for you. So, Devon called my sister who called the rest of the family and…

And my nightmare began. I just need to get this stuff out because it really was a nightmare Mom.

I know honey. I'm here. Talk to me.

The entire family met, behind my back, to see how much they could each pitch in and help me out. Sounds like a good family, right?

No, it doesn't because I know what you were about to go through to get that money.

Yes, you go it. I got phone call after phone call from your family that for three years, didn't bother to return my calls and now wanted to know everything about my spine and/or procedures. In each phone call, whomever I had the displeasure of speaking with demanded answers to one question after another about everything from my spine to my personal life. This was only because someone (Devon) that had been present in my life throughout all these procedures, innocently called them as a last resort for help because he truly cared about me. Not the other way around. Since you crossed, not only were they incorrigible to me but they never gave a shit about me. You don't know how much I despised them Mom and how much I kicked myself for ever trying to keep in contact with them. I regretted not cutting them off the second you crossed. I tried, in some ways, I tried. By going back to school, graduating and then going on to graduate school. Yet I never felt like I could fully separate from them. The only person I really kept in contact with was Grandma and she loved me no matter what, always.

Of course, she did honey.

Like I've said before, for a long time, I just felt so scared of being completely alone with no family and the, you know, "what if's" such as this. Yet, now I was seeing just how awful they were and how better off I was without them. I already knew this, but I guess I needed it slammed in my face again, huh? I mean, in all that time I was over thinking the "what if's" and that over thinking kept me in the very situation I wanted to get out of.

Sometimes it takes a few unpleasant experiences with people before we get the lesson. This is heart breaking. I hoped my sisters and your cousins would be there for you but something in me knew they wouldn't.

I feel the same way. I hoped just because I felt so lost without you but having them in my life was turning out to be a nightmare on top of the spinal nightmare I was already enduring. The barrage of questions was infuriating.

It is very upsetting for me to hear what they did to you. I need to know. What did they ask you?

"What part of my spine was injured? What type of surgery did I have? Who was my doctor? Did I get second opinions? Should I have even had those surgeries?" Again, with the, "Why aren't you and Devon getting married," and had I gotten married I wouldn't be in this predicament. Why did I lose my job, and didn't I have anyone else to ask for money? Why I didn't have any savings? Why did I move to New York City in the first place? My favorite was, "You wanted to be independent like your mother. Look where it got her."

What the heck was that supposed to mean?

Well, it seems mother, both of us were put down in the same sentence for wanting more for ourselves than the miserable life your family ended up with. The fact that they could say and do these things was yet another way they showed how cold-hearted, thoughtless, insensitive, narrow minded, judgmental, ignorant, mean and cowardly they are.

Oh, my goodness! Who did they think they were saying such horrible things and asking such questions of you when they promised me, they'd help my children if they ever needed it? It's not as if their children didn't fall on hard times. Messing up was the norm for some of my nieces and nephews and as you noted, they still relied on my sisters well into their thirties and forties. They had no right to ask you those questions. They had no right to treat you so terribly period!

I agree and felt ganged up on too. It was just me taking all these phone calls while I was in excruciating pain. They had no compassion for what I was dealing with. I wanted to tell them all to take whatever help they may or may not give me and go fuck themselves. My personal life and all the decisions I made in it was none of their business. Everyone now knew my painful situation and were less than empathetic. To make matters worse, that lawyer cousin I have got involved and do you know what happened next?

Tell me.

Pratt, Louisa's son, lived in New Jersey at the time and he and his girlfriend (now wife) came to my apartment, unannounced, supposedly to see how I was. Devon and I were both like, "These two haven't so much as picked up the phone to call in over three years and now all of a sudden they're concerned and at my doorstep?" I didn't feel concern. I felt like since they were sending money, they sent my little cousin to check up on me to make sure I wasn't lying about what I was going through. Unfortunately, it just so happened that when my cousin came over, I was in the midst of an emotional meltdown.

What brought on the breakdown?

After Devon called them and prior to my cousin's unannounced visit, your family started playing these mind games.

Oh, you have got to be kidding me.

No.

What did they do?

At first, they would assure me they would help by sending me a few dollars for this or help with that. My cousin Darlene said she would help me get a prescription filled through her Pharmacist husband and so on, but no help came. When I called, I was told, "I thought I could help but I just can't right now." Then they would do it again. They'd assure me they'd help with this or that. Again, no help would come, and I'd make a follow up call only to get the same excuses. A few hours before Pratt came over, I called Carolyn and told her to tell the rest of the family, "If someone is going to help me then do it but don't tell me you're going to help me, not just once but a few times, and not do it. That's cruel and I don't deserve it. What I'm dealing with is no joke." Then she yelled back at me, "Don't you yell at me! Who do you think you are? You don't speak to me that way…" and she started ranting on. I had to hang up. I was so frustrated and angry with her and your entire family.

Who wouldn't be? I just don't know how they could do this to my child. That is just like her to deflect the situation by not taking any responsibility and instead putting it off on someone else. In this case you. Honey, this breakdown wasn't just something out of the blue. It was building up.

I know and I was trying to keep myself together and I did, for a long time but your family just added way too much stress to me. Before this I never asked them for help, ever. Now, the only person that cared about me was asking them for help on my behalf and they all lost their shit and, in the process, brought me to my breaking point. All because they can't handle anything, including their own lives and they think they have the right to ever say to me that they can't talk to me. Really?

Honey, you're human and I think, given what you were dealing with, you kept yourself together longer than most could. Also, they all had each other to lean on. You had yourself, Devon and your animals.

That was all I needed.

I know. What made you call her?

I called to tell someone what I mentioned before. If you're going to help me than do it because I'm going through serious physical pain. Carolyn was the only one I got a hold of. They were being their asshole selves by putting me through so much stress and aggravation. They actually drove me to the point where I was on my knees, crying from the bottom of my gut and pleading with them for help. On top of that they kept bombarding me with all those questions about my personal life, my spine and what not. Then they'd go back to, "We're not going to help you when you don't even call us." I mean it was a never ending crazy dysfunctional circle they were trying to rope me in. The same crap they did with you.

Are you kidding me? You'd think they'd get sick of their own mind games.

No, it feeds them. They like to make other people feel worthless and drive them to the point of a breakdown because it makes them feel better about their own low self-esteem and shit lives. I knew what they were doing. That's why I reveled in living so far from them.

Honey, they always told me, "Your daughter thinks she's better than us." And do you know what my response was?

What?

"She is" and you are. I know what they were trying to do too. It's just what I said earlier. They were trying to find an excuse not to help you. They just have to take everything to such a dramatic, horrible extreme.

I prided myself on never having to ask for financial help from your family, especially while I was going through my spine surgeries and this is the reason why. They acted like I was some drug addict that came to them for money on a regular basis as opposed to a person dealing with three successive spine surgeries whose companion asked them for help for monetary help. Here I was making it on my own and my cousins were still running to their parents for money, a place to stay, help with their drug problems, girlfriends getting slapped around, abortions, etc. My older cousins relied on their parents for childcare for Christ sakes and it was when they had their kids on the weekends. They didn't want being a parent to get in the way of their partying/drug use. Whatever situation my cousins were in they've always had the help of their parents and I never begrudged them as Darlene so generously accused me of. I never judged them because mommy was always there to protect them. I just despised the fact that they thought they could treat me so badly because my mother crossed over. It's a point they never got and still don't. I needed this one time help and it became a huge, drama situation as everything is with your family and guess who they blamed for all the drama.

You.

Of course. According to them I was depressed, angry, and a failure. My so-called godfather went so far as to tell me, not that I had a dark cloud hanging over me but that I WAS a dark cloud with no light in her life. Louisa, that fucking drunk, suggested I go live in Darlene's basement until…

Until what?

Apparently until I crossed over because that's what she felt my final outcome would be. I was so offended she would even suggest something so fundamentally stupid. Darlene has never lived on her own a day in her life. She had no business making such a demeaning statement. Darlene went from her parents to college to her husband. Here they are trying to bring me down for supporting myself since the age of 19 and enduring three spinal surgeries, all while working full time for all but this one time. I never felt so belittled by people so blatantly incompetent. I felt like, "Who are these people to be so condescending to me after all the shit they pulled in their lives?" Your family hates to help people. I've seen it firsthand. If someone, be it a relative or friend, asked them for help, to their face they would pretend it was fine, they were there for that person and cared about them. Behind their backs they criticized and complained about any "help" they had to give that person. Here again is the difference between you and your sisters. You cared about people and taught me the same. Your family cares only about their selves.

You're right. They were all about themselves and the only thing that mattered to them was THEIR family and no one else. I never agreed with that way of life and I got a lot of criticism for it too. I don't know who my sister or any of my family thought they were to treat my child like this. I would have never treated any of their children so badly. They only did this because I wasn't there that's it, Kristin?

What?

You did nothing wrong but have a spine injury and fall on hard times that lasted far too long.

I felt like a criminal. They got bad but did they ever get this bad with you?

Oh yes, they did honey. I got all those same questions, but I had the house as my income and disability so that saved me from being dependent on them, but they would still ask more questions than they had a right to. Many times, I told my sisters to mind their business but…

But what?

I tend to be more of an appeaser for the sake of not arguing. I also had you to stick up for me. You, my beautiful strong girl, don't take shit if I may say so and as I've said. That doesn't go over well with the family.

Too bad. So, getting back to when Pratt and his girlfriend showed up, unannounced, I told Devon to tell him he should have called first and to come back because I didn't want him to see me so distraught. My cousin heard me crying and telling Devon these things from the hall and he and his girlfriend just stood there. I actually slammed the door in his face. Devon tried to help him understand where I was coming from, but he didn't get it. He's too small minded.

Did he ever come back?

No, and if that were me, and my cousin was in such an emotional state I would respect their space and even be concerned. I'd also call again because this was one cousin, I never had any problems with, until now. All my life I always succeeded, did well in school, excelled in dance and was strong and independent. I slammed the door in his face because I had to draw the line somewhere or they would have taken my dignity. I was going to do whatever I had to in order to preserve my dignity and self-respect. Granted I wish I would have been in a better state of mind when I drew the line but that's why it's always good to call before you stop by someone's house. I had every right to feel as I did. Pratt wasn't there out of concern. If he was ever truly concerned, I would have heard from him prior to this night. I didn't and never heard from him after either. Instead, Pratt shared how upset I was with his mother (Louisa) and how "unstable" he thought I was. She, in turn, shared this with the rest of the family and poof! Now I was unable to handle my life or make decisions.

What were they going to do put you in a nuthouse?

That's what I thought! My feeling was, "I'm having a hard time I'm not a crazy person!" The drama was out of control. Then that lawyer cousin called me and stated that the family got together and each pitched "x" amount of dollars in to help me. However, there were a couple of stipulations for me to get this money.

Oh know. This just gets worse and worse. What were the stipulations?

First, I had to apply for disability even though I wasn't disabled and was never diagnosed as such. I also had to show them proof in the form of the filled-out application that I applied. Secondly, the lawyer cousin wasn't going to give the money to me. Rather, he felt he should contact my landlord by phone and mail and tell them that I'm having a hard time with my health and job loss, and that he was acting on my behalf and to accept "x" amount of dollars which covered two months of my rent and utilities. I asked him over and over to just send the money to me. That I was always dependable and more than capable of sending the money to my landlord. I told him he wasn't permitted to speak on my behalf and that my having a hard time didn't mean he could. I also expressed to him how important it was for me to keep my personal life private from my landlord and that if he told them all these things, they would be calling me, asking me questions they had no right to ask about my health and job situation. He was literally violating my privacy. Still, the egotistical lawyer insisted on getting his way. I felt them trying to silence my every word. I also felt like I was losing my strong sense of self the way you did when we moved to Buffalo.

You think that's what happened to me?

Yes.

As hard as this is for me to admit I think you're right. I mean I was never quite as fierce as you, but I was getting stronger in Syracuse and certainly feeling more independent that I'd ever felt before in my life. I think my cancer diagnosis coupled with having to go back to a place [Buffalo] that held some not so pleasant memories for me made me feel as you just described. I, too, felt like whatever strength I did have I had to fight to keep it. The family has a way of making you feel weak and second guess yourself.

Yes, because there are so many of them and only one of you and me.

Shame on them. How was Devon reacting to all of this?

He was at a loss for words. He immediately regretted calling them. I told him, "I tried to tell you how they are. They're manipulative and controlling. That's why I moved away from them."

What did he say?

"You're telling me." He felt horrible as he listened to all these phone calls and the way they were treating me. Here he was only trying to help. You should have seen his face after a conversation with them. He thought they were crazy people.

He's right.

Devon was a big man with a big heart and a gentle soul. It took a lot to upset him but if and when you did, boy you'd better watch out. He wanted to go up there and make some noise.

He probably should have.

Yeah, well if we had a car he probably would have. Devon couldn't believe them, but he's had his share of family problems which caused him to not speak with his extended family either. He understood. Devon never left my side and was always there for me surgery after surgery after surgery, so supportive and caring. Every time I had a decision to make about a procedure or anything, for that matter, the only thing he'd say to me was, "This is your decision. Whatever you want or need to do I'll support you," and he did. He was the only person that, having seen me on a day to day basis, understood what I was going through and saw beyond the heartache I was in. I thought of not accepting the money from your family but with Monte sick I was thinking like a mother. I decided that I would bite the bullet and for the time being and the sake of my kids, accept the money. At the end of it all they stated, "This is the one and only time we'll help you."

You never asked them for help before, ever and that's what they said to you!

Yeah! I felt like saying, "Yeah, great because I've never asked you for help before you crazy fucks!" At this point, I didn't care what your family said or felt about me. I really didn't. They were and still are just plain rotten people that I refuse to let into my mind and heart. Not to mention all the things they said about me were/are wrong. I knew that. Devon knew that and that's all that mattered to me. Your family IS a cancer.

Well I knew they were wrong too! Still, they didn't have make you feel worse or put you through all that. As I said, they should be ashamed of their selves but what's sad is they're not.

You said it and Devon used to say that he wanted to be a part of my family because it reminded him of the Godfather, his favorite films and how close all the family was in those movies.

Did you remind him that Sicilian families also violently kill each other if double crossed?

I did. His response was classic. "Oh yeah," he said, "It's good we don't live in Buffalo." I couldn't have agreed more. So, unfortunately, that ego maniac lawyer went ahead and contacted my landlord and true to form, they called me asking all these questions. I had to reassure them that everything was fine, and I just hit a rough spot, that's all. Still, they asked me, "Well, are you paralyzed? Can you walk? Your lawyer called and said he was sending the rent on your behalf? Will you be working again?" I assured them that I was going to be okay and more importantly, the man that called WASN'T my lawyer. He was an over-zealous, controlling cousin by marriage whose ego was in dire need of some serious checking.

Your cousin way overstepped his boundary. His behavior is shameful, and he should take my name off his first child's birth certificate. I would never treat his children so badly, and I won't have my daughter being so disrespected without me there to protect her.

After all the crap they put me through, I still made a point to call the family, one by one, and say thank you for the help they gave me. I wasn't going to play into the negative things they said of me.

Good. Good for you. That's how you do things honey. Be your best self and let them be their ugly, rotten selves.

With my rent paid for a couple of months, I felt like I could breathe. Prior to this, even though I lent my savings to Andrea who never bothered to pay me back. I still managed to put some money into my savings account every paycheck. However, between the co-pays, balances left over from what the insurance didn't cover of my procedures, Rx's and so on, having an illness/ailment costs a lot of money. It wiped out my savings.

You don't have to tell me that.

Yeah, and I didn't have that much to begin with. Then there were two last interactions with your family that were indicative of what I could no longer take.

I know. You got to a point where enough is enough. Yes, So, what was the first interaction?

I had one last conversation with Carolyn where she said she couldn't talk to me anymore.

What? Why would she say that?

I don't know it was weird. With all their horribleness, I told you, I called each of those that lent me money and said, "thank you". I asked Carolyn why everyone treated me so badly.

And?

She said, "You have to ask them." I told her I couldn't ask them because no one even bother to see if I was okay and I never did anything to them to deserve how they treated me. Then do you know what she said?

No, what?

She said she did all she could to "help me" and "that's that," as she put it. I asked her what she meant by that and she said, "I can't talk to you anymore. I just can't. I've done everything I could." I couldn't believe what I was hearing. Again, as if I were an addict they'd been carrying. We started to argue and before you know it. I finally didn't give a shit and told her what I'd been wanting to say for years.

Which was?

"You and the rest of your fucked-up family can go fuck yourselves! Don't ever call me again!" Then I hung up.

It pains me to say this but good. You had to honey.

She sickened me, and it would be the last time I'd ever speak to her. I was so pissed about how she treated me but now, all these feelings I kept inside about how deeply she hurt you flooded to the surface.

What do you mean, how she hurt me?

You know exactly what I mean. Do you want me to say it?

I wish you wouldn't Kristin.

Looking back, I couldn't believe you moved us into her house. How could you even live upstairs from her! How did you stay in relation with her, help her and love her as you did after all the pain, she caused you? Now I figured it out. Now it all made sense. I no longer wondered why she needed to come down and help me when I was going through my second spinal surgery. It was out of long-standing guilt.

You know, this is very painful for me to discuss. You realize, that don't you?

I'm sorry. We can drop it if you want.

No. You brought it up. I encourage you to talk about things that have been festering. I need to do the same. She was my sister. I had to, for myself, I had to forgive her, but we weren't as close as she led others to believe.

I know. That was apparent but Mom; you could have forgiven her just the same without moving us into the apartment above her house. She fucked your husband for Christ sakes! What a low-life, disgusting thing to do to someone let alone your own sister. I don't care if she is your family. That's unforgiveable.

Nothing is unforgiveable. Well, almost nothing.

So, you say.

Yes, I do. Anyway, that was years ago Kristin.

I know but my feelings were coming up like a damn that broke. As I was thinking about things, I remembered one specific incident.

What incident?

There was always this tension between you and Carolyn. Like you said, she used to brag about how close you two were, and even more so, after you crossed over. That never made any sense to me because while you were here, I could see that wasn't the case. That tension was never more apparent than the day Carolyn came over to the house. We had, thankfully, moved from her apartment. She was ranting and raving about her ex-husband that was leaving her for another woman, a younger woman who just happened to be pregnant with his child. She vacillated between rage and hysteria. She was expressing how angry she was, as if you couldn't tell by the tight lips, beady black eyes and grinding teeth even when she spoke. You always have such empathy for people. Yet as I watched her rant on you sat in your lazy boy chair, unphased, cutting coupons and not even looking at her. You just let her go on and on. Until she paused and said, "Mary! Are you listening to me! Why aren't you saying anything? I'm in pain and you're not saying anything!" You turned to her, looked her directly in the eye and with a disdain I'd never seen in you said, "What would you like me to do?" This enraged Carolyn even more and she just continued to go off until you calmly interrupted her and said. "Carolyn, I need to rest now." Your very polite way of telling her to leave. Boy was she pissed, and I was left thinking, "Wow, I just saw my Mom give a very non-empathic response for the first time in my life." Then, I remembered a conversation we had years before.

Hmm, I forgot about that. She was very upset that day but all I could think was, "What comes around goes around."

Yes, I could see that on your face and so could she. She didn't even argue. She just picked up her things and stormed out. The conversation we had years before was where you disclosed her indiscretions.

I think I remember now.

Yes, it was an unforgettable time. We were living in Cobblestone Apartments. This was right after you were diagnosed with breast cancer.

Oh yes, I do remember.

Yeah, right? Anyway, we were in the bathroom and I was crying. I was angry about the pain you were about to go through and how Dad wasn't helping us. The only reason you disclosed this was because you didn't want me to harbor anger. Your analogy for me to forgive what felt like was unforgiveable was to share with me how Carolyn made this horrible "mistake" and slept with Dad, and how you had to forgive them both. Yet, here you were in your lazy boy chair, feeling anger you had every right to feel. It's not that you harbored it Mom. It's just that you moved us above the reminder (Carolyn) of such a painful time in your life. Now, that pain was in your face every day. I have to admit. I was always confused as to why we moved there as I, too, carried a disdain for Carolyn. I just sucked it down for the same reason you did.

To try and keep peace.

Yes.

And did it?

Not for me.

Me either. Still, I couldn't just stop talking to my sister even though the thought did cross my mind several times. There was too much family between us. Like I said honey, I had to, for myself, forgive her. I hoped the guilt she felt for her stupid, thoughtless, heartless mistake was enough suffering for her but listening to the way she treated my daughter, it seems that it wasn't.

Things were never the same between you two, were they?

Of course not. Besides, my sister owed me. If it helped us, I was going to take whatever she offered. Don't think I wanted to move into that apartment? I hated every second we were there, but it allowed me to save some money and get us our own place much faster.

It hurts me that you had to make all these painful choices that in reality, weren't really choices. Your back always seemed to be against the wall and your choices were between one rotten situation over another. I wanted more for you Mom. You deserved better. What? I can see the thoughts rolling around in your head. What is it Mom?

My sister hurt me immensely and while she may try to lie about this what we're talking about is the truth. I had to forgive her because, again, I was afraid any anger or resentments I had for others would feed my cancer, but I don't think I ever really forgave her. I swallowed a lot of pain, anguish and anger others caused me over the years thinking that if I didn't express those feelings then they weren't there but that's not the case. Unexpressed negative emotions only build up. It's not healthy. I know the family has come down on you a lot in the past for how self-expressive you can be but I'm glad you don't hold your feelings in like Mom did. I'm proud of you for always standing your ground.

Remember when Andrea and I had that fight after I came back from traveling? When I came back, and she rented out my room and I went to stay with Carolyn for the night?

Yes, yes, I remember.

I asked Carolyn if you guys ever fought like that and she lied to my face and said, "Oh no! I've never fought with my sisters they way you girls do." I knew she was lying. I could tell by the way she stuttered when she said it. Why would she lie like that?

My sister has her own way of keeping things together in her head. Plus, that's not something she's ever going to admit. Not to anyone.

I know but she could have at least admitted that she had arguments just as bad as the ones Andrea and I had. Your family has this trait that's been passed down from one generation to another. They go out of their way to make others look and feel like they're so dysfunctional.

As you so eloquently noted, they do that to make themselves feel better about their own dysfunctions.

I'm sorry you swallowed so much crap Mom. I really am. That's why I hated being in Buffalo. You took us away from all the things that made us happy in the hopes that you'd find comfort and support with your family, but they gave us just the opposite. Your family acted like they've done no wrong. People would be shocked at these things we're speaking of because they put on such a good façade.

I hoped my family would be supportive and help us but, they weren't. They couldn't handle their own stuff let alone help me or anyone else. Before moving to Buffalo I had to learn to be strong in my life. I was alone and fending for myself and my three children from very early on while my sisters had their husbands and ex-husbands to help them and their children. My sisters seem to have forgotten that about me. I had my moments. I had a few breakdowns here and there and rightfully so, but I was also independent, self-sufficient, resourceful…

Strong, caring, loving, giving, warm, non-judgmental, generous, nurturing, sincere amongst many other things your sisters weren't and still aren't. They were never half the woman you were. When you crossed over, they did the same thing with you that they were doing to me.

What's that?

They'd only remember and speak of your imperfections and frailties and they did it in such a way that made them think they were above you. It's sickening. They're sickening.

So, the conversation with your aunt was one of the last of two interactions you had with the family before you completely cut them off. What was the second one?

Shortly after my conversation with Carolyn, Louisa and Darlene came down to Jersey to visit Pratt. They called me to see if they could come visit.

Really?

Yeah, that was my reaction but then I thought maybe we could have a conversation and bring some closure to all that happened. I said, "fine." The night they were supposed to come, Louisa called to tell me they were too tired. I told her that was fine and welcomed them to stop by before they left. She told me she didn't think she would have time to visit me while she was there. She said she and Darlene thought I was too depressing to them. Again, with this shit and this was coming from a thirty plus year alcoholic, pill popping child that relied on help from others all her life. I can't even recall a conversation with your sister where her words weren't slurred. So, I took the opportunity to express that I felt belittled when she thought so little of me as to even suggest my living in Darlene's basement until the "what if." Now mind you, I was talking calmly, not yelling or anything like that. Your sister, on the other hand, drunk as anything and in her usual slurred manner of speech, went on this rant about what was wrong in her life.

My sister has her own issues to deal with and I don't think that will happen in this lifetime, particularly if she's still drinking. It's quite apparent that the family has two forms of communication; anger and rage. Rarely did I ever experience positive communication in our family. Louisa's drinking is for her to figure out but you're right about her always having someone in her life to rely on. My sister could never be alone. She needed to be in a relationship and usually it was with someone that was able to help her with money. We used to argue about that.

About her always needing to be with someone.

About her inability to be independent. I wanted her to learn how to stand on her own two feet, but she chose not to. I survived far better than my sisters and with much less help, if I had it at all.

This was really uncalled for. I mean it. They could have just politely said they couldn't make it and apologized.

Yeah but that's what nice people do Mom. We're talking about the lowest of the low.

Oh honey, please tell me you stopped this nonsense once and for all.

Yeah, I'd had enough. I cut her off and said, "Louisa, as I told your sister, go fuck yourself and don't ever call me again." Needless to say, that was the last interaction I would, thankfully, ever have with your family again! At least for a number of years anyway.

Finally!

I was so relieved too. It was as though a huge weight were lifted from my mind and spirit. Yet between the pain from my neck and all the changes my body was going through. I longed for my old body, prior to my surgeries. I, essentially, lost my ability to be carefree and express myself with movement. I was having such a hard time getting used to this new body with all these limitations, which seemed foreign to me.

What kind of limitations babe?

In addition to never being able to dance again I'm limited with everyday tasks as well. I can't sleep on my stomach or right side because of the placement of the titanium and the permanent pain and weakness from the sprain. I'm unable to run, jog, turn my head abruptly, lift or carry anything 5lbs. or over. No more aerobics or hardcore workouts which I loved. I have to sleep on a stupid orthopedic pillow because my neck has to be aligned just right so I don't wake up with a muscle spasm or migraine. I'm prone to migraines a few times a week and they're not fun.

Do you take anything for them?

I used to take Imitrex but now I found that Excedrin Migraine works just as well if I take it at the onset. I forgot what it's like to go a day without pain. I'll never have that again. Also, this is unrelated to my neck surgeries, but it happens and affects my neck.

What is it honey?

I have these recurring nightmares that continue until this day.

What are they?

It's not so much what they are but how they make me feel. They vacillate between someone sitting on my chest, covering my mouth or me drowning. All of them have to do with not being able to breathe. Sometimes I'm so embedded in the nightmare that while I'm in it, part of the nightmare is me trying to wake myself up or trying to take a breath and I can't. In the nightmare I feel myself trying to breathe and I can't. It's like I'm trying so hard to wake up and I just can't until I finally bolt upright, sweating and gasping for air. It's scary and it throws my neck into a severe spasm for days.

Oh Kristin. I know you know what that is.

Yes, that's my body remembering the abuse your son put me through. Part of the abuse was him covering my mouth as I tried to scream and fought to get away. His hand would be so tight over my mouth that I couldn't breathe, and his body was so heavy on mine that I could barely move. That's why, in the nightmare I'm unable to move or breathe until I bolt upright.

Sweetheart come here. I love you. I love you. You did nothing to deserve any of these horrible things and yet you've still come out so much better than the people that hurt you. The way they treated you was wrong. I know I've said it many times, but I'll keep saying it. They never would have behaved this way if I were there, NEVER! You weren't the problem, they were. You were just outnumbered that's all, and that's enough when it comes to them. You are my daughter. You chose to walk away from them. Not hurt them back or take your pain out on others. That's dignity and self-respect. Something they'll never have. You were getting betrayed left and right on some very deep levels by people you should have been able to trust.

Yes, but I hurt Mom, still and it makes me feel like they've won.

There is no winning, only over-coming and you are over-coming severe abuse from more than one person. You will always be one of God's little angels and that's all that matters.

You know, when I was going through the surgeries, there were many times where I'd take a pill and then get this sudden panic feeling and start questioning myself; "Did I already take this? Will it have an adverse reaction with the other pill I just took a half hour ago?" I developed a fear of the medications I was on and their subsequent reaction I would get, if any, even though I'd been taking them for so long. Many nights I went to bed scared that I wouldn't wake up because of all the meds I was on, and the worst part was that I took the risk. I had to because the pain was unbearable.

When you're on the kinds of pills you were on, they can start to mess with your head. I felt the same way. You know how much I hated taking my pills. I always felt like if I didn't space them far enough apart, I would accidentally overdose. That was a scary feeling.

That's how I felt! I think that panic feeling had more to do with my fear of overdosing and not being prepared to leave this earth and my babies, than any reaction I would get from the meds.

Those were my fears too. That's why I fought so hard to stay.

I know. Are you okay Mom? Listening and talking about all of this I mean?

Yes, I am. Let's keep going. This is so good for both of us. As painful as this is to hear I need too, and you need to keep getting as much out of you as possible.

So, on top of my fears I thought about all the things I wanted to do that are no longer possible for me unless I want to risk being paralyzed.

Like what sweetie?

Aside from the obvious and most important which is dance; things I wanted to do like skydive. Then there were the things I did that were now out of the question such as: aerobics, jogging, lift weights, calisthenics and any other exercise. I'm not even able to do yoga because of the way the equipment is placed. I can walk and every day I have to remind myself to be grateful for that.

I'm sorry you're not able to do these things. I know it's hard for you.

I'll always feel a deep sense of grief for the body I had.

That's natural and to be expected.

Yeah, but I didn't think...

It would happen. I know.

In addition to the loss and grief I felt from not having full use of my body I missed you so much.

I know you did babe. I missed you too.

That was hard for me. Holding on to your urn and crying became a ritual for me. I needed to feel your love and support because I was starting to feel like this ugly, unworthy person who didn't deserve anything good. I thought about all the things your family didn't remember.

Like what?

Like the times I made any one of your nieces and nephews and your sisters laugh when they were going through some of their worst times. Or the fact that, for my older cousins, I was their "go to" babysitter because Darlene and my sister were always out partying. If they did get Andrea to babysit, she used to pack the babies in the car at 10:00 or 11:00 at night, when they were supposed to be in bed, and take them to the worst part of Buffalo to "hang out" on the street no less. Are you kidding me on that?

She did do that I remember that. One of her many irresponsible acts.

Yeah, I remember it too, but the rest of your family's selective memory doesn't. I used to be the one they'd call to watch their kids overnight because they knew I was responsible. They knew their kids were safe with me, and they were. After you crossed over, Carolyn's daughter came to visit me when I was living in Queens. Well, she didn't come to visit me. She came under the guise of "visiting me." Her girlfriend broke up with her and she went into a complete depression. She found out her ex moved to NYC, so she came to "visit me." What we really did was go to all the bars she thought her ex-girlfriend would be at. I even held her at night while she cried that pathetic asshole. Or the myriad of times I empathically listened to your sisters as they complained about their ex-husbands/boyfriends/girlfriends and anyone else they were fucking or fucking over as well as anything else about their spoiled lives.

Most importantly Mom, no one would recall the amount of time I spent with Grandma but Grandma. I loved being with her. I used to go to her house and cook with her and for her. I'd help her with her laundry or take her to get her hair done. Your family accused me of not spending enough time with my own grandmother yet who was with her all the years you were sick. My siblings and your nieces and nephews were out partying, and your sisters were going through their shit. No one wanted to "deal" with Grandma. As soon as I could drive, I was taking Grandma wherever she needed or wanted to go more than anyone else. I know there were some stretches where I didn't call Grandma while I was going through my spine stuff, but that was because I was in so much pain and I didn't want her to hear it in my voice. Sometimes those stretches sometimes lasted a few months. It was hard.

I know and I can vouch for all that you did for your Grandmother.

Your sisters spoke of their mother with a hatred in their voices that sent chills down my spine.

Honey, Grandma knows you love her. She wanted to hear from you more often but that's only because she worried about you. She missed you but she knew you were going through something terrible.

I hope so because I would feel awful if she thought I purposely didn't call her. I would never, ever do that. Grandma was there for me all the times I wanted to get away from Cody and would have even let me live with her. She was my safe place. I've missed her.

Babe, she doesn't hold the same feelings the family does and that's all that matters.

There was no need for the way your family behaved and the nonsense they put me through. To me, there's nothing respectable about your family. The horrible things they said to me made me feel like I was pulled into their own self-hatred. They added one layer of insult after another of how little they thought of me for an injury which led to a disease that I was working so hard to overcome. I felt knocked to the ground but no more. Your family never truly cared about me and basically threw money at me. I don't forgive them because they've never expressed one ounce of remorse for all that they put me through. Never again would I ever have to defend myself, my life or my decisions to your family or anyone for that matter. I was going to do whatever I had to in order to maintain my independence. You always told me, "The only person you can depend on is yourself." You're right. I wasn't made to be dependent on anyone but myself. As long as I'm breathing that's how things are going to stay for me.

I do love this side of you honey. I mean I accept all of you, but you are a fighter through thick, thin and everything in-between.

That I am. I spent the first part of my life training to be a strong, disciplined and powerful dancer. I achieved that. I lost my ability to dance but I never lost the dancer in me. It was time for me to put all that strength, discipline and power to use. For me, the dance is never over. When things get tough, even unbearable, there is only one thing left to do…

FIGHTING BACK

2004 - 2005

"Dance is the art wherein
we ourselves are the stuff of which it is made."

Kenneth Grooms

Fight back! I wanted my life back Mom. I couldn't take any more of the darkness I felt submerged in.

You mean by the family?

Not just them but the doctors, hospitalizations, emergency room visits, agonizing pain and the pain killers. All of it took the best parts of me and turned me upside down and inside out. I felt like I was losing control of my life.

You almost did.

Yeah and it was time for me to take my life back. I got caught up by your family.

Like I did.

Yeah. Your family had no business asking me for proof that I filed for disability and then backing me against the wall threatening to not help me if I didn't file when I wasn't even disabled.

That's what they said to you. That they wouldn't help you if you didn't file for disability?

Yes, remember? That was the reason I got the paperwork in the first place. It was part of the "conditions" under which they would give me any financial help.

Boy oh boy. My sisters thought so little of me that they could treat my daughter like she was some, thing, without value or feelings. That hurts me. You know why they said that don't you?

I don't know and I don't care. Any decisions about my body were for me to make, not them.

I agree but I know why and so should you.

If you need to tell me, then okay.

In their minds, by you filing for disability it was their way of ensuring they wouldn't have to help you again.

I'm telling you Mom. I knew this the moment we moved to Buffalo. Your family is a bunch of fucking losers, all the way. Here I am, more than capable of walking, getting from one place to another, working and they're telling me to file for disability, not because they care but because they don't want to be bothered which is exactly how they acted. I would have never gone to the low lives in the first place had Devon not made this call.

I know and they'll deny all this, of course…

Of course.

But I know them. I know how they work and think.

Well, contrary to their ignorant mindset, I knew if I really put my mind to it, I could make my body stronger. I knew I wouldn't be as strong as I was prior to my surgeries but I could be stronger and that was all the hope I needed, and I knew exactly where to start.

Where was that?

By ripping up that stupid disability application. I never had any intention of sending it in. I just filled it out so they could see it and I could get that money. Ripping it up felt good, real good!

That's it sweetheart. When you make the decision to get well and the decision is yours for the taking.

I thought about my dance training and looked through all my old dance books and other books I had on the body. This was my starting point. I have a book on the Alexander Technique which focuses on proper body alignment. I also have books on Kinesiology from college. I remembered how unlimited I was prior to my spine surgeries. Now I needed to find where my limitations were after my surgeries. Being mindful of proper body alignment and awareness I began little stretches with my head. I thought about the placement of the titanium in my neck and most of the places I lost ROM (range of motion) in my neck. I lost the most ROM moving my head ear to shoulder. However, I still have a decent amount of ROM when turning my head side to side and some up and down.

What about rotating your head in a circle?

Not a good idea. Titanium isn't flexible. I can only bend and stretch as far as the implants let me and that's not far at all when it comes to head rotations. Thinking about my limitations I devised simple, gentle stretching exercises with what I can do. I rotated my head very slowly and gently, looking left then right as well as up and down. Although I'm limited in this area, I still included some lateral resistance exercises where I place my hand on one side of my temple and press against it but resist the hand that's pushing. This helped with strengthening my neck. I did two sets of eight repetitions in each direction for each exercise. Then I started on my arms and upper body. Believe it or not when you want to use a resistance band to strengthen your upper body, you're still using your neck muscles.

Oh sure, everything is connected.

That's right. I had to hold off on the resistance bands until my neck healed more. I couldn't believe how much we use our neck muscles for every movement. You don't realize it until you hurt your neck in some way.

I remember when I got whiplash from my car accident. I felt it everywhere.

Exactly. I realized how much I had to learn how to isolate the other parts of my body to strengthen and ultimately use them.

What kind of arm and upper body stretches did you do?

Very simple ones where I'd stretch my arms up, sideways and across my chest. I did the same with my legs. My goal was to "awaken" my muscles. Muscles have memory and mine were, ever so slowly, beginning to remember how far they were stretched, used and just how strong they were. I also wanted to get my blood going again. Movement brings oxygen to the blood which, in turn, brings nutrients the body is lacking due to illness and/or medications.

Kristin, you were so fortunate you had all those years of dance training. dance saved you.

It did. It really did.

When I say dance, I mean you. You saved you honey.

Thank you but you know. I was thinking, what if I didn't have a dance background? Not everyone does and what if you have to go through spinal fusions and you don't have "body movement" background? If you don't have insurance, like I didn't at the time, it's hard to know where or how to begin healing yourself.

What would you say to someone who wanted to heal and didn't have dance background?

I would say first have a conversation with your doctor. Find out what your limitations are. Then, working with your limitations in mind, start with what feels good and what doesn't. Go by that simple rule, if it hurts don't do it! Whatever does feel okay, do it mildly and work your way up. With all my dance background that's what I did. If an exercise hurt, I stopped, regrouped and started again but not to the point of pain. Sometimes it's good to push pass the pain but not when you're still healing because you can hurt yourself and destroy your healing process permanently.

That's a good rule to go by. So, what was one exercise that was painful for you?

Bending over to stretch my back or my back-leg muscles was uncomfortable but also scary too.

How so?

Until my neck was fully healed and fused, anytime I bent over I felt like my head was going to fall off, literally. It was a weird feeling.

Oooh, that does sound scary.

The exercises were working. I felt like my body was "waking up" for all intents and purposes. I know Devon was relieved that I was taking the initiative to get myself well again.

I'll bet.

Yeah, because for so long I was depressed and barked at anything he suggested that might help me get well. I hate to keep saying it, but pain is a difficult, excruciating thing to overcome. Pain impulses take over your thought process because their attacking all or certain parts of your body. When pain is strong enough all you can think about is how to get rid of it and fast. Things like Yoga (which I couldn't do anyway), stretching and any other body work take time. When you're in pain, time is the last thing you have.

You say it as many as you want because no one understands the pain you were going through better than me. It's like you want to get well but there's this agonizing thing that's blocking you, draining you and turning you into someone you never knew existed. Someone you'd rather not know or be familiar with for too long.

You nailed it. I felt terrible when Devon would suggest something like the stretches I started doing and I would snap at him. I didn't mean too, and I always apologized but that doesn't lessen the hurt. I was just so frustrated and upset that I had all these limitations on my body where there were none before. It was extremely difficult to accept and get used too.

I'm sure but you were trying Kristin. Devon knew that and he knew the real you. Not the person on pain pills and in pain. Let me ask you before I forget, why can't you do Yoga? It seems like that would be good for you.

No, Yoga contains strenuous stretching in inverted positions that I'm absolutely unable to do, unless I want to break my neck.

Oh, I see. So, what do you think led you to being able to do these exercises now as opposed to before?

My neck kept growing those bone spurs and that's mainly what was causing me so much pain. I was in the midst of three surgeries within a four-year period and the healing was taking a very long time. At this time, my neck was finally beginning to heal and fuse properly. As I began to heal, I started to feel upset that my doctor never offered me any assistance or helped me get on a healthier path to get me off the pills I was on. He left all that to me and I was clueless as to where to begin. During one of our appointments I questioned him as to whether he performed the first surgery properly and with the latest equipment, which I don't believe he did. I thought and still think if he did, I wouldn't have gone through so much.

Do you think he screwed up on you?

I don't feel I was in the best hands possible but like I said. Once you begin a procedure with a doctor it's hard to switch.

Right. No one wants to work on someone that's already been worked and has fears that a mistake was made.

Exactly.

What did he say?

He was offended that I was questioning him, but I had every right too.

So, what was his response?

He gave me a blank stare and asked me if there was anything else. No explanation, nothing. Next thing I know I get a call from him the next night telling me he's called in an extra script to my pharmacy and that he wouldn't be treating me anymore, that I had to find a new doctor. I was pissed. So was Devon.

You mean to tell me your doctor left you high and dry because you questioned the procedures, he performed on you?

Yup, fucker.

Is that legal?

No. You have to be a "non-compliant" or truly difficult patient for them to pull a stunt like that and I was neither of those things. This guy was just as asshole right to the bone.

It's your job to question your doctor. You should have sued that doctor. He's not God.

Apparently, he thought he was, and I didn't have the energy or patience to deal with a lawsuit, which is what I'm sure he was banking on, but you know what?

What?

It sucked and I was devastated but after I got over the shock of what he did, it turned out to be a blessing in disguise and one I needed. I was unhappy with this guy. Even Devon said, "This could be a good thing. You've wanted to find someone new for a long time. Now you can." I'll be honest. As much as I wanted a new doctor I was scared. I was afraid I would get someone worse. Also, I knew it would be hard. Would I find a doctor that would treat me after another surgeon already did? Still, I tried to look on the bright side. While this doctor was completely unprofessional to discontinue my treatment as he did, I benefitted from his shit behavior. I didn't feel like I was getting the best care with him and I wasn't. Now, I had the freedom to find a doctor who cared about his patients and their well-being and hard or not, I was determined to find her/him. I felt this resurgence of hope that, contrary to his stupid, arrogant and worthless opinion, I would have a life and it would be as good a life as I was going to make it. There was no reason for me to not want, deserve or strive for a good life just because I was going through something so horrible. These things were still possible for me. I was just surrounded by bad company that had to go.

Good for you Kristin. You are so brave.

Thank you but I was scared too. I didn't have a doctor. I didn't have insurance and I was still on all these damn medications. The script my doctor called in was for 120 Vicodin's which were to last me one month.

That's a lot of Vicodin's to be taking in one month. Did you take them all?

I had to. The pain was gradually lessening but I still needed something to keep it bearable.

I was concerned for you taking all those pills. I was afraid you'd get addicted.

I don't have an addictive personality. My mind is my strongest muscle and it's very disciplined. When I want to do something, I put my mind to it and do it, no if's, and's or but's. If I want to stop something I will. When I was in graduate school one of the questions, I raised to one of my professors was the difference between an addictive personality and having a physical addiction to something.

Aren't they one and the same?

That's what he thought but I don't feel that way. My body needed the pills to keep the pain at bay. My mind wanted off them. I knew I would be off them once the pain got better. While I believe in body/mind connection this was one area where my mind was working independent of my body. My goal was to get them on the same page. Even with all the emotional turmoil I was in at the time I never developed any kind of addiction because I knew I had emotional conflicts I wanted to deal with head on and in my own time, and I knew I could. I think this is where my need to control things in my life and within me worked in my favor.

That was very smart of you Kristin.

I found the more I stretched the less I needed to take the Percocet's. Pretty soon I was only taking the Vicodin's and my anti-inflammatory (Celebrex) for my arthritis. The good thing about going from the Percocet's to the Vicodin's was that the

Vicodin's weren't as strong. I only needed a muscle relaxer from time to time. So, there was some improvement there. I worked for things to only get better. I kept envisioning myself drug free.

You were working hard.

I was and I wasn't going to stop there. I felt well enough to look for work being mindful not to overexert myself. If I had to lift something, I continued with keeping things close to my body so as to use my inner core to help me. Or, I would lean the object against a wall and gradually lower it to the floor with my legs and use both my feet and legs to move it. It's kind of hard to envision, I know, but trust me, it's possible and it works.

I believe you.

I did this for things like Lilli and Monte's big bags of food. This also helped strengthen me as well. To make things easier for myself I had my groceries delivered and mail ordering everything helped a lot too.

That was smart of you. How were you and Devon doing? I know before you said you two were more like companions. Was that still true?

Yes. Unfortunately, we couldn't get the passion back. We went through so much, too much. We remained friends and were still together almost every day. Sometimes I felt guilty Devon stayed with me so long. Maybe he stayed out of guilt, maybe out of love, he stayed and that's more than anyone has ever done for me, with the exception of you.

He stayed because he loved you Kristin. He could have said at any time, "I can't do this." He didn't.

I tried to be the best person I could while I was going through all this stuff; for me, Devon and my animals. It was just so damn hard. Those pills are very strong. I don't mean to use them as an excuse for any of the times I lost it but when I took them, I was up and not feeling the pain. When they wore off it's like someone was dragging a jagged knife across every muscle on the inside of my neck. So, I'd take another pill and the cycle just went on and on.

Honey, I understand, believe you/me. You remember how many pills Mom used to take just to get me through the day. I couldn't even care if I was addicted or not. I had this debilitating and life-threatening disease hanging over my head. Unless you experience this kind of thing firsthand, you're not going to get it and many people aren't sympathetic to what you're going through either, as you discovered with your job and the family.

Well here comes the good news. This is the part that I'm sure you were thrilled about.

If it's what I think it is I was beyond thrilled. I was ecstatic!

Yup. Along with strengthening I knew it was also time to make an important and necessary change.

You finally quit smoking!

You guessed it. It took about four different times, but I did it!

I am so proud of you. I was so upset when you started Kristin you don't know. I...

I know Mom let's not go there. Let's focus on the positive. I quit!

I know how hard it is to quit. How did you do it?

I used the patch. You know the little sticky thing you put on your arm while it delivers a small amount of nicotine to your body. What's good about it is that you scale down by using smaller patches which deliver smaller amounts of nicotine until you don't need them anymore. I stuck with it. It took me about four months, but boy did I feel a difference once I was completely smoke free. I felt my breathing improve 80% that first week and it just went up from there.

Good for you honey. Was there something specific that made you quit?

There were a few reasons actually. The first, of course, being my health and the second was something that happened that really stuck out for me.

What's that?

Sometimes I would place my ashtray on top of the back of the couch because I smoked while watching T.V. Often, I would forget it was there and leave it there. One day Devon sat on the couch, leaned back and the whole ashtray spilled on top of him.

Oh yuck! Poor Devon. What did he do?

He wasn't too phased, but I felt horrible and disgusted. All I thought was, "All that shit is going into my body and killing me as I'm trying to get well." Not to mention what it was doing to my animals. Another reason had to, specifically, deal with my heart. I was getting these palpitations which may have also been caused by the Celebrex, that's one of its known side effects if you're on it for a long time. I'm sure the other was stress but I know the smoking didn't help matters at all. All these reasons were enough to scare me into cleaning my body out. Once I stopped smoking, I wanted to start a vitamin regimen to cleanse, strengthen and rebuild myself from the inside out. My body and mind were ready to be drug free.

Like mother like daughter! How many vitamins and herbs were Mom on again?

A ton. I still have all your vitamin and herb books. They're what I used to help me figure out which ones to use along with internet research. I looked up which herbs and vitamins helped with arthritis. There's an overwhelming amount of information on the internet but I kept at it. Sometimes I would spend hours on the computer sifting through what seemed like would work best for me. Then I would call the companies that made the products I was interested in and told them what I was dealing with. All of them were really nice and answered all of my questions. Through a lot of trial and error I finally found a vitamin/herbal regimen that works for me.

Well, let's hear it.

I start my day, every day with a vegan combo of Glucosamine/Chondroitin/MSM, another vegan joint supreme, a vegan collagen plant builder and turmeric. All these help with the osteoarthritis and work as natural anti-inflammatories. I also take Grapeseed extract which works well for rebuilding and strengthening muscles after a period of non-activity as well as managing stress and keeping your blood pressure low. I added liquid Calcium Magnesium with Vitamin D which helps bring oxygen to my body and also aids in alleviating pain. Then I added a multivitamin which helps absorb all the other herbs and vitamins and milk thistle to help clean my liver. I also take Kava Kava. Another herb to keep the body/mind calm and centered. Lastly, I take Senna because all of the above combined can cause constipation and digestive Enzymes just to help my digestive tract be healthier and work better. I needed them due to my lack of exercise.

That's some regimen! That must have been a ton of research?

It was.

Do you take them all at once?

No, no. I spread them out and take five at a time within a two-hour period. It's better to take them that way in order to get the most optimal results.

That's what I thought.

The more I took them, along with stretching and walking as much as I could, the less I took my Vicodin until I was down to only three Vicodin a day.

You were making such incredible progress.

I felt like I was. Without the negativity of your family I felt limitless and back in control of my life. That was really important to me. When I felt strong enough, I made the decision to go completely off the Vicodin so that the only synthetic pill I was taking was the Celebrex. I knew my body would go through some withdrawal, but I wasn't prepared for how much.

You talked with your doctor before doing this didn't you honey? Kristin?

The schmuck stopped treating me, remember?

Oh no you didn't talk to anyone before doing this?

No, I called my primary physician who knew all the meds I was on and everything I was going through and she gave me some helpful advice.

What was that?

Do it on a weekend. Make some food ahead of time because she said I probably wouldn't be in the cooking mind (as if I ever am☺), keep a pale next to me with a plastic bag in it, buy some

Gatorade to drink afterward and keep the phone handy in case I had to call 911 or she said I could call her.

That's pretty good advice. I know this was hard for you, but you do have a strong mind. Once you put your mind to something you do it. You make the decision and the decision is done. Nothing and no one will stop you.

I just wanted to get well, that's all. I wanted to, for once in long time, think clearly and get all this shit that was being pumped into my body for five years, out. The withdrawal wasn't easy. I told Devon what I was doing and that I wanted to go through this alone, that I didn't want him seeing me go through anymore ugliness.

How did he feel about that?

He was nervous for me, but I knew I could call him if I needed anything. He was glad I was doing this. He didn't like me on all those pills any more than I did. It was scary. I had no idea what I was about to go through.

I'm sure. I wanted to talk with you, but you still weren't able to talk with me as you are now. It was more like you'd talk to me as if I wasn't there, but I was with you baby girl, every step of the way.

I know you were.

Do you want to talk about the withdrawal and what you went through?

I guess, like all these other things we're talking about, it would help. It just makes me sad because it was pretty terrible.

I know but, you're right. It will help. So, start with the first day. What did you do?

The first day, just the day, wasn't too bad. I had Lilli and Monte and I played with them. I basically kept myself busy throughout the day. I thought, "This is nothing. I'm good. I'm handling this way better than I thought."

The calm before the storm.

Yes, but I didn't think there would be a storm. I thought that first day was the worse it was going to get. How naïve was I?

You didn't know. You'd never gone through withdrawal from anything before.

The day turned into evening and I was watching T.V. when I started to feel this general uneasiness, which turned into restlessness, which turned into an angst that wouldn't go away. Then my legs started to feel itchy but there was no itch when I went to scratch them. Then I felt the same thing in my arms, hips, buttocks, chest, stomach and pretty much everywhere else on my body but it was just beneath the surface of my skin. As the synthetics were leaving my body, my body was asking for more. Since I wasn't feeding it anymore junk it started to crave it. This itchy sensation got stronger until I felt like I had thousands of teeny, tiny bugs crawling underneath my skin starting from my head and on down to my toes and everything in between. Nothing was left untouched by the teeny bugs crawling underneath my skin.

Oh boy.

That's how it felt. I rubbed my legs, took a shower, paced the apartment, rubbed my legs and arms some more but nothing helped. Then I felt myself break out into a dripping sweat as if I'd been exercising for hours. Night turned into early morning and my stomach started to cramp bad, to the point where I was doubled over. I curled up in a fetal position on my bed, Lilli and Monte lay with me. I couldn't move. Every time I moved it felt like someone had a sharp object to the inside of my gut and dragged it across my stomach with each move. So, I remained still.

Oh Kristin, as if you hadn't been through enough already.

Right. After a few hours of this I needed the pale. I threw up whatever was in my stomach and when there was nothing left, I had the dry heaves just like I did when I was in Corfu, remember?

I remember.

My head was pounding, and I got one of my migraines from throwing up so much. I really hugged that toilet. I mean my head was so far in that thing I could have drank the water with my tongue. At the same time, I got diarrhea, so I had to…

It's okay. Get it out.

It's gross but I had to vomit into a bag while I was on the toilet. This was so disgusting, all of it. I remember, clear as day, feeling as though I was being hallowed out. I felt like I was dying.

In a way you were; that part of you that was unhealthy and had all those pills in you was literally leaving your body. You were going through so much. I wanted you to feel me holding you and telling you I loved you. Did you feel or hear me at all?

No. I'm sorry.

Why not? Why wouldn't you let me in?

I was scared. I needed you so much, but I felt like I failed you.

Why would you feel that you failed me?

I was supposed to be a famous dancer or choreographer or someone important. Instead, I was job hopping just to maintain insurance so I could try, with everything I had in me, to recover from spine injuries and learn how to live with Spondylosis, Degenerative Disc Disease and Osteoarthritis. That's a pretty far cry from being a dancer. I couldn't have felt more like a failure.

Honey listen to me. You were handling three spinal surgeries and all that they entailed, you kicked a cigarette habit and now you were kicking pain killers, not to mention you had a family that gave you no support, were negative, critical and mean and did their best to make your life as bad as they were obviously feeling inside, and you had only one person as your support system. I'd hardly call that a failure. You were a success at surviving what I'm sure seemed impossible circumstances and pressure at the time. Besides, you could never, ever be a failure in my eyes, ever! Please don't down yourself. You were doing. You were doing! How long did the withdrawal period last? It was more than the weekend, right?

Yeah, all these symptoms lasted a few days. My body was purging all that crap out and I was so tired. Every muscle in my body ached and my stomach was killing me from all the vomiting. I didn't even have the energy to heat up the prepared food I made. I drank a lot of Gatorade and thankfully, I was smart and just on a whim bought some baby food.

That was smart. At least you put something in you although it would have been better if you put something solid in your stomach.

I couldn't keep anything down until the fourth day.

I wanted to physically be there for you, hold you and tell you how much I loved you; that you were going to be okay and we were doing this together. I know there were a few moments you wondered if I was there. You asked if I was present and I told you yes. Sometimes you got angry because you thought I left you alone. I didn't and I never will.

I'm sorry I got angry. I felt like death. I didn't want to be going through any of this. I worked so hard to have a different kind of life, one that was successful. Things didn't turn out as I hoped.

You don't have to apologize. I know the feeling. You have dreams, hopes and work hard for the kind of life you envision for yourself but sometimes life takes you down a very different path. You can either fight it and fall into a pit of depression, anger and destruction. Or, you can take the high road and discover your worth more than the challenges that are put forth to you, work with what you've got and deal all the emotions that brings. I'm so proud of you that you chose the latter. I truly am Kristin.

That says a lot about you as a Mother.

That says a lot about you as a woman.

I'm glad I was naïve about the realities of withdrawal because lord knows I wouldn't want to know about any of this beforehand. Devon was so sweet. He checked on me a few times, but I couldn't talk long with him. I just let him know I was okay, and I'd call him if I needed anything. When I felt well enough to see him, I felt like I was seeing him for the first time in years. He looked so clear, everything did. In the five years I was dealing with my spine and on all these meds my thoughts became blurred, tangled up and hard to focus on. I had no idea how all this was affecting me emotionally too because being so drugged up the only emotions that were distinguishable to me were sadness, pain and anger. Do you know what I'm saying? Prior to this detox, everything was so, what's the word I'm looking for…

Foggy?

Yes, foggy.

Baby doll?

What?

Both me and God heard you when you said you were being given too much. We heard you. I think there is this general impression in humans that God has the ability to take this away and give that to you, but once the spirit and soul enter the physical body, the journey is then up to the individual. God would never do anything to hurt you. God is love and loves you, always, from the moment you enter to the moment you leave your physical body.

I know.

Do you?

Sometimes, other times I wondered about God and all that you taught me.

What do you mean?

I wondered how God could create humans and give them the ability to be so cruel, just in general you know.

That's the ego. God also gave humans the ability to be loving, caring, compassionate human beings. Again, it's up to the individual to decide which path they'll choose. Do you remember when we did Transcendental Meditation? Where you transcend your negative thoughts and move past them to get to love.

Yes. I was in my teens and it was another group we went to that started god-awful early and I never remembered to eat before☺.

That's the one. Well now you're a woman. Now that you've cleaned your body out, I want you to eat healthy and transcend to love.

I'm really trying Mom. I am.

I know sweetheart. I see that. So does God.

You know as my body cleaned out, I literally felt like colors were brighter. Conversations were clearer too. Before, it was hard to have a conversation with anyone even on the simplest topics. I had to really listen hard and focus in order to intelligently respond to people. This was mostly at work. I couldn't afford screw-ups. That's why I would come home so exhausted too. Many times, I would get home and think, "Phew, I made it through the day!"

I bet. Your mind was working just as hard as your body and you did it! You cleaned your body out just as you wanted.

Yes, I did.

Do you think you were a good employee at your last job?

I do. I do my best to be a good employee. I like to help my co-workers, go beyond my responsibilities and be as creative as I can within the rigid confines of the corporate world.

I know it was hard for you to be in the corporate world. It wasn't the place for you, at all but you were making it work for the sake of your health and your animals. I think it was a blessing that you weren't working at this time. Some people go to the movies on the weekend. Not my kid. She completely cuts out a five-year run with pain killers on her own! You are someone to be in awe of honey. I mean that.

Thank you but you know what I was saying before about not really knowing or understanding how this experience with my spine was affecting me emotionally?

Mmm, mmm.

Well, being clearer about things also brought with it its own challenges.

What do you mean?

One night, I think it must have been a month or so after not being on any pain pill except for the anti-inflammatories I was watching T.V. Devon fell asleep on the couch. Lilli and Monte were also sleeping peacefully. Everything was good, or so it seemed. All of a sudden, out of where, my heart began to race so fast I thought it was going to burst out of my chest. I broke out into a sweat, my hands started shaking and my auditory senses became severely distorted.

I know what was happening. Say a little bit more about this.

The voices on the television sounded like the teacher in the Peanuts cartoons, remember her? She had that waap, waap, waap, waap sound.

Oh yes.

A fear and panic set in so strong and fast it forced me to abruptly spring up from the couch.

What were you afraid of?

Everything. Every thought I had was fear based. "What if I move the wrong way and hurt my neck again? What if I grow more bone spurs and need another surgery? What if I never find a full-time job? What if people don't wise up and realize we can't use all our natural resources. How will we grow vegetables if we continue to destroy our land through mass farming and all the chemicals that entails which get emitted into the environment? What if I grow more bone spurs and have to have another surgery? What if I'm on one of the elevated subways and the train falls off the track? What if I grow more bone spurs and have to have another surgery? What if someone breaks into my apartment and Devon isn't here and I'm unable to defend myself? What if I grow more bone spurs and have to have another surgery? I can't go through the pain. I can't do it. I won't do it. I'd rather die before I have to go through another surgery." On and on my thoughts went. They jumped from past to present to logical then abstract but mainly was the fear of hurting my neck and needing another surgery. I kept coming back to the same question over and over, "What if I grow more bone spurs and have to have another surgery?" The thought itself sent me into a panic state.

Those surgeries really knocked you for a loop.

You can say that again. I didn't realize how frightened I became of something going wrong with my neck. I pushed all my feelings down about the fear, despair and anger I felt from having gone through such a horrible journey and for five years. Now, my breath was taken away, literally. I couldn't catch my breath. I literally could not catch a full breath. I freaked out. So much so that I woke Devon up and asked him to feel my chest. He felt my heartbeat and my wet shirt from my sweat drenched body. I kept asking him, "Am I dying? Am I dying? I'm not dying right? I'm okay, aren't I? Aren't I? Am I okay?" I asked him what was wrong with me. He didn't know. He could only try to calm me down and help me relax but I couldn't. I felt like my thoughts were uncontrollable and I was going to end up being committed. I really did. I never experienced anything like this before in my whole life. You know what was happening to me right?

I sure do. It happened the same way it did with Mom. That's what you call a panic/anxiety attack and they are scary.

Holy cow! You're telling me. It took the entire night for my heart rate slow up. Poor Devon. It was just one thing after another with me.

Poor Devon? Poor you.

The blinds of darkness from pain killers revealed the light of hope. In that light rest the true meaning of a panic/anxiety attack.

Like you said you were going through so much, physically and emotionally that you didn't have the time or energy to focus on how this experience with your spine was affecting you. I know that all those drugs numbed a lot of that sadness and anger too. Once you start that healing process you have to travel backward in order to figure out what you were numbing and why.

Wow. Who knew? You said yours happened the same way?

Oh goodness yes and at the time I was with Spencer. You know how she could get. Her way of supporting me was to tell me to relax in a militant voice; not very reassuring when you're in the midst of a panic/anxiety attack. Of course, all they did back then was prescribe you medicine. One of the very reasons I was having these attacks in the first place. I was on all these medications for my back, depression and then cancer. I was on so many pills I didn't know what to take when. Not remembering anything about what and when to take my meds, I was afraid I would mix the wrong ones because the doctors never told me what medicines I shouldn't take together and often, I never remembered to ask. Thank goodness I had you to help me keep things straight. You knew what I took, when I last took it and how many for the day and/or night. You'd tell me, "Now Mom, you have to take this one at this time and wait this amount of time before you take this one and don't forget to eat in-between." Things got to the point where every bit of information entering my brain was too much and put me on overload. I'd hear you but everything went into my subconscious. I couldn't remember a thing.

I felt the same way Mom. It's like okay, hurry up and stop talking person because I'm about to fall asleep just as a means of coping.

Exactly.

All that you said is the main reason I wanted off the pain pills too. They're so strong and if you mix them with the wrong thing, even cold medicine, you might not wake up. I didn't want to leave my animals. They've always been my reason for living.

They're a mighty good reason too. You kids were my reason. What other symptoms did you get from these panic/anxiety attacks?

There are some attacks that are episodic and some that last a duration of time. Mine was long lasting, sometimes weeks. I went weeks feeling frightened to even walk out the door because my breathing was so off. I couldn't catch a full breath and had to take little breaths. Every time I tried to take a deep breath my lungs felt like they would only expand so far. Sometimes I felt disoriented, like I couldn't remember where I was going or what I'd just done. I thought I was going insane. The fact that I wasn't hearing other voices was my only reassurance that, at the very least, I wasn't "losing it." I was scared all the time and my heart wouldn't slow down. My body would break out into hot and cold sweats and trembled all the time. There were moments I thought I was dying or having a heart attack. Sometimes I'd be talking with someone and feel all of the above and wonder if they knew what I was going through in the midst of our conversation. I felt naked, as though people could see right through me and see all the panic happening inside me.

You weren't losing it although I know the feeling; particularly that feeling that people know you're panicking. Panic comes from pushing the feelings that are too hard to handle emotionally, down.

I didn't know what to do or where to turn because I'd never had a panic/anxiety attack before. So, I went to my doctor, my crappy Medicaid doctor who was short tempered, unhappy and didn't seem to care anything at all about his patients. Devon came with me. You know what my doctor said?

What?

I told him all my symptoms and he said, "Sounds like your classic panic/anxiety attack. Here's a prescription for Lexapro. Take it." I told him part of my anxiety was all these pills I'd been on and that I was trying to get off pills. In a sarcastic voice he said, "Well, the Lexapro will help that. Call me if it doesn't work." Devon and I left the office. I was disgusted by his indifference. I was hoping he might be able to point me in the direction of an alternative to pills when dealing with panic/anxiety attacks. I even asked him if he knew of alternative medicine or healing or anything like that, but he didn't. I wondered if Medicaid ever really checked the licenses on the doctors they put on their roster because all the Medicaid doctors I saw sucked and if they didn't suck then I was being treated by whatever ten-year-old intern they had. I hated having to deal with all this shit Mom. I really did.

I know. I truly know how you were feeling babe. It's interesting because I remember when you were a little girl and we'd been in therapy a few years. I think you must have been about eight years old or so. The therapist wanted to put you on some anti-depressant drug, but I wasn't sure, so I asked you. Do you remember this?

I do, yes. You asked me on our way home from our therapy appointment. We discussed it the whole way home. I vividly remember us pulling into the driveway and then, after you got out of the car and crossed in front of the garage door you said, "So what do you think honey? Do you want to try the medication?" You followed it with, "You don't have to if you don't want too. It's up to you." I remember feeling happy that you cared enough to involve me in such a big decision that most parents would have just made for their kids, without asking how they felt.

I felt it was only appropriate since those sessions were about empowering ourselves and each other. How could I empower my daughter if I didn't trust or respect her enough to know that she knew her body and mind best, even at your tender age. Do you remember your response?

"No, Mom. I want to feel my feelings. I don't want drugs in my body."

That's right. That response right there affirmed even more why I asked you.

Which is?

You were way more advanced than your age and knew what your mind and body needed to begin to heal inside and out. So, do I even need to ask what you did with the prescription?

I put it in a drawer and went online to try and research alternative medicines or healing techniques for panic/anxiety.

That's my Kristin.

I didn't find anything that helped get to the root of the problem. I'm sure therapy would have helped but I didn't have the money and Medicaid only employs Psychiatrists, more pills!

Oh my gosh! It's like a never-ending circle of bad treatment.

Like I've said, it's fine if others want to use medication and I'd never judge but that's not the route I wanted to go. I just feel like the healthcare industry relies too heavily on pharmaceuticals to "help" people. As you said, it was and still is a never-ending cycle of bad treatment. I so wanted some sign of hope. I knew other people experienced panic/anxiety attacks but what if pills are part of your panic/anxiety triggers? Where do you go? I wanted something that would help me help myself. I wanted to walk through the process of my panic/anxiety attacks, see where they started from, how to cope with them and ultimately, overcome them. I missed you so much because I knew you experienced the same thing and even though you went on pills it was a different time now. If you were here, we could have figured something out together.

There was a lot I wanted to do for you and couldn't. That was hard for me too.

I was going through one challenge after another but my biggest challenge, always, was not having you with me. One night, again while I was watching T.V., I saw an infomercial. You know how I love my infomercials. I have so many "As seen on T.V." products.

You're a trip Kristin. Do they work?

Yeah, many do. This product was different. It was called "Attacking Anxiety and Depression." It was the first sign of hope I had in a long time. Buying something for Anxiety and Depression from an infomercial seemed so silly but I thought, "I have nothing to lose. I'm going to try it. I can always send it back in thirty days if I don't like it."

Sounds like something I would have liked.

This was right up your alley. I knew from my years of therapy there was going to be a lot of work involved and working out my panic/anxiety would take time. I was willing to do the work and since I was still looking for work, I had time.

It sounds interesting. Tell me about it.

I was so excited when the package came. It came with a big workbook and sixteen CDs. A woman by the name of Lucinda Bassett started the program at a place called the Midwest Center for Stress & Anxiety, Inc. in Oak Harbor, Ohio. I looked through the workbook which contained several different question and answer sections. Then I checked out the CD's and immediately began with the introduction CD. On it was Lucinda Bassett and a few other people that worked the program who successfully overcame their panic/anxiety. I knew the second I heard Lucinda's voice and the other people talking about their experiences that I was going to be okay so long as I put in the effort. I loved this CD because listening to other people talk about their symptoms made me feel like I wasn't alone. There was another CD that was none other than, go ahead, guess?

A relaxation CD.

You got it. My first thought was "Please don't let this be the sound of waves."

The sound of waves can be very relaxing honey.

They are but I needed something…

Tangible.

Yes. Waves can only take me so far. I needed a plan, a schedule, a time frame to get on the path of feeling better and that's exactly what this program gave me; stability when I was feeling so unstable. I was already physically keeping up with my stretching and toning exercises and I continued with my myriad of herbs. Now what I needed to do was take care of my mind and heart. I had a good feeling about this program. I was right.

That's smart of you and you know what you need. What was on the relaxation CD?

It was the sound of Lucinda's voice which in and of itself was relaxing. Her voice is soft and nurturing. The relaxation CD had to be listened to every night as part of the program because it conditions you to work through your panic/anxiety with your breath. The first week of listening to my relaxation CD I was able to take a full, deep, big, long breath for the first time in months, just by listening to Lucinda's voice and doing the exercises she gave. I, eventually, fell asleep to my relaxation CDs as opposed to staying awake until morning and getting one or two hours sleep due to fear and panic. It was amazing.

Oh my gosh honey that's wonderful.

You don't know how good it felt to finally be able to take a full breath. In addition to using my relaxation CD's I also worked each CD along with the booklet every night. I mean I worked this program, every day, like you wouldn't believe. I'd be on my CD's, doing whatever lesson I had for the day, then writing in my booklet answering questions and then the relaxation CD's at night.

Wow. You really were working this program. If it's one thing you are it's a good student. You're diligent in your efforts to succeed at whatever it is you're doing. So, you see babe. "Failure, could never be a word to describe you."

You were the same way. I think I get my love of learning from you. You were always taking me with you to learn about something new or experience something different.

You loved being with me. Anything I did you did too and loved it☺.

I think if we knew about the Attacking Anxiety & Depression Program, we would have done it, together.

Oh absolutely. So how did it help you exactly? I'm curious

It was an amazing program that did exactly what I was hoping for.

Which was?

It helped me help myself. It took me to the root of my panic/anxiety and even depression and forced me to deal with them by taking me through different exercises on the CD's. Then the program has you process those exercises through questions you have to answer in the workbook. There were fifteen lessons in all.

Well, tell me a little bit about them.

Okay. I feel so excited when I talk about them because they truly helped me. One of the ways they made such an impact on me is that at the end of each Lesson there was a section on how each Lesson can be applied to dealing with depression. This was invaluable information for me.

Kristin this sounds like exactly what you needed. No wonder you get excited about it. Everyone deals with anger, depression and anxiety. Boy, I wish I had this when I was going through my stuff.

Me too. I still have the book. I can read you the lessons if you like. Not every single detail but enough so you can see how the program worked.

Yes, please.

Okay, so Lesson 1. This was an introduction on Panic and Anxiety Attacks. This was good because they immediately started you off with understanding why Panic and Anxiety Attacks happen and how to deal with them, i.e. breathing exercises, positive self-dialogue and understanding panic and anxiety attacks.[19] Lesson 2 gave six steps to putting an end to Panic and Anxiety attacks. I loved this chapter because it works if you work it.

Oh, the breathing exercises are right up my alley.

I know, right?

That must have been a good lesson for you too

It was.

What were the six steps?

So, the six steps were, well how about I just read them to you along with a little blurb of what they are.

Sounds like a plan. I just love that you were doing this. This is so what Mom was doing. We are so much alike.

Yes, we are. Okay, first step…

First step…

"ACCEPT - recognize that you are feeling anxious. PERMISSION - Give yourself permission to feel anxious about whatever it is that is bothering you. BREATHE - First, inhale through your nose slowly for two-seconds, mentally counting one, one-thousand, two, one thousand. Then exhale through your mouth to a mental count of four-seconds - again by one-thousands." These help move you through your attack. "INNER DIALOGUE" - here they gave a couple of phrases for you to talk yourself through the anxious time. One of the phrases I use if I feel an attack coming on is, "It's just anxiety. It will go away. I will not lose control. I can still go about my business feeling spaced-out. It won't hurt me." "DISTRACT" - keep myself busy during an attack and last but not least, "LET TIME PASS "- give yourself time to deal with and let your panic/anxiety attack pass.[20] Sometimes if I needed to spend an extra week on a lesson I did.

I feel the healing already. These are excellent tools. Did they work?

Oh my gosh yes. Like I said, they worked the first week for me. I think because, for me, it was all about changing my thought patterns from negative to positive and ultimately changing my behavior as well. Lesson 3 dealt with negative and positive dialogue. How negative dialogue can cause and keep you in your panic/anxiety, and how the positive self-dialogue can move you through it.[21] Lesson 4 was about Expectations. "To become more effective and less affected. To understand that our expectations are usually too high which creates much of our anxiety and depression. To be able to set realistic goals. To realize we are responsible for how we feel." Lesson 4 also talked about understanding how our beliefs and misbeliefs are responsible for our stress, anxiety and depression.[22] Lesson 5 was another good one. This one dealt with Diet, Nutrition & Exercise. This is where I learned about the different foods that can contribute to panic/anxiety.[23] From this lesson I decided to, are you ready for this?

I'm ready.

I cut out all refined sugar and switched to decaf coffee and you know how much I like to drink coffee!

What! I'm in shock! You cut out sugar and coffee!

Caffeinated coffee.

Oh, my goodness. These attacks scared you into making yourself well, physically and emotionally as opposed to giving in to them which is what some people do. For the record, I'm thinking more of the family that tried to take you down as opposed to help you. More than half of the family deals with extreme panic/anxiety disorders and what do you think they did about it?

Uh, let me guess, pills!

Bingo and blame everyone else for their problems.

That's the other thing I liked about this program. It makes you take responsibility for your actions which I firmly believe in and practice every day. I can't tell you how much of a positive difference I felt in my energy level after cutting out sugar and caffeine.

How so?

Well for starters, I was gaining control of my panic and anxiety. I also felt calmer, not tired or anything like that, just calmer without all that sugar and caffeine in my bloodstream pumping me up.

That's exactly what you needed honey. You needed something to help you calm your nerves and get your thoughts to a more positive place.

Yes. That's where I was headed. The last lesson, Lesson 6, dealt with Anger. This was another of my favorite topics. They were all my favorite topics, but some spoke more to me than others; anger was one of them.

Another challenging area for you.

Yeah. This lesson had several good techniques such as, "To begin to break the bad habit of anger. To learn how to think before you react. To recognize that beneath most anger we find fear." I have to also add sadness there too. "To become less affected and more effective." It also helped me to understand that when turned inward, anger causes my depression. With this chapter I taught myself how to control my responses at the onset of a situation where I feel anger coming on by responding with confidence and assertiveness so I can express myself clearly.[24]

Dealing with anger and depression is hard for everyone. I know it was for me. Everyone blows up, everyone. This program sounds like it was helping you to also get your bearings on your feelings and really pinpoint why you were feeling the way you did, and ultimately respond to others in ways that were respectful to you as opposed to harming yourself. When you get angry and upset you hurt yourself and at the end of the day, whomever or whatever you're angry at still has to be dealt with.

Right. I spent a few weeks on this chapter. Lesson 7 dealt with learning Assertive Behavior; "To understand the difference between being assertive and being aggressive, To use assertiveness to decrease anxiety and depression," and "To see that being used and manipulated can't happen without your cooperation.[25] I liked that last one.

"Being used and manipulated can't happen without your cooperation." I like that too. That's deep and so true. That's a good one to keep in your mind.

Yeah, I agree. All of these are excellent tools that I use to this day, particularly in tense situations where I need to get my point across without getting riled up. Lesson 8 was about Anticipatory Anxiety and learning, "To understand that the "what if" thinking creates fear, anxiety and sadness, that it rarely happens," and that counteracting the "what if" is by living in the present moment and using realistic positive inner dialogue. In addition to that, understanding limitations and addressing them with a plan of action. Lastly, recognizing the worth of small, steady steps through slow change.[26]

"Small, steady steps" babe. That's you.

I know. Lesson 9 was about Guilt and Worry. "To see that guilt and worry are behaviors that cause anxiety and depression. To understand guilt and worry can be positives if used wisely. To practice present moment living. To practice shifting from negative guilt and worry behavior to problem solving action mode."[27]

This one is one I definitely had a problem with my whole life. All I did was worry. I worried about cancer, my kids, my health, money and so on and so on. All this negative energy is toxic.

It is and it's hard to change when you've been engaged in the behavior for so long, but I wanted to change, for the better. That's why I did this every night. I had to retrain my thought process and that doesn't happen overnight. In fact, I continue to work on all these lessons every day.

That's it honey. You just nailed it. These lessons are lifelong.

Yes. Lesson 10 was the one that affected me the most because these are what triggered my panic/anxiety attacks. It dealt with Obsessive, Scary Thoughts. The key points in this lesson were, "To understand that obsessive, depressive, scary thoughts are a distraction; to determine the real concern behind over-reactive illogical thoughts; to acquire, through practice, the ability to defuse the power of your obsessive thoughts; to use 'replace' rather than 'stop' when dealing with obsessive thinking; and to realize that we are not our thoughts. We are our actions. To find the themes in your obsessive thoughts and address them."[28] Whenever I would get one of the scary thoughts, I was talking about earlier such as needing another neck surgery. I'd play it over and over in my head until I allowed it to work me into a panic/anxiety attack. I had to learn to acknowledge them but not give them any power.

That's right. I know that can be hard for you living alone too. You don't have anyone to really bounce things off of. You're very much on your own with everything from your physical to emotional recovery. That's not easy but you did it and you're still doing it.

I try and I'll keep trying until I leave this world. Lesson 11 talked about Medication and Alcohol. It asks you to "assess your level of depression and dissatisfaction with life." This way you can determine if you need anti-depressants. It also asks you to assess your consumption of alcohol and determine if it's masking your reality.[29] Neither of these applied to me since I don't drink, and I didn't want to go on anti-depressants. Nonetheless, I still found the information helpful.

Lesson 12 talked about Resisting Change. Its key points were, "To understand that all changes cause some discomfort. To acknowledge that every thought, work, and action is connected to a 'payoff.' To stop using your anxiety as an excuse for anything." This last point is my favorite. "To consciously resolve to take personal responsibility for our own healing." I felt a real connection to this lesson because I'm so resistant to change. Any kind of change makes me anxious, so I was able to put all the lessons prior to this one to good use anytime there was a change in my life regardless of how big or little.[30]

I know my little creature of habit. You were never one to cope with change very well. Every time we had to move you would get so anxious, you'd start packing the apartment up that night even if we weren't moving until months down the road. You gave Mom anxiety. You just wanted it done and over with.

I know, sorry. I hated all those moves we had; uprooting only to get settled only to get uprooted again. It was hard.

Do you think all our moves were part of the reason you had this anxiety?

Partly, yes and I'm not blaming you at all. There was just a lot of instability in our home both physical and emotional.

I know and that's exactly what I was striving not to have happen.

Well, no one knows better than us that life doesn't turn out as we'd like it too, right?

Right.

Now that my body was clean of pain killers, I was feeling every emotion I had, including the ones that were stored in my subconscious for years because I was unable to deal with them for one reason or another. I wasn't liking what I was feeling, at all. What I liked about this Lesson and this program as a whole is taking responsibility. I know I mentioned it before but it's important for me to take responsibility for myself, my feelings and my actions interpersonally and intrapersonal. I work on this as well.

Lesson 13 dealt with Time Management. It talked about understanding "that we choose how our time is spent. To get comfortable with 'self' time. To become more comfortable asking for help." I've always been pretty comfortable with that one. You were always asking me to ask someone for directions or a question or something. I got used to asking for help. Now, it comes in handy in my life. It also brought up a key point and that is that "over-scheduling can be an avoidance. To learn how our body, mind and spirit communicate, 'Enough for today!'" and "To become more efficient and less anxious."[31]

You're good with your time management.

Yeah. I've always been good with time. Lesson 14 was How to Keep Stress from Becoming Anxiety. I liked this lesson too because it's easy to allow stress to turn into a full- blown panic/anxiety attack. Its key points asked you, "To understand that stress is an attitude. To recognize environmental stressors and emotional stressors. To be able to use healthy reactions to stress. To learn the power that comes from under-reacting. To understand that stress is a message you give to yourself. To understand that we always have choices: eliminate, modify or change attitude."[32]

Stress can be a powerful emotion if you let it. If you don't manage your stress level it can be the downfall of your physical and emotional health. I think most disease, be it mental or physical, stems from the amount of stress in our lives from the time we're born. By the way, I'm glad you don't hold it against me that I used to ask you to ask others to help us with something. Perhaps it was my way of making sure you never allowed yourself to get "stuck" or be completely alone.

It was a little embarrassing at times but, I'm glad you did. I'm a better person for it and I never mind helping someone else when they need it.

Good, that's my girl.

I think Americans have the worst work habits. We work these crazy hours, get totally stressed out and accomplish what most Europeans do in a few hours. I'm done with being stressed. I'll never go back to that life again.

Good because a stressful life is no life at all.

Amen. Lastly, Lesson 15, Getting beyond a Growth Spurt, was a culmination of all the other lessons. Its key points were, "To completely understand that you hold the key to overcoming your anxiety and depression. To be aware of the courage and tenacity ever present in the person who sets out to change life-long habits in thinking and behavior. To be open to growth spurts. To see that this is only the beginning. You aren't done yet; you will never be 'done' learning about you. To see that: 'you are the lock, and you are the key.'"[33]

Wow, this is amazing work. All these lessons are incredible tools to a healthier you. They're different from the psychoanalytical paradigms that I used to do but I like them. They're...

Tangible!

Exactly.

Yeah, I'm used to the same psychoanalytical paradigm as well but there's only so much analysis you can do before you finally get fed up and need something more concrete that's going to bring about change. That's what this program did for me. It helped me understand my thinking and the resulting behavior and change the negatives to positives. I worked this program for a few months. Toward the end they ask you to perform a challenging exercise.

What was that?

To purposely put yourself in a situation where you know a panic/anxiety attack may happen so you can practice your new skills. It was scary for me to do at first, but this was the most life changing part of the program and to see, "Have I really progressed or not?"

Did you?

Yes, I did.

I just love that you took this route instead of taking more pills. This was so brave and disciplined of you Kristin. What was so life changing about the exercise?

To move beyond panic/anxiety and realize I have the power to conquer my fears, over and over, is empowering at its best. When I truly understood how in control I am of my panic/anxiety and my emotions overall, I felt like a 1,000 pounds was lifted from me. In the packet was a wallet sized card to carry around with you in case you have a panic/anxiety attack. It reads ten pertinent points to help you through your attack:

1. Accept the feeling – it cannot hurt you.
2. Give yourself permission to feel anxious.
3. Breathe slowly through your nose.
4. Calm yourself with positive self-talk.
5. Let go, float and flow.
6. Distract yourself, it is only anxiety.
7. Use the adrenalin in a positive pursuit.
8. Don't let a bad day scare you.
9. Give yourself credit for how far you've come.
10. Let time pass. IT WILL GO AWAY!

I love it! How healing this is!

Exactly, and that's all I wanted. I just wanted my independent life back through positive means. I didn't think there was anything wrong with that. There's nothing impossible about empowering oneself, nothing at all.

The family put you through a lot and they had no right too, Kristin, you did nothing wrong. When someone hurts you or backs you into a corner, you're a fighter. You come out swinging. The family doesn't like fighters. When you're in need they want you to be complacent and do as you're told. You're completely the opposite.

I know who I am, and I would never be purposely difficult, rude or hurtful to anyone unless I'm in a situation where I have to defend myself or fight for what's right. I was on my way back to a healthier me. While I was working on a healthier mind/body I found temporary work as a legal assistant.

Kristin, that's great!

Yeah, it was only temporary but it sure helped. The first few weeks were painful, but my body was holding up, meaning I wasn't taking any trips to the emergency room. In fact, I was going on public transportation and even able to carry a light bag. I was grateful to be able to work again. I don't like staying home doing nothing all day, every day.

I know you don't.

After temping for a few months, I was finally able to secure a job working as a Legal Assistant and the best part was that my benefits started the day of my hire. I worked hard to get to overcome my physical challenges, the pain and limitation and everything that spinal surgeries brings but I was doing it!

Yes, you were/are!

It was hard Mom. Your family used to tell me "No one can talk to you without you getting angry." Yet whether I was angry or not everything I felt and said was criticized by them and my words twisted. Who wouldn't get upset at that?

I know honey. I've been there.

I'd had enough of their manipulative ways. I wasn't going to let them make me think I was something I'm not, which was angry and depressed. These are feelings I had, not who I was or am. When you crossed over, I suddenly became a free-for-all with them; someone they thought they could treat like dirt. They were stupid enough to think I would stand by and let that happen. They forgot whose daughter I am.

That's right.

Your family lacks morals, principles, empathy, compassion and courage. There is nothing admirable or respectable about them. I've had some of your friends say the same thing to me.

The important thing is you didn't let them deter you from getting well. That was my biggest concern, but I knew you would come through strong and healthy if that's what you wanted, and you did.

I made my own way and lived my life on my terms. I knew I could, I just got knocked down, a few times and hard. Getting away from your family was like an escape. During all this stuff with my spine, before experiencing the family for who they truly are, Devon asked me if I thought it might be a good idea for me to go back to Buffalo with Carolyn when she came down to stay with me. He saw the look of defiance that came over me and quickly took his suggestion back.

I wanted to ask you how you felt about your aunt. She came down to help you and then turned around and cut you off. That must have been painful for you. It sure is for me. Lord knows I could never do that to her child and her helping you doesn't lessen the pain she caused afterward.

You're right about that but she's on her own with her shit actions. That's her but I don't have to nor do I ever want to deal with her or any member of your family again. I could never behave in the ways your family and my sister did. Never.

One of the lessons I got from the Attacking Anxiety and Depression program is that, like some circumstances and situations, you can't change people but you can change yourself and your life by getting rid of what's negative and replacing it with something positive, no matter how big or small. Your family or anyone else for that matter will never shake me, make me or break me. Only I can. The only person that holds any power over me is me.

That's right honey. How about your sister?

The same for her, she's on her own with her very sad self. Remember when I told you I had ulterior motives with regard to your ashes; when I took them from Andrea?

I do.

Well, it was around this time that I did what you originally wanted to be done with them. I released you.

I know. THANK YOU! I knew you would if you were given the chance and you did.

I had to. I wasn't going to let them keep you like that. Enough was enough with their bullshit.

Your aunts must have been pissed!

I'm sure they were but I don't care. I stayed as far away from them as possible. I was thinking about how only a few years after you crossed over Trudi's husband crossed too. This was before all this stuff happened with my spine.

I know. I helped him over. He was so dazed about where he was. We all are when we cross over. That's why someone from your past helps you with the transition.

I think that's beautiful. Well, here on earth, I was nothing but supportive of your sisters and my cousins during this time. I didn't demand funeral flowers or barge into their home demanding items belonging to my Uncle as they did me. I didn't' intrude on their pain as they did mine. I respected their pain and their privacy, yet they were so self-righteous and cold when you passed. I'll never forget these painful memories. I was protective of you in life and I remain protective of you in spirit. Andrea was reluctant to give me your ashes, but my feeling was, "This is my mother too and I'm going to fulfill her wishes if it's the last thing I do." My feelings weren't out of malice. It was just time for them to stop disrespecting you, get a backbone and work out the issues they had with you for themselves, not through your ashes. You asked me to make sure your crossing over was handled exactly as you wished, and I let you down by letting your family railroad your every wish. I wasn't going to let that happen again, ever. You said you wanted your ashes scattered in a serene, beautiful place, somewhere in nature. I released you and Sophie's ashes together in a place that's serene, beautiful and peaceful. I hope it was okay.

The place was fine. The fact that my remains were released is what matters. It's not healthy to keep the ashes of those that have crossed over. I never wanted my remains to be cooped up in an urn. I didn't believe in that.

I know.

I know your sister didn't handle it well.

Yes, mostly because I told her after the fact. I know that wasn't nice, but it was necessary.

Why?

She would have tried to stop me, argued with me, brought the family up and use them as an excuse and that's exactly what she did when I told her. All I heard was "I" this and "me" that. One of the things she said to me was, "Trudi is going to be so mad," and this and that person has a say and blah, blah, blah. Releasing your ashes wasn't about me, my siblings or any other member of your family. It was about you and what you wanted. You are the only one who had a say in what you wanted done with your remains after you crossed. You made your wishes known and it fell on deaf ears when it came to my siblings and your sisters. I couldn't stomach one more person disregarding your wishes because you were no longer able to speak for yourself. I did it because that's what you told me you wanted.

Thank you for hearing me.

You're welcome. It felt good to know you were finally free. Besides it was time for me to be done with your family and all their negativity and that included my sister. I overlooked a lot when it came to her antics which were getting tiresome and harder to overlook.

I'm listening.

Throughout each and every procedure and my subsequent healing time my sister kept telling me she didn't have the money to come see me or that she couldn't get the time off work. Yet I found out, through a conversation with Carolyn, that she'd been to visit them several times driving right past me because remember she was living in North Carolina at the time.

Oh right.

I couldn't believe it and by now we weren't even talking. I'm glad because I know if I asked her why she didn't visit me she would have found a way to say it was me. The sound of her voice was nauseating to me. My breaking point came with one last and very sad event.

What happened?

While I get it that when you're not talking with family there's tension, but no one could bring themselves to be, even decent to me and that's sad, for your family because this next event sums them up pretty well.

What do you mean? Oh no, what happened?

Grandma Territo crossed over and no one, not even my sister had the common decency to let me know.

Are you serious?

Yes. Talk about a knife in the back.

You don't know how much I hate that you were going through all this with them and I couldn't be there to help you.

Me too.

I cannot believe the things they were pulling. I feel like I don't even know who these people are.

Yeah, right? It was also bullshit! Here I was going through spinal surgeries and trying with everything inside me to recover and they still found a way to blame me for their inability to be decent. Grandma crossed over May 8, 2001. It wasn't until two years later that I received this information from Andrea, and I was pretty stunned.

You have every right to be so upset. I would be.

Yeah, I mean I take responsibility for the fact that I wasn't in contact with your family or my sister but for crying out loud do the right thing, be decent for fucking once. With all the bullshit they put me through I didn't have any reason to call them but my grandmother crossing over is certainly reason enough for someone, anyone to, at the very least, send an email to let me know. I wasn't even given the opportunity to say goodbye. I never received anything of Grandma's, not one stitch of clothing, not a tube of lipstick, a picture, not even the cards or letters I sent her - nothing.

Nothing!

Nope and I would have liked to have something of hers that I could have held onto as part of my memory of her. I'll tell you Mom; I don't have it in me to be as cruel as your family is. I just don't and that's what finally made me see how lucky I was to be strong enough to get away from them.

Honey, you just nailed it. I know my daughter and I know the things the family has pulled on you would never even cross your mind. I know that. I don't know what else to say here Kris except Grandma knows you love her. She always has even when you weren't able to call her as often as you wanted. She knew you were going through something terrible and that hurt her because she knew you didn't have me, and you also didn't have her. She was too old and fragile while you were going through your surgeries.

I know.

Screw them. What they did they'll have to live with for the rest of their lives.

That's the thing though Mom. Your family doesn't see anything that they did to me as wrong. They feel themselves in the right.

So what? Let them. Let them. At some point down the line their conscious will catch up with them and you'll be way beyond all this.

I think about Grandma all the time and miss her. I have all these great photos I took of her with the camera Aaron bought me. Some she's posing with her glasses, some without. I have all these wonderful memories of her all the times I went to visit her when I was little. The lunches we used to have with her friends, the little dinners I'd make for us, the walks we'd take in the park. I have something of hers that's more priceless than any material item, something your family will never have.

What's that?

Grandma's life story. I wrote a paper on her in college. I tape recorded Grandma recalling her life as a little girl, her parents, meeting your father and so many other wonderful, funny excursions she shared with me that belong to her and I. I still listen to her from time to time. I cherish the hours I spent listening to her recall her life, with tears and laughter.

Oh honey, that's beautiful. I'm so glad you did that, and I bet Grandma loved it at the time. She loved being the center of attention!

She did and we had fun doing it. She really liked talking about her life.

I bet. You really went through a lot and with very little outlet for self-expression you came through stronger than ever honey. You should be proud of yourself. I am.

I am. Now my outlet is writing. I write because I have to. I used to dance my feelings out. Now I write them.

Your writing is playing a big part in your healing process and, it's working. Wouldn't you say?

I would, definitely. I continued to write in my novel in-between surgeries. It was the only hope I had for having a life with meaning, for me at least. I knew I could get well from my spinal surgeries. I felt it at a gut level. If it's one thing I've realized it's this. When you're alone, vulnerable and in need of help and you're trying to climb out of the well of darkness, it's easy to feel like you're the one causing all the problems, and everything is your fault. However, there is cause and action as well as reaction.

Unfortunately, I've discovered people can be controlling, demeaning and do some pretty cruel things to you when you're already down. That's why it's important for me to walk away from negativity and never engage it.

Those are words of encouragement for someone that might be going through something similar. You did a great job getting yourself well honey. I couldn't have been any prouder. I see your mind wandering off. What are you thinking about?

Do you remember that dream I had of you? It wasn't too long after you crossed.

The one where we had our day together?

That's the one. In addition to that dream I've had this recurring dream of you.

What is it?

Well it's two things; it's what it is and when it happened. The dream is you packing me up in whatever apartment I'm in. You're getting me ready to move somewhere. I'm usually hesitant to go but you keep packing away and reassuring me everything is going to be okay. What's interesting is that the dream happened every time I had a life changing event. I had it before my move to New Hampshire, when I moved back to Buffalo, before my move to New York City, whenever I changed jobs and even when I stopped communicating with your family. Sometimes if I awoke from one of them, I'd feel this sinking feeling in my heart because I knew something significant were about to happen and wondered to myself, "Oh no, what other shit am I going to be put through now?"

Sometimes you hold yourself back by being so resistant to change, whatever the change may be. I just wanted you to know that I'm here, helping you to let go of whatever was moving out of your life because it's no longer necessary for your growth, particularly when it came to the family.

I didn't realize how angry I was at them from way back. I needed to get these feelings out.

I know you did. Well, how do you feel?

Okay.

Okay.

This is hard, talking about all this stuff.

I know it is.

It's hard but it's good for me. The more we talk the lighter I feel.

I knew you would. Celebrate the healing you've accomplished thus far. Hey?

Yeah?

I know you said you needed to talk but you're not the only one. You've recognized and dealt with some things that have long since been buried but there's more. We have some very important things to talk about. In fact, it's the most important stuff.

What makes you say that?

Because baby girl, it's the stuff that's holding you back from having that beautiful life. We need to deal with some things, you and me kiddo. That dream you had of me packing you up. You had it again right before another life changing event. Are you ready for this next part of our conversation?

I have to be if I want peace in my life. Mom, I'm scared.

I'd be worried if you weren't. I'm right here sweet pea. I'm right here. Mom's got you. I'm not going anywhere.

Just tell me. Did you know what was going to happen to me? Mom?

Continued in Book III

END NOTES

[1] The Buffalo General Hospital, 100 High Street, Buffalo, New York 14203. *Medical Records*, (September 25, 1990).

[2] Ibid, (September 26, 1990).

[3] Ibid, (September 27, 1990).

[4] Ibid, (September 29, 1990).

[5] Ibid, (October 5, 1990).

[6] Ibid, (October 25, 1990).

[7] Ibid, (November 30, 1990).

[8] *Haldol Oral: Uses, Side Effects, Interactions, Pictures, Warnings & Doses*. www.WebMD.com 2005-2016 WebMD, LLC.

[9]https://www.oneonta.edu/faculty/farberas/arth/smarthistory/arch_constantine.htm

[10] https://en.wikipedia.org/wiki/Parthenon#Destruction. Tomkinson, John L. "*Venetian Athens: Venetian Interlude (1684-1689)*" Anagnosis Books. (August 14, 2012).

[11]Petit-Palais Museum, https://en.wikiarquitectura.com/building/petit-palais-museum/

[12] Inter-County Imaging, 955 Yonkers Avenue, Yonkers, New York 10704. *X-ray Report*, (May 10, 1999).

[13] Phelps Memorial Hospital Center, 701 North Broadway, Sleepy Hollow, New York 10591-1096. *Medical Records*, (August 31, 2000).

[14] DeNoon, J. Daniel and Reviewed by Chang, Louise, MD, *WebMD Health News*, (November 19, 2010).

[15] Delgado, Amanda and Nall, Rachel. *What is Cervical Spondylosis?* Medically Reviewed by Steven Kim, MD , (October 27, 2015). www.healthline.com.

[16] Ibid.

[17] St. John's Riverside Hospital Andrus Pavilion, 967 North Broadway, Yonkers, NY 10701. *Medical Records*, (January 9, 2002).

[18] Ibid, (May 28, 2003).

[19] The Midwest Center for Stress and Anxiety, Inc., *Attacking Anxiety & Depression*, Copyright 1985. Revised 1989, 1992, 1994, 1996, 1997, 1999, 2001, 2002, 2003. The Midwest Center for Stress and Anxiety, Inc. 112 N. Church St., P.O. Box 205, Oak Harbor, OH 43449, pgs. 1-1 – 1-17.

[20] Ibid, pgs. 2-1 – 2-19.

[21] Ibid, pgs. 3-1 – 3-16.

[22] Ibid, pgs. 4-1 – 4-16.

[23] Ibid, pgs. 5-1 – 5-22.

[24] Ibid, pgs. 6-1 – 6-10.
[25] Ibid, pgs. 7-1 – 7-18.
[26] Ibid, pgs. 8-1 – 8-12.
[27] Ibid, pgs. 9-1 – 9-14.
[28] Ibid, pgs. 10-1 – 10-16.
[29] Ibid, pgs. 11-1 – 11-14.
[30] Ibid, pgs. 12-1 – 12-16.
[31] Ibid, pgs. 13-1 – 13-12.
[32] Ibid, pgs. 14-1 – 14-14.
[33] Ibid, pgs. 15-1 – 15-14.

www.ingramcontent.com/pod-product-compliance
Lightning Source LLC
Chambersburg PA
CBHW070152120726
47909CB00001B/78

* 9 7 8 0 5 7 8 6 7 6 4 5 6 *